Equality and Ethnic Identities

Studies of Self-Concept, Child Abuse and Education in a Changing English Culture

Alice Akoshia Ayikaaley Sawyerr
University of Oxford, UK

and

Christopher Adam Bagley
Liverpool John Moores University, UK

SENSE PUBLISHERS
ROTTERDAM/BOSTON/TAIPEI

A C.I.P. record for this book is available from the Library of Congress.

ISBN: 978-94-6351-078-3 (paperback)
ISBN: 978-94-6351-079-0 (hardback)
ISBN: 978-94-6351-080-6 (e-book)

Published by: Sense Publishers,
P.O. Box 21858,
3001 AW Rotterdam,
The Netherlands
https://www.sensepublishers.com/

All chapters in this book have undergone peer review.

Printed on acid-free paper

Equality and Ethnic Identities

We dedicate this book, with gratitude and affection, to the memory of our colleague Dr. Kanka Mallick of Manchester Metropolitan University, and to the futures of our own children, Richard, Jessica, Michael, Daniel and Abigail. And we pray for the healthy, joyous and prosperous futures of the 22 wonderful children whom we studied in St. John's nursery school in London.

TABLE OF CONTENTS

LIST OF FIGURES AND TABLES

FIGURE

ABBREVIATIONS AND ACRONYMS

ACE	Adverse Childhood Event
ANOVA	Analysis of Variance
BTEC	Secondary school-leaving certificate focussing on practice rather than theory
CCH	Child-Centred Humanism
CCEA	Children's Centres in England Evaluation
CECA	Childhood Experiences of Care and Abuse scale
CEVQ	Childhood Events Questionnaire
CNS	Central Nervous System
CR	Critical Realism
CSA	Child Sexual Abuse
DCP	Day Care Provider
DCR	Dialectical Critical Realism
DfE	Department for Education
DFEE	Department for Education and Employment
DoE	Department of Education
DES	Department of Education and Science
DfES	Department for Education and Skills
DoH	Department of Health
EYFS	Early Years Foundation Stage
GBCS	Great Britain Class Survey
GTC	General Teaching Council
HEFCE	Higher Education Funding Council
HMG	Her Majesty's Government
IPPR	Institute of Public Policy Research
MELD	Acronym for the 4 levels of DCR: 1M, 2E, 3L, 4D
MENCAP	'Mentally Handicapped' Charity Organisation
MERN	Manchester Educational Research Network
NAO	National Audit Office
NESS	National Evaluation of Sure Start
NHS	National Health Service of England and Wales
NNEB	Nursery Nursing Examination Board
NVQ	English term for National Vocational Qualification. NVQ 3 is a first year college level qualification.

OECD	Organisation for Economic Co-operation and Development
OFSTED	Office for Standards in Education
ONS	Office for National Statistics
Power1	In DCR: enabling, emancipatory power
Power2	In DCR: coercive, repressive power
PRU	Pupil Referral Units
PSHE	Personal, Social and Health Education curriculum
PISA	Programme for International Student Assessment
PTSD	Post-Traumatic Stress Disorder
QCA	Qualifications and Curriculum Authority
RE	Religious Education
RSES	Rosenberg Self-Esteem Scale
SATS	Scholastic Attainment Tests
SEN	Special Educational Needs
SEU	School Exclusions Unit
SSCC	Sure Start Child-Care Centre
SSLP	Sure Start Local Programmes
StJ's	St. John's Nursery School
UN	United Nations
UNESCO	United Nations Education, Science and Cultural Organisaton
WHO	World Health Organisation
1M	In DCR, the first level: Non-Identity, Absence
2E	In DCR, the second level: Second Edge, Negativity 'absenting absences'
3L	In DCR, the third level: Totality of Social Structure
4D	In DCR, the fourth level: Inner Being and Transformative Agency

CHAPTER 1

AFRICAN AND RUSSIAN JOURNEYS

Reflections on Autoethnography

INTRODUCTION

This chapter is in essence our attempt to chronicle and understand the role which our own identities have played in planning, undertaking, and writing about ethnic identity, disadvantage and racism. Our twin research journeys began for Christopher (CAB) in 1968 when he began researching ethnicity in England, and continued that journey in Canada, The Caribbean, India, The Philippines, Bangladesh and Hong Kong. Early in Christopher's academic journey two students arrived separately in England to begin nursing studies: one, Alice (AAAS) had origins in Sierra Leone and Ghana, and began her research journey which resulted in 2016 in the PhD in psychology on which this book is based. The second nurse, Loretta Young (LY) from Jamaica went on to study sociology, and became the partner of CAB.

Loretta's ideas and research have contributed to our own perspectives which has culminated in the research of the two of us, Alice and Christopher, which has become increasingly focused on ethnic identity, including our own ethnicities as we journey in the world, have partners of differing colours, and children of mixed ethnicities. Alice and Christopher have been research partners since 2008, working together on projects on identity, education and ethnicity within the Manchester Educational Research Network (MERN). A member of this network, Dr. Kanka Mallick died before her due time, and this book carries forward work which she designed and initiated. Christopher and Loretta, together with Kanka and others, engaged in work on child abuse, and on the identity and adjustments of children in contrasted social and cultural settings (Bagley & Mallick, 1979–2001; Bagley & Young, 1979–1999). These joint endeavours have provided the intellectual grounding for this book, based on Alice Sawyerr's interpretation of the issues of ethnicity, identity and child maltreatment addressed by members of the MERN.

Our subjective-objective approach is emboldened by the literature on autoethnography, defined by Ellis et al. (2011) as: "... an approach to

1

research and writing that seeks to describe and systematically analyse personal experience ... this approach treats research as a potential, socially-conscious act" (p. 1). In this model, autoethnography is both process and product. For Alice and Christopher, autoethnography is an *implicit* intellectual process which informs their intuition as they write, construct studies, and interpret data. For us, at least, an approach which is grounded in qualitative sociology and psychology does permit us to undertake "mixed methods" research, which includes quantitative research on such topics as self-esteem, child maltreatment, ethnicity and adjustment. Our value assumptions, manifested through our biographies, are incorporated into the research model of dialectical critical realism, which is discussed in detail in a later chapter. An excellent example of autoethnography coupled with critical realism comes from the Aboriginal scholar Chris Sarra, who in his book *Strong and Smart: Towards a Pedagogy of Emancipation* (2011), writes an autobiography of his experience as head teacher of a rural Australian school, and how his identity as an Aboriginal Australian informed his pedagogy. Excellent examples of successful autoethnography are found in the educational and social research papers written and edited by Hughes (2011), Short et al. (2013) and Pillay et al. (2016).

AN AFRICAN JOURNEY

Alice Sawyerr writes: The role I have played in this research reflects my belief and understanding that research is never a neutral matter: it is important to make the researcher's role as visible to the reader as possible. Such information is valuable in indicating *'where the researcher is coming from'*, making apparent her value perspectives and biases (Evans, 1998). In particular, I do not wish to distance myself from the multi-ethnic nursery practitioners, children, parents and carers at the nursery that I worked with as a clinician over a ten year period (1994–2004), work which also included the *Identity Project on "Myself"* in 1998 with the practitioners, parents and pre-school children (Sawyerr, 1999).

Evans (1998) observes that: *Researchers using ethnographic and biographical approaches often include reflexive accounts describing how they came to their topics and giving some personal details in order to situate themselves in relation to their work.* Connelly and Clandinin (1994) also observe that texts written as if the researcher had no autobiographical presence result in: *"... Deception about the epistemological status of the research. Such a study lacks validity."*

It would be unseemly for me as an African researcher to write a historical case study on my participatory observations and interviews with multi-ethnic nursery practitioners and children from diverse ethnic and cultural backgrounds, which did not include a reflexive account of my personal experience of 'colour and ethnicity'. Distancing myself from participants in this study would be what Fine (1994) describes as 'othering'. It is for all these reasons that I include the following account of myself in '*An African Journey*' in this chapter, and '*not for reasons of self-publicity*' (Evans, 1998).

My journey begins in Freetown, Sierra Leone in West Africa, where I was born. My parents were Creoles (Krios) from Freetown. My upbringing in the first five years of life was in Freetown, and then my parents moved to the then Gold Coast (now Ghana) where I attended primary and secondary boarding school.

I came to the UK to study nursing at age 19. During my training at The London Teaching Hospital in Whitechapel (now the Royal London Hospital), I developed an interest in psychology, but was persuaded by my parents to complete nurse training in the UK first before beginning degree studies in psychology. After becoming a State Registered Nurse at the London Teaching Hospital, I left for university education in Ontario, Canada in 1974. There I completed a four-year full time psychology degree in three years in 1977 (attending summer school each year) in Toronto. I married after graduation, and worked as a clinician at a juvenile correction system in Ontario, providing assessments and writing reports on young offenders for court hearings. By this time, I had two children.

I returned to university in Toronto in 1981, and completed postgraduate studies in social work in 1983. I then worked in the largest statutory Child Protection System in Canada, the Children's Aid Society of Metropolitan Toronto, until moving back to the UK in 1987. In the UK, I initially worked in child protection in the Royal Borough of Kensington and Chelsea in London, from 1988–1994. I continued postgraduate work, training in Psychology and Systemic Family Therapy at University College London (UCL), where I graduated in 1993.

I left child protection social work in 1994 to work, for 10 years as a clinician in a multidisciplinary outpatient specialist all-age National Health Service (NHS) Mental Health Trust Clinic, with the added responsibility for service provision for all six local authority day nurseries in a generally affluent area of central London, but with pockets of extreme deprivation. I initially taught part-time at Royal Holloway, University of London (RHUL) for nine years (1995–2004), while also working full time with the NHS Mental Health Trust.

Subsequently I worked full time at RHUL for 11 years (2004–2015) teaching Psychology, Family Therapy and Mental Health.

Now, I consider some of the key developmental stages in my life. I reflect on where I lived in the world, whether I was in a predominantly black or white environment, and whether or not it made a difference to me personally, educationally or professionally. I continue 'An African Journey' on a personal note, with the unveiling of cultural and ethnic origins and the importance of this historical background in my understanding of the concept of ethnic identity, and my subsequent professional and research development.

As far back as I can remember, between ages 5 to19 years I was living in the Gold Coast (now Ghana) a predominantly (black) African society. I had no reason to doubt my identity and I was conscious and proud of the fact that I was black and African, like every citizen in the country. My parents were, of course, black and African. My dad was darker in complexion, while my mum was quite light in her skin colour. My complexion is halfway between that of my mum and my dad's. My mum had long wavy soft hair. I have softer curlier hair than my dad. I did not attach any value or significance to either of my parents' complexion or hair texture at the time, or wondered about their ethnic origins. I was aware that my mum's relatives were all light skinned, and my dad's relatives were all darker in complexion.

On reflection now, I do not remember ever thinking of myself as being different in any way, because some of my friends that I grew up and attended boarding school with had parents with similarly "different" complexions, like those of my parents. I was never asked at school about my ethnicity or identity, only my name and the names of my parents. There isn't even a word for ethnicity or identity in the Creole (Krio) language which is my mother tongue (a Sierra Leonean dialect), or in the Ga dialect which I am fluent in, spoken in Accra, Ghana where I lived with my parents for 14 years.

When I arrived in the UK at age 19, I lived with my uncle (my dad's younger brother) and his Nigerian wife in a flat in Earls Court, in Southwest London which although predominantly white, had a mixture of black and other ethnic minorities. We moved later to Golders Green, North West London, which is predominantly 'white', and is also the main residential area for London's affluent Jewish population. We had many family members visiting from West Africa. Local family friends and former school mates, mostly students would visit us regularly to have dinner, which we referred to as our favourite dinner parties. The house was always lively at weekends which I looked forward to when I visited my extended family, from my nursing residence in Whitechapel, East London.

The hospital patients and the community in Whitechapel were a mixture of English, Irish, blacks from Africa and the Caribbean, Asians and other ethnic minorities. The staff and students at the hospital were also from multi-ethnic backgrounds. This was once the area off residence of newly arrived Jewish refugees, who later moved to Golders Green; now it is the home of a relatively new population from Bangladesh. My friends and student colleagues were a mixture of whites, blacks and individuals from different parts of the world. I never saw myself as being different and have no recollection of being made by others to feel 'different' because I was black.

On completion of nurse training in the UK I left for Canada where I was a full-time undergraduate psychology student. Being an international student I was given priority for accommodation on campus for three years. Toronto is a cosmopolitan city, similar to London with students from all over the world. There were blacks who identified themselves as black Canadians, or as African Canadians and West Indians.

I was perceived and referred to by my white and non-white friends and work colleagues during my stay in Canada, as an African Canadian, because of my Canadian citizenship. I did not have any experience of being an isolated black person during my student days, or during professional life as a clinician working in statutory settings with white children, adolescents and young adults and their families from diverse cultural backgrounds. Again I never saw myself as being different and have no recollection of being made by others to feel different (or disadvantaged) because I was black.

On my return to the UK in 1987 with my family, I worked as a clinician with children and their families from multi-ethnic backgrounds in Ladbroke Grove in West London. I also conducted joint assessments and investigations with Kensington and Chelsea Social Services, working collaboratively with health visitors and local community organizations and interpreters. The fellow staff team members were from diverse ethnic, cultural and multi-faith backgrounds. During this stage in my life, I have no recollection of being made by others to feel different: my ethnicity did not seem to matter. It was my qualifications, ability, skills and professional experience that counted.

When I joined the NHS (National Health Service) children's mental health clinical centre I did not give much thought to the fact that I was going to be the only black clinician on site. This was a highly respected centre of excellence staffed by a team of all-white clinicians and administrative staff. Most had been working there for more than a decade. The clinic was headed by a psychiatrist, and I was familiar with all of the staff members in the clinic, and was warmly welcomed when I joined.

The only transition I had to make was from that of a former joint student/ trainee from University College, London, to the status of a colleague in the NHS children's mental health centre. The clinic provided free NHS Mental Health outpatient services to all who would self-refer, or be referred by various health, legal and welfare agencies, including managers of local day nurseries in the borough, for child and parent assessments, and whatever therapy was considered necessary. During my first months at the clinic I began to notice and experience a strange pattern of behaviour from referred clients, who were all new to me. I would go to the reception room to call out the name/s of the referred individuals, couples or family members, greet them and lead them to the consulting room, close the door after them, introduce myself, sit down and attempt to begin the session. However, the individuals, couples or family members would fix their eyes at the consulting room door as though they were expecting "the real clinician" to join them in the session. I would reintroduce myself, ask them to introduce themselves and go through standard assessment and routine interviews with them before starting to engage them in a conversation about their reasons for attending the initial sessions and how they would want to use the sessions. I noted that these clients were all white.

I also observed different reactions from black and mixed parentage children, couples and families, who had also been referred to the clinic. They reacted in the following ways:

- Some black Africans and African Caribbean clients after entering the consulting room would turn around and shake my hand congratulating me for being the first black clinician at the clinic. They used words like: *You have made it, you have arrived Sis. It's good to have some colour in this place.*
- Others presented themselves as quiet, polite, respectful and watchful. They would not refer to me by my first name but as: *Miss Alice, Mrs Sawyerr, Miss, Madam* or *Ma'am.*

However, there was a notable non-attendance by some white clients who having met me, did not call to cancel their subsequent, missed appointment. This was in contrast to all of the black clients. I raised this in a staff meeting when all of the clinicians were present and tried to find out whether this was a familiar pattern. Colleagues informed me they had never had similar experiences in all the years they had been working at the clinic.

Only the director of the clinic, a consultant psychiatrist remarked that it could be related to my ethnicity i.e. my being black in a visibly all-white clinic – even though some of the clinicians were Jewish, others were European or South American. Although the 'absentee' behaviours of some clients, and reactions from ethnic minorities had not been anticipated, they had to be given serious consideration. With time, as some of the clients began to settle in the sessions they also began to open up with me, which involved taking risks in sharing their feelings and becoming more reflective. This gradually extended to the sharing of the following with me.

For the white clients:

- They did not mean to be rude or disrespectful in the initial session when they were staring at the consulting room door.
- They were expecting a white clinician, as the clinic has never had an ethnic minority clinician in the staff team.
- Some had been referred to the clinic previously and were familiar with the ethnic composition of the staff team.
- My name on the appointment letter did not indicate to them that I was non-white so they may have been shocked to see me, and thought I was a new secretary or a student on placement, taking them to the consulting room before the arrival of the clinician.

For the black clients:

- They said it was a pleasant surprise for them to finally see a black clinician at the clinic – that was why they congratulated me.
- Some expressed their belief that a black clinician would be more able to take into consideration other cultural and traditional perspectives other than Eurocentric ones. This would include different child rearing practices, hierarchical structures in black families as well as the struggles, prejudices and injustice that black families face in society, especially when involved with social service, the police and the school systems.
- Others said they were surprised and could not help but wonder how I had managed to get a clinical post at that clinic. They thought I must be knowledgeable and well experienced.

Most of my colleagues admitted that they had never thought of my ethnicity becoming an issue, or had expected these reactions from white and ethnic minority clients. When I began clinical work with referred children and their parents and carers on site at the day nurseries (rather than at the clinic as my colleagues had done previously), all the nursery practitioners presented themselves to me as relaxed and friendly. They would ask me to join them in the staff room during my lunch break. I also became aware that the nursery practitioners whose children and their parents I was working with jointly (with the clinic and the nursery), were giving feedback to the other nursery practitioners about the work we were doing together. These included:

- Positive changes they were observing in the children's behaviour,
- The fact that the parents were fully engaged in the work with their children at the nursery,
- Also, they appreciated that they did not have to collect their children from nursery and travel with them on two buses each way, to and from the NHS Mental Health Trust Clinic.

The preschool group room nursery practitioners also began to join me in the staff room during the lunch breaks and invited me to their group room for afternoon tea with the children. They eventually told me that they had initially thought that I would be *'a coconut, brown on the outside but white on the inside in my thinking, attitude as well as behaviour'*. But they admitted that over time they had come to realize that their assumptions about me were wrong! The nursery workers also felt able to express their concerns to me about the number of black and mixed parentage children who were being referred to the NHS Mental Health Trust clinic rather than to Family Centres. They were concerned that the children were being 'pathologised' and labelled before starting school at age five.

During the identity project on 'myself', one of the preschool group room's black practitioners played an important and leading role in getting her colleagues, the children and parents to work collaboratively with her on completing the project tasks, concerning their children's ethnicity and identity, since some of the children seemed confused concerning these areas. In one of the identity project staff consultation sessions, we talked about our own ethnic backgrounds and identity. We gave permission to each other to ask clarifying questions. When it was my turn, I described my ethnicity and cultural background as 'black African, Creole from Sierra Leone'. However when I was asked which section of the Creole ethnic group in Freetown I belonged to, I could not answer, as I had never asked my parents about this.

I was able to ask my mother about this. She informed me that her ancestors were the freed slave settlers in Nova Scotia who had escaped from slavery in the USA. The British government had subsequently resettled many of this population in the western part of Freetown, although many remained in Halifax, Nova Scotia, where most of Canada's black population live, only overtaken in size in recent years by African-Caribbean settlers in Toronto, and Haitians in Montreal. She also explained that there had been a lot of interracial marriages (between 'blacks' and people of various shades of colour) over the generations on her side of the family, hence the lighter skin complexion which prevailed in her family.

She also explained (as dad had passed on by then) that, my father's ancestors were originally from Nigeria, from the Yoruba people. They had been settled by the British government in the Eastern part of Freetown shortly after emancipation was declared by Britain. They had been taken from Nigeria but had subsequently escaped being sent to the Americas or Europe, so had not been involved in interracial marriages, which she pointed out explained their darker complexion and their retention of their Nigerian, Yoruba first names. Their surname had been changed to 'SAWYERR', and the family has maintained a particular spelling of the surname which has remained a prominent name in Sierra Leone, Ghana and in Nigeria (spelled with a double R at the end).[1]

'*An African Journey*' started with my birth in Sierra Leone, travels through Ghana, England, Canada, and back to England where my interest in ethnic identity issues developed and led me to the discovery of my ancestral historical roots in Nigeria, and in the freed slave populations of Nova Scotia. Despite these diversities of background, I came to have a consciousness of "colour" and of ethnic difference and how others react to personal ethnicity, only in my postgraduate studies and professional work. I had been largely protected by my family, my social class position, and the cultures in which I grew up and began my career. Only in Britain did I come to understand, emotionally, how racism works and how it could disadvantage minority individuals, and their children.

In 2002 my colleague Fola Shogbamimu introduced me to Professor Christopher Bagley, his former teacher and research supervisor. Professor Bagley and his Jamaican partner Loretta Young had a keen interest in ethnicity and cross-cultural psychological issues (the topic of Loretta's thesis), and since 2008 I have been associated with Professor Bagley's *Manchester Educational Research Network*. This collaboration explains the convergence of Christopher Bagley's ideas with my own approach, and my use of materials and data available from the Manchester group, including material collected by Dr Kanka Mallick.

CHRISTOPHER BAGLEY: ASHKENAZI EXODUS – MULTICULTURAL AND MULTIFAITH JOURNEYS

Christopher Bagley writes: My great-grandfather, Abraham Abramsky arrived in London in 1876 with his wife and two young sons, settling first in Bethnal Green. They were escaping pogroms inflicted in a town in what is now Belarus, in the region 'Beyond the Pale', to which Ashkenazi Jews were relegated. The two young boys – one of them my grandfather, one of them my grand-uncle – chose different routes in adapting to English society. My grand-uncle chose the "integration" route, maintaining a strong and overt Jewish identity, while adapting to the public legal and social norms of British society. He made good in the rag-trade (the slang term for the garment and fashion industry), and moved to Golders Green, where his family descendants are Orthodox Jews.

My grandfather chose the route of "assimilation", which my father and I have inherited. My granny used to say: "Good Jews make it in the rag-trade, and move north to Golders Green. Bad Jews [meaning my family] make it in car-breaking, and move south to Charlton." I am a Bad Jew, even though I retain remnants of our secret language (Yiddish). My grandfather changed his name to the Anglo-Saxon sounding "Bagley", and his sons were enrolled (like me) in the local Church of England school. Having the name Christopher allowed me to pass for Christian, even though I remained a Secret Jew.[2] "Passing", pretending to have an Anglo-Saxon ethnic and Anglican religious identity to which I was not really committed, gives me I think, a duality of thought and identity, which makes one open to new ideas and cultures. My father graduated from car-breaking to car-making, and worked on the production line of Morris Motors (now British Leyland) in Oxford, and was a Communist shop-steward. Like my dad, I joined the Communist Party, but kept a dual identity (my hallmark) as a Christian-Marxist. It was not only social and economic equality I took from Prophet Jesus, but pacifism as well. Unlike my "Christian" peers, I took the message of Jesus seriously, and became a lifelong pacifist.

Pacifism led me to Quakers, and as an alternative to compulsory military service in the 1950s I became a psychiatric nurse at the Quaker hospital, The Retreat at York. My early training in social psychiatry inspired the ambition to become a psychiatric social worker, in which profession I initially qualified after studies at Exeter University, where I also obtained the Certificate in Education, enabling me to teach in secondary schools. Again, the duality, teaching *and* social work. I have always believed that schools and teachers are important agencies in social work and social care, a passion shared with Professor Colin Pritchard at Southampton University (Bagley & Pritchard, 1996a, b). The marriage of educational studies and multiculturalism has also resulted in a fruitful collaboration with Professor Gajendra Verma at Manchester, and we have co-edited many books in this field.

My dad died young, and we moved to London to live with my more-or-less Jewish grandfather when I was 16. His house was close to Clapham Common in South London. Grandad explained that during the war a huge air raid shelter was constructed beneath Clapham Common. When the Empire Windrush, a troopship taking Caribbean soldiers and airmen back to the islands, filled her empty hold in 1948 with the first group of African-Caribbean migrants to Britain on her return journey. The new arrivals had to be housed somewhere. In the shelter beneath Clapham Common was the "ideal" place for the authorities (out of sight, out of mind). And this is why there is a large settlement of Jamaicans in the houses around Clapham Common, based on the original 500 settlers from the Windrush, and subsequent "chain migration". It was natural that my sister and I should spend our teenaged years in the Jamaican culture transported to London. (My Jamaican creole is about as good as my Yiddish).

When doing research on children with epilepsy, I was greatly intrigued (and privileged) in being able to review files completed by Anna Freud (Sigmund Freud's daughter) on her patients at the Hampstead Child Guidance Clinic (Bagley, 1972).[3] At the Institute of Neurology in London I was the bibliographic research assistant to Dr. Eliot Slater, whose textbook on psychiatry I had used a few years before as a student psychiatric nurse. My task was to translate from German the neglected neuropsychiatric literature on schizophrenia for the revision of his textbook, and for a clinical review of this literature (Davison & Bagley, 1969). Yiddish certainly helped in reading and translating modern German. This experience has left me with an obsession for systematic reviews of academic literature (eg, Bagley & Thurston, 1996a, 1996b).

My fascination with spatial relationships and urban geography stems from my first teachers of sociology, at Exeter University, which led to research on my first publication whilst still an undergraduate (Bagley, 1965), and to later research on behavioural ecology of Brighton, Sussex and then in Calgary, Canada. Maps (and Descartes) excite me: the Cartesian conceptualisation of number and space brings feelings of control and achievement: *I draw maps, therefore I am.* I was inspired too in a Master's in urban education, by my teacher Colin Ward, the anarchist and sociologist of the city (Ward, 1988) – there's a tension of course between my love of Descartes, and my reverence for socialist anarchy. Intellectual tensions too, are stimulating and paradoxes lead to strange and exciting solutions, such as critical realism. My favoured ecological approach is illustrated in the contrasting of social disadvantage and achievement in two schools in Greater Manchester, reported in Chapter 8. I found that many of the 'zones of deprivation' identified by Friedrich Engels in Manchester in 1845 still contained pockets of deprivation, in 2008.

My Jamaican partner, Loretta Young, was first my graduate student, and then my wife. It was a nice coincidence that my doctoral supervisor at Sussex University was the Jamaican sociologist Fernando Henriques, a black Sephardic Jew with Brazilian-Portuguese origins. Fernando used to say, with irony: "If there's anything worse than being black, it's being Jewish and black." My doctoral thesis was on the social and psychological antecedents of racial prejudice. Though I immersed myself in the literature of social psychology in writing the thesis, I regard myself as *both* a sociologist and a psychologist, separate but merging identities.

Psychology I learned from Hans Eysenck, when I was at the MRC Social Psychiatry Unit at the Institute of Psychiatry, based at the Maudsley Hospital in South London. I was intrigued by Hans' passionate opposition to psychoanalysis. Could it be that bad? My reading said no, so I had a brief, didactic Freudian analysis at the Tavistock Clinic. Again duality: behaviourism *and* psychodynamic psychology as complementary approaches to understanding human endeavour. And ultimately from psychoanalysis and its extension into Jungian and Adlerian ideas of the self, I know that my true self can never be adequately revealed: only G-d is aware of the contents of that self, its struggles, its doubts, its despair, its heights. But the Tavistock analysis gave me the confidence to 'come out' as a confident multidisciplinary scholar, and as a Jewish-Quaker. At the Maudsley, it was my privilege to work with the Quaker social psychiatrist Michael Rutter, co-publishing with him work on the African-Caribbean population of Camberwell, South London (Rutter, Yule & Bagley, 1973).

Loretta and I have wandered through the world, spending most of our professional lives in Canada. We are now resident in both Manchester and Amsterdam, where our daughter Abbie (now Dr. Abbie Vandivere) is a lecturer in technical art history at the University of Amsterdam (probably the only black person working in this field in Europe).[4]

While serving at the University of the West Indies I had a salutary experience in perceiving colour. Towards the end of long committee meeting I glanced at my watch and saw an arm extending from a short-sleeved shirt. I had a moment of existential panic: *my arm had turned white*. All of the other arms in the room were shades of rich dark and light brown. My own arm had palsied, withered, turned white. Then I realised that all of me was white! I have been immersed for many years in a black, Jamaican kinship that oftentimes I forget about being white, about being the odd one out. My sister also married a Jamaican partner, and we are delighted by the various shades of brown of our children and grandchildren, the varied texture of their hair, and so forth.

In the East, Gajendra Verma, Kanka Mallick and I have researched education and cross-cultural psychology in India, including an ecological study of murder in Mumbai. The years I spent in Hong Kong provided a fruitful partnership with John Tse, including our book on suicidal behaviours in Chinese adolescents (Tse & Bagley, 2002). My interest in suicide stems from undergraduate sociological study of Durkheim's *Suicide*, and this interest has resulted in much fruitful collaboration with social psychiatrists, with publications too numerous to mention here. From Hong Kong I administered Canadian charitable funds which enabled young sex workers in The Philippines to return to high school (Bagley, 1999), work which has proved fruitful in saving young lives (Bagley et al., 2017). Suffice it to say that the former adolescent sex workers, "rescued" by our scholarship funding, now name any first-born son "Christopher", and nominate me as honorary godfather! I have a book full of birthdays, and linking with my godsons is an exercise in spiritual joy.

My spiritual journey led me to examine concepts of G-d, and I found the Islamic concept the most interesting and attractive. Five years ago, I converted to Islam, becoming a Muslim-Quaker (Bagley, 2015). I remain a pacifist, and my involvement with Palestine has led me to try and elaborate a philosophy of Islamic pacifism (Bagley, 2017).[5] With Muslim colleagues, I am also trying to elaborate the concept of an Islamic society in which women have equality with men, and children and adolescents are not sexually exploited (Bagley et al., 2017).

In conclusion, I find *differences* in ethnic identity, in cultures, in religion, in disciplines of research, intensely interesting and exciting. Different ideas and nuggets of identity spark against one another, merge, and then part again with new form and identity. Life is so rich, so exciting, so full of space and colour! We are all different, and all the same as Quakers would say, within the divine body, the Divine Kingdom on earth.

Alice and Christopher aver that their intellectual partnership has been rich and rewarding. Neither of us could have produced this work on their own, and we have through an academic partnership, been synergistic in developing interesting intellectual ideas on identity, and on dialectical critical realism. Read on!

NOTES

[1] My father's younger brother Professor Akilagpa Sawyerr, an academic lawyer, was Vice Chancellor of the University of Ghana from 1985 to 1992. He was honoured in 2016 by having a campus thoroughfare named after him. The eulogy at the public ceremony said of him: "After leaving office, he continued with service through the Association of African Universities where the campaign to pressure academic freedom in African Universities was given greater voice. This has ensured that many universities, to a large extent, are able to operate without much political interference." *StarrFMonline*, April 18, 2016 www.starrfmonline.com

[2] Except that, forced into the showers at my grammar school, I had to explain what circumcision was all about.

[3] I am 'a person with epilepsy', which is an inherited, family condition. My mother was permanently excluded from school at the age of 10, when she had a seizure in front of her classmates. Teachers feared that this gentle child would 'become violent'. My research on racial prejudice has been paralleled by work on prejudice and discrimination against people with visible disabilities (e.g. Bagley & King, 2005).

[4] www.fromthegroundup.nl When I told Abbie that she would have reduced fees if she enrolled at the University of Calgary, where I worked, she replied: "Any university which employs you can't be worth attending." She was probably right.

[5] I am also elaborating a Muslim account of 'gay identity', arguing from Qu'ranic and Sunnah sources how Islam can uphold gay partnership. This is work in progress.

CHAPTER 2

SOCIAL CLASS, IDEOLOGY AND IDENTITY

INTRODUCTION

The research embodied in this book began in the late 1990s when Alice Sawyerr was developing a programme of identity enhancement for preschool children in nurseries in an Inner London Borough. This stemmed from work in a child, adolescent and adult NHS Mental Health clinic which served two distinct areas in the borough – very affluent area and predominantly white (group) population and a multi-ethnic client group from one of the most disadvantaged areas of London. It was clear from my (that is, Alice's) clinical work that some black children were confused about their ethnicity and their identity, and they had obviously been influenced by the stereotypes of black ethnicity held by the majority of white persons around them. A number of the children I[1] was working with were attending the local authority day nursery, which I will call St. John's (StJ's). It was closed some years ago, when the Local Authority replaced the nursery with a Sure Start Children's Centre.

But in 1998 the preschool age children (3–5 year olds) including some of the children in my clinical caseload, were showing some confusion about their ethnicity and identity. So, I devised an identity enhancement programme which might counter the negative stereotypes about ethnicity and skin colour that the children seemed to be identifying with. I described this programme's success in a book chapter (Sawyerr, 1999), and my work seemed to have had some influence.

In 2002 I began a linked research project, focussing initially on all of the children in StJ's, overtly examining how the "Six Early Learning Goals" prescribed by government, were being implemented in this multi-ethnic day nursery. Included in the goals were "Knowledge and understanding of the world" and "Social and emotional development", and I wanted to see how these goals included, if at all, any understanding of issues of colour and ethnicity. This research was only partially completed, since the nursery was arbitrarily closed, and was then re-opened a few months later as a Sure Start nursery, with an entirely new group of children. The politics underlying these changes we discuss below.

I analysed in detail video-recorded interactions of staff and children, interactions between the children and the audio recorded semi structured interviews with staff. More recently I have been able to focus the lens of research on to a Britain that seems to be changing rapidly in terms of ethnicity, migration, class, politics and social service provision, and I review the nursery school observational data in the light of these changes. Because the research spans a long period of time, we decided to place the two pieces of research presented below (including the study of Northern Schools carried out in 2006–2007) within the context of a historical review of equality, ethnicity and gender in Britain, with special reference to issues of education, health and community development. The period 1968 to 2008 has been chosen since it fits well with the review of literature on education, inclusion and inequality which Christopher Bagley and I were undertaking as part of the Manchester Educational Research Network programme of research.

This book embodies two "empirical studies" on ethnicity, identity and self-esteem, which are developed and discussed within three intellectual contexts. First of all, the remainder of the present chapter will set out a perspective on equality in Britain today, looked at from the perspectives of social class divisions, which are analysed within a Marxian framework which discusses the role of ethnicity, gender and occupational status in forming the strata of society. The purpose of this initial discussion is to establish a value position, in which concern is expressed for the life chances and social mobility of the lowest strata of society.

Secondly, Chapter 3 elaborates the theoretical framework of Critical Realism, a philosophy of social science research which assumes that (contrary to positivist or social constructionist methodologies) that *reality* exists independently of the researcher, and can be elaborated and understood within the framework of critical realism, whose ultimate goal is the emancipation of individuals and institutions through a self-conscious, freely chosen process of *morphogenesis*.

Thirdly reflecting our value grounding of identity studies, Chapter 4 establishes the basis of the value position which *underlabours* the critical realist model, informing and evaluating the actions of individuals in the matrix of critical realism. This chosen value position is called *Child-Centred Humanism*, which argues that all human institutions and actions should be evaluated according to the degree that they regard children's interests as having primacy in all of society's institutions: the needs and rights of children must be considered, implicitly or explicitly, as the building blocks of all of humanity's social institutions.

Chapter 5 is concerned with episodes of equality and ethnicity in the period 1968 to 2008. This time period was chosen firstly since the empirical materials considered in this volume were planned for and gathered in a ten-year period occurring within this time frame (1998 to 2008); this entire period is also one of significant change and development in research and policies concerning ethnicity, gender and equality in British society. In order to do justice to this perspective, we have to consider, historically speaking, the preceding decade as well. Since other scholars have written systematic reviews of this history, we summarise their accounts, and instead focus in detail on specific episodes and themes, such as the history of medicine, the history of childhood, equality and exclusion of youth in British society, and specific episodes and themes in the movement towards ethnic equality. This Chapter should be read in parallel with Appendix A of the thesis, which is a lengthy and systematic review of the literature on equality and exclusion of youths in the period 1968 to 2008.

Chapter 6 establishes the themes of ethnicity, gender and identity in charting "the evolution and development of self-esteem research in Britain and America", observing significant changes which these studies have identified, through the decades from the 1960s onwards, from the pessimistic findings of "doll studies" to recent decades in which positive self-esteem in ethnic minority children has made remarkable gains. Our empirical work in this field is outlined in Chapter 7, which presents the findings of an observational study of a multicultural day nursery, following our development of a programme for enhancement of ethnic identity in young children. The findings of this study are placed within the context of a critical realist case analysis.

Chapter 8 extends the review of literature to older children and adolescents, including American studies showing that African American adolescents now have excellent levels of self-esteem. This review in addition, focusses on gender, including literature showing that adolescent females have significantly lower levels of self-esteem (as measured in particular by the Rosenberg Self-Esteem Scale: the RSES). Reasons for this are explored, including the literature on the negative impact of sexual abuse on self-esteem in females. It is argued that differential levels of self-esteem observed in many cultures might be explained by the incidence and impact which child sexual abuse has on adolescent girls.

Issues of ethnicity and gender are explored in the second empirical study of this thesis, including the analysis of a previously unpublished data set collected in 2006 to 2007, in ten Northern English Schools, focussing on 2,025 school students aged 11 to 18. Using standardised measures of self-reported abusive events, the study showed that the RSES is indeed a structurally reliable measure when used with English students, and correlated significantly with validated measures of mental health. When history of sexual abuse was taken into account, self-esteem differences between the genders did not reach statistical significance. Within boys, ethnicity was not correlated with self-esteem, but in girls, those of African-Caribbean origin had higher levels of self-esteem than their female peers.

In the final Chapter, the importance of treating the school as a unique community which can address the social and psychological needs of all students is stressed. This is illustrated by two schools in the Northern Schools sample, which had marked differences in terms of histories of sexual and physical abuse, self-esteem and psychological adjustment. It is advocated, using the critical realist model, that schools and the communities they serve, should be unique centres for social action research which address problems of the families and children they serve.

CONCEPTS OF CLASS, ETHNICITY, INEQUALITY, GENDER AND EXPLOITATION

It will rapidly become apparent to the reader that a concern with Marx's idea of class oppression, alienation and 'the reserve army of labour' frequently occurs in the pages that follow. The work of Marx which we have drawn on is his political humanism and freedom from economic determinism, and not Marx's frequently misunderstood and misapplied writings on economic reform (Singer, 1996).

It is possible to be a Marxist scholar, and not to mention Marx, or Marxian concepts at all. Thus in Brian Simon's *Education and the Social Order 1940–1990* (published in 1991) Simon simply spells out in great detail how educational systems control and socialize young people in ways which make them acquiescent and useful for the prevailing social, political and economic order of Britain. This is despite periods of educational reform and "break out" (such as the beginning of comprehensives, and the expansion of the university sector). The established order of capital clearly, in Simon's historical analysis, re-imposes itself and reorders changing institutions, in a phase which Simon labels "downhill all the way" beginning in the 1970s with the re-imposition of neoliberalism, which reflected, according to Clarke (2007) the crisis of capitalism brought about by America's prosecution of the Vietnam war, bringing in its wake "neoliberalism globalisation, imperialism with empires" (Radice, 2007).

Despite a New Labour government slogan that an era of "education, education, education" would be initiated in Britain (Wragg, 2004a), the decrease in funding for education and social services has continued (in Britain and other capitalist economies) inexorably from 1980 into a condition which Tomlinson (2013) describes as the increasing globalisation of capitalist enterprise:

> Governments in modern capitalist nation-states are overseeing and encouraging a vast expansion of education and training, for reasons which those in control of policy and practice are not always clear about. Groups who were previously excluded or received minimal schooling are now included in formal schooling for longer and longer periods. Groups who previously monopolised privileged kinds of education leading to guaranteed employment now face threats of status and employment competition with larger numbers who aspire or are coerced into more formal schooling and its assessments. In order to retain privileges, elite groups support the reconstitution of segregative policies and provisions. (Tomlinson, 2013, p. 5)

In Britain, it seems that in the long run educational systems will continue to serve the global economic power systems.

The educational system is changing, and so are the manifestations of social class in Britain, as Mike Savage and his team (2015) make clear in their Great British Class Survey (GBCS) which obtained surprisingly full accounts of many social, cultural and economic aspects of their lives from some 161,000 respondents who completed a media-sponsored internet survey in 2011. The data allowed Savage and colleagues to construct a seven-fold schema of social class, with the Elite at the top, and the precariously-living proletariat, mostly poor, often unemployed at the bottom of the scale: this "precarious proletariat" was dubbed (following Standing, 2011) the Precariat, and are estimated to number about 15 percent of Britain's population. (Only one percent of the internet responders fell into this class, so the team led by Savage carried out direct sampling to get an accurate profile of this group). They are sneered at, derided, looked down on by many in the classes above them, and called Scum, Chavs and Yobs, in modern slang. On the three bases of social class grouping in Savage's (2015) analysis: income and wealth; cultural capital; and social capital, the Precariat are at the bottom of the class system, blamed for their own poverty. These are the 'reserve army of labour', useful cheap labour for capitalism in times of boom, and useful scapegoats in times of bust. They occupy, in Savage's sociology, "worlds of shame and stigma":

> ... The rise in rents in the neighbourhood caused them great anxiety. Owning a home was not something they could even dare to imagine.

The devastating impact of the bedroom tax, benefit caps and austerity cuts to local community services have had on their families and themselves were and are, felt sharply and painfully. They raise their voices and shout and swear; they are angry with – and frightened by – these precarious times. (Savage, 2015, p. 342)

Savage and his team have surprisingly little to say about gender – how women conceptualise themselves within systems of material wealth and reward, cultural capital, and social interactions, and the differences which partnerships or marriage might make, nor about what being single or in gay partnership means in terms of class profiles. But they imply that in the Precariat, women dislike self-conceptions of class, citing earlier research: women tend to reject ideas of being "working class". These young women "… invested in femininity and respectability in response to the (real or imagined) judgement of others – *judgements based on the values and morals associated with the dominant class*. Yet they did not possess the required sorts of capital – economic, cultural or social – to be anything other than working class women" (Savage, 2015, pp. 365–366, italics in original). Moreover, drawing on the work of Skeggs (1997) Savage says that within the 'emotional politics' surrounding the identity of Precariat women there is "… fear, desire, resentment and humiliation" (Skeggs, 1997). It also reminds us that aspects of class identifiers are also shaped in particular ways by gender (along with race and sexuality) (Savage, 2015, p. 366).[2]

Guy Standing (2011, 2014) divides the precariat (15% of the population, according to Savage) into two groups: at the bottom are the group he terms "the lumpen proletariat" whom the established order sees as "dangerous" in terms of their socially destructive anarchy, based on their psychological, social and political disarray, their dangerously figurative and literal fire-setting of the property and ideas of the respectable economic classes. Following Marx, Standing – Professor of Development Studies at the University of London's School of Oriental and African Studies – echoes Marx and Engels in writing a manifesto on behalf of the precariat whom he describes as a 'trans-European, bastard child of global capitalism' (Standing, 2011, 2014). They are, he says, a true class created by capitalism, following the economic logic of Marx's historical analyses.

Where do *ethnic minorities* cluster within Savage's class systems? Certainly not randomly. They are over-represented in two class groups: Technical Middle Class; and Emerging Service Workers. And they are under-represented amongst the Precariat. However, Savage is not very specific about types of ethnic minority within the class groupings, and this is obviously a field for further research. It seems likely that ethnic minorities will maximise their educational opportunities, their reserves of cultural and social capital, and will increasingly move out of the lowest status groupings into the better paid technical sectors, even though they are more than a generation away from achieving parity in the Elite and Established Middle Class groups described by Savage (2015). Heath (2014) uses census and labour force survey data to show how ethnic minorities in Britain are slowly climbing occupational and status ladders, despite the factors that there continues to be a significant amount of racial discrimination in employment (Bagley & Abubaker, 2017). In this latter research we showed that the ethnic minority candidate for employment has to apply for twice the number of jobs as the 'white' candidate, before even being offered an interview.

Educational sociologists, following Standing's, and Savage's class analyses, have coined the term "precarity", in discussing the fate of some school leavers. Dovermark and Beach (2016) in referring to the classic study by Willis (1978) on working class boys "learning to labour", title their article: "From learning to labour to learning for precarity." They observed: *"A demand on national economies in the 1970s [during the Thatcher era] was that they should begin to increase their labour market flexibility, which came to mean transferring risks of insecurity on to workers. Education was one way to prepare future workers for Precarity ..."* (p. 174) Their analysis concerns not only Britain, but the whole of Europe. Batsleer (2016) in an incisive ethnographic study of young NEETS in Manchester show that living off food bank handouts was (for the capitalist class) a useful way by which low-achieving youth were ritually subjugated at a very basic level (nutrition) into membership of the underclass.

Tomlinson (2013) addresses the interesting issue of how middle class parents may cope with the potentially downward mobility of their children who are not particularly successful in school: it is crucially important for middle class parents that their children should not join the ranks of "the ignorant yobs", of the precariat, who in British society are usually blamed for their own failure. Middle class parents can maximise wealth and social capital by gaining either private education, or a favoured state school (through choice of where they live), private tuition and psychological help, and if necessary getting special educational status for their children (e.g. getting extra help because of dyslexia). The social capital of the middle and upper classes helps them to access the best routes in further education and training, and in using social influences to gain employment for children who would in consequence be able to escape joining the ranks of the precariat.

From her international survey Tomlinson points to the case of Finland, in which high scores on international tests of achievement (e.g. PISA) are gained by teaching which effectively truncates the standard deviation of the measures, so that that most pupils achieve close to the group's high average marks. In Britain, the low educational achievers are often blamed for their own failures (Johnston, 2007): a chaotic and ever-changing system of educational initiatives for youth who are or who will become NEETS (Not in Education, Employment of Training), and the frequent failure of these programmes, often leads to denigration of the underachievers (Tomlinson, 2013, pp. 125–126).

Chronic poverty, the continuation of life in the underclass from one generation to the next, demeans the culture of life and its social meaning for up to 15 percent of England's population. It diminishes health, it promotes family brokenness, individual malaise and despair, the neglect and maltreatment of children, the abuse of the body, the frequency of illness, and the prematurity of death (Marmot 2008, 2010, 2015). Healing poverty through initiatives such as a universal, living wage (Flaschel et al., 2012; Standing, 2014) could be hugely cost effective in public health terms (Bellis et al., 2014a).

But England is unlikely to adopt the policy of a living wage. Instead, policy researchers focus on absolute poverty and destitution in the land. The leading advocates in this field from the Rowntree Trust present considerable evidence from the research they have funded, that chronic poverty is demeaning, and eats away at the basis for mental and social health (Unwin, 2013). Pointing to the general economic structure, they argue that poverty is both unnecessary, and easy to solve through fiscal measures. But they fail to address the more fundamental political or value question: who benefits from the institution of poverty in Britain?

The same question: who benefits? Must be asked of Gender and Ethnic inequalities. It is certainly in men's interests to have a class of humans who will satisfy their sexual needs, ensuring that their genetic prowess is transmitted through children, and to have women who will care for and socialise those children in satisfactory ways, cook and clean the dwelling place, and supplement household income through some kind of external labour. Feminism is clearly a threat to this comfortable male hegemony. The widespread sexual exploitation of girls and adolescent women, which we discuss at some length later in this book, is the crude expression of this male hegemony.

In the past, ethnic minority groups in Britain may have been trained to serve the dominant classes through special kinds of socialisation and control, through which those of "inferior" colour, nationality or religion (Catholics and Muslims for example), were trained to accept the stereotypes placed upon them, but nevertheless had to become cheerful hewers of wood, and drawers of water. The Tottenham riots of 2011 finally consigned that model of socialization to the flames (Unwin, 2011, 2013; Standing, 2014).

In a fascinating account of the sociology of popular culture in Britain, Jones, (2011) analyses media and political accounts of *chavs*,[3] an apparently flamboyant group sometimes with temporary wealth, but allegedly little taste, who are trying to rise out of the precariat, but who are sneered at and stigmatised for trying to cohere as a cultural group.[4] The media-inspired campaign of denigration of this lower class group parallels the rise in income inequality in Britain, and the dismembering of the welfare state. According to Jones' political analysis these events are connected, and the chavs are a group to be kicked around by respectable folk whose aspiration for cultural capital glances enviously at the class above them, without sympathy for the sneered-at class below. These chavs are the welfare recipients, the scroungers, the welfare cheats, the deceitful layabouts and criminals, 'the feral underclass'. Middle Britain loves the class above them, and despises the class below. This mix of media and popular hatred is extremely functional for the capitalist social order. Chav-hate is, arguably, a greater problem than Islamophobia (Kundari, 2007; Fekete, 2009). Muslims have a solid ethical and spiritual tradition which assures them that they have moral surety in the face of hatred (Al-Refai & Bagley, 2008). Chavs, on the available evidence, have a much weaker identity formation (Jones, 2011).

CONCLUSIONS

The Chapters on self-esteem, identity and self-concept in ethnic minorities – the literature that we review and analyse, and our empirical reports of studies with children and adolescents – show that in this field, at least, there has been considerable, positive change. No longer do black and ethnic minority children and adolescents have an inferiorised self-concept thrust upon them. This is not however the situation for many females, especially white females.

Our argument will be that our greatest concern should not be merely, or primarily, with the cultural and social development of the self-concept of black and ethnic minority children. Our concern should not be only with ethnic minorities, but also with the "poor whites", and their children who are making up the bulk of Britain's 'perpetual underclass'.

Furthermore, we want to know why in a recent WHO international comparison of 42 world nations of young people aged 11, 13 and 15 (Inchley et al., 2016) the group with the *poorest* emotional health were 15-year-olds in Britain. British adolescent girls were also close to last in the nations surveyed in terms of physical health (measured by poor diet, exercise, obesity, sexual health, and alcohol and substance use). And why, in *every* nation and age-profile studied in the WHO survey, did females have poorer mental health than males? Is this connected with the prevalence and impact of child maltreatment, and sexual abuse experienced by females, which we explore in a later chapter?

Britain and America of all the developed nations have the most unequal distribution of wealth, as measured by the Gini coefficient (UN, 2005; Booth, 2008a). Do these two nations (which also come at the bottom of league tables for child and adolescent health indicators – Wilkinson, 2005; UNESCO, 2007; Currie et al., 2008; OECD, 2008; Friedli, 2009; Wilkinson & Pickett, 2009) have integral or systemic links between inequality and the chronically poor health and adjustment in their underclass? Certainly, these two nations appear to be the most prominent of the developed nations in which global capitalism has imposed itself, and in which the situation of an underclass perpetuated by lack of social mobility is, among the developed nations, the most enduring (Sawyerr & Bagley, 2016).[5]

The underlying economic forces of neoliberalism underpin ("require") these class-based differences in life chances, and informed the economic and social policies (recreated from earlier ideas of economists such as Adam Smith) of the Conservative government's agenda in Britain in the period from 1979 to 1995. These policies were largely continued by a New Labour government attempting to occupy the 'middle ground' of politics. This neoliberalism, as defined by Saad-Filho and Johnston (2005),

> … is the ideology of the market and private interests as opposed to state intervention. Although it is true that neoliberalism conveys an ideology and a propaganda of its own, it is fundamentally a new social order in which the power and income of the upper fractions of the ruling classes – the wealthiest persons – was re-established in the wake of a setback … this upper capitalist class and the financial institutions through which its power is enforced is a hegemonic force. Although the conditions which accounted for the structural crisis were gradually superseded, most of the world economy remained plagued by slow growth and unemployment, and inequality increased. (p. 2)

This inequality, we argue, is most enduring in the neoliberal economies of the USA and the UK, and thrives on the lack of social mobility of the poorest social classes (Sawyerr & Bagley, 2016).

Finally: in leading the reader on this research journey we have needed to tell "my story", explaining how our own identities and research interests have been formed; and how we have come to explore the research philosophy of Critical Realism, which has allowed us to assert with some confidence an underlying value premise which informs how we interpret all research findings in the human sciences: the philosophy of *Child-Centred Humanism*.

NOTES

[1]   The term 'I' in this chapter refers to Alice Sawyerr.

[2]   Clearly, Bourdieu's sociology is influential in Savage's analysis: "... the thinking of the French sociologist Pierre Bourdieu [offers] the most perceptive approach to unravelling the complexities of class today" (Savage, 2015, p. 19). That, concedes Savage, is why the original research questions explored in detail ideas about "cultural capital", which may shroud ("mask" in Marxian terminology) the layers of social class. The upper two classes inherit cultural capital; the other classes gaze adoringly, with longing and admiration, over the invisible fence, or within the pages in the popular organs of social control, at the dream world of their masters.

[3]   A word derived from the Romany language, meaning "kid".

[4]   For example, the *Mirror* newspaper of July 7th, 2016 gloated over the suicide attempt of "the King of the Chavs" who squandered his £9.7 million lottery win in 11 years, and is now "a penniless drug addict".

[5]   Global capitalism's negative 'neo-liberal' impact is greatest for the countries of the *developing* world, as the relevant essays among the 30 chapters in Saad-Filho and Johnston's (2005) edited volume, show.

CHAPTER 3

CRITICAL REALISM AND DIALECTICAL CRITICAL REALISM

Grounded Values and Reflexivity in Social Research

INTRODUCTION

The concept of Critical Realism (and its later development using concepts from Hegel and Marx) known as dialectical critical realism (DCR), comes from philosophy, and not from social science. It uses philosophical language and reasoning, which is often challenging for the social scientist who has had no grounding in formal logic, or in the discipline of philosophical analysis. DCR is not an account of social science, but rather a philosophy of how knowledge about people and their social structures may be construed, interpreted, described and fitted together. DCR assumes that although the ground of knowledge is real, it also has a value base: there is no such thing as value-free social science.

Critical Realism (CR) clearly prefers social science research which employs qualitative, case-study methods, but acknowledges that multiple methods (including surveys and statistical analyses) can be used in order to gain the fullest information about "a case" (Alderson, 2013).

Critical Realism emerged from the writings of the philosopher Roy Bhaskar who was seeking an alternative to what he saw as ambiguous and often confusing models of scientific methodology, particularly, the Popperian doctrine of "falsifying hypotheses" (Popper, 1992). He extended his critique to the methodologies of social science (Bhaskar, 1975), attempting to find a way forward from what he saw as the stultification and confusion of "positivism", "phenomenology", "post-modernism", and "social constructionism". Critical realism has been attractive to social researchers, and theorists who are committed to a firm ideological basis for viewing human action (e.g. Marxists, Muslims, Catholics) in asserting that *structures* within society are real and although their influence may be debated, their *being* or ontology (e.g. class exploitation, alienation, the nature of spiritual being) is not in doubt.

It is of course possible that Marxists and Catholics will disagree profoundly on what is or should be salient (Creaven, 2007) but CR nevertheless also lays the way open for dialogue and compromise between seemingly incompatible systems through the process of dialectical critical realism (Bhaskar, 1993/2008). Bhaskar adapts the Hegelian model of dialectical debate (traditionally: thesis, antithesis, synthesis) and goes beyond this model in positing a fourth level in the dialectical process which leads to action for, or advocacy of change. Moreover, this process of dialectical critical realism (DCR) is a continuous process in the lives of social systems, dyads and individuals, and there is continuous feedback between the 'agents' (the actors or individuals in DCR), or between various individuals: through these reflexive ideas and exchanges, organisations are in a process of continuous change and adjustment to new feedbacks, and the changing of social structures.

At this stage, a challenge in reading CR theoretical texts and research emerging from that theory should be mentioned: Critical Realism has developed its own vocabulary, and has coined new words ('neologisms') which the student may have difficulty in learning, or retaining. Furthermore, common English words are used in a way which attributes a rather different meaning to that of everyday language. The use of the word *absence* is a case in point. The difficulty of grasping CR concepts may be illustrated by this quotation from Anderson (2016): *"Absence as a noun or verb is central to the DCR process of absenting absences, constraints, ills, contradictions, oppressive power, relations or inequities. Absence is the crucial empty physical, social and mental space that enables movement, imagined alternatives, processes and change"* (p. 166). Thus "absence" actually means (in some, but not in all situations) the presence or existence of some positive force for social change.[1] Despite the complexities of her CR model, Anderson in her two volumes on *The Politics of Childhood Real and Imagined* (2013, 2016) has many valuable things to say, and we have tried to utilise her insights in this book.

What one finds in CR writing is an absence of dogma, and a willingness to engage in debate (the essence of DCR) to reach compromise. Thus Collier (1994) offers a useful synthesis of Weber's "individualism" and Durkheim's "collectivism" showing (pp. 144–145) that these are not alternative models of individuals within social systems, but in the DCR mode, interactive ones, which coexist and offer simultaneously, ways of promoting social action for change: individuals co-operate collectively, but remain individuals, is the message. Thus, in Collier's (1994) analysis of Marx's writing on *Capital*, most wage earners are mystified by the nature of capitalism that exploits them: their alienation remains unmasked. But in the Dialectical Critical Realist model they are capable of understanding and changing both their modes of thought and their social actions, their necessary "underlabouring" (using a term borrowed from Locke) in addressing capitalist exploitation. The worker who fails to grasp the nature of his or her exploitation remains in a state of "non-realism", asserts Collier (1994, p. 12).

In response to critics of this Marxian approach, Collier (1994) says:

> ... modern non-realists often accuse realists of dogmatism because of our defence of objectivity. They accuse us of arrogance in claiming truth for our theories ... [but] ... To claim objective truth for one's statements is to lay one's cards on the table, to expose oneself to the possibility of refutation. (p. 13)

This bold claim to recognise "reality" (which is, of course, initially an intuitional process) rejects postmodern ideas of the relativity of knowledge and the impossibility of constructing linear models of basic cause; and the rejection of social constructivist ideas that knowledge and values are relative, and are generated through unique sets of social interactions. One understands why CR has proved attractive to the Muslim scholar Matthew Wilkinson (2015). In "making sense" of his experience of teaching in a Muslim school he says:

> ... this book draws upon the tradition of dialectical European philosophy, epitomised by Hegel ... Most recently, this tradition has been brought with great energy and conceptual sophistication into the contemporary academy by the founding figure of the philosophy of critical realism, Roy Bhaskar, as well as others following his lead, such as Alan Norrie, Andrew Wright and Margaret Archer. Critical realism is exceptional in its coherent articulation of a contemporary philosophy of being, of knowing and real personal, ethical and social change, and its *refusal* to reduce being of all types, including spiritual being, to socially constructed epistemology or merely psychological or semantic meaning. This makes the philosophy of critical realism at its original, dialectical and spiritual moments an ideal vehicle for the development of a systematic rationale to interpret Islam and Islam-in-education in a multi-faith world. (p. 10)

Wilkinson draws on both Islamic and critical realist thinking in arguing that Muslim education should be "a philosophy for success", or empowerment (or, as Marxists would put it, the unmasking of alienation). *Success* is seen by Wilkinson as embedded in the multidimensional development and self-realisation of human social interaction within and between the four planes of social being defined by CR theorists. These planes are:

The Real: Material transactions with nature (e.g. "the ground of being", "the essence of humans", "the uniqueness of each human being" counterpoised with forces of nature, polity and economy which impose themselves on humans; and the divine revelations of various world religions);

The Actual: Inter-subjective (interpersonal) transactions between individuals or 'human agents' in different settings, including socialization and social control, the imposition of racialized identities; economic deprivation; forced migration *et alia*: and the understandings which humans have of these controlling forces, in dialogue, in writing, in protest, in political movements;

The Empirical: Social relations at the *non-reducible* level of structures, institutions and forms;

The Transcendent: The embodied personality's liberation through mutual tolerance, the shedding of false consciousness, spiritual fulfilment; awareness of self-potential, self-actualization. (Adapted from Bhaskar, 1993/2008 – this is also the basis of Alderson's MELD model, explained below).

Wilkinson focuses his analysis on "the embodied personality" and his or her spiritual, intellectual, affective-cultural, civic, and instrumental dimensions. Each of these dimensions has distinct and interrelated or "articulated" ontologies. "Ontological realism" concerns the philosophical study of *being* (the first level of being in CR theory), and is a central concept within DCR:

> A basic understanding of critical realist ontology, the philosophical study of being is … that being exists independently of our knowledge of it and in particular, our ability to describe it, so that it cannot be reduced to discourse, nor is it merely contained or constructed in the semiotics of our speech. (p. 50)

Alderson (2016) in construing "the politics of childhood" offers the following explanations of DCR's 4-levels of analysis, which, following Bhaskar, she terms *MELD*. The first level is *1M* – DCR concepts of basic reality e.g. moral realism, which consists (in social science) of ethical naturalism. The 'moral realism' inherent at this basic level of DCR

> … accepts that harm and benefit are universal, causal, moral realities, which are defined and experienced in varied local and personal ways. To deny moral realism would set up theory/practice inconsistency … Because humans are vulnerable, sensitive, social beings, able to flourish and to suffer, moral realism is part of human nature and daily life, and is not artificially introduced (Archer, 2003; Bhaskar, 1986; Collier, 1999) … 1M seeks to avoid the anthropic fallacy that places humans at the centre of the purpose and meaning of the universe

(Bhaskar, 2000, p. 26). Instead, 1M sees that we are part of nature ... A related problem is the adultist fallacy. This sets rational adults at the apex of morality, and regards childhood as a slow climb up from lower, natural, pre-social, pre-moral babyhood to higher, socialised, moral adulthood. (Alderson, 2016, pp. 28–29)

Priscilla Alderson in her two volumes on 'the politics of childhood' offers a vigorous and often moving account of the children she has been involved with in her research over a 30-year-period, but admits that she is a recent 'convert' to DCR: "The challenge of rethinking my past research in relation to DCR, and of writing this book, has helped me, and I hope it will help readers, to see how DCR enlarges research theory and analysis. Since learning about DCR, I have revised some of my former ideas and discarded others, on the continuing journey of learning and changing" (Alderson, 2013, p. 8).

Alderson terms the second level in her DCR analysis *2E* (second edge) "... which concerns the transition into intervention and *process in product. 2E* concerns actively negating problems that were identified at 1M (Bhaskar, 2008, pp. 97–98). This involves absenting *aporia* (contradictions and constraints, ills and untruths) ..." (Alderson, 2016, p. 34). Exactly how this is done is problematic however, and often one is challenged to know where to "fit" one's research findings within the four levels of analysis, and how to interpret findings (and undertake further research) in terms of absence, dialogue, dialectic or change – for example, the research studies on children which Alderson presents us with. She continues (p. 36): "A seven-scale DCR framework for interdisciplinary analysis (Bhaskar & Danemark, 2006) helps to connect many themes ..."

We move to Alderson's third level called *3L*. She terms this level the *totality of change*, and comments " ... 3L *recognizes that we all share the core universal human nature, our common humanity, and we are all unique and ethically different ... We are interconnected and interdependent, dialectic replaces dichotomy, 'is' connects to 'ought', and 'ought' connects to 'can'* (Bhaskar, 2010, pp. 146–8) ... " (Alderson, 2016, p. 41). It is at this level of understanding social structure that Margaret Archer's ideas (1995, 2000, 2003) of *morphogenesis* (personal change through dialectic interchange, and self-reflection) may become increasingly important. And then at the level of the fourth dimension 4D, there occurs the fullest realisation of *reflexive analysis*.

The transformative agency of *4D* aims for *"...emancipation ... in the free society where each individual's flourishing depends on everyone flourishing. 4D works to overcome the false sense of self as separate and isolated. We relate to the world and to other people through recognising what we share in common* (Bhaskar, 2002, p. 305). *The key questions concern identity (who am I?) and agency (what am I to do?)"* (Alderson, 2016, p. 46). At this stage then, false consciousness is shed, and alienation is unmasked.

The combined model is thus called *MELD* – in summary:

1M: Basic values, which are often unseen or unrecognized, but which inform or control action (e.g. covert power systems and alienation)

2E: Seeds of hope, and the dawning of understanding and dialectics. The realisation of *absence,* of lack of fulfilment, and yearning for change.

3L: Understanding of how social structures constrain us.

4D: Critical reflection and social change.

Clearly, this is an ideal (and idealistic) model, and Bhaskar (2000, pp. 8–9) warns us of the possibility of "malign MELD", in which negative, coercive powers subvert consciousness, control debates (e.g. through newspaper campaigns), and ensure that the powers of capital are unassailed, however much information we have (e.g. on health inequalities, on educational underachievement, or on poor quality schools). The 'seeds of hope' of 2E are often dashed.

Alderson devotes her two volumes to accounts of how, effectively, to liberate children so that their rights are fully realised. She uses the 1E assumptions about the "real" world and its state in nature (what Wilkinson in his Islamic formulation would call the original garden of paradise in which, following the acquisition of knowledge, Adam and Eve are charged with "naming all things").

> Childhood and nature overlap in symbol and in practice ... ways in which children are treated reflect activities towards nature. These range from neglect and abuse to violence that wastes potential and ends the lives of millions of children. (Alderson, 2016, p. 46)

Alderson then devotes her volumes to analysing children's lives (especially those in contact with health care systems) in detail, explaining how their condition is perceived and classified, and how they are treated – fit into the MELD hierarchy.

> The DCR aim of promoting utopias is to negate alienation ... schools are particularly good places for transformation, having the time, space and long-term relations to nurture utopian work ... DCR concepts can assist teachers in being reflective, self-critical, and collegial ... DCR's concrete utopian imagination is not a prescription for the future, but for an open

society where individuals decide what to do with their freedom. It is an inner urge that flows universally from the lack of elemental absence (lack, need, want desire). (pp. 157–158)

Considering alienation's ending, Alderson speculates about the 'natural communism' that would follow – what Quakers would call the Kingdom of Heaven existing on earth now, through the process of constructive relationships.[2] In Alderson's formulation this communism goes beyond Marx (who merely wanted 'from each according to his ability, to each according to his need'): "Marx's ... generous giving and taking is not possible if everything is already shared"[3] (p. 159). In this model, the needs, rights and interests of children are not separate, but shared, in the utopia which Alderson anticipates. Alderson's (2013) chapter on "Inner Being: Alienation and Flourishing" sums up, for us what is most inspirational in Alderson's critical realist theory of social science. She comprehensively demolishes the myth of "value free social science". Research with children, she argues, is not only value-informed: its entire goal in showing how children can "flourish" at the highest level of the MELD model is, as Bhaskar put it "value saturated" at each step in the MELD framework:

Having reviewed support for value-informed social research, I now summarise MELD 4D, fourth dimension, where values are central ... the traditional Hegelian dialectic is taken towards logical, consistent completeness ... To include real being (ontology) and real transformation, MELD 1M first moment begins with non-identity and absence; 2E second edge involves negativity and oppressive power; 3L, third level, concerns open, dynamic totalities [of social structure] which move on to 4D, fourth dimension, of praxis, transformative agency in ethical practice and liberating power, the dialectic that is 'the pulse of freedom'. I hope that this chapter, by showing all the MELD moments, will help to clarify the meaning and relevance of some earlier parts of this book. They all relate to the DCR logic that human beings inevitably desire and move towards freedom and justice, and that this is or should be the central concern of social science ... When individuals are out of touch and alienated from their body and nature (plane 1), from other people (plane 2), and from structures and institutions (plane 3) they can become unable to act in order to absent the absences and power2 [of oppressive forces], and they are denied the capacity for transformation at MELD 4D. (Alderson, 2013, p. 138)

Although DCR is a complex philosophy for social science research, Alderson's reconstruction of her previous research with children using the DCR framework, which she elucidates in the passage quoted above, is both enlightening and enervating. The reader's journey in following this difficult intellectual model seems justified. According to Bhaskar (1993/2008): "Practical, concrete utopianism stands in contrast to abstract, intellectual utopianism ... being practical involves absenting constraining absences, as each in their own way, human beings try to overcome power2 and 'master-slave' relations' in society and nature ... the dialectic is an inner urge that flows universally from the logic of elemental absence (lack, need, want, desire) ... against power relations towards freedom as flourishing" (p. 14).

The critic will say that Alderson has taken a winding and intellectually convoluted path to reach an inspiring conclusion. But there is no denying that her work *is* inspirational. Priscilla Alderson's (2013) reflections on the religious origins of "theories of the self" in critical realist theory is fascinating too, for the student of self-concept: she writes that: "Ideas about the self also illuminate the fourth plane of social being, the inner self, and MELD *4D* on *flourishing*, and its converse, *misery*" (p. 140).

Consideration of the soul, the inner or spiritual self, may be outside of the bounds of conventional sociology, but for Alderson "DCR explores unseen deeper realities, and shows the problems in social research that ignores them ... Without some explicit theories of human nature and the young self ... [research] ignores concepts of harm and benefit to children ... ideas from religion and philosophy seep into common imaginings of the self ... they [Jesus, Muhammad, Buddha] exemplified 'childlike' humility, poverty, humility , vulnerability, willingness to admit ignorance and to learn, with obedience to a transcendent goodness and an innocent detachment from worldly power" (pp. 141–142). Alderson then turns back to her mentor, Roy Bhaskar (2002) who "theorised an embodied personality, a psychic being or soul or anima, and a ground state, all three striving for humanity."

Brad Shipway (2010) writing about critical realism's contribution to the discipline of education comments on CR as a philosophical and a transcendental (spiritual) model that "encompasses educational administrators and policy makers, teacher educators, and philosophers of education in what they do and think." CR uncouples itself from postmodernism, enabling researchers to describe the 'real' world through a grounded, value-based ontology. Shipway quotes Collier (1994):

> ... critical realism is an ongoing research programme within the
> human sciences, and in particular in their theoretically and politically

contentious border areas. It is certainly not a completed system which can be applied in these fields to solve all problems: on the contrary, by treating scientific projects as explorations of realities with inexhaustible depths, it helps to keep these projects open for self-criticism and development" (Collier, 1994, p. 236). According to Shipway (2010) CR has "an emancipatory mission" for research and practice in education. "Critical realism supports a stratified, democratic use of homology,[4] and the exercise of power is a vital condition for the possibility of emancipation of students and those who work with them. (p. 5)[5]

MATTHEW WILKINSON: DIALECTICAL CRITICAL REALISM AND ISLAM

The generosity of the shared dialectical process also flows from Wilkinson's (2015) analysis of Islam. He too uses the MELD hierarchy, and concludes his *1E* analysis: "*The Islamic Critical Realism (ICR) fulcrum offers the philosophical possibility that God may have granted genuine spiritual insight to those who fall outside one's own religious tradition and this can enrich rather than threaten one's own commitment to faith and facilitate a genuinely respectful engagement with the 'other'*" (p. 64).

Moving to *2E*, Wilkinson observes how Bhaskar (1993/2008) adapted Hegel:

He radically alters the phases of dialectic into non-identity, to absence, to totality to transformative praxis in an extension of the 'revindication' of ontology and the positing of a new ontology of original critical realism" (p. 66). Further, on absence, Wilkinson observes: "According to critical realist thinkers, absence, negativity and change are essential parts of the duality of presence and absence in being (Norris, 2010). For example silence is the precondition of speech, rests are indispensable to musical sound, and as we know from natural science, empty space is a necessary condition of solid objects. In the experience of selfhood, a sense/knowledge/belief that 'I am this' necessarily entails a sense/knowledge/belief that 'I am *not* that.' (p. 66)

In DCR absence is, crucially, transformative. "Indeed, dialectical change is understood by critical realists as the process … of remedying or removing absence" (Bhaskar, 1993/2008). For Bhaskar, positive change is often the removal of, or progression from, something negative. The archetype of this movement is the process of abolishing (i.e. absenting) the conditions of slavery – and on the meaning of the "master-slave" relationship Bhaskar has much to say.

In Wilkinson's (2015) account of the journey towards combining British and Islamic citizenship in Muslim adolescents, he first paints the *2E* picture of absence, and the 'absence' of seriousness' in National Curriculum goals concerning citizenship education. But as his research progressed, Wilkinson moved to 3L, the level of 'seriousness'. As an example, he cites Lovelock's (1979) idea of *Gaia*, the self-regulating, self-healing universe, which he relates to the Qur'anic idea of *kalifa* or stewardship of the earth. At this level, DCR concepts allowed Wilkinson to focus on transformative ideas, on the notion of the primacy of structure over individual agency. At the *4D* level, the meaning (and pedagogy) of citizenship education was taken outside of the classroom into 'the world', so that

> ... unity-in-diversity is the bedrock of society, in which institutional structure both predominates over individual agency and can be transformed by it. This task of linking agency with structure means that more than any other subject at the level of 4D (Fourth Dimension – transformative praxis), citizenship education needs to be carried outside of the classroom into the community. (Wilkinson, 2015, p. 246)

MARGARET SCOTFORD ARCHER

Archer is, in our reading, the most impressive of the sociologists who have been inspired by Bhaskar's critical realism, and its unfolding from and through Marxism and Hegel, into dialectical critical realism, into realms of theology, and how in critical realist theory, we may understand and apprehend notions of the divine (Archer et al., 2004).

Bhaskar's (1993/2008) earlier consideration of (and modification of) Marxian theory had led some American commentators to label him as a Marxist (and hence the virtual boycott of DCR by American sociologists – Gorski, 2013). Transcending the purely material concerns of Marxian ideology, he embarked on a spiritual journey, exploring Hindu and Buddhist concepts of self and soul (Bhaskar, 2002). Certainly, as Wilkinson (2013, 2015) saw in adapting DCR in Islamic terms, there are profound possibilities of DCR transcendence in reconceptualising Islamic (and other theologies') approaches to citizenship education.

Archer's fullest and most eloquent account of "the internal conversation" for us is her 2003 volume *Structure, Agency and the Internal Conversation*. Her arguments concern "structure" (which has variable meaning in philosophy and sociology, but is seen as an enduring form), and "agency" (with similar debates about its meaning, but intuitively, how individuals relate, subjectively, to structure). Both structure and agency exist independently (i.e. have ontological reality), and causal relations between them remain to be investigated. Structure and agency "are two distinctive and irreducible properties and powers, and ... human reflexive deliberations play a crucial role in mediating between them" (p. 14). Thus *reflexivity* is central in Margaret Archer's sociology:

> Were we humans not reflexive beings there could be no such thing as society. This is because any form of social interaction, from the dyad to the global system, requires that subjects know themselves to be themselves. Otherwise they could not acknowledge that their words were their own nor their intentions, undertakings and reactions belonged to them ... not one social obligation, expectation or norm could be owned by a single 'member' of society. (p. 19)

Moreover, the reflexive, internal conversations and self-appraisals of individuals in their interactions with others have, in Archer's model, causal power in modifying structures: these "extrinsic effects ... mediating cultural and social properties of their societies ... and the private lives of social subjects are indispensable to the very existence and working of society" (p. 52).

Archer draws ideas and insights on the social psychology of the self, described in the writings of William James (1890) and George H. Mead (1934/1974), whose ideas of self-other, and I-myself she analyses in detail, and is critical of their ideas of "personal reflexivity": their idea of the "inner world" lacks autonomy in relation to the individual's "outer world" – a crucial shortcoming, in Archer's goal to "reclaim the internal conversation" as talking "to" society, not merely "about" society. Only then, Archer proposes "... we are in a position from which properly to consider the potentialities of our reflexive deliberations as the process which mediates between 'structure and agency'." (p. 129) Archer illustrates her thesis by analysing the "internal conversations" of twenty adults, making each a unique case study, in showing *inter alia*, "How the different *individual* modes of reflexivity, which mediate constraints and enablements in quite distinctive ways, are also related to *collective* action" (p. 166).

Reflexivity does not usually lead to structural change, of course, and Archer illustrates why this is so in her analysis of types of reflexivity. But, reflections upon reflections, refined, shared and polished reflexives, "'meta-reflexives'... are such because they pursue cultural ideals that cannot be accommodated by the current social structure and the array of contexts it defines ... By personifying their ideals of truth and goodness, the meta-reflexives awaken them and re-present them to society. In so doing they re-stock the pool of societal values, by displaying alternatives to the aridity of third-way thinking – and its repressive consensus ..." (Archer, 2003, p. 361).

A useful critique of Archer's "reflexivity and conduct of the self" has been offered by Akram and Hogan (2015), who examine among things, how Archer's idea of self-reflexion may challenge ideas of the "taken-for-granted" everyday events in the lives of individuals which form part of Bourdieu's (1986) account of *habitus*. Bourdieu downplays ideas of freely willed choice in making decisions, focussing instead on how social and economic classes create reserves of social capital, through socialising those below them into "unconscious acceptance" of everyday lifestyles. It's almost as if some wealthy elite had devised a newspaper called *The Sun*, which the workers may enjoy as their daily intellectual succour: this same cabal would have been responsible for creating 'sink estates' and poor quality comprehensives. This habitus of the labouring classes, and of the reserve army of labour is deeply entrenched. The proletariat's only mode of upward mobility, like that of the proles in Orwell's *1984*, is to win the lottery. Yet despite this gloomy continuity of class, Bourdieu allows that 'misrecognition' (akin to Marx's 'false consciousness') can change over quite lengthy periods of time, or change in response to sudden upheavals, such as war. Bourdieu has appeal for some radical sociologists in that he seems to have identified how socio-economic classes perpetuate themselves through symbolic rituals which can be enduring across generations: but these rituals may also be identified, and changed (e.g. Carlisle, 2013; Garth, 2015; Savage, 2015).

Archer's idea of morphogenesis, as part of a self-reflexive change in self-concept, a path to "social mobility" seems a light year away (or perhaps a "second edge" away in CR terms) from the rather depressing portraits of everyday social life which come from detailed ethnographic portraits of working class life which students of Bourdieu paint. For Akram and Hogan (2015) Archer proposes "... a seismic shift [from Bourdieu's account] in how people form and conduct themselves in everyday life, a process that would result in the realization of extremely high levels of *ethical autonomy* ... she goes beyond Giddens' and Bourdieu's notions of everyday, routinized taken-for-granted actions ... offering an entirely new view of how people form, manage and understand themselves in everyday life" (p. 610).

Archer (like Alderson, 2013, p. 80) does not reject Bourdieu's account of "everyday habitus", but offers instead a novel form of social psychology of everyday life. What is novel (among other things) is Archer's idea of *agency*, which is developed within the framework of Bhaskar's dialectical critical realism. Personal reflexivity (renewing one's own thoughts, feelings and actions in relation to those of others) is shared, according to Archer, by all people who find themselves in a common social situation. Akram and Hogan (2015) sum up their understanding of Archer's position:

> Reflexivity is the regular ability, shared by all normal people, to consider themselves in relation to their social contexts and vice versa … Reflexivity in modern society means a transition from a morphostatic to a morphogenetic society of constant change. Reflexivity is also linked to our emotional commitments and our moral concerns … all of which help to maintain 'the internal conversation' which reflects ongoing conversations in agents about who they are, and how they see their lives progressing … Archer's work raises the idea that individuals think about who they are (in the sense of personal and social identity) and modify their identity in the course of everyday being … Central to such a practice of the self is a deep sense of awareness of who one is, how one became who they are, and the benefits of pursuing such new performative aspects of identity. (Akram & Hogan, p. 620)

In this new world (for it seems to be too exciting to be like the old world which we all remember):

> Reflexivity emerges from a new social and cultural order, which creates novel situational contexts, and which they must negotiate … In such a scenario, agents draw upon their socially dependent, but nevertheless personal powers of reflexivity to define their courses of action … Reflexivity is not necessarily positive, because it can also have negative outcomes … some will be taking the best course, but may make mistakes … not all reflexion is successful, but all are crucially trying to be reflexive. (Archer, 1995, p. 110)

In *Making our Way through the World* (1995) Archer argues that there is movement between modes of reflexivity, taking the agent through the various levels of the MELD model (or not, as the case may be). But at each level the individual's "internal conversation" is crucial. Archer (2013, p. 13) defines four types of reflexivity, which can occur at any of the MELD levels: *"Communicative Reflexivity (conversations with others, before they can lead to action); Autonomous Reflexivity (internal conversations that are self-contained, leading directly to action); Meta-Reflexivity (internal conversations about critical actions within society); Fractured Reflexivity (broken or negative conversations). And reflexivity can assume crucial importance in times of stress and change. Progress and change are not inevitable."*

Akram and Hogan (2015) are impressed by Archer's thesis, and comment: "*Archer's work raises the idea that individuals think about the way they are (in the sense of personal social identity) modifying their identity in the course of everyday being … But what does it mean when she says that agents regularly rethink and evaluate their everyday being? … Central to such a practice of self-reflexion is a deep sense of awareness of who one is, how one became who they are, and the benefits of pursuing such new performative aspects of identity*" (p. 621). Akram and Hogan raise important questions of how different Archer's idea of self-reflexion is from Bourdieu's notion of habitus: or at least, how one moves from one state of being, or knowledge, to another status. Archer's objections seem to be to Bourdieu's philosophical assumptions in his methodology (which Bhaskar would likely have rejected as flawed) in arriving at his model: she does not object to Bourdieu's moral impulse, which at the end of the day, seems close to her own.

This is a fascinating area for qualitative research, for eliciting extended accounts of how people in specific communities, or with shared pasts (e.g. ethnicities, childhood experiences) construe themselves through their intellectual, moral and emotional histories, their reactions to others, how they share thoughts, feelings and opinions. The agents in such a study might be people undergoing change in their lives and who are making choices for the future, reflecting on their past: a population of senior high school students might be ideal for such a study. Would the results confirm Archer's idea of achieving social mobility through self-reflection, or Bourdieu's idea of achieving personal change through the absorption of new ideas? We suspect that both ideas might be confirmed, or a new synthesis of both views might emerge: perhaps the four stage MELD model might even be applied to the results!

One problem which such research might face however, is that if the researcher interviewed her informants repeatedly over a period of time, she herself would be part of the reflexive process, and might mould a set of ideas in her respondents simply by asking questions *about* key issues, without expecting particular answers. And of course, in the interim her informants would be set on a train of thinking. The intelligent respondent might make an electronic search on being reflexive, and might begin to discuss Archer's, Bhaskar's and Bourdieu's ideas with her fellow students. And where would that lead us?

Margaret Archer (2014) replaces the idea of postmodernism with that of "late modernity", enabling a "trajectory towards a morphogenetic society". That, in Marxist terms, would be a society liberated from the oppression forces of alienation.

CRITICAL REALISM'S MARXIST DIMENSION

Throughout Critical Realist writing there is mention of Marx, much of it critical, although Roy Bhaskar (1992/2008) clearly draws inspiration from Marx and Hegel, even when he is moulding their ideas creatively into an entirely new way of understanding "society and nature." Collier (1994) writing about critical realism before Bhaskar developed his influential ideas concerning dialectical critical realism, observed: "On the basis of the critical realist solutions to these questions [e.g. how to reconcile structural causality with effective human agency] I suggest that Marxian social science is about *constraints on the reproduction and transformation of social structures.* The knowledge of these constraints is the ground for political judgements: constraints on the reproduction of society show how it cannot reproduce itself without developing certain destructive features …" (p. 234: italics in original).

This implies that critical realism should, like Marxism, be concerned with alienation, the separation of the individual from the 'natural' status implied by their relationship to the social equity required by 'labour' (employed, for example, in schools in the world of subordinated learning, or employment). This alienation, a form of habitus, is an "enslaving ideology" transmitted between generations: CR's (and DCR's task) is to 'unmask' this alienation, and replace 'false consciousness' with reflexive knowledge which enables social structures, and individuals interacting with structures, to reach a state of self-hood that melds them in the utopian awareness that may be the natural state of humankind.

There is lyrical parallel to morphogenetic insights, in the model of "wonder" which Ahmed (2004) derives from the writing of Descartes (on the body's first passions of cognitive surprise) and the "sensuous certainty" which Marx describes in the first dawning of consciousness in the unmasking of alienation:

> The body opens as the world opens up before it; the body unfolds into the unfolding of a world that becomes approached as another body. This opening is not without its risks: wonder can be closed down if what we approach is unwelcome … But wonder is a passion that motivates the desire to keep looking; it keeps alive the possibility of freshness, and vitality of living that can live as if for the first time … wonder involves the radicalisation of our relation to the past, which is transformed into that which lives and breathes in the present. (Ahmed, 2004, p. 180)

Critical Realism, in Daniel Little's (2012) analysis sees critical thinking as "emancipatory". In both Marxist and CR traditions the term "critical" has specific meaning. Bhaskar cites Marx's Feurbach thesis: "The philosophers have sought to understand the world: the point however is to change it." In this model, critical science is an engaged or committed scientific endeavour, aiming to construct knowledge that may be, according to CR's emancipatory paradigm, for humanity's long-term benefit. Like Marx's *Capital*, which was subtitled "a critique of political economy", CR also attempts to expose the underlying ideologies of powerful interest groups, and to expose "false consciousness".

On the difficulties of research findings actually leading to change, Alderson (2013) observes: *"Many childhood researchers are disappointed that their 'participative research' [that] ends with the neat reported findings (words) seldom leading to real, messy, transformative change (deeds). DCR helps to identify and remedy this problem, in following Marx by identifying five types of practical contradictions to be resolved if real change is to occur"* (p. 91). Alderson continues her analysis of DCR in Marxist mode in discussing Bhaskar's (1993/2008) borrowing from Marx of the idea of "the master-slave relationship", which goes beyond the power of "masters" in older societies to all kinds of power relationships:

'Master-slave' relationships involve Marx's understanding of concepts that are central to DCR [identifying] ... forms that have immanent contradictions that can suggest an ideal and misleading representation of the world; and also a real world that can be described, classified and explained in various, changing and developing ways. Marx, as a scientific realist, believed that explanatory structures are essentially not only distinct from, but are often ... in opposition to the phenomena they generate. Examples include the way many schools fail many of their students ... (p. 111)

Marxist scholars who have identified "master-slave" relationships in schools are, for example Coard (1971, 2004) on the labelling of Black children as "subnormal"; Willis (1979) on working class boys "learning to labour"; and more recently, Grant Banfield, (2016). But the educational administrators of England will usually[6] maintain that authority in schools must be preserved, if we are to produce workers for a functioning economy. For Bhaskar (1993, 2008), "The ruling classes claim their enduring power, far from being abuse of the slave by his master, is their right and duty (like the colonial 'white man's burden') and is also in everyone's best interests. This Marxist idea of false-consciousness, or *mystifying* of the reality, is propagated as a routine part of class power" (Alderson, 2013, p. 116).

Grant Banfield (2016) in his *Critical Realism for Marxist Sociology of Education* uses the terms "Marxist" and "Marxian" interchangeably. This, we infer, is a way of saying that although he is a Marxist, he is certainly not a Marxist-Leninist. He defers to Roy Bhaskar's 'spiritual socialism', quoting Bhaskar's early (1989) writing:

> I take it that whatever our politics ... socialists can agree that what we must be about today is the building of a movement for socialism – in which socialism wins a cultural hegemony, so that it becomes the enlightened common-sense of our age. (p. 1)

Banfield tells us that his 'starting premise' is that Marxian education is in Marx's words 'revolutionary practice.' According to Banfield

> Education is part of what Gramsci has actually called 'the war of position' ... where the trenches of civil society are won in classrooms, workplaces, pubs and on street corners, that socialism becomes ... the enlightened common-sense of our age. According to Bhaskar, not only is there an elective affinity between critical realism and historical realism, but also the original intent of critical realism was to support the science of history that Marx had opened up ... it is in their differences that the real possibilities of a working relationship between critical realism and Marxism are established. (p. 1)

This last point is important: DCR may draw on Marxist ideas, but it goes beyond Marx's interpretation, e.g. his use of Hegel. Furthermore, "*A crucial defining feature of critical realism is the seriousness with which it takes ontology. This seriousness is an antidote to what we will see as tendencies in fields like the sociology of education (and Marxist sociology of education) to ontological shyness*" (Banfield, 2016, p. 3).

An ontology based on the stratified, four-level MELD model permits

> ... Bhaskar's stratified, differentiated ... real ontology indicating that what appears and is immediately experienced are only surface features of deeper realities ... Bhaskar's emergentist ontology allowed him to advance an emancipatory critique of human-harming social structures ... with understanding of the structural causal relations underlying them comes an ethical responsibility to negate and overturn them. Science is simultaneously a social and emancipatory practice: the underlying methodological content common to both the natural and

social sciences is emancipation: Bhaskar's dialectic of 'the pulse to freedom. (Banfield, 2016, p. 4)

As Brad Shipway (2013) observes in his *A Critical Realist Perspective of Education*, schools are particularly appropriate places for a (Marxian) critical realist analysis and reconstruction. They contain, and control (and often harm) our precious children; they are the state's agents of socialization; they control and discipline, preparing the young to be rulers, administrators, technicians, labourers, excluded minorities, or the reserve army of labour – according to their various rituals, and social structures ranging from those of the 'public' schools to the 'crumbling comprehensive' servicing sink estates (Sawyerr & Bagley, 2016).

The conclusion is that critical realism enriches and humanises Marxism, and counters the development of reactionary themes such as "the dictatorship of the masses". DCR's spiritual aspirations concerning the soul and the self also enrich the insights of Marxism. Alderson's use (2013, 2015) of Bhaskar's four level-analysis in writing about children and their emancipation, their flourishment, and their possibilities for fulfilled and non-alienated lives is profoundly creative, and inspirational. Collier (2002) argues that critical realism "can add to Marxism without taking anything away" – but he acknowledges that some of his fellow authors (in an edited volume on *Critical Realism and Marxism*), may disagree.

We conclude this section with the views of Creaven (2007), who is the most enthusiastic of the "Marxist critical realists". Examining how Marx and Engels worked together, he observed that Engel's was the "underlabourer", clearing away the underbrush of false ideas and philosophical nonsense that impeded the clarity of Marxian ontological analysis. (Wilkinson, 2015, too uses the idea of underlabouring, which clarifies the road to emancipation in the critical realist model). Engels' survey of "the condition of the working class in England" was one of the underlabouring tasks for Marx's theory of *Capital*, for instance. In Creaven's (2007) analysis "Marxism was already, implicitly a critical realist social theory." Thus Bhaskar's evaluative realism, "… provides (in Marx's phrase) 'an ethical basis for championing the struggles of the oppressed' as a natural principle of justice" (p. 29).

In his most recent writing, Creaven (2015) uses Bhaskar's dialectical model to resolve the tensions between the "two Marxisms" – structuralism, and humanism – to show that there is a "coherent unity" between the two forms.

APPLICATION OF CRITICAL REALISM MODELS IN DIFFERENT
FIELDS OF RESEARCH

Critical realism and 'social ontology' models have become increasingly popular with researchers in several areas of social science research, although the bulk of research is still undertaken with children and adolescents in educational, health and social care settings. One interesting development is the growth of CR research in the area of industrial sociology, and human relations management (Zacharialis, Scott & Barrett, 2010), and a recent textbook (Edwards, O'Mahoney & Vincent, 2014) includes case examples of how to approach research settings in the CR mode, to collect relevant data, and interpret it using dialectical critical realism.

Easton (2010) offers a useful guide to case study research using critical realism, for use in organisational, business and human relations management (for an example of this application see, for instance, Abubaker & Bagley, 2016). In Easton's CR model, the case study must be grounded on a firm ontological basis of "truth", of a description of the nature and implicit values of the organisation studied. He recites the "basic assumptions" of CR: "Firstly, the world exists independently of our knowledge of it; secondly, our knowledge of the world is fallible, self-deceiving, cloaked in implicit or poorly-organised theories whose assumptions are not often explicit – thus our initial concepts of truth and falsity often fail to provide a coherent view of the relationship between knowledge and its object; thirdly, the realm we wish to research is differentiated and stratified ... by actions, texts and institutions, and they are all *concept dependent*" (p. 120).

Easton urges: "Critical realism first of all makes the ontological assumption that there is a reality, but it is usually difficult to apprehend. I distinguish between the real world, the actual events that are created by the real world and the empirical events which we can actually capture and record. Thus we will always be surprised about the nature of the real ... The research process is one of continuous cycles of research and reflection. The final result is the identification of one or more mechanisms that can be regarded as having caused events" (Easton, 2010, p. 128).

Following Easton, we have attempted to construct a case study of a preschool day nursery, in which the ontological assumptions about 'reality', causal processes, and the potentials for reflexive morphogenesis which are at different levels of the MELD framework, for the different agents (Alderson, 2016). These agents are:

The child: is enrolled in the nursery according to some special criteria; plays, is fed, grows, learns, acquires beginnings of selfhood and ethnic

45

identity, shares thoughts and feelings with peers. He or she begins to acquire concepts of gender, and values concerning a presumed place in the world.

The nursery worker: is burdened with social values, and implicit assumptions about how and what children should do and learn, in order for them to conform to the norms of the school into which they will graduate.

The manager: brings to the nursery group the values from above on who shall be admitted, and how they shall be handled and taught, and how parents should be dealt with.

The researcher: observes, learns from, cares about the children and their workers, engages in reflexive dialogue with herself and the workers and the managers, beginning to understand the patina of 'false consciousness', the web of deceit, which the social structure is using to control the children, who will soon 'learn to labour'.

The bureaucrat: the faceless ones, who manipulate, control and deceive, who close the nursery and dismiss the children, because they are offered a large financial reward for so doing; they issue documents justifying this, which are cloaked in deceit and false assumptions. The 'dismissed' children learn their first lesson in the master-slave relationship, of being temporary or reserve workers in the capitalist social order.

In the Chapter on the nursery school case study, we try, *post facto* to elaborate this model, even though when AS undertook that fieldwork, she had not come across the Critical Realist model of social research.

CONCLUSIONS AND REFLECTIONS ON CRITICAL REALISM

In reading Bhaskar, Alderson, Wilkinson and Archer and other critical realists, we have been struck by a new facet of communication and information which influences all of our lives: the electronic information system of the web from which we are constantly gleaning information; and as well as sending frequent e-mails and texts, the sharing of ideas and images with friends (and others) on sites such as Face Book, Twitter etc. The youngsters among us are no longer truly part of themselves: we share ourselves, reflexively, with a much wider world than when Roy Bhaskar published his first book, in 1978. What is the meaning of this electronic world? Alderson (2013, p. 102) is worried about the covert collection of children's electronic data as a means of controlling them, an electronic version of Bhaskar's (1993/2008) 'master-slave' relationship. But there is also a powerful anarchy in the data which is collected on all of us, and liberation when it is released through the integrity of 'whistle-blowing'.

And finally, what of the older adolescents whose "souls have been murdered" (as Schatzman, 1973 puts it). We are referring to results later in this study which have identified a group of adolescent women who lead 'shadow lives' because of the chronic physical and sexual abuse they have endured. The qualitative researcher would likely elicit these accounts from her informants. But then, how should she intervene (as intervene she must)? And, returning to Alderson's (2013, 2016) reconstruction of her earlier work with children, how might the researcher help these adolescent women achieve a self-actualization of identity?[7]

Alderson observes that: *"Children and adults learn about their needs through their bodily experiences within relationships; they express their needs and views through their bodies; and they are respected or disrespected in the casual or harsh ways in which their bodies are treated in practice"* (Alderson, 2013, p. 94). She is writing about her research with physically challenged children: but these words could have been written of physically and sexually abused children. And how can Archer's inspiring message of personal growth help us in bringing these children and adolescents through 'absence' to their fullest potential?

Finally, we want to emphasise how exciting and life-changing critical realist theory may be . Once you have absorbed it (or your personal version of it, since different actors will perceive DCR writings differently, and take away different aspects of the model in their quest for truth-telling and social change) your life, your thinking and feeling about the world will never again be the same. Reflecting, thinking, feeling, relating to one's own thoughts and those of others is exciting, a daily excitement which is never lost.

We are empowered in being confident that *our* value judgements and the actions that derive from them can be important: in research we now move easily from 'is' to 'ought', and reflexively through dialogue and debate with our academic and professional partners, set new goals and horizons for achieving liberation, and see ways of escape from alienation and 'false consciousness' imposed on myself and others.

Critical realism gives to the student what Ahmed (2004) calls a sense of "wonder" in rediscovering and redesigning the social matrix of her world:

This critical wonder is about recognising that nothing in the world can be taken for granted, which includes the very political movements to which we are attached. It is this critical wonder about the forms of political struggle that makes Black feminism such an important intervention, by showing that categories of knowledge (such as

47

patriarchy or 'women') have political effects, which can exclude others from the collective … (Ahmed, 2004, p. 182)

We note that other scholars and activists in the field of "race relations" have used the idea of realism somewhat differently from later DCR theorsts (e.g. Carter, 2000), but there is certainly a case for merging "critical race theory" (Taylor, Gillborn & Ladson-Billings, 2016) with the DCR approach.

NOTES

[1] "At its philosophical core lies a theory of *absence*, which Bhaskar combines with his pre-existing arguments from critical realism for the significance of ontology. This is a basis for the realist understanding of human *being* in society and in nature which, through the account of absence, is aligned to a theory of *becoming* and change in a spatio-temporal world. The alignment of being and becoming is achieved in a manner that displays both a uniqueness of individual philosophical voice and boldness of intellectual vision, and these gave Bhaskar a fair claim to stand … in the first rank of western philosophy today" (Norrie, 2010, p. 3).

[2] Anderson is in fact a Quaker – see her account of "respecting children" in a Quaker publication (Alderson, 2017).

[3] There is an intriguing parallel with Flaschel's (2009) idea that Marx's "reserve army of labour" will disappear if the social democratic state gives *all* citizens, whether working or not a generous living allowance, in his model of 'flexisecurity'.

[4] "Homology" is a term borrowed from biology which explains the link between "the transcendental realist world view", and Roy Bhaskar's political model of socialism (Collier, 1998, p. 469).

[5] It would be interesting to have a critical realist account of "emancipation" in the world of children's friendships described by George and Clay (2013) and their idea of "challenging pedagogy".

[6] Tim Brighouse (QVINE.org.uk), is an inspiring exception.

[7] This is, alas, not an academic speculation but one based upon my anguish at the results, reported in a later chapter of this thesis, concerning the "Northern Schools Study" which found that some five percent of adolescent women had "devastated self-esteem", often reflecting prolonged physical and sexual harassment, maltreatment, and abuse.

CHAPTER 4

CHILD-CENTRED HUMANISM (CCH)

A Guiding Value

The final and unavoidable conclusion is that education-like all our social institutions must be concerned with final values, and this in turn is just about the same as speaking of what have been called 'spiritual values' or 'higher values'. These are principles of choice which help us to answer the age-old 'spiritual' (philosophical? humanistic? ethical?) questions: What is the good life? What is the good man? The good woman? What is best for children? What is justice? Truth? Virtue? What is my relation to nature, to death, to ageing, to pain, to illness? How can I live a zestful, enjoyable, meaningful life? What is my responsibility to my brothers? Who are my brothers? What shall I be loyal to? What must I be ready to die for?

(Maslow, 1964/2014, p. 64)

INTRODUCTION

We employ the principle of Child-Centred Humanism (CCH) as an ethical ground which *underlabours* throughout this thesis. The concept of underlabouring is part of a Critical Realist (CR) research model. Within CR, what underlabouring is concerned with is the general ethical model, the working model through which structures and their elements are considered, examined and judged. The under-labourers are the everyday workers, of good-will who in Collier's (1994) script:

… aim to remove the idols (Bacon), obstacles (Locke) or ideologies (Marx) that stand in the way of, new knowledge to be produced by the [social] sciences. (p. 19)

Every person is their *own* philosopher in Critical Realism, not just the professor in her ivory tower. And Alderson observed that critics "… overlook how philosophy is integral to everyday and research thinking, and that a main task of philosophy is to be an under-labourer, clearing away rubbish and laying foundations. The philosopher Mary Midgley (1996) compares philosophy with plumbing. These can both be ignored and taken for granted until they are not working well … and plumbing's equivalent in clear logical thinking, has to be fixed" (Alderson, 2013, p. 20).

For the Muslim Critical Realist (Wilkinson, 2015), underlabouring is both literally and figuratively, doing good deeds like clearing the highway of rubbish, effectively implementing the *Sunnah*, the life and teaching of Prophet Muhammad. In Hadith 26 of Imam Nawawi's collection, for example: "Every joint of a person must perform a charity each day that the sun rises … every good word is a charity … and removing a harmful object from the road is a charity." Every step, every action, must serve others, and in Child Centred Humanism every action, thought, deed and intention must 'underlabour' the principle: *Children First*.

An understanding of CCH grew out of Bagley's (1973) review of the literature on legal decisions surrounding child adoption, in which it became clear that the higher courts in Britain were increasingly likely to put the child's interests first, when the rights (or demands) of adults for possession and control of the child conflicted with what judges thought were the child's best needs and interests. Bagley translated this idea of "children first" into a more general philosophy of child welfare and child care (e.g. Bagley, Young & Scully, 1993), termed "total child welfare" meaning that all human institutions and actions should be designed and operated on the principle of "children first".

Inspirational here was Colin Ward's (1979) book of joyful anarchy *The Child in the City*, which showed how children adapted to, and then took over, city spaces. Bagley expressed outrage at the violation of children's space and movement, this "absent" army of victims, invaded by the power given to an adult-centred, materialist world in which the motor vehicle, and its right to move speedily through children's spaces, had primacy. He showed that in Canadian and in British cities (1992, 1993) that many thousands of children were killed or severely injured each year by these steel assassins as the children ran, played, crossed roads to reach play spaces or schools, or cycled on city roads. Moreover, it was children of the economically poor who were most likely to be killed in this way, since they perforce lived in areas most cut through by traffic.

Bagley extended the concept of CCH into a more general humanistic doctrine, arguing that such humanism could have either a secular or a religious basis, and could be founded in Quaker ideas of universalism which, in application, always made children's needs and interests primary

(Lampen, 2015), ideas also extended to the humanistic treatment of child victims of sexual assault whom Bagley (1995a, 1999b) saw as frequent victims of the panicked processing of a system designed to help them. The humanist principle was also extended to the treatment of child sexual abuse offenders (following Hank Giarretto's (1981) humanistic treatment model (Bagley, 2003; Bagley & LeChance, 2000).

CCH has *psychological roots* in Carl Rogers' humanist psychology, the "third way" (the middle ground of integration between behaviourism and psychodynamics). From Rogers CCH draws pedagogic ideals of knowing each *individual* child in a group, and caring deeply about their needs, strengths and aspirations. This is why CCH is a firm advocate of small school classes, assuming that the teacher cannot know adequately each pupil when class sizes rise above, say 15 per teacher.

Abraham Maslow's humanistic idea of positive psychology fits well within the CCH philosophy of serving the developing needs of the child, adolescent and adult for nurturing, physical care, safety, love, esteem, and stimulation, so as to reach the fullest fulfilment for both the child and the adult. This *Psychology of Being* (1968) is embedded in religious ideals and values which enable "peak experiences" of actualization (Maslow, 1964/2014).

CCH has a *theological underpinning*, assuming (with Quakers and Muslims) that all children are born,not sinful, but are joyfully seeking from, birth with their inmost spirit, the spirit in others "playing cheerfully in the world" (to paraphrase George Fox).

CCH treats each child as a unique and special human being, with a unique combination of needs, abilities, strengths, and aspirations. The parent, the teacher and the counsellor need to understand, in the Thomas-Chess account, the uniqueness of each child in the developmental matrix. This model offers the principle that adult actions and interactions regarding the child must be modelled on the "goodness of fit" between the unique demands of each child's biological, personal and social gifts, and the responsibility of adults in nurturing of those gifts (Chess & Thomas, 1999). Bagley and Mallick (2000b) tried to apply this model in their longitudinal study of child temperament (replicating Chess & Thomas), showing with case studies and statistical data, that two children with identical needs at birth could "spiral up" or "spiral down" (e.g. into delinquency) according to how adults interacted with them. The child's uniqueness in the psychological matrix through which we understand human motivation is also fruitfully elaborated in the ideographic methodology of Gordon Allport (1968).

Chilldren's rights are central in the CCH model. There are three kinds of rights: transcendental or absolute (e.g. the right to have one's basic needs for nutrition, safety and love to be met); contractual (e.g. those mutual rights and obligations as the child grows older, and becomes of age, defined in a legal contract); and social (e.g. the developing citizen's right to freedom, and their obligation to respect the freedom of others, in the social contract on which society is implicitly founded.) Children have a special set of rights, and for a definition of these we turn to the developmental psychology of Maslow (1954/1970). Maslow's pyramidal diagram of human needs is well-known, and we will not reproduce it here. At its base, are the child's physiological needs for food, water, warmth, safety and security: in the CCH model the child has an *absolute right* to have those needs met by surrounding adults. There cannot be any reciprocal basis to the meeting of those needs. As the child grows older, she or he is socialized and educated, with a growing body of reciprocal relationships. "I help you" is implicit in the relationship in which "you help me."

These reciprocal relationships grow into a set of interactions which make up the social contract. Society has a duty to enable young people to maximise their talents, and to esteem themselves (and others) psychologically. At the apex of the pyramid is *self-actualization*, making the most of the talents and the psychological, social and material wealth which society has given us, for the benefit of our own spiritual growth, in ways which maximise the welfare of our common citizens: and of course, the welfare of the most precious citizens who are our children.

THE TRADITION OF CARL ROGERS

Abraham Maslow, George Kelly and Carl Rogers have been categorized as "phenomenological personality theorists" (Chamorro-Premuzic, 2007), who are philosophically grounded in notions of personal freedom and individual personal development (the essence of CCH).

Carl Rogers' humanistic psychology which focuses on individual uniqueness, and the possibilities for "harmonic growth" – that is, achieving fulfilment through meeting ethical goals involving other people – is important in CCH and DCR *provided that* self-development is intimately linked to social development. Rogers teaches the psychology of human development not by statistical materials, but by a series of individual case studies of adults reflecting on how they experienced challenge in childhood and young adulthood (Rogers & Stevens, 1967).

We learn, says Rogers "to be free" through our parents' care, the kindliness of our teachers, and the reciprocal rewards that being a good citizen brings. "Trust" and "empathy" are the markers of the progress of the adult. "Being free" has to be learned, through self-discipline. It is a reflexive process, in which learning to love ourselves, we love others: we love "our" child, we love children, we love "your" child. In this reflexive social contract we seek the equality of all citizens (Rogers, 1961, 1980; Kirschenbaum & Henderson, 1990). In the Rogerian model of social exchange, each person "opens the spirit" to others in a trusting and creative manner, absorbing the goodness and goodwill of the other person. In this process the individual acts freely (i.e. exercises free will, and in the course of doing this, self-discipline, or 'discernment' as Quakers would say). 'Free will' in the Critical Realistic dialectical model which we are applying here, is not merely an abstract decision or choice: it is based on dialogue, communication and questioning, making sense of oneself in relation to one's past, and one's current interactions, and fresh information on the meaning and effects of one's choices. Anderson (2013) illustrates this beautifully in her accounts of children making choices concerning life-changing surgery for conditions such as scoliosis.

CCH as applied to education follows Rogers and Freiberg (1980) in insisting that teachers should know their children as *individuals*, and be focused on the child's individual development within the classroom group. This is only possible if the class of children is small enough for the teacher to know each child well, and engage in an individual teaching plan for each child in the classroom. In this model, a school class should not contain more than 15 children, large enough for children to play creatively with others, and to learn co-operation with the larger group. 'The fifteen' may also contain children with challenging psychological and physical needs. Research on class sizes (the pupil-teacher ratio) shows, perhaps unsurprisingly, that in smaller classes there are fewer 'off task' interactions amongst children, more focus by teachers on individual needs of children, and in the long-term enhanced scholastic and social skills in the child and in the adolescent and adult that they become (Blatchford, 2003).

The critic of Rogers may argue that this is a bourgeois, individualistic concept of self-realisation, unavailable to "ordinary" working people and their families (Sawyerr & Bagley, 2016). This is certainly true, and it is true also that being a pupil in a class of 15 students or less, is usually the privilege of those whose parents have been able to purchase a private education. But it does not deny T. H. Green's social democratic principle that *every* child should be enabled to enjoy the privileges of the most wealthy in the land. Rich countries such as Britain, as we argue in our paper on equality (Sawyerr & Bagley, 2016) can easily afford to fund such a quality of education for *every* child.

John Lampen, an advocate of Quaker schools founded on Quaker educational principles argues that we must look not at the schools themselves, but at:

> ... the environmental therapy movement which Friends and others developed to meet the needs of 'difficult' children evacuated during 1939–1945 War. Their practice recognised each child's innate worth and capacity for good by creating systems of governance and discipline which embodied Quaker testimonies to peace and equality ... this is one of the great Quaker contributions to education in the last 200 years.

Within Quakers there is currently a vigorous debate ongoing about what exactly Quaker values in education are, or should be, and the organisation and practice of the seven Quaker secondary schools in Britain and Ireland is being examined in detail (Newton & Broadfoot, 2016). What is common in these schools is that classes are small, and teachers focus on "the inner worth and capacity for good" of each child.[1]

The dialectical critical realist model's perspective on moral realism (Bhaskar, 2008; Archer, 2016) seeks "to avoid the *anthropic fallacy* that places humans at the centre of the purpose and meaning of the universe" (Bhaskar, 2000, p. 26). Following this principle, CCH is not an individualist goal, even though it adopts Rogerian principles of phenomenology in child and adult development: it has a universalistic purpose, applying not merely to individuals, your children and my children, but to all of humanity's children, past and present.

Thus CCH has a view of the history of childhood, which western society has only recently come to understand as a separate area for concern (Mayall, 2013). This suppression of childhood's history is a form of alienation: in Alderson's (2016) words: "The present estranged, destructive relations between humans and nature suggest that many people are alienated from their physical human nature in different ways that need to be researched separately and together ... The effects of alienation were evident in the severe ill-health of children and adults in Victorian slums and factories ... and are replicated today in many majority world cities" (p. 27). Friedrich Engels (1845) in his *The Condition of the Working Class in England* drew ecological maps of Manchester showing the worst zones of deprivation. Today some of those zones of deprivation in Manchester are sited *in exactly the same city zones* (Sawyerr & Bagley, 2016).

THOMAS HILL GREEN, 1836 TO 1882

The nineteenth century English *political theorist* Thomas Green (1999) may seem an odd intellectual pairing with the humanist self-theorists of twentieth century America. Green was however, a remarkable thinker, laying the intellectual and moral ground for the development of the British welfare state by Beveridge and his followers. Green argued that the twin goals of human activity ought to be to maximise the citizen's welfare, *and* to maximise that citizen's freedom. Green argued passionately that being economically poor, being poorly educated, enduring degraded housing environments and working conditions, undermined the citizen's freedom, including that citizen's ability to contribute interactively in any kind of metaphysical social contract, to the welfare of others (Wempe, 2004). Green stated: "An interest in the common good is the ground of political society, in the sense that without it no body of people would recognise any authority as having a claim on their common obedience" (Green, 1942, pp. 45–46).

Green's ethical socialism had a metaphysical ground, which he took from Hegel's *Propaedeutik*: that in self-reflection the individual citizen recreates himself or herself in daily reflection in acknowledging his or her own duty (maximising concern for others, and the freedom in oneself), and eliciting such actions in one's fellow citizens, in a dialectical system of interchange with oneself and with one's compatriots seeking, as Quakers would say, that of God in everyone (indeed, Green was a fervently religious socialist – Boucher & Vincent, 2006). It should be said that Green took on board Hegel's "naïve idealism", which is criticised and reformulated by Roy Bhaskar (2008) in his marriage of critical realism and the dialectical method (Norrie, 2010). But it should also be said that for all its challenging complexity, Roy Bhaskar's *The Philosophy of Metareality: Creativity, Love and Freedom* (2012) also has much to commend itself to CCH. And we are glad to sign up T.H. Green as a patron of CCH, since his heir, the British welfare state, is a crucially important element in fostering child welfare (just as dismantling the welfare state is an attack on children and their welfare).

In Green's personal self-development in supporting a benevolent social contract, there is an interesting parallel in Margaret Archer's (2003) idea of morphogenesis, part of the critical realist model. Indeed, Green's model of metaphysical introspection and recreation of the self-other bond of mutual generosity in daily thought and interaction, seems to us to fit remarkably well with Archer's idea of a social structure grounded in a process of continuous reflexivity.

Archer's ideas (Archer 1995 to 2012) on reflexivity fit well within the Child-Centred Humanism (CCH) model outlined here, and also with the ideas of loving interchange between human beings advocated by Rogers. The critical realism that Archer proposes is a revolutionary model (following Bhaskar, 2008) of how humans conduct themselves in everyday life, achieving high levels of "ethical autonomy" in which one appraises oneself in relation to other agents in the wider social system. This reflexive self-other system is a "morphogenetic" one of continuous change. Each individual, in this reflexive process, engages in "internal conversations" which are shared with the reflexivity of others who are also reflecting on and communicating their own internal conversations about novel situations. Each day these collaborating individuals in their networks of support and friendship, both negotiate, and create the matrix of change (Power 1, *liberation* versus Power 2, *oppression*, in Bhaskar's model).

While of course evil remains in the world, and existing power systems of rich over poor, and of ignored or exploited children remain, Archer's emphasis on liberation and 'upward mobility' through an increasing self-consciousness in all of our actions, is clearly an optimistic one. One is struck by some remarkable similarities between Thomas Green's Hegelian dialectic in recreating selfhood on a daily basis (in Green's case, through daily prayer and contemplation), and Margaret Archer's perpetual reflexivity in finding ethical pathways for oneself in relation to one's fellow citizens. For both Green and Archer, the goals seem to be freedom, choice, and autonomy in reaching goals of social justice.[2]

Margaret Archer's work grew out of her concern with comparative studies of educational sociology in Europe, including the struggles of working class children to achieve upward social mobility (Archer & Giner, 1971; Archer, 1979). Her work has expanded in its moral compass to possess a very complete ethical domain. Like other critical realists (e.g. Bhaskar, Collier, & Wilkinson) she is both radical in a political sense (Scambler, 2012), but nevertheless, also appears to be strongly influenced by (as was Green) "the ontology of God".

Although Archer does not make explicit her theological position (except in one joint publication – Archer, Collier & Porpora, 2014, on "the divine ontology" replacing positivist agnosticism), we detect elements of the Vincentian *will* in her position: each human being, however wretched their situation (e.g. as a slave, or a prisoner) has moral challenges each day, possibilities of kindness and mercy to others which they may act upon, reflect upon, and recreate themselves in, despite their wretched situation: spiritually at least, their pattern was one, as Archer would put it, of 'upward mobility'. (Vincent de Paul, himself a slave for many years, argued that even the 'poorest' human was capable of daily acts of kindness – Pujo, 1998).

Reflecting on one's past, the events of yesterday, the events of childhood is a core part of Roy Bhaskar's dialectical interchange in which the passive past ("the absence") is pondered and recreated in a new present. In this model we recreate not merely ourselves, but also the ethic that childhood is primary. This self-reflective pathway to ethical behaviour is grounded psychologically, in Mead's idea of the reflexive self, modified and extended by Archer (2003).

CONCLUSIONS

Finally, we add to CCH Marx's idea of alienation from the self, imposed by a capitalistic society in which making profit is the dominant motive, explicit or implicit, ordering how human values are *officially* framed, and how social institutions and public debates are moulded. In Marxian theory, the capitalist system has created an underclass, a 'reserve army of labour' who are chronically under-employed and under-skilled but who can be called on it times of economic boom or growth to become labourers and service workers, for the benefit of capital and the minimisation of wages (for the reserve army is constantly looking for work, at or below minimum wage level). The children of the poor, in this model, must be segregated into 'sink' estates of public housing, in which they can be observed, ordered, contained and controlled. Some of these children would, as Engels (1845) observed, graduate into being career criminals and can then be safely contained in penal institutions. Others can be given a decent second class education which will enable them, when required, to be hewers of wood and drawers of water.

CCH is passionately concerned with the unmasking of the alienation which clouds the consciousness of these families and children (in urban areas which contain ethnic and religious minorities, and refugees; but with a solid phalanx of 'poor whites'). As Scambler (2013) writes of Margaret Archer's view of Marxian theory: "To introduce the concept of ideology it is necessarily to introduce that of false-consciousness." And dialectic critical materialism's reflexive model can in its reflexive, morphogenetic mode, help those with "fractured reflexivities" to grasp "true-consciousness", sharing with those in the ghettoized sink estate a fuller realisation of their position.

Everyone, in T.H. Green's and M.S. Archer's models of social action, may achieve upward mobility, to the life of the gentle-person. In Wilkinson's Islamic CR model, it is the journey on the Straight Path (the focus of each of the five daily prayers) that ensures that the faithful imitate Prophet

Muhammad's peaceful example, on the straight road to Paradise. For Muslims, the soul given by God resides in all human beings, not merely in other Muslims, and the Muslim's task is to seek out and serve (as do Quakers) the soul of everyone (Bagley, 2015). Again CCH's model of reciprocal love, and CR's reflexive morphgenesis seem to converge.

NOTES

1 www.qvine.org.uk
2 Wilkinson (2015) uses an Islamic model of critical realism in a rather similar way: the five daily prayers and reflection on The Qur'an and Sunnah (life and teaching of the Prophet Muhammad) are models by which human reflection can be liberating, allowing the ideal society created by the Prophet Adam to roll out across the earth. There are similar, parallel themes in Franciscan and Quaker theologies.

APPENDIX: THE CHILDREN'S CHARTER OF DEVELOPMENTAL RIGHTS

The following Children's Charter, some of which we reproduce here since it fits so well with CCH principles, has been produced by the Save Childhood Movement, reflecting Article 3 of the UN Convention of the Rights of the Child: "In all actions concerning children, whether undertaken by public or private social welfare institutions, courts or administrative bodies, the best interests of the child shall be of primary consideration." The Children's Charter advocates:

Awareness: Children have the right to live in societies that are fully informed about the evidence supporting healthy human learning and development, societies which take action to protect children's rights and freedoms based on this awareness.

Health and Wellbeing: National and local decision makers have the duty to provide environments that maximise children's physical, mental, emotional and spiritual wellbeing. In doing so they should recognise the vital importance of parents, families and local communities and the intrinsic human need for belonging and contribution.

New Technology: Policy makers have the duty to ensure that young people's development is safeguarded from the unintended developmental consequences of living in a digital world.

Learning and development: Children have the right to be protected from any system that might inhibit their innate curiosity, creativity and love of learning ….

Adult Well-being is essential for child wellbeing: Adults have the right to expect the cultural and social systems within which they live to support their own learning and self development. Children ... have the right to be protected from any relationships that are uninformed or harmful to their health and well-being.

Pre-Birth: ... mothers and babies have the right to be protected from all factors that might compromise their health perinatal and birth experiences.

Engagement and Encouragement: Children have the right to be in the company of informed and encouraging adults who help to enhance the ways in which they can relate to and understand the world.

Physical Activity: Children have the right to be provided with environments that enable them to develop all of their senses and physical capacities.

Body Image: Children have the right to be protected from negative media and commercial influences that might undermine their confidence and self-worth.

Play: Children have the right to be provided with the time and space to explore their environments in unstructured ways that nurture their creativity, independence, self-confidence, self-expression, cooperation and emotional resilience.

Risk-Taking: Children have the right to learn from challenge, to experience failure as learning, and to become confident and adventurous explorers of the environment.

Wonder and Awe: Children have the right to maintain a deep connection with the natural world that helps them feel part of something greater than themselves and fosters compassion and empathy ...

Stewardship: Children have the right to be protected from systems that endanger their own future. They need to learn about plants, animals and ecosystems so that they understand the importance of balance and sustainability and can grow up as stewards of the environment.

For the full text from which the above quotations are taken, see: www.savechildhood.net and (http:bit.ly/ChildrensCharter)

EQUALITY AND ETHNICITY IN ENGLAND 1968 TO 2008

INTRODUCTION

> There are perhaps three kinds of books one can write on the subject
> of 'history' ... One is a 'how-to' guide to practice. Another is a
> philosophical investigation into theories of knowledge. The third is a
> polemic supporting a particular approach. (Arnold, 2000, p. i)

This section on aspects and elements of the recent history of ethnicity
and equality contains elements of the third of Arnold's approaches. It is
a polemic undertaken using some of the assumptions of Bhaskar's (2008)
dialectical critical realism, as identified by Archer (2008) and Alderson
(2013, 2016).

The events of yesterday are past: everything is history. Ethnographers
(e.g. Glass, 2016) argue that we should address this history not merely from
documented, external facts, but from individual, life-time memories which
become embodied in folk memories (the "history from below" described by
Jordonova, 2006).

The Jamaican teenager on the former slave-island of Jamaica, on finally
leaving secondary school triumphantly shouts, "Free paper come!" This
free paper, the document of manumission is the release from slavery *and*
later from the oppression of a grinding discipline of educational systems
still infected with the ghost of colonial values, with set books for English
examination boards which ignored the literature of the Caribbean underclass,
and the history of slavery and colonial oppression (Searle, 1973). The pain
of that slavery is transmuted into the wail of Bob Marley, and the song of
"Sallow Brown" the child of a slave and a white owner, who is separated
forever from family through being sold. In the Caribbean psyche, in its patois
and folktales derived from West Africa's *Anansi*, who defied capture by the
slavers, there is a hidden theme of alienation (the imposed separation of
body, social being and spirit) that has to be resolved. But, as the Critical
Realist model teaches, individuals are often "alienated from their past" by
powerful structural forces (Alderson, 2016). Folk memories may reintegrate
that past.

The past recalled by the ethnographer is both an account of her own past, and the past memories and current ideologies of those with whom she engages in research (Glass, 2016).

The history of education, identity and ethnicity in Britain since the late 1960s is part of our folk memory, our own ethnic identity, personal accounts expressed through reviewing and recollecting the events surrounding "colonial immigration" and the adaptation of a British class system to order and control these immigrant vestiges of empire. British society was, and still is psychologically, a colonial power whose wealth was enhanced by the slave trade. As Fekete (2009) argues, Britain's "new McCarthyism" is founded on deeply embedded ideas in British history of the need for conformity to white, British values and the desire to root out dissidents, extremists, and religious non-conformists (e.g. Muslims).The strata of English society are (at the highest level) the hidden holders of wealth, an international cabal whose wealth is largely hidden in their offshore accounts; then there are the white administrators, politicians and professionals who maintain (or at least order) the tradition of British values, and the smooth working of the capitalist system; their underlings are the middle whites, senior clerks and overseers who administer this class-based capitalist system; and then the workers artificially divided into several sectors. First are the lower whites, heirs of colonial clerks and tradesmen, and their siblings – heirs of the soldiers and sailors who administered the empire; then there are the imported colonial subjects and their descendants; and at the lowest level, a permanent underclass who serve various functions – as scapegoats for economic inequalities, and as a 'reserve army' who can be used to depress wages and enable capitalism to function efficiently.

There are small, but important, fragmented 'status' groups and their 'parties', in Weberian terminology: the artists; the intellectuals; the critics, the scholars whose commentary is safely ritualised within their collegiate holding-pens; the rabble of journalists; the trade unionists of uncertain power; and the spiritual leaders who hold in check the confused anger of any congregation they are able to muster. Finally there is the important seed of refugees, and the newly-nascent Islamic groups who are now the fashionable targets of disdain and hatred amongst the middle- and lower-whites, and their organs of information.

The popular history of England is a falsified one, unconsciously embedded in the language which lauds the ephemeral British values which must be taught to children so they will not become radical,[1] for a radical is dangerous:

... is it better to 'think' without having critical awareness, in a disjointed or episodic way? In other words, is it better to take part in a conception of the world mechanically imposed by the external environment, i.e. by one of the many social groups in which everyone is automatically involved from the moment of his [sic] entry into the conscious world ... Or on the other hand, is it better to work out consciously and critically one's own conception of the world and thus, in connection with the labours of one's own brain, choose one's sphere of activity, take an active part in the creation of the history of the world, be one's own guide, refusing to accept passively and supinely from outside, the moulding of one's own personality? (Gramsci, 1971, pp. 323–324, quoted by Collier, 1994)

This then, is the theme of radical education: writing, thinking, exchanging ideas to form a set of values wherein the individual's alienation might become unmasked. To know the world in this way is to desire its change. Chris Searle, the radical teacher and headmaster who was dismissed from his headship for trying to 'unmask' the alienation of schoolchildren in England, sets out five brilliant principles of a radical, 'inclusive education':

An 'inclusive school' cannot exist if it accommodates itself within a system of market competition and rivalry. Such a system needs its failures to balance its successes, its unsaleable goods to complement its retail profits... Secondly, and fundamentally, there is the question of curriculum. An inclusive curriculum starts from the breadth of the lives of its students and their communities, and goes on broadening. The inclusive school is a school of the world: it does not stop at being the school of the nation. Its curriculum includes the narratives of all who impact upon it. It does not restrict itself to a canon of established work – it is a tool of discovery, a creative mechanism by which the autobiographies of all of the lives of the school can be told or explored; all their histories, languages, beliefs and skills. It goes beyond the personal, institutional and national boundaries that it breaks through ... Thirdly, the inclusive school is a critical school. It takes nothing from above on trust. It uses its languages to examine and critique. It educates young scholars – who are also young critics – and teaches them – to quote Brecht, to 'grab hold of a book. It's a weapon. You must take over the leadership.' ... Fourthly, there is the relationship the 'inclusive school' has with its community of learners and their families, who often become the teachers of the teachers. This community offers a depth of support, involvement, knowledge and governance which can build such a symbiosis, that school and community become one ... Fifthly, there is the dimension of a school's ethos: an inclusive school should be a place of trust, care and intercommunal friendship. It should be a bulwark against division ... a centre of active participation and democracy, where its constituents have their own fora – and, most pertinent, it should be a centre of growth in co-operative empowerment among students and teachers, and an incentive towards the empowerment of the community it serves. (Searle, 2001, pp. 149–150)

Fifteen years after Searle was writing, concepts of "inclusive school values" had taken a significant turn, with the passing of the Counter Terrorism and Security Act of 2015, which has led to schools (state and private) being issued with the Prevent Duty Guidance, in which teachers were required to teach 'British values' which required verbal conformity to the British state. Any teacher or school governor who deviated from these guidelines was liable to be issued with a letter declaring him or her to be a "non-violent extremist" – the case of the governor of a Birmingham primary school caught up in the "Trojan Horse" affair is a case in point (Bagley, 2016). This is not a climate in which Chris Searle would survive as a teacher, offering his pupils ideas derived from Berthold Brecht.

One of our tasks then, in this writing, is to provide glimpses of a historical account through a radical lens, of the origins of education for minority children in England from 1968 to 2008. The final year of that review was still a time of hope.

By 'minority' we mean *children* whose ethnic identity, language, or legal status as children of refugees, is different from the majority. We also include in this population, children from all ethnic groups, with physical and cognitive challenges. These latter are important minority groups, greatly neglected in educational discourse (Bagley, 2008; Tomlinson, 1981, 2013, 2014).

POLITICAL, ECONOMIC AND SOCIAL PHILOSOPHIES: PERSPECTIVE ON EVOLVING IDEAS

We like change, evolution and synthesis in ideas, and this in part accounts for our liking for Roy Bhaskar's Critical Realism. Bhaskar uses, for example Marxian and Hegelian concepts, but also goes beyond them in the evolving model of dialectical realism. For those concerned with equality of groups as the starting point for discussions of education, ethnicity and gender, Marx's ideas are an important starting point: "The concept of a 'reserve army of labour' has been much discussed since Karl Marx referred to this as a way in which capitalists have a pool of cheaper workers (women and children in his day):[2] this pool of labour can be useful for profit-making in times when they become an 'overworked part of the working class, which swells the reserve army of labour' (Marx, 1887, p. 636)" (Tomlinson, 2013, p. 16).

This Marxian idea is used frequently throughout this book, including Marx's idea of alienation (the separation of the worker from a natural mode of social habitus, imposed by the conditions of labour, and the masking of that oppression through the creation of false ideologies). Tomlinson (2013) describes in detail how modern day youth are persuaded by government ideology and media that failure to find employment when their 'skill' is lacking, is their own fault, and not that of a neoliberal, capitalist system. Blaming the victim is a powerful way of remaining in power.

The ideas we want to synthesise include not only ideas of class oppression, but ideas of personal freedom as well, which have emerged from the writings of the English philosopher T.H. Green, emphasising the twin goals of maximising both human freedom *and* human welfare, ideas which have led to the founding of the British welfare state. Some religious groups (notably Quakers) excluded from universities and professions, moreover tried to prove that religious ideals could inform the ethics of private enterprise, trying to show that the natural inclination of humans is not towards exploitative capitalism.[3]

Peter Flaschel (2009) the German social economist, offers an ingenious synthesis of Marx, Keynes and Schumpeter in developing the idea of "flexisecurity", which offers within a capitalist, but social democratic framework, the ideas of "putting Marx to bed", by guaranteeing the "reserve army" not merely a living wage but a comfortable freedom from the "wants" described by Green and Beveridge, but also a stake in the monetary economy through spending power in the model of Keynes, as adapted by Schumpeter in liberating the spirit of "the restless entrepreneur" in a social democratic, market economy (Flaschel et al., 2012).

It is not our purpose to critique or build on Tomlinson's (2008) major review of the literature in the field of ethnicity and educational policy prior to 2008. Rather, we offer brief case studies of people and events – accounts and stories which seem to me to enliven and enrich the understanding and appreciation of issues surrounding ethnicity, identity and equality in the field of British educational and cultural systems.

However, we cannot proceed until we have summarised Tomlinson's major conclusions. First of all, she points to the "negative, defensive and contradictory central government policies directed towards racial and ethnic minorities in Britain" (2008, p. 177). Policies seem to have been piecemeal, often well-meaning, but poorly conceptualized with ideas about "pluralism" and "multiculturalism", "assimilation" and "integration" being weakly defined, but strongly debated. The underlying pressures of xenophobia, prejudice and racism have meant that policies in relation to "migrants" have been harsh. But at the same time, attitudes to the required "assimilation" by ethnic and religious minorities of "British values" have been confused, and contested.

Tomlinson (2008) concludes that:

A continuity throughout the book has been the contradictions between political encouragement of immigrant labour, while at the same time enacting legislation to control immigration, and allowing a discourse of antagonism to 'immigration' in general to dominate public and media discussion ... Policies have been influenced by xenophobic and racist reactions within the indigenous population ... (p. 177)

In Tomlinson's (2008) analysis of government policies (including those of Labour and New Labour governments) there was, she observes "a continued attempt to deflect attention away from the situation of racial minorities by claims they were simply part of the disadvantaged sector of society" (p. 178). This is the 'Bethnal Green' model, in which different groups of immigrants, from Jews in the nineteenth century, to Bangladeshis in the twentieth settled in the cheapest available housing, gradually making good, and then moving on to professional jobs, and middle class areas of settlement (Glynn, 2005). Certainly "... minorities settled in inner cities and towns among sectors of a working class where jobs were available but then disappeared, [and] there was competition for decent housing, schools were neglected and under-resourced and not intended to be educated to high levels." But governments rarely made consistent efforts to absorb immigrants into housing and jobs in systematic ways which reflected policies for equity. Disadvantaged white, working class groups in these areas (typically, northern cities in which textile industries had declined) often blamed the minorities for their own disadvantages.

"The most critical failure" that Tomlinson (2008) identified has been the chronic failure or neglect of policies for the education of African and Caribbean heritage, black children and adolescents. The emergence of a black (and other ethnic minority) middle class may not be of much assistance

… for black children segregated on poor housing estates and in less successful schools … The endless production of research and government reports on the lower achievements of black young people and the subsequent minimal and grudging adoption of measures to raise their attainment levels have now gone beyond blame and exhortation. It is no longer acceptable that as a group young black citizens can be allowed to fall behind other groups in education and employment, and be regarded as potential criminals. (pp. 178–179)

A further policy theme identified by Tomlinson (2008) was "… the minimal and grudging preparation of teachers to teach in a multi-ethnic society." Despite some progress

From the mid-1980s a general devaluing of the teaching profession, merged with right wing attacks on any multicultural, anti-racist or equality courses led to a disappearance of most university, college and local authority or in-service work [on multiculturalism] … The lack of any national strategy to prepare and develop all teachers for a society and a world now experiencing more ethnic, racial and religious conflicts and tensions … is a serious omission. (p. 179)

Tomlinson continues: "A major discontinuity for teachers, however, was the absence in Britain from the 1990s of a discourse and a language concerning the preparation of all young people for a democratic multicultural society" (p. 180). While she refers earlier in her review to The Crick Report, and the beginning of the Citizenship Education curriculum, she accurately observes the unevenness of the adoption of this curriculum in English schools, and its confusing overlap with Religious Education, and other curricula.

However, this flexibility has been welcomed by Muslim schools who teach Citizenship as part of the Muslim Education curriculum (Al-Refai & Bagley, 2008). But in England since 2015, any school which becomes an Academy is no longer required to follow the National Curriculum, of which Citizenship Education is a part. How then will schools, as an institution, address Citizenship Education and the idea that "… education in a democratic, plural, multicultural society be shaped by a public service culture relevant to the whole society, not one that encourages private, faith, business or an particular group interest" (Tomlinson, 2008, p. 180)? We can accept that some faith schools (e.g. Muslim schools, Quaker schools) prepare their students for magnanimous and public-spirited participation in public life (e.g. Bagley & Al-Refai, 2014; Newton & Broadfoot, 2016). But will this be true of business-led Academies?

Tomlinson's (2008) somewhat optimistic conclusion is that a British government might engage in "… more direct political organisation and engagement to ensure that equality in terms of citizenship rights and responsibilities, and the removal of structural and institutional treatment …" (p. 181). This was written at the cusp of government change, when the continuation of a New Labour government was a possibility. The same was true of the review of policies on equality and inclusion we undertook, with a final perspective on the fiscal and school year 2008–2009 (Sawyerr & Bagley, 2016). By 2017, there were stronger grounds for pessimism than there were in 2008.

EPISODES IN THE HISTORY OF ETHNICITY IN ENGLAND, 1968 TO 2008

We have chosen to explore through salient episodes, the history of British minority education (and often, more specifically, English education) over the past 50 years, a period covered by our lifetimes. This is personal perspective, and task, shared with my colleague and different, systematic and integrated accounts of this history have been offered by others (Tomlinson, 2008; Warmington, 2014).

During these 50 years we have been an African-born child, a migrant, with Caribbean slave forbearers, a nurse, a teacher, a scholar, a child of empire in Canada and Africa, a professional psychologist, a child and family therapist, and a lecturer in psychology; and a Jewish, quasi-intellectual immersed in academic disciplines and action which advocate equality and social change. This historical account is inevitably selective and focuses on key studies, and the profiles of scholars we have found interesting and influential. Only very recently have we discovered the exciting perspectives of analysing knowledge and actions implied by the work of Critical Realism (Bhaskar, Archer, Crieghton, Alderson), a challenging set of philosophical ideas which has been taken up by some Marxists (e.g. Crieghton, 2007), Muslim scholars and researchers (Wilkinson, 2015), and Catholic feminists (Archer, 2014). All of these exponents of Critical Realism seem to have in common a grounded ontology, which allows us to form types of dialectical critical realism in which Hegel's model of thesis, anti-thesis and synthesis is modified into a reflexive, four-factor model that leads to an advocacy of change.

Our theme, then, is of an underclass upon which the middle and lower whites have tried to impose an inferiorized self-concept not only on some ethnic minorities but also on 'poor whites', for whom their alienation (sometimes based on racialized, class oppression)[4] remains largely unmasked. Added to the 'poor whites', and the ethnic minority underclass are the downwardly mobile groups of the physically and cognitively challenged. The issue of inclusive education for these children is an interesting case of groups whose disadvantaged status cuts across class and ethnic lines, but whose difficulty in becoming productive wage earners means that they too must often serve the economic system by downward mobility, being transferred into the underclass (Tomlinson, 2013).

WHY STUDY RECENT HISTORY?

This perennial question has many answers. A nation often defines itself by its "public history", in which events, facts and accounts of events are selectively construed, and often falsified (Jordanova, 2006). Radical (e.g. Marxist) historians try to construct a "people's view of history" (e.g. Morton's *People's History of England*, 1938). But the "periodization" in such accounts may involve naïve abstractions which, according to Popper's (1957) critique of Marx and Engels, creates a 'poverty of explanation', a value schema imposed on events, rather than a schema emerging heuristically from "the people's" accounts of history. Popper argued that since "my" actions can never be predicted (because "I" have free will), the future events and life course of the mass of the people can never be predicted from historical events events (Popper & Eccles, 1977).[5] This idea would fit with Archer's (2008) reflexive critical realist account of individuals(and groups of individuals) taking charge of their destiny.

Max Weber's classic argument on the bases of stratification (Bendix, 1978), is also based on his historical analysis: while it is not based on accounts of the actors of history, nevertheless it has an intellectual appeal in offering three bases for stratification: class (relationships to the economy); status (political influence, sometimes independently of wealth); and party (the social organisation of political struggle, which is not merely based on economic factors). This model seems to us to offer an intuitively attractive way forward in trying to explain the interplay of historical events, in which economic interests and forces, and popular struggles to reconstruct an identity, offer the opportunity for oppressed groups to break free of agencies which implicitly or explicitly, engender a "false consciousness". And Weber's model of social class and bureaucracy does not intellectually oppose Durkheim's idea of society as a set (or sets) of collective social systems in which group values and identity powerfully influence individuals. Rather, in the Critical Realist model both are relevant, and coexist in an interactive and reflexive manner. Creaven (2007) neatly marries Weber and Marx in his critical realist exposition of Marxism.

Ultimately in this sketch of recent history we acknowledge the critical realist view that "I" am part of the values of history, and reflexively "I" am part of this account, as we recreate or retell history, we are also influenced also influenced by our newly-created, reflexive accounts. We acknowledge, with Scambler (2014):

> For Bhaskar, the 'transformational model of social action' outperforms, sees off, the individualism of Weber, the collectivism of Durkheim and the phenomenology of Berger … The transformational model of social action goes hand in hand with a relational, rather than individualistic collectivism or interactionist concept of society.

The ontological basis on which we build this historical sketch is value-laden: the belief that Britain is governed by socioeconomic class interests, and the racialialization and stigmatising of minorities reflects a government policy serving economic or class interests. We believe, nevertheless, that human beings can, through reflexive 'conversations' with themselves and others, achieve special "status islands" (or "parties" in the Weberian model), in which social change ("upward mobility" in Margaret Archer terms, 2003, 2014) is possible.

Understanding and attempting to break free of the false consciousness, by deprived minorities whose self-perceptions and aspirations have been de-based by a capitalist class system, is one of the themes of this book. Part of this shedding of a false consciousness also involves the shedding of a "false history" (as Tosh, 2002 terms it) by the lower whites and the exploited minorities. And in this enterprise, while Marx and Engels (1848/2008) may be criticized for their predictions concerning the decay of capitalism, their humanist conclusions, their use of the Hegelian ideas of thesis-antithesis-synthesis in analysing social histories deserve close attention (Collier, 1992), adaptation, and reformulation (Creaven, 2007; Bhaskar, 2008).[6]

SPECIFIC EPISODES IN RECENT HISTORY

Histories of Childhood, and the Sociology of Childhood

Aries (1962) is a starting point in analysing how cultures and societies have over time, viewed and treated children. These ideas have changed profoundly over the centuries, from an era where infanticide of "unwanted" children was common, to the emergence of ideas that when the rights of adults and children conflict, the rights of children are paramount, and should prevail. This is well illustrated by changes in the law concerning adoption in

England and Wales, when landmark House of Lords' decisions established the primacy of children's interests and rights in contested cases of adoption, which has led to the establishment of the professional *guardian ad litem*, who advises judges on how they might proceed in cases where custody of a child is contested (Bagley, 1973).

Mayall (2013) offers a view on "the sociology of childhood" from a historical perspective. The literature of import is quite recent, and usually dates from the 1970s onwards, when researchers moved beyond 'laboratory' studies of child development to concepts of how children perceived and interacted with, and possibly influenced, their wider environment. Another type of work Mayall identifies is that of the longitudinal study, in which children are followed up from birth until middle or even old 'age' – the 1946 birth cohort originally studied by Douglas (1969) is a case in point. This is a special kind of 'historical' study: findings from some of these important British longitudinal studies are reported in a later chapter, on child maltreatment as an antecedent of mental health problems as an adult.

Mayall (2013) concludes her essay with observations on the often bewildering interactions between children and various forms of social media, and portable electronic devices. It seems not uncommon for grandparents to be instructed in the use of such media by their young grandchildren (a type of relationship which is worth further study). Mayall argues that studies of the sociology of childhood have directly and indirectly, exposed the strengths and weaknesses of social policies on behalf of children: *'While this may be a long journey, with many setbacks and some doubting commentators, it has to be undertaken patiently and thoroughly. The analogy with feminism holds: since the early 1970s, women have faced a huge task ... Sociological approaches to childhood, it can be argued, face even greater difficulties. However, some progress has been made and even more can be achieved'* (pp. 37–8). Priscilla Alderson's two-volume account (2013, 2016) of her 30 years of research with children, refocussed through a critical realist lens, is a bold contribution to this challenging task.

The Social History of Medicine

One approach which will interest the social scientist is that of focus on a specific topic in science, or on policies related to a particular group. In this respect, 'medicine' has been the most intensively studied (Porter, 1997), and shows how medical ideas, irrationalities, 'desperate remedies', and progress has reflected major trends in society, in terms of theology, philosophy, conquest and war, social control and punishment (as in the case of psychiatry), and the slow emergence of ethical conduct in medicine and medical research, epidemiology and public health, and the modern emergence of "evidence based medicine". The astonished reader may ask: how could medical practice be other than 'evidence-based'; but it is salutary to note that 'treatments' were often driven by bizarre theories, untested, and often cruel.

Porter (1997) ends his massive historical survey thus:

> The close of my history suggests that medicine's finest hour is the dawn of its dilemma. For centuries medicine was impotent and thus unproblematic. From the Greeks to the first world war, its tasks were simple: to grapple with lethal disease and gross disabilities, to ensure live births and manage pain ... Medicine [today] has led to inflated expectations, which the public have eagerly swallowed ... (p. 718)

Porter does not adopt any particular "philosophy of history": rather, his accounts of human folly and failure in coping with sickness simply reflect various phases of conventionally-described history (Jordanova, 2006, Chapter 5). Better treatments of illness came not from physicians but from nurses in the care of those injured in battle (e.g. Florence Nightingale); and of evangelical Quakers in the care of the mentally ill in developments such as *The Retreat* in York (Porter, 1997, p. 497). Today *The Retreat* now specializes in treatment of adolescents whose behaviour (e.g. repeated self-harm; eating disorders) has made them unacceptable in mainstream schooling.[7]

Alderson (2013) offers a striking example in the history of medicine: the identification by Semmelweis in the mid-19th century, of the causes of high rates of maternal mortality through poor hygiene procedures – an evidence-based finding rejected by medical ideologues.[8] Alderson, in observing that the children killed by this medical malpractice were entirely absent from the historical account writes of this 'absence' that: 'Absence is a central concept in dialectical critical realism (DCR) and this book is concerned with the absence of children and childhood from almost any report ... [in] major topics of public concern. Yet children and their interests are actually central to all of these 'adult' matters' (Alderson, 2013, p. 3). Similar points are made by Fekete (2009) in her analysis of how European state policies have, over 20 years, changed and developed to control the inflow of 'alien' groups: the children within the asylum seekers, the drowned refugees, and the deportees are children too. Or, as the Charlie Hebdo cartoon ironically put it, the little drowned boy on the shores of Greece would have grown up to be an adult terrorist in Europe, and could be classified by default among the general group of "terrorist suspects". Children are only relevant for the official policy makers in the field of immigration if they hinder or assist the procedures of acceptance or deportation: "Only a miniscule fraction of the world's orphaned, abandoned or separated children make it to Europe; their presence should evoke curiosity or sympathy. Instead, governments want them to disappear" (Fekete, 2009, p. 185).

Medicine, in Foucault's (1976) analysis has been enveloped in "a cloud of unknowing" so far as its true values and purpose are concerned, and "the clinic" which has emerged is hyper-rational, but not hyper-humane. But, according to Scambler (2016): "Foucault is stronger on *how* power works than on *why* ... His notion of 'governmentality' for all its purchase, glosses over what people with capital 'do' to those unable to resist being exploited – largely due to what Margaret Archer calls their *natal* or 'involuntary' placement in society (via relations of class) or oppressed (via relations of state command)." Certainly Foucault has inspired considerable debate amongst academic historians, who often appear to resent this sociological intrusion into their territory (Porter & Jones, 1998). Foucault's emphasis on "power and humanity" has upset some, and energised others (McGowen, 1999).

Large populations of children are ignored by modern medical practice, since they live in economically marginalized, and politically troubled areas (Sawyerr & Bagley, 2016): as Alderson (2013, 2016) puts it in critical realist terminology, they are "absent". For example, the huge toll of malarial infection on children's CNS development in Africa and Asia goes largely unremarked in the annals of medicine (Bagley, 2008).

In the review of literature on the development of self-esteem, later in this book, we examine the potential effects of sexual and physical abuse on the adjustment and mental health of adolescent women. It is astonishing that mainstream psychiatry only became alerted to this widespread public health problem through the work of sociologists in Canada and the U.S.A. (Badgley, 1984; Finkelhor, 1979). Sexually abused children are in critical realist terms, *absent* figures in the history of childhood (Alderson, 2013).

Finally, it is clear from the evidence we have reviewed (Sawyerr & Bagley, 2016) that poor psychological and physical health in Britain is transmitted over time (perhaps even over centuries) through the perpetuation of an underclass in which the health of parents is intimately linked to the poor health of their children. While this relationship is not absolute or deterministic (the cycle can be broken) – in a capitalist-controlled society it may well be in the interests of the ruling group to have a permanently degraded tier of individuals whose marginal skills can be used whenever the demand for labour would otherwise drive up wages, through shortage of unskilled labour.

Some Relevant Historical Studies of Ethnicity and Education

The Marxist scholar Chris Searle (2001) writes about "race, class and exclusion in British schools". This is not a difficult history to write, for there are numerous examples to draw on in policy documents and descriptions of practice. But after his initial chapter on educational and governmental policies, Searle chooses to draw on narrative accounts (his autobiography as a head teacher, and the writings of pupils themselves). Searle, an English teacher, draws extensively on his pupils' poetry. The refugee boy wrote: "I used to swim down on the beach on the river. Then the war started again when I was ten years old,/ And I was frightened, it was a bad war. My Uncle Issa Haq[9] was shot by the soldiers/ You could see dead people everywhere". In Britain said Searle, "many young Somalis were confused, unsettled and fragile". One bullied Somali boy reacted angrily to racist abuse and punching, and was excluded from school (Searle, 2001, p. 70). Exclusion Searle sees as a "moral façade", a strategic tool in the unmasked poverty of English education, the creation of a special class of *absent* children. This moral façade is a whited wall, upon which in 2016 a government daubed a pastiche of "British values".

Searle, a head teacher of a secondary school in Sheffield, was dismissed from the school when he finally refused to exclude pupils for *any* reason. A Yemini, 'now English', boy wrote of this school: "If the world was like our school:/Then the sun would shine/And racism would die/Beauty would rise/And the darkness would hide." Searle's approach, for me, is a brilliant way of seeking historical truth by means of poetic biography, by the autoethnography of his students.

Searle's philosophy of the Inclusive School, quoted earlier, seems to us an ideal way in which a school should be inspired by its teachers, through which the 'absence', the alienation of pupils, becomes unmasked. Schools should be gentle places, and no pupils should exploit or abuse any other person, physically, psychologically, or sexually.

Telling It Like It Was: Forty Scholars and Activists Speaking Out

This stirring volume edited by Brian Richardson (2005) contains the text of Bernard Coard's original monograph of "How the West Indian child is made educationally subnormal by the British educational system" which demonstrated with data how children with African-Caribbean ancestry were wrongly labelled as "stupid" and denied educational opportunity.

The contributors reflect on various themes stemming from Coard's seminal work, and Coard contributed (from his prison cell) a chapter making the following points: Quality education should be available for all children; Education is the most important form of wealth for families and nations; Discriminatory education is a tool by which women, and minorities, are subjugated; Income, wealth, power and privilege maintains its own, self-perpetuating system of elites; Break the link between capitalist interests and its connections to race and education:

> Some may ask whether the nation has sufficient resources to spend so as to bring all schools throughout the country up to high educational standards so that all children can enjoy exposure to these standards. The answer is an unqualified yes. Britain is a wealthy country with more than sufficient resources to do this. It is all a question of priorities. (Coard, 2005, p. 189)

Although a Marxist, Coard couches his arguments in terms of Britain's national interest in developing *all* of its citizens into skilled workers. He does not discuss issues of alienation and false consciousness. This task is left, in this edited volume, to Mahamdallie, who echoes the Brechtian phrase in his chapter title *Is this as good as it gets?* He, like other contributors, makes it clear that the institutional racism in education that Coard exposed "became the analytical touchstone for the Black Parents Movement of the 1970s." The issue that Coard exposed (the creation of a large group of African Caribbean children as 'educationally subormal') remained, in different form, in "Thatcher's Britain". Continuous political activity, campaigning by the Lawrence family on behalf of their murdered son (Doreen Lawrence contributes to this volume), and the Macpherson report exposing institutional racism, have changed the nature of the debate, and of educational practice.

It is unlikely that there are many teachers today who are actively racist: it is the educational policy makers who control systems, who are racist by default, offering third rate education to 'poor whites' and 'poor blacks' alike. Wally Brown (2005) a black educator, writes that "the future belongs to us". Yes, the battle on behalf of black youth is nearly won, it is the poor whites we have to worry about. This book contains great poetry by black poets, and interesting accounts of supplementary education schemes. This is a cheerful and stirring book which convinces one that black youth in Britain are on an upward trajectory (just as their Muslim peers, described by Ramadan (2010), are moving out of the ghetto, as Islamic educational systems bed down in Britain). This book is a piece of history, looking backwards with anger, and forwards with hope. For the 'poor whites' it has little to offer.

Chris Searle writes angrily in his chapter that a disproportionate number of black youth were (in 2003) being excluded from school: but the very fact that they are black means that they are numbered, noticed, counted, and cared about. While our historical review ends in the period 2008–2009, we would venture the guess that exclusion rates for black children are now (in 2016) falling. But for the underclass of 'poor whites', and for the white children with special needs, for the children who have been through the care [sic] system our hypothesis is that their rates of exclusion from school on arbitrary, cruel and illogical grounds are *not* falling (Sawyerr & Bagley, 2016).

Issues of Institutional Racism

Direct Racism involves conscious, direct and deliberate actions by individuals (or their social institutions) which denigrate and disadvantage a person of an ethnic, religious or perceived racial (or racialized) group, or indeed a whole group of people, through organised propaganda, and direct discrimination. The evidence on such racism in Britain was described by a team of researchers at The Institute of Race Relations (IRR) in London, which led to the publication of a lengthy, well-researched and widely publicised book by Jim Rose and Nicholas Deakin, and others called *Colour and Citizenship: A Report on British Race Relations* by the Oxford University Press in 1969. This long report was widely read and favourably reviewed, and its research on racial discrimination, for example, led to the strengthening of the laws which made racial discrimination in access to housing, services and employment, illegal.

Warmington (2014) in his review of the roles of "black intellectuals" in this process observes that however earnest and well-directed, the IRR at that time was directed, run and staffed mainly by "white liberals". However, the IRR could only survive on private foundation grants, and some government contracts: it declined to be an arm of government, and following the publication of its massive report, funding greatly diminished. The IRR survived as a much smaller institution, now led by its radical librarian A. Sivanandan, who described how a core of radical staff took over the IRR (1975). The Institute is now known internationally for its radical, Marxian approach. The IRR's academic journal *Race* changed its name to *Race and Class*, and now has a healthy world-wide circulation under the auspices of its new (capitalist) publisher SAGE Journals Inc.

The approach of the IRR can be gauged by an article by Sivandandan in 2005 entitled "Why Muslims reject British values": *"As the IRR pointed out at the time, the fight against racism cannot be reduced to a fight for culture; nor does learning about other people's cultures make racists less racist ... the racism that needs to be contested is not personal prejudice, which has no authority behind it, but institutionalized racism, woven over centuries of colonialism and slavery into the structures of society and government."* In this analysis, institutional racism is part of class warfare, ignored until "unexpectedly" it was given "official currency" by the Macpherson Report of 1999.

Since that time the IRR has produced a number of excellent reports, including comprehensive studies by its new co-director, Liz Fekete (2009) of Europe's "new racism", Islamophobia. This further analysis sees working class racism and anti-immigrant rhetoric of the right, and Islamic radicalism as "useful diversions" serving the ends of international capitalism, which divert energy away from workers uniting in a common, anti-imperialist cause (see Bagley & Al-Refai, 2017, for a fuller discussion).

Ironically "liberal" legislation such as the Race Relations Acts and subsequent legislation on behalf of ethnic, gender and physically challenged groups may be functional for capitalist enterprise, since they enable the most qualified workers (e.g. ethnic minorities) to be recruited without worrying about obstructions by the white proletariat. It enables too, stereotyping of "industrious and intelligent" ethnic groups such as Indians and Chinese who are channelled into sectors of labour (technical, engineering, medical) where their skills are much needed (Phillips, 2011). None of this liberal patina denies the fact of the profound *absence* (in CR terms) which is the Level 1 tier of Institutional Racism: that is, institutional racism thrives on the denial of the concepts of ethnicity and race. We illustrate this in a study of racial discrimination in England in 2015 (Bagley & Abubaker, 2017).

The liberal ethos of the IRR's first manifestation has continued in the work of the Runnymede Trust, with Professor Nicholas Deakin being involved in 2016, as he was in 1969, in this organisation's scholarly work. The Runnymede Trust (a private charity) is credited with defining the term "Islamophobia" in 1997, and continues to monitor this important aspect of British racism (Runnymede, 2016).[10]

Institutional racism silently infects institutions and their norms, values and actions which are translated into everyday behaviours in which it is assumed that certain groups (e.g. Muslims, Refugees, Migrant Workers, African-Caribbeans et alia) by their nature, or because of their embedded beliefs, or their current circumstances are bound to behave in a certain way. Thus it behoves public officials (e.g. police, teachers) to 'stop-and-search', or report to the police any student apparently behaving oddly, or expressing opinions incompatible with 'British values'. Under the Prevention of Terrorism Act of 2015, for example, any teacher or school governor who does not do so may be issued with a formal letter from the British Home Secretary declaring them to be a "Non-Violent Extremist", in consequence of which they will be barred from being a school governor, or lose their licence to teach.[11]

The Marxist scholars of the Institute of Race Relations have long argued that this deep layer of racism has been ignored by the 'white liberals' who merely describe the surface layers of the racist society. The Macpherson Report (1999) was (as Sivandandan observed) a surprise in pointing to layers of institutional racism in police reaction to the murder of a black teenager (Stephen Lawrence) by a gang of white youths. Tomlinson (2008) describes this report, which identified "institutionalised racism" (in the metropolitan police, and by implication in other British institutions) as "a defining moment in British race relations." Certainly, the government responded with an amendment to the existing Race Relations Act. This required institutions such as police, health services and educational institutions to work towards providing "equal, fair and just services to all groups."

The ethos of "equality" implied by this, resulted in the collection of statistics on "ethnic origins", and fed in part into the development of the Sure Start programmes for preschool children, which were modelled on the American Head Start movement of providing preschool monitoring and provision for children from disadvantaged groups (Eisenstadt, 2011; Sawyerr & Bagley, 2017b).[12]

The ideas apparently underlying the concept of institutional racism have been analysed in detail by Celia Phillips (2011) who after identifying some conceptual ambiguities (What kind of racism? What kind of institutions?) concludes:

> ... Institutional racism can be retained to assist our understanding of persistent ethnic inequalities in key areas of social policy ... institutional racism needs to be situated within a conceptual framework which acknowledges the role of racialization [the imposition of racial labels] at the micro, meso and macro levels ... and can explain ethnic inequalities in education (e.g. attainment), and policing (e.g. stop-and-search practices). (p. 187)

She is pessimistic however, of practices which are functional for changing a class-based social system, except in the long run. One problem in the official data she presents is that the many children of mixed ethnic ancestry (Platt, 2009) are not adequately identified: are they counted by officials (or themselves) as white, or black, mixed, or other? This dilemma points to some intriguing research possibilities.

Educating "Our" Black Children (2001)

Who are "we"? We are all teachers, all professionals, all people of good will – the parent-figures of all children in the land (and in the world). The idea implicit in the title of Richard Majors (2001) book is pleasing, and fits with our idea of Child-Centred Humanism, that everyone, and all of humanity's institutions, should address humanity's primary value, of putting the needs and interests of children first. Richard Majors was an American educator working in Manchester when he edited this book, which has 15 well-researched and incisive chapters, including several by Americans who offer interesting insights into positive trends for enhancing Black achievement and identity in the United States. Issues addressed include 'black masculinity', 'Afrikan-centred curriculum', supplementary education, 'ego-recovery' in African-Caribbean adolescents, Black feminism, school exclusions, and successful schools.

This book is a stimulating blend of scholarship and moral fervour, which addresses, for example the (im) moral bases for excluding anyone, of whatever ethnicity or status, from schooling. Figures are cited from the 1990s showing that Black adolescent males were 15 times more likely than others to be excluded. But it is important that these boys could be identified, and advocated for. Poor White boys excluded from school are less identifiable, and have fewer advocates.[13]

Two years before this edited volume was published, the MacPherson report on institutional racism was published. This was certainly a turning point in ethnic minority relations in Britain. African Caribbean children and their parents (who, with increasing frequency, included one white parent) who were 'standing up to be counted', forming a distinct and coherent pressure group. Institutional racism was on the run: David Gillborn's inaugural professorial lecture at the Institute of Education, London in 2002 was on Education and Institutional Racism. Gillborn was pessimistic about the educational future for African Caribbeans in Britain, but events seem to have taken somewhat different turn. Fortunately for the racists, a new target had appeared on the horizon, Muslims (Fekete, 2009).

CHAPTER 5

Can Individual Schools Make a Difference?

> By the 1990s, a new educational phenomenon had appeared in Britain. This was the failing school, a demonized institution whose head, teachers and governors were deemed to be personally responsible for failing whole communities ... (Sally Tomlinson, 1998, p. 157)

> The unashamedly normative desiderata are (i) to define a good school or society in relation to an expected and continuing increase in the variety of resources; (ii) in a manner to allow this variety to translate into a distribution of opportunities that furnishes the social conditions for a good life for all members of the school or society; (iii) and proves resistant to the recrudescence of the current actualist state of affairs Margaret Archer. (2015, p. 22)

In their much-cited monograph *Fifteen Thousand Hours: Secondary Schools and their Effects on Children*, Michael Rutter, Barbara Maughan, Peter Mortimore and Janet Ouston (1979) take their title from the number of hours the average child would spend away from home, in educational institutions being taught by teachers, and interacting with peers. This, surely is an important piece of the environment that must have a powerful influence on children and adolescents, for good or ill. Yet it was remarkable that little was known about the effects of schools, *qua* schools, on the youngsters they contained. Before embarking on this work Rutter had compared samples of children from an inner London borough (Camberwell) with similar aged groups in a quiet, semi-rural environment (Isle of Wight), and had shown for instance, that the lives of "West Indian" children in Camberwell were marked and marred, by a variety of institutional features of the school (Rutter, Yule & Bagley, 1975).

Building on this work, Rutter et al. (1979) studied some of the schools in the Camberwell study, plus others in contiguous Boroughs to form a group of 12 schools whose institutional processes, and social, scholastic and behavioural processes and outcomes were intensively studied. Rutter had validated a short measure of behavioural and emotional problems for completion by teachers and/or parents, and the profiles of groups of children varied significantly between schools, for unknown reasons. Moreover, in the previous longitudinal work in "School A" 30.8% of pupils had behavioural difficulties according to this scale, at age 11, but this proportion had *fallen* to 9.2% at age 14; but in "School B" in the same Borough, 34.0% had behaviour problems at age 11, *rising* to 48.0% at age 14 – all highly significant differences. Reasons for this were at the outset of the research, unknown.

It was clear to Rutter's team in studying the "school effect" that characteristics of pupils enrolling at age 11 had to be controlled for, in statistical terms, if any school effect was to be identified. Within each school a considerable amount of questionnaire data was generated, included pupil-completed questionnaires on (for example) how well the school "Helps you develop your personality and character." There was significant variation in the measures across schools, as well as between pupils according to age, gender, achievement, ethnicity and other individualised variables.

> Our finding that secondary schools varied greatly with respect to rates of examination success, attendance, misbehaviour and delinquency is entirely in keeping with the evidence from other research. However, our investigation has taken matters a stage further by showing that these differences were not explicable in terms of the children's characteristics prior to secondary transfer. Rather, they stemmed from experiences during the secondary school years. (Rutter et al., 1979, p. 179)

The findings of Rutter's team were salient: some schools had many pupils who were disgruntled, sad or rebellious; others had rather few. The differences *could not be wholly accounted for* by the behavioural profiles of pupils entering at age 11. This "school effect" was stable over time, and was not linked to the physical quality of the school buildings, or spaces (e.g. playing fields) surrounding the school. There was however, a cumulative or additive effect in terms of "success" (fewer behavioural problems, more examination successes, more pupil and teacher satisfaction). There was, clearly a "school process effect", a school ethos associated with success. Pupils were calmer, teachers praised them more; teachers stayed in post longer; after school clubs and activities thrived. "Happiness" was the order of the day, and the successful schools had an implicit but enduring set of values which were independent of the often decayed urban settings in which these "flagship schools" were moored. These were outstanding schools, but there was an equal number of secondary schools in the area studied, which were "beached wrecks" as educational institutions. This remarkable study has had a number of effects in that often reactionary educational administrators have adduced the policy that a new, highly-paid head can "turn a school around" (a philosophy that survives in the current obsession with creating new, so-called Academies).

Disappointingly, Rutter's ground-breaking research has stimulated rather few ethnographic studies of schools, which could have added qualitative flesh to the sturdy bones of Rutter's quantitative work – for example, the contributors to the edited volume on *School Effectiveness for Whom?* (Smith & Tomlinson, 1998) replicate but do not seem to build, in theoretical or ethnographic terms, on Rutter's models of successful inner-city schools.

Michael Rutter himself deserves special mentioned. He is the world's leading child and adolescent psychiatrist, and now in his eighties still (in 2017) was publishing several scholarly papers a year. He has made breakthroughs in the genetic study of psychiatric disorder, particularly autism. But he is also well known for his work in social psychiatry, especially his longitudinal work on Romanian adoptees. Most remarkable is the sociological dimension he brings to his clinical work, which is quite unparalleled in Western medical research.

One of Rutter's team, Peter Mortimore (1988) reported on "school effectiveness" in a sample of 50 English primary schools, and showed that some schools were much more effective than others in supporting pupils' personal and intellectual development, when the variable intake to the schools was controlled for. In another replication, Smith and Tomlinson (1989) in a study of 18 "multiracial comprehensives" replicated Rutter's design, and also showed that 'the school effect' could be strong:

> … the results confirm the finding of Fifteen Thousand Hours, that different secondary schools achieve substantially different results with children who are comparable in terms of background and attainment at an earlier time … [We] also show that these affects are more important than any differences between black and white children, and they provide a more detailed and reliable account than has yet been available of the progress from the age of 11 of children belonging to racial minority groups. The study was much less successful in explaining why the differences in explaining why the differences bet schools occur … (p. 3)

Again parallel ethnographic work would be most welcome, but none of the schools studied by Rutter, Mortimore or Smith and Tomlinson seem to have been studied in this way. Instead research analysts (e.g. Brighouse & Tomlinson, 1991; Slee et al., 1998) have examined administrative procedures, and interpersonal relationships between staff, and between teachers and staff in trying to construct profiles of successful schools. Valuable though this kind of work is, we would love to know in more detail of how, at the heart, these schools throb.

It is relevant to mention here recent research by Newton and Broadfoot (2016) on "the school effect" in five Quaker secondary schools in England.

Using a combination of qualitative and quantitative methods, they show that the Quaker ethos (respecting and nurturing one another in a community devoted to learning, and service) has prevailed over the years, despite the majority of students and teachers not now being Quakers themselves. The origins of this philosophy of education are described by Lampen (2015).

Subsequent sociological research (e.g. Searle, 2001; Carlisle, 2013) has followed the tradition of Paul Willis in showing why some (perhaps most?) secondary schools are relatively unsuccessful in meeting the needs of all of their students.

Adding Resources: Quasi-Experiments in School Evaluations

A different kind of research on "quality schooling" is the experimental one: choosing a 'failing school' and a similar control school, and supplying the target school with extra resources, teachers, and social work support. Such projects have shown that when target and control schools are compared, to be very successful, and are likely to be cost effective: initial costs are easily offset in the medium run in saved costs of youth delinquency, dropping out of school, lack of skills, unwanted pregnancies, unemployment etc. In the Appendix on "Excluded Youth" (Sawyerr & Bagley, 2016) the methodology and results from some of these studies are presented, and reviewed.

We offer a brief overview of the "experimental" study undertaken by Bagley and Pritchard (1999a, 1999b). They selected for intensive study two matched secondary schools and feeder primary schools, in separate parts of the same urban area, serving communities several miles apart. Both communities were marked by high delinquency rates in children and adults in public housing projects. Both communities also had high rates of mental illness in adults, and child care referrals associated with families who were barely coping with the challenges of everyday life. In the focus schools funding allowed for an additional teacher to be placed in the primary school in the most deprived sub-area, who focussed in particular on learning and behavioural problems in young children. A half-time teacher was added to the staff of the secondary school, who specialised in work with learning-challenged children, and those with emotional and behavioural difficulties. A full-time social worker addressed problems of families of selected pupils attending both the secondary and the feeder primary school, focussing especially on sibling groups from particularly disorganised families, using the "family service" model of working intensively with a small case load of "high risk" families (Starkey, 2002).

The programme lasted for three years, and both focus and comparison schools were monitored regularly by the researchers using both pupil questionnaires, and teacher reports. In the focus secondary school exclusion rates fell to zero by the third year; pupils reported less bullying and fighting, and said they enjoyed school more; formal delinquency rates were down; in the families of the focus school children, rates of abuse, neglect and removal to care dropped dramatically; no 'unwanted' pregnancies were identified; absenteeism rates fell; self-reported drug use dropped. None of these indicators improved in the contrast school, where rates of pupil problems became worse rather than better. The researchers' cost-benefit analyses showed that that even in the short run, the experimental inputs into the school were highly cost effective, and if applied nationally would have yield savings of many millions of pounds. In retrospect however, the researchers reflected that it was not merely the additional inputs that had helped: the ethos of the school seemed to change, and all of the teachers know that their school had been singled out for special treatment. They had discovered, once again, the joy of teaching! This mood of optimism was catching, for pupils and teachers alike.

Williams and Pritchard (2006) in the first part of their challenging book *Breaking the Cycle of Educational Alienation: A Multi-Professional Approach* give fuller details of qualitative and case study data collected in the experimental study described above, and stress that a school-based social worker was crucially pivotal in the multi-professional approach. This worker could act immediately in giving support to families, whose son or daughter was manifesting problematic behaviour in school. In the second part of this book, the authors review further British studies which had achieved somewhat similar results, and elaborate a model for the caring, inclusive comprehensive school.

Jamaica Rising: The Power of Juk[14]

The extraordinary island of Jamaica was the receiving port for African slaves, where they were broken in before being shipped to plantations across the British-ruled Caribbean. Jamaica has long had a reputation for the severity of its regime and its punishments to make black people conform to servitude. The African spirit has survived however, in Jamaica as in nowhere else.

In the West African system of religious drumming, of the five ritual drums the big, father drum is the Jah drum which when pounded evokes the spirit of Jah (or Jahweh, as Rastafarians say). This religious metaphor of sound survives powerfully in Jamaica today. Life is lived outdoors, and the throb of electronic sound-systems pulse from the bush a mile away.[15] Jah is the god of fertility, of sex, of power. His thrust is Juk, and has music is Jazz. Juk means to hit, to thrust, to strike, to sing, to dance, to strive, to have sex, to create, to be fertile, to *survive*. Juk has guile and cunning, like the Anansi figure from West African folk stories who always outwits his opponents, just as Jamaicans will always defeat slavery and oppression, ancient or modern.

When the European colonialists raped North and South America, they first tried to enslave the Amerindians. In this they failed entirely: when enslaved, North American Indians and the Caribbean islands' aboriginal dwellers, all died within a few months or years: deprived of a traditional culture they simply could not survive. The cultural story that this embodies will not be retold here. Suffice it to say that on an island like Newfoundland (sic) in the land which the British appropriated and called "Canada", Amerindians were unable to flee, were herded into the centre of the island, and put down. In this Canadian province (as was the case with Tasmania's aboriginals) Native Indians were entirely exterminated; the same happened in all of the Caribbean islands, although in Jamaica some of the "Maroons" (hiding in the mountains) intermarried with escaped slaves.

African slaves survived, we speculate, because of their outgoing, thrusting culture, the culture of *Juk*, which strikes back, which lies in wait for opportunity in whatever form it takes, including taking white names, white manners and white professions, even submitting to concubinage and various values of 'whiteness'. Yet many profoundly African cultural forms survive in Jamaica, including *pocomania* (a shamanist-style of group worship with drumming, dancing and singing, and a few Christian accoutrements). Ancestor worship (burying one's dead on family property, with grave ornaments favoured by the dead ancestor), animal sacrifice in times of change and stress, and many other African rituals have been hidden from western anthropologists. Only Fernando Henriques, the Sephardic-African anthropologist from Brazil was able to describe some of these with any perceptive accuracy (Henriques, 1967).

In Britain a 'black history' movement drew on several African and Caribbean strands to form supplementary and Saturday schooling for black youth (e.g. Stone, 1979; Richardson, 2005). Foremost amongst this movement has been the Jamaican Dr. Vince Hines, whose Brixton-based foundation led to the publication of *How Black People Overcame Fifty Years of Repression in Britain 1945–1995* (1998). Other leading activists in London deserve mention, especially Chris Mullard (Mullard, 1985) an academic whose community organisation strengthened the black cultural roots of the Nottting Hill Carnival in London.

We end this section with two brief case histories of Jamaican families in London, Canada and the United States (the three countries to which Jamaicans have in large numbers, emigrated). First of all, the 'B' family: Mr. and Mrs. B arrived in London in 1960 with their two Jamaican-born children, and settled in Brixton, and had four more children. All attended the same "successful" Roman Catholic secondary school. Mr. B was a chauffeur for a West African country's Ambassador in London, who passed on to Mr. B a signed photograph of Marcus Garvey, which he proudly displayed in his living room. Mrs. B worked as a primary school's cook. All of their children are professionally qualified; and three have academic or medical doctorates. The professional achievements of these six children have ranged from College Director, Dean of Surgery (at a leading US University), Attorney General of a Caribbean nation, two Professors, and a Director of Nursing in a large hospital. Mr. B has now passed, but his wife attributes her children's success to the good school that they had attended. The question must be asked: why have these children (and many other Jamaican children) achieved so well? The answer probably lies in the happy coincidence of a "good" secondary school attended, and high levels of achievement motivation (like that of the Jamaican-American Colin Powell, and like Obama, child of immigrants). This survival is a sophisticated form of Juk.

Now, consider the 'W' family. Poppa W has passed now, but he was the successful inheritor of land in rural Jamaica, on which he grew sugar cane, refined rum, and leased some of his land for bauxite mining. In the West African polygamous tradition he had four wives: each wife took his surname, and each lived in her own house in the village compound. By his first wife he had 12 children, but only 13 children by his other three wives. All lived quiet, Anglican lives, and attended Sunday services. Girls and boys lived at various times in the different houses, according to space, and needs (e.g. for an older girl to help with young children). All but one of the 12 children of the senior wife have become professionals in Britain, Canada, the United States, Jamaica, and other Caribbean islands. They are teachers, accountants, paramedics, professors, land surveyors, senior nurses: all (but one) have degrees, including four master's degree, and one doctorate. The one exception is the oldest son of the senior wife, who in his turn has inherited the family land, has acquired more properties, has four wives, and (at the last count) is father of 36 children by these four wives. Only the marriage of the first, or senior wife was solemnized in the Anglican

Church in this rural Jamaican parish (This extended family in its second and third cousins, includes an Olympic bronze medallist sprinter from the 2012 games; and an Olympic gold medallist from the 'seventies').

We draw several lessons from these case studies: Africa survives in rural Jamaica, and this form of polygamy has not been described in any published ethnographic work; diverse cultural systems both run in parallel, and happily intertwine; this cultural complexity by no means inhibits upward social and occupational mobility; and only quite wealthy people (with traditional, African chief-like status) can afford to be successful polygamists!

These are, we submit, not isolated or unique case histories; they may not be typical, but they are certainly not atypical either. They are Jamaica rising, out of the children of Africa, a people making the best of themselves.[16] Jamaica is one of the most successful of the Caribbean islands. Its music, born in Africa, is refined and flows back to Africa, so the reggae beat is now common in West Africa. Jamaican athletes and professionals are the strongest in the world: Juk survives. And becoming middle class presents Jamaicans (and other African-Caribbeans in Britain) new challenges in self-perception and identity (Rollock et al., 2015).

THE POVERTY OF EDUCATION IN BRITAIN

This historical review ends, arbitrarily, in 2008–2009. In undertaking this review, we wanted to form an impression of the development and change of how inequality and deprivation (both absolute and relative) impacted on the lives and achievements of families, children and adolescents in what seemed to be a Britain divided along lines of social class and ethnicity. The purpose of this exploration was to 'unmask' not only our own alienation in this divided, complex society but also the alienation imposed on the 22 children who are at the heart of the study reported in the next Chapter, of a nursery school in a deprived (i.e. oppressed) area of Inner London. We wanted to understand the nature of the forces that oppressed them and their families, forces which must be understood and unmasked if we are to create a society in which the selfhood of each individual becomes self-actualized.

We have put this lengthy review (appended to this book) in the past tense, since the account is a form of history. The state of Britain in 2008 may be significantly different from that of Britain (or of England) in 2016. Numerous supportive references are cited, and for these the reader is referred to the Appendix. The summary of this overview is reproduced here:

Britain offered the promise of a quality education from preschool to university, but currently youth in the population who formed a more or less permanent underclass (at least ten percent of the population) rarely took full advantage of these educational opportunities, due to a variety of negative pressures in their lives. Up to 2008, Britain was one of the world's wealthiest countries, both in terms of gross national income, and average income per head – but this wealth was distributed much more unequally than in all countries of the developed world, with the exception of the United States. In Britain, health indicators – rates of illness and death from various diseases and "accidents" in the first two decades of life – illustrated the chronic disadvantages experienced by the poorest income quintile of the population. Differences between rich and poor families in this regard were actually increasing. The poor remained economically poor and in relatively poorer health, decade upon decade, while the incomes and good health of the richest quintile improved year by year. The rich were becoming richer, but the poor remained poor.

There were powerful structural problems within British society which created enduring economic poverty, which persisted between generations, with its associated educational poverty: at least half of children from families in the poorest income quintile endured second-rate conditions of living, second-rate educational provision, and restricted occupational opportunities. These were "the excluded youth" of Britain. This sector of the population also suffered disproportionately from chronically poor health, maladaptive behaviour, exclusions from school because of their 'special educational needs', and various long-term neurological disorders.

Children from the underclass were much more likely to live in areas of large cities in Britain marked by social or poor housing, high levels of criminality, intergenerational family problems, and psychiatric illness in adults. The schools which serve their "sink" estates were often of poor quality, "crumbling schools" with high rates of teacher turnover, and the lack of specialist teachers in maths, science and languages in secondary schools. Classes in these schools were often too large for effective teaching, and teacher morale was often low. 'Troublesome' pupils from these schools were often subject to temporary or permanent exclusion from the educational system, and if they completed schooling they only atypically gained examination successes which enabled them to proceed to college or university. They were likely to become a chronically under-employed underclass, leading disorganized lifestyles marked by petty criminality, as well the drift into begetting the next generation of the underclass.

Britain could offer focussed school-based educational and social work intervention services for families and children otherwise destined for school exclusion and educational failure. These demonstration projects have shown that although such interventions are costly in the short term they are nevertheless frequently successful in diverting young people from depressed and self-defeating lifestyles. Because of the criminal justice and social service costs saved, in the long-run these interventions could have profound psychological and fiscal benefits.

The 'poverty of education' in Britain in the period under review was illustrated by international comparisons which highlighted Britain's comparative failure on a number of indicators of achievement, health and well-being in children and adolescents. Two groups were identified as having especially high levels of stress and failure within the educational system: children growing up in (or having recently left) residential child care; and children with 'special educational needs'. High levels of permanent and temporary school exclusions identified an educational system which practised exclusion rather than inclusion. Children were particularly likely to be excluded from mainstream schools on grounds of alleged disruption, poor academic performance, disability of various kinds, or the simple fact of being bullied. Britain, although a signatory to the UN Commission on the Rights of Disabled Children (2006), in practice violated this convention through its high levels of educational exclusion of children because of their cognitive, emotional or behavioural challenges. The plight of children with autistic spectrum disorders was particularly dire in this regard.

International literature on school class sizes has been reviewed, showing clearly that in smaller classes (18 or less) teachers could focus on the learning, emotional and behavioural needs of each pupil, without the need for forced exclusions. However, in Britain many school classes contained 30 or more pupils, and in secondary schools classes could be up to 60 in size, because of the shortage of specialist teachers in mathematics and science (so that classes had to 'double-up' for the one qualified teacher). It was argued that one of the crucial investments needed in a rich nation is that of halving school class sizes.

We commended the government's Sure Start initiatives for under-fives in families in deprived areas, but almost certainly these programmes although successful in some applications, were underfunded and not comprehensive enough in scope to be fully effective. We described an alternative type of intervention in which social workers and specialist teachers are attached to primary and secondary schools serving deprived areas. Such interventions could be highly cost-effective in reducing school exclusions, problem behaviours in school and community, school drop-out and later problems such as unwanted pregnancy, drug use, unemployment and criminality. Here, we argued, was a way of preventing children of the poorest families becoming the next generation of the underclass.

THE MULTICULTURALISM DEBATE

We argue (Bagley & Al-Refai, 2017) that the attack, both popular and political, on the concept of multiculturalism is fundamentally racist and xenophobic in nature. This semi-intellectual critique of some politicians and the popular press, while failing to define in coherent terms what is meant by "culture", attacks the idea that there could be more than one version of the concept of English or British culture and identity. As Modood (2013) says, multiculturalism is here in Britain to stay: live with it. Afro-Caribbeans, Asians, Muslims and many other cultural groups (including Scots, Irish and Welsh) are here in England for all time. And they will marry your children, and your grandchildren.

Demands for "integration" are often actually demands for assimilated subordination, and the giving up of 'alien' languages, customs, religions, dress styles, and skin colours. Fortunately these views are firmly held by only a minority of the white English population, Many African-Caribbeans are in fact assimilating through intermarriage with non-racist whites; and an increasing number of former Christians are converting to (assimilating with) Islam. Islam itself is non-racist, a wonderful mix of ethnicities.

The nature of racism in Britain is changing, and anti-black prejudice is now morphing into Islamophobia. Islam itself is a religion of non-violence, a religion of dignity and good deeds, loving neighbours including Christians, whom Islam from its very beginnings, has accepted with tolerance and respect. This is illustrated by the studies on citizenship education and religion of Al-Refai and Bagley (2008), Wilson (2014) and Wilkinson (2015), and in the pluralist theology of Tariq Ramadan (2010).

CONCLUSIONS

This is a partial and subjective, value-based view of episodes in British multicultural history from 1968 to 2008. In constructing it we have used a variety of informants, scholars, immigrants and their descendanta like ourselves, and published accounts in our special areas of interest, including medicine which was the first profession for both of us. The review of inequality of education focusses on "the underclass" who with now with *decreasing* frequency, contain the ethnic minority children of immigrants. Black British and Asians in Britain are rising up, not in revolt, but through their aspirations to succeed in educational and occupational sectors. How long will it be before Britain has a Prime Minister who is 'non-white', a Muslim, and whose grandparents were born in Pakistan?

Nevertheless, Britain more than any other European country, has a rigid class system in which "poor whites" often attend the worst schools, with lives blighted by many negative factors in family and environment. Ethnic minorities may reside temporarily in this ghetto of the underclass, but the poor whites, without a clear ethnic or religious identity with which to dignify themselves, are effectively required by the forces of capital, to remain in the 'reserve army of labour', in which Bhaskar's (2008) master-slave relationship and its supporting ideologies, remain unmasked.

Good schools can help children to be upwardly mobile (including children from 'poor' white families), and putting extra resources into schools can "break the cycle of alienation" (Williams & Pritchard, 2006). African-Caribbean children, we argue, have strong motivations to succeed academically and the combination of such pupils and a "successful" secondary school can lead to powerful achievement and upward mobility in Black (and Asian) students. For the future of Blacks and Asians in Britain we are optimistic; on the future (*pace* Tomlinson, 2013) of the "poor white yobs" we are more worried. They have a much weaker ethnic or religious identity, apart from a broad nationalist spirit. Their religious and value affiliations are often weak or confused, and they generally do not have aspirations to be upwardly mobile (Tomlinson, 2013).

These "poor whites" are part of the segment of social class which Guy Standing refers to as "the precariat". Writing of recent social changes in Britain, and the danger that the precariat might become the foot soldiers in "emerging neo-fascist movements" in Europe and North America, Standing observes: "The precariat is most exposed to a crisis of identity ... [but] the precariat must not desert multiculturalism or the legitimation of multiple identities. However, it must do more, in that it must have its interests represented in all identity structures and institutions. This is not a plea for a new form of corporatism. It is a call for the precariat to become a class-for-itself" (Standing, 2014, p. 274).

That this form of identity has not yet evolved is clear from the research of Goodwin and Heath (2016) who analysed data from a panel study of more than 31,000 voters following the UK Referendum vote which resulted in a majority opting, in 2016, to leave the European Union. The 'Brexit' group (voting to leave) in many ways resembled those who favoured the right-wing United Kingdom Independence Party in previous studies using this panel of voters. The Brexit group were significantly more likely to have incomes below the median for the country; they had many fewer educational qualifications; they lived in neighbourhoods where their neighbours were also "... often unskilled and in precarious, insecure and poorly paid employment; they were, in ethnic terms, predominantly white." What united this group of Brexit voters was their strong sense of "an English ethnicity". This seemed, in 2016, to be the current identity focus of the precariat class.

We will try and integrate this historical review within the research findings that follow. Meanwhile, we want to express our disappointment at the lack of good ethnographic studies of ethnicity in British schools in the period 1968 to 2008. Only the qualitative work of Connolly, 1998, and Searle, 2001 stands out – but we are enlivened by Chris Sarra's 2013 critical realistic ethnography of the education of First People in an Australian high school.[17]

We are disappointed too by the lack of studies in the tradition of urban sociology pioneered by Morris (1957), which could have focussed on ethnicity as a major variable, and which might illuminate aspects of the lives of children, youth and their families in British cities, through spatial analysis of how disadvantaged conditions cluster together, within the catchment areas of certain schools, which may themselves by disadvantaged.

NOTES

[1] *Fundamental British Values in the Early Years* (2015) and *Prevent Duty Guidance* (2015) available at https//www.gov.uk
[2] And in the twentieth century, as Gaine and George (1999) observe.
[3] The work of the chocolate companies, in particular Cadbury and Rowntree, and the systematic efforts by The Rowntree Foundation to research the nature, extent and effects of economic poverty, and to lobby governments in this regard, are cases in point (see J. Unwin *A UK Without Poverty*, 2014, www.jrf.org.uk): 39% of Britons over 18 do not have a secure job, or one that pays a 'living wage' (www.neweconomics.org).

[4] Working class racism – blaming ethnic minorities for their ills – is highly functional for the capitalist class system (Fekete, 2009).

[5] Popper's partnership with the neuropsychologist John Eccles is an interesting departure from Popper's previous writing, and this foray into the world of the spirit has not had the consideration that it deserves. His autobiography *Unended Quest* (1976) shows Popper to be a man of warmth and complex ideas, who is not merely a purveyor of anti-marxist or positivist ideologies.

[6] Capitalism, in the form of neoliberalism, has resurged triumphant in the 21st century (Campbell, 2007; Arestis & Sawyer, 2007; Steger & Roy, 2010). Marx and Engels (1848) had observed that sectors of the failed underclass could safely be contained in prisons. In America, the failure of "the war on poverty" was replaced with the "war on crime", and the incarceration of the lower classes on an unprecedented scale (Hinton, 2016).

[7] Smith (1993) in his history of the "human sciences" grounds modern psychological and social science in a dialectical process, engaging with the unfolding philosophical and theological traditions of the Greeks, the Catholic Schoolmen, and the Enlightenment and later philosophers (including Quakers).

[8] This spread of infection was caused by lack of hand-washing hygiene by 19th century physicians. Muslims, in their critique of Western medical practice, point out that Muslims wash their hands (and other body parts) five times a day prior to their ritual prayers, and thus introduced practices which minimized cross-infection in Islamic medical practice from the 7th century onwards. See: http://bit.ly/1LEoEBd

[9] Haq is one of the names of Allah, and is often taken as a surname by Muslims. It means "teller of truth".

[10] It is pleasing to note that the major funding for *both* the radical Institute of Race Relations, and the liberally minded think-tank, The Runnymede Trust in the past five years, has been the Quaker foundation, the Joseph Rowntree Charitable Trust.

[11] Bagley (2016) reports that several such letters have been issued to Muslim school governors in the wake of the 'Trojan Horse' affair (see Bagley & Al-Refai, 2017, for details).

[12] Despite (or because of) the success of Sure Start, the Coalition Government in Britain from 2010 onwards initiated fiscal policies which have led to the steady decline of the Sure Start Centres (Campbell et al., 2016; Torjeson, 2016).

[13] Research published by the Department for Education in 2012 showed that 1996 was the peak year for exclusions. By 2009–2010 African Caribbean males were four times more likely than other pupils to be excluded. The most frequently excluded groups were (a) Roma and Traveller children; (b) children of any ethnicity, receiving 'free school meals'. On achievement, Perera et al. (2016) constructed a 'benchmark' measure from GCSE results, to compare with international data. On this index English pupils, collectively, were achieving at about 60% of the level

of the highest scoring countries internationally. On ethnicity, African-Caribbeans were scoring in the middle range (as were English Whites), but all ethnic minority groups were achieving higher scores over time. 'Social disadvantage' (regardless of ethnicity) and being schooled in the Midlands or North of England, depressed achievements by more than 10%. If these trends continue, it is 'poor whites' who will be England's most disadvantaged ethnic group within a decade.

14 We are relying for these accounts on Jamaican friends and colleagues in Britain, our own Jamaican extended family, and the Vince Hines Foundation (www.ubol.com)

15 In Trinidad it is the percussive sound of open-air steel bands which seduce the listener.

16 Another under-researched factor concerns the spread of migrant Jamaican families across countries (Canada, USA, Britain, Trinidad), their network contacts in the age of Skype, and their 'social capital'. An additional intriguing project for research are the 'Windrush' families and those arriving before 1960 in London, who (faced with discrimination in access to rented housing) with the aid of low-interest local government (GLC) loans bought large Victorian houses around Clapham, Brixton, Streatham and Tooting Commons, which sell today for £1 million or more. I have been informed of several Caribbean millionaires now enjoying comfortable retirement in Jamaica, or on other Caribbean islands, based on their London property sales. As Young (2005) says, 'accentuate the positive'. If you can't overthrow capitalism, at least you can slide into its ranks. Other Caribbean property millionaires, I am told, have moved to quieter English suburbs or cities, and are funding the house-buying and education of their children and grandchildren.

17 Peter Woods' excellent textbook *Inside Schools: Ethnography in Educational Research* (1986) had, according to *Google Scholar* been cited by only 104 researchers up to 2016. About half of the research using Wood's approach was in the Dutch language (including research on bilingualism in Dutch immigrant children). Very few of the cited references were in the fields of ethnicity, and none was from the UK. Searching the articles in *Anthropology and Education Quarterly* (an American journal) we could not find any notable articles on UK educational settings. The textbook by Goetz and LeCompe (1984) on ethnographic research in education has several hundred links on *Google Scholar*, but not a single study that we could locate focussed on an English school of any type. A much more fruitful resource proved to be the UK journal *Ethnography and Education*, which began publishing in 2005. Special issue Vol. 6 No. 2 (2011) on *Race, Ethnography and Education*; and Special issue Vol 11, No. 2 (2016) on *Precarity, Ethnography and Education*, we found particularly valuable, and discuss some of these articles in the text of this thesis.

ETHNICITY, GENDER AND IDENTITY

The Evolution and Development of Self-Esteem Research in Britain,
Canada and America

The world experienced (otherwise called the 'field of consciousness') comes at all times with our body as its center of vision, center of action, center of interest. Where the body is, is 'here" when the body acts is 'now" what the body touches is 'this" all other things are 'there' and 'then' and 'that'. These words of emphasized position imply a systematization of things with reference to a focus of and interest which lies in the body ... The body is the storm center, the origin of coordinates, the constant place of stress in all that experience-train. Everything circles round it, and is felt from its point of view. The word 'I', then, is primarily a noun of position, just like 'this' and 'there'.

(William James, 1890, pp. 154–155)

INTRODUCTION

In the model of child-centred humanism (CCH) the aim of studying children, their interactions and their development, is to understand ways in which their beginning levels of self-esteem can be built into a self-concept which is aware, intelligent, comprehensive, confident and compassionate in ways which allow each of the stages of life's challenge defined by Erikson (1965, 1968) to become, at each developmental stage, actualized in ways which allow the child to become confident and magnanimous with regard of self and others, and in ways which (in Maslow's model) are self-actualizing, helping the child to become an adult full of love and wonder at the marvellous world which they have inherited.

This growth of self-actualization (Maslow, 1970) is based in the core being of the child, his or her body, skin colour, hair texture, the dynamics of movement, the nervous system, sensory impressions, linguistic and visual pathways, touch and taste, movement and breath: every child is not merely special, every child is unique, and the self-concept of each child is unique too as he or she makes sense of the myriad of interactions of daily life, and the endless, joyous reflexivity of reshaping the self-other matrix. Each interaction produces a new 'self', according to the symbolic interactionist George Mead (1934). Although Mead suggested that oftentimes we reflect, internalise or modify the views which others have of us, the self as agent is nevertheless powerful. As James (1985) had argued: "Our self-feelings in this world depend entirely on what we back ourselves to be and do" (p. 4). James maintained that individuals have free choice (or free will) in these matters, and Vincent de Paul would agree.

Margaret Archer (2003) develops the ideas of the reflexive self from the writings of James and Mead into the idea of the dialectical, morphogenic self in which the I-Me dyad engages continuously with others in formulating ideas about their shared world. The critical realist Priscilla Alderson (2013) also grounds her ontology in the physical being of the child:

Children and adults learn about their bodily experiences within relationships; they express their needs and views through their bodies; and they are respected or disrespected in the sensitive or casual or harsh ways in which their bodies are treated. (p. 9)

In reviewing the recent literature on self-esteem and self-concept, we cannot detect much change in basic theory concerning self-esteem (e.g. in Owens, Stryker & Goodman's 2001, *Extending Self-Esteem Theory and Research*). Rosenberg's self-esteem scale (the RSES), developed in the 1960s, is still widely used internationally, in educational and clinical settings, and is well validated in terms of how it correlates with (predicts, or is predicted by) measures of depression, anxiety, and emotional and behavioural problems in children, adolescents and adults (Robins et al., 2001). Self-evaluation (a description in evaluative terms of what the individual assumes their basic characteristics to be) is measured most frequently in the literature of clinical and social psychology, by Rosenberg's (1965) simply-worded, 10-point scale. Self-esteem levels (as measured by the Rosenberg Self-Esteem Scale – RSES) both predict and reflect emotional instability, and scholastic success within different age groups, and within different demographic groups (categorized by gender, social class) in Americans, and across the world at about the same levels, even though mean RSES scores sometimes differ between the various groups studied.

It was clear in Hewitt's (1976) overview of the idea of 'self' in social, clinical and educational psychology that 'self-esteem' had dynamic and interacting relationships with ideas of identity and self-actualization. we reproduce (with permission) the figure which Loretta Young (in Young & Bagley, 1982) constructed in her review of "self-esteem, self-concept and the development of black identity". This seems to me to draw together the strands of research quite succinctly, and provided the basis for the cross-cultural studies of 'racial identification' using the Color Meanings Test (CMT), and the Preschool Racial Attitudes Measure (PRAM) designed by Williams and Morland (1976).

In her idea of "global identity" as a preliminary to presenting data on "children and race", Young (1982) usefully draws together the degree to which an individual has, at various ages (infancy through to adolescence, mid-life, old age) tackled the identity challenges which all humans face – with Maslow's hierarchical model of life-stage needs, with "self-actualization" at the pinnacle of Maslow's well-known triangular depiction of progress in human development. Many individuals, because of for example, their position in social structure, fail to achieve this highest level in which the person the best of their talents in magnanimous self-development. As in Erikson's system, there is often 'premature identity foreclosure'. Carl Rogers' person-centred approach does not incorporate stages of development, but is reflexive and context dependent at each moment of an individual's life. For the adult, there is a duty (in the Child-Centred Humanism model) to creative conditions of growth for the child to proceed from "absence" (in Bhaskar's critical realist model) to a realization of self in the phase of 'upward mobility' described by Archer (2003).

In Young's model (reproduced in Figure 6.1, below) identity is clearly related to self-concept and self-esteem. Identity has both cognitive (knowledge) and affective (evaluation) aspects. The higher order concept combining these two aspects of self is what Young terms *global identity*, the highest-order concept, incorporating both self-concept and self-esteem in an integrated whole. Within global identity are the parts of the self, related to one another in particular configurations representing varying degrees of ego integration. The degree and type of integration at any point in time depend, Young argues, on the ways in which the various developmental "crises" or challenges in Erikson's (1968) schema have been solved, and the degree to which the parallel needs outlined by Maslow (1954/1970) – e.g. for love and belonginess, have been is equivalent to the idea met. The term global identity is equivalent to the idea of global self-concept elaborated by Coopersmith (1975).

STUDIES OF 'RACIAL' IDENTITY IN YOUNG CHILDREN USING DOLLS, AND FIGURES WITH CONTRASTED ETHNICITY

Since our own research (Sawyerr, 1999) and the work in this book stemmed from efforts in helping minority children achieve an adequate sense of

GLOBAL IDENTITY OR THE GLOBAL SELF-CONCEPT

The parts of the self, related to one another in particular configurations representing varying degrees of ego integration, and differing degrees of success in the resolution of Erikson's life-crises, or fulfilment of Maslow's life-stage needs – in the parallel models below, elements in one column are equivalent to the elements in the facing column.

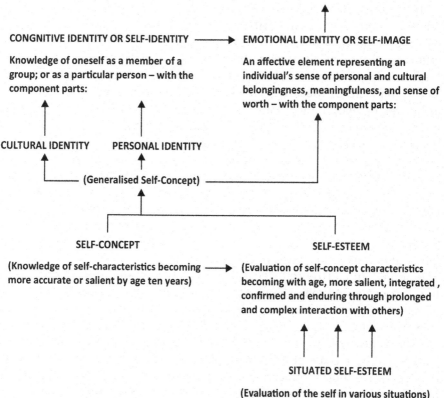

CONGNITIVE IDENTITY OR SELF-IDENTITY ⟶ EMOTIONAL IDENTITY OR SELF-IMAGE

Knowledge of oneself as a member of a group; or as a particular person – with the component parts:

An affective element representing an individual's sense of personal and cultural belongingness, meaningfulness, and sense of worth – with the component parts:

CULTURAL IDENTITY   PERSONAL IDENTITY

(Generalised Self-Concept)

SELF-CONCEPT

SELF-ESTEEM

(Knowledge of self-characteristics becoming ⟶ more accurate or salient by age ten years)

(Evaluation of self-concept characteristics becoming with age, more salient, integrated , confirmed and enduring through prolonged and complex interaction with others)

SITUATED SELF-ESTEEM

(Evaluation of the self in various situations)

Figure 6.1. Relationships of identity and aspects of the self

self, using dolls and other materials, we have a particular interest in this literature. The American doll studies of the twentieth century, asking children (usually aged five or less) of different ethnicities which doll they preferred had produced gloomy findings, showing that many African-American children preferred the "white" doll or figure (Clark, 1966; Porter, 1971; Fox & Jordan, 1973) – although a substantial minority or sometimes even a majority preferred a doll which looked like them. The point was in the comparison – some 90 percent of white children preferred the "white" doll, and also attributed positive characteristics to the doll which looked like them, and saw black figures (and children) in stereotypically negative terms.

Milner (1973, 1975) was the first British psychologist to replicate this type of study in an English setting. He studied 100 African-Caribbean, 100 Asian (mainly Indian), and 100 European children (presumably white) in South and West London. He adapted the classic doll figures described by Clark (1966) and Morland (1966), asking the questions "which doll looks most like you?"; 'Which one do you like the best?', and of the adult figures questions such as 'Which one of these two men is the bad man?' All of the white children chose the white doll when responding to being asked to choose the doll 'like them'; but only 52 percent of the black children, and 76 percent of the Asians made the 'correct' choice. Similar patterns occurred in identifying figures who resembled parents.

All of the white children would 'rather be' the white figure – but so would 82 percent of the black children, and 65 percent of the Asians. Concerning 'out-group' preferences, six percent of the white children thought it would be fun to be part of a black family, compared with 74 percent of Asian children, and 72 percent of black children. None of the white children held negative stereotypes about their own group; but 65 percent of Asian children, and 72 percent of black children, had negative stereotypes of African-Caribbeans. Milner concluded that this misidentification was not the result of cognitive confusion (there were no cognitive test differences between groups), but rather reflected the incipiently poor self-esteem of the minority children. In later writing Milner (1996, 1997) argued that certainly in America, the impact of racial self-derogation in young children using the doll test had greatly diminished, reflecting the growth of the "Black Pride" movement. For Britain however, Owusu-Bempah and Howitt (1999) remained pessimistic.

The most recent English study using dolls or photographs that I can locate (Lam et al., 2010) does however give rise for optimism, however. These researchers used eight stimulus photographs with 124 black, white and Asian 3 to 5-year-olds in London. The older the child, and the better their performance on a symbol recognition test, the more likely were they to identify their own "race" correctly. But whatever the children's ethnicity, they did *not* display any pattern of rejection of their own ethnicity, or preference for a different ethnicity. Another optimistic study comes from Rutland et al. (2005) who studied the self-perceptions of 136 white, English 3 to 5-year-olds from contrasted environments: housing in which all residents were white; and housing where residents were a mixture of both black and white families. Only the children who had little inter-ethnic contact showed negative evaluations of the black individuals displayed in the stimulus material. Children from the mixed-ethnicity environment showed no biases. The authors interpret these findings in the light of Allport's (1954) well-known paradigm that "equal status interaction produces liking." We speculate that children who grow up to enter the growing number of mixed-ethnicity partnerships in England (Platt, 2009) often come from' mixed-race' urban areas.

IDENTITY AND INSTITUTIONAL RACISM

One of the most significant government policies developed in response to the recommendations of the Macpherson Inquiry Report (1999), on the death of Stephen Lawrence, was the recognition that education has a crucial role to play in eliminating racism and promoting and valuing racial diversity.

The National Curriculum was legally established in England through the Education Reform Act of 1988, and allowed governments to make curriculum changes which all state schools had to follow, as evidence or policy required. Thus, after the Macpherson Report was published in 1999, The national government required schools to ensure that they take account of responsibilities for addressing issues of institutional racism, in curriculum planning and delivery. "Early Stage" inspectors in Wales, and Office for Standards in Education inspectors in England now had to evaluate and report on a range of racial equality issues. The governmental body, the Commission for Racial Equality (CRE), launched a government initiative for Racial Equality, *Learning For All: Standards for Racial Equality in Schools*, (2000) in England and Wales in February 2000 as a first step in addressing the Macpherson Report's recommendations.

The Macpherson Inquiry Report's major contribution has been the provision of a clear definition of 'Institutional Racism' and its implications for all educational and related organisations to examine and tackle subtle and covert forms of discrimination. The report defined 'Institutional Racism' (p. 6,34), as:

> The collective failure of an organisation to provide an appropriate and professional service to people because of their colour, culture, or ethnic origin. It can be seen or detected in processes, attitudes and behaviours which amount to discrimination through unwitting prejudice, ignorance, thoughtlessness and racist stereotyping which disadvantage minority ethnic people. It persists because of the failure of the organisation openly and adequately to recognise and address its existence and causes by policy, example and leadership. Without

recognition and action to eliminate such racism it can prevail as part of the ethos or culture of the organisation. It is a corrosive disease.

While the nursery school research study Alice Sawyerr undertook in 2002–2004 did not focus on, or measure institutional or individual racism directly, it explored the following: how learning was facilitated, how positive self-esteem, positive self-concept and values of racial diversity might be communicated between practitioners, and to children, through the implementation of the foundation stage curriculum. This we felt was important since these areas could influence the learning process of all children (i.e. Black, White, Mixed-Parentage and other Ethnic Minorities) in positive ways in a multi-ethnic day nursery; or they could have negative consequences for minority children (Milner, 1997).

The study reported in detail in the following chapter, was especially concerned with early learning and influences, because of the potentially life influencing experiences that young children can have. The literature reviewed prior to the inception of that study suggested that the younger children were, the more vulnerable they might be in internalising racism from subtle or overtly discriminatory practices (Rist, 1970; Adams 1978; Ingram, 1982; Brophy, 1980; Ogilvy et al., 1990; Connolly, 1998).

During the four decades prior to 2002, there had been a growing interest in the study of ethnicity and childcare, by psychologists, sociologists and social policy researchers in Britain. Researchers had focused on such areas as: differential treatment of children, children's self-identity, children's cultural identity and children's racial and gender identity: e.g. Adams (1978), Verma and Bagley (1982), Bagley and Verma (1982), Milner (1983), Troyna and Williams (1986) Wilson (1987), Tizard and Phoenix (1993), Barn (1993), Owusu-Bempah (1994), Owusu-Bempah and Howitt (1998), Barn, Sinclair and Ferdinand (1997), and Connolly (1998).

These empirical research studies highlighted concerns, and heightened awareness of how negative experiences in interacting with others and absorbing messages from the wider culture, could negatively impact Black and Ethnic Minority children's psychological, emotional and identity development. These studies also emphasised the need for educational and local authority social service departments to address the identity needs of children of all ages from Black and Ethnic Minority backgrounds. Specific research studies carried out in nursery education contexts had shown that the quality of childcare was vitally important in the pre-five stage (Ogilvy et al., 1990). Children at that age depended on adults to provide both a stimulating psychosocial environment which offered opportunities for positive developmental experiences, and most crucially, their developing self-esteem.

The special role of adult contact in children's cognitive and language development had been stressed by many authors (e.g. Schaffer, 1984; Wells, 1986). For ethnic minority children the quality of their interactions with adults at nursery school was likely to be of particular importance, since nursery school was not only the ethnic minority child's first encounter with the education system, but often also their first contact with a predominantly White English-speaking environment.

In reviewing this literature we were particularly charmed by an American doctoral thesis by Rosenzweig (1998) titled *I have a new friend in me: the effect of a multicultural/anti-bias curriculum on the development of social cognition in pre-schoolers*. Working with three and four-year-olds in a multicultural nursery setting, Rosenzweig helped each child develop a positive story about an imaginary friend of the same ethnicity, who had many positive characteristics. Then, she helped each child "transfer" this super-person-like-them inside of themselves, as an invisible helper. I like the morphogenetic, critical realism implied by this approach, the beginning of the internal conversation which becomes reflexive, assisting assured, confident friendships.

Teacher-Child Interactions

In a British study of staff attitudes and perceptions in multicultural nursery schools, Ogilvy and colleagues (1990) had shown that staff were less likely to respond contingently to these children than to indigenous i.e. White children. Rather, they adopted a controlling style of interaction as a blanket strategy, irrespective of individual differences in the children's ability. Tizard et al. (1972), in their study of young children in long-stay residential nurseries, found that the way in which staff behaved and talked was positively or negatively influenced both by its organisational structure and by its aims. In a later study of staff behaviour in pre-school centres, Tizard and colleagues (1976), found that the avowed educational aims of pre-school centres were related to both the cognitive content of staff talk, and to children's cognitive needs. Children's test scores were highest in nurseries with clear educational aims, particularly those which incorporated daily language instruction sessions, and lowest in centres without educational aims, where staff talked to and taught the children less. Tizard and Hughes (1984) further showed that the home-school partnership was crucial, since parents are the first (and probably the best) teachers of their young children.

Bruner (1980) had earlier commented on 'the absence of a sense of lively purpose in what they are doing' in many pre-school staff (p. 74) and lamented the paucity of adult-child talk. Ingram (1982) confirmed that individual children's contact with adults in the day nurseries she studied was surprisingly low. She found, moreover, that there were significant differences in the amount and type of adult-child contact according to the child's sex and ethnicity, with Black children, especially West Indian boys receiving little adult attention. Similarly Connolly (1998), in his study of racism and gender identities of young children in an inner city primary school discovered disturbing degrees of racism affecting the lives of five and six year old children. His data came from in-depth interviews using an ethnographic methodology which gave primacy to the voices of young children, giving them the space to articulate their own experiences and concerns. His findings showed not only that many young children were capable of dealing with quite complex ideas about 'race', but that they were already doing so, exemplified by the fact that children's racialised attitudes and behaviours were inextricably bound up in everyday experience in classroom and playground.

His findings further support the ideas of Epstein (1993) and Siraj-Blatchford (1994) that with the right kind of analytical 'scaffolding', important work can be done in the positive building of children's racial attitudes and perceptions of self and others. Epstein also noted that while such work was already going on with older children, his data suggested that it needed to incorporate young children at the start of their schooling careers.

It was therefore, we felt (in reviewing the literature prior to 2000), an important area for nursery school practitioners to address, given their direct involvement in activities with the under fives at the foundation stage of the curriculum in nursery settings, and in reception classes in schools. Adults' expectations of children appeared, from the literature published before 2000, as important and worth investigating, since their expectations and attitudes might inadvertently shape and influence the perceptions and behaviours of all the children they interact with at the foundation, preschool or kindergarten level.

Teachers' Expectations

Braun (1976) and Good (1987) commented on a potential influence on differential treatment of children, embedded in the expectations that teachers hold. Expectations of individual children's behaviour may be based on first impressions and/or any other available information pertaining to the child, such as knowledge of family background. Teachers actions may also be based on generalised beliefs held in relation to a particular social or ethnic group, which are then applied to individual members of that group (Rogers, 1982). This is another basis of prejudice: individuals are prejudged on the basis of their ethnic group membership and expected to behave in accordance with a stereotype.

Adams (1978) found racial stereotype could influence pre-school teachers' expectations of both children's academic performance and their social behaviour. For example on the basis of photographic evidence, staff pre-judged White children to be more intelligent and less disruptive than Black children. The British and American literature reviewed in 2002, further suggested that teachers' expectations and perceptions of their pupils might affect the type of teacher-pupil relationship and that this effect could be strongest in the early years of schooling, influencing both the quantity and the quality of adult-child interaction (Rist, 1970; Brophy, 1980).

This idea of low-self esteem developing, and continuing in minority children in English schools was supported by findings from Bagley and Coard (1975), and Bagley et al. (1979). In this latter study however, a group of African-Caribbean children was identified who had adequate levels of self-esteem, *and* whose parents were highly critical of the English educational system: alienation unmasked, so to speak. Coard (1971) had identified practices in British schools in which African-Caribbean children had been falsely labelled as 'educationally sub-normal'. This linked to later findings from a national study which showed that teacher stereotyping of pupils could lead to their poor scholastic performance, regardless of their ability (Pidgeon, 1970).

In further English research using photographs, Davey (1982) found that black children frequently 'preferred' the photographs of white children of similar age and sex, a 'bias' not shown by white children. These were results based on group testing of several thousand children, the person handing out and collecting the tests being white. These findings prompted Maxime, a black psychologist, to devise pictorial figures in story books which she thought were more appropriate for enhancing minority children's identity, in multi-ethnic situations (Maxime, 1986 to 1991).

Alice Sawyerr used Maxime's books and pictures in work in counselling young children (Sawyerr, 1999), work which led her to undertake the observational study of the multi-ethnic nursery school described later in this book. Wilson (1987) also used specially designed photographs as projective measures in her study of 'mixed race' children, and showed that several different types of 'colour preference' were expressed by children of black-white marriages. Bagley et al. (1993) also found, in work with transracially and interculturally adopted children, and in children of racially mixed marriages, various kinds of ethnic and colour identification were possible: but they could not show that any particular type of racial or ethnic identification was connected to any kind of psychological outcome or adjustment in these children.

Loretta Young's English and Cross-National Work Using the Preschool Racial Attitudes Measure (PRAM)

The monograph by Williams and Morland (1976) collected together the earlier American studies, both substantively and theoretically, and offered a developmental model for countering "colour bias" amongst young black children in America, suggesting that the growth of positive role models in the African-American community could result in the development of positive self-concepts in African-American youth: their results did offer a challenge to American educators to offer a curriculum that was free of racial stereotyping and "colour bias".

Young and Bagley (1982) carried out cross-cultural studies using the Williams and Morland Color Meanings Test (CMT) and Preschool Racial Attitudes Measure (PRAM) in 468 young children (aged 4 to 7) in London, and in rural Jamaica. The CMT measured preferences for various colours, whilst the PRAM elicited young children's evaluative perceptions of drawings of Black and White adults and children.

The tests were administered by Young, a female, Black Jamaican who had been resident in the UK for about 12 years when testing took place. Besides the tests of colour and ethnic perception, and ethnic-identification choices, the children completed Ziller's (1972) self-esteem test for young children, which involved placing a figure representing "myself" in relation to the figure of the "bad" boy or girl. Of the children tested, 117 were resident in rural Jamaica. The UK-based group included 100 who were "white English", 113 black children with parents whose origins were in the Caribbean, 23 black children whose parents were born in Africa, 30 children with parents of Cypriot origin, and 17 with Asian parents. The results (which across the ethnic groups, showed high levels of statistically significant variation) indicated that:

The large majority of responses of white children fall into the pro-white range (consistent with adequate levels of self-esteem in this group) ...

but only a small proportion of the responses of the UK West Indian Group (which includes 69 children with Jamaican parents) fall into the pro-black range. Similarly, only a small proportion of the responses of the children in rural Jamaica fall into this group. The only group to manifest more pro-black than pro-white bias is the small group of African children ... In the white English, West Indian, Asian, Cypriot and rural Jamaican groups there was a significant tendency for pro-white bias to increase with age. (Young & Bagley, 1982, p. 200)

The Ziller self-esteem measure showed significant cross-ethnic variations, and was associated with colour and ethnic preference – implying that choosing a figure which resembled one's own ethnic group was in some children associated to a certain degree, with 'better' self-esteem. However, these correlations rarely exceeded 0.2, and explained very little common variance. The validity of the Ziller test in children as young as these might be in question, an issue taken up by Stone (1979).

The apparent puzzle in these results was the strong tendency of black children in rural Jamaica to reject their identity in favour of the white figures, even though they rarely saw white people, and at that period had very little access to visual media. Young explains this by reference to the culture of Jamaica in which post-slavery, "fair" people (i.e. light-skinned African-Caribbeans) had higher economic and social status in a society still rigidly stratified by racial layers (Wilson, 1973; Foner, 1977). Henriques (1968, 1974), a Jamaican anthropologist observed:

My research over the last ten years in the Caribbean suggests the mythology of the superiority of the white is still being upheld in terms of marriage. That is to say a coloured or black man will generally tend, particularly in the middle classes, to marry a woman who is lighter than himself. This not only improves his own social status but creates greater opportunities for his children. It is in fact a historical pattern. (1974, p. 113)

Young and Bagley (1989) extended their research using the CMT and the PRAM with 5 to 7 year-olds, to African children in Accra, Ghana, and to black children of Jamaican parents who had migrated from Jamaica to urban Toronto, Canada (around 100 children in each group). Results were interesting, showing first that the black Ghanaian children regarding black figures and ethnicity in a wholly positive light, clearly having a secure identity focussed on their own ethnic group. And the children of Jamaican parents in Toronto also had much more positive views of their personal ethnicity than did children in rural Jamaica, and in black children of Jamaican parents in London.

The authors, in discussing these results, point to the research by Elizabeth Thomas-Hope (1982) which compared adult samples of migrants from the English-speaking Caribbean (including Jamaica) to England, America (New York and Boston), and Canada (mainly to Toronto). All of those whom Thomas-Hope interviewed had generally similar educational and social class profiles before migrating. She compared their personal satisfaction with the achievement of the goals of their migration, which were chiefly to improve occupational and educational status for themselves and their children. Migrants to America and Canada were much more likely than immigrants to England to be "satisfied" or "very satisfied" with achieving the goals of their migration: some 50 percent of migrants to England expressed satisfaction with goal achievement, compared with over 85 per cent of those migrating to North America.

In discussion of these findings, Lowenthal's (1967) study of West Indian migrants in New York was recalled: at that time Caribbean migrants made up some 12 percent of New York's ethnically black population; but they made up one third of New York's black professionals. Lowenthal, himself a Jew, dubbed these migrants "The black Jews of New York". In Britain, unlike in Canada and America, a racist social structure had tried to push its Caribbean migrants into the status of an underclass.

Maureen Stone's "The Education of the Black Child in Britain" (1981)

Maureen Stone's book, based on her doctoral thesis, deserves to be better known. Stone (cousin of Bernard Coard, then imprisoned for life in Granada for being a revolutionary Marxist), criticized the current policies of "multiracial education" which she saw as stemming from white liberal concerns about racialized minorities, whose place in the class system put them at greater disadvantage than racism per se. Stone criticized British work which purportedly saw African-Caribbean children as having poorer self-esteem and identity problems as a reflection of a racist social structure, arguing that such work (e.g. Milner, 1975) tended to pathologise black children. She examined these previous studies, showing that in fact many (and often the majority) of black children in these studies had perfectly 'normal' self-esteem and positive choices in the projective studies.

Stone studied African-Caribbean children in a variety of 'cultural enrichment' programmes in London, including Saturday Schools, and argued that Caribbean culture was rich and thriving in Britain. She used the Ziller and Piers-Harris measures of self-esteem with a variety of populations, and could not show that overall, there were significant differences in self-esteem profiles between various ethnic groups. When Black children did underperform scholastically, or had identity problems, Stone blamed the failure of existing 'multiracial' education policies. Ultimately, she identified Britain's class system with its ritualized demeaning of the aspirations of the poorest classes, those intended to be 'the reserve army of labour', the underclass who would be recruited into low-wage employment when the forces of capital required – as the structural mechanism responsible for depressing the personal and academic aspirations of black children in Britain.

In this focus she draws on Paul Willis' (1978) impressive (but also neglected) study of how working class children in Britain 'learn to labour', a study cited by Banfield (2016) in his focus on critical realism for a Marxist study of education, deriving his analysis from Roy Bhaskar's earlier work. In reading Maureen Stone's study, one has a distinct sense that a critical realist approach would have strengthened her theoretical model, and ultimately, the impact of her study.

Mirza (1992) studied "black girls", African-Caribbean adolescents in two multicultural comprehensive secondary schools in England, and found them, contrary to popular stereotype (but in line with Stone's findings) to be generally confident, achieving well, and with a secure sense of identity.

Updates and Critiques of the Doll and Figure Studies of Racial Identity

How children are socialized, in certain historical phases of social structures, to accept and 'internalize' society's stereotypes of them is usefully summarized by Milner (1983), who also analyses the stereotypes of "race" which the white, English schoolchild had absorbed throughout the days of empire. How do children of these colonies, born to immigrant parents, avoid internalizing these stereotypes? On this topic there is surprisingly little research in Europe and North America. Milner (1983), critically reviewing Maureen Stone's work, and reflecting on his earlier pessimistic studies using dolls, reported that there was a flux of change since his 1975 monograph which showed that many African-Caribbean children were internalising the stereotypes projected not only by their peers, but apparently by many institutions of society. Milner further commented on progress in teacher awareness, and the use of multicultural materials, as well as improvements in teacher training (Milner, 1996). Research flowing from the research group of the Indian-born academic, G.K. Verma at Manchester University (e.g. Verma & Bagley, 1982) was becoming widely known, and was increasingly available (and influential) in colleges concerned with teacher education.[1]

Youth culture itself was changing, and the music of *Rastafari* (African-rooted, Jamaican folk music) was becoming increasingly popular amongst youth of all cultures, as were cross-ethnic friendships, and eventually, marriages (Bagley & Young, 1984). Bagley et al. (1979) on the basis of several national studies of racist attitudes estimated that about a quarter of British adults were liberal and accepting of minorities of various kinds; but another quarter were extremely hostile, or racist, while the remaining 50 percent of the population had half-formed, unarticulated attitudes which could in theory be manipulated into "anti-immigrant" fugues by political demagogues.[2] Not surprisingly, it was the 'non-racist' quarter of the population who were most likely to be in a mixed marriage.[3] For minority people in Britain there has developed an enduring phalanx of 'liberal whites' who provide a sector of British social structure in which people of various ethnic and religious origins can mix on terms of acceptance and equality. By 2008, a quarter of the population who formed the racist group of the 1980s (and their now adult children) had evolved (according to various attitude surveys) into an Islamophobic sector of the population (Fenetke, 2009; Bagley & Al-Refai, 2017).

Ethnic Mixing: Black and White Are Both Beautiful

British research on self-esteem and "race" since the 1990s has focused mainly on 'mixed-race' children, and adopted children whose ethnicity is different from that of their parents (Wilson, 1987; Bagley, 1995). In Britain a pressure-group called *Harmony*, founded in the 1960s, has thrived through various government and foundation grants, and lobbies educational and social service sectors on behalf of 'mixed' children. Tizard and Phoenix (2002) studied a group of children of black-white marriages, and argued that "mixed race" deserves to be category of identity which is unique, with individuals choosing what aspects of their racial and cultural heritages to blend and present to the world. The "misidentification" of the Blackness or Whiteness (of the mixed-race individual) according to context appears to be a more salient topic in America than in Britain (Wright, 2015).

The most recent census data (2011) for England and Wales indicated that 48 percent of African-Caribbean males and 34 percent of African-Caribbean females were in a partnership with a White (usually British) European partner. In England and Wales some nine percent of the population, around 2.3 millions, were in a mixed, black-white partnerships. These partners tended to be younger than the population average, and most had at least one "mixed race" child (Platt, 2009; ONS, 2014). The "Harmony Child" is common in many schools in British conurbations. Muttarak and Heath (2010) Heath et al. (2013) put this unique form of intercultural mixing into sociological context in their analysis of data from 115,494 successive respondents in the General Household Surveys in Britain, from 1998 to 2006. They showed that ethnic intermarriage was taking place at an increasing rate in second- and third-generation immigrants. Even in 'conservative' Muslim and Hindu populations, intermarriage occurs more often when the children of these immigrant groups live (and go to school) in ethnically mixed neighbourhoods.

This apparently remarkable success in British 'race relations' has received little attention from press, public, and university researchers, and the very normality of this mixing is, one supposes, an indicator of the assimilation of immigrants which politicians seem to desire (Bagley & Al-Refai, 2017). One basis for the marital mixing of White European and African-Caribbean populations might be due to the fact that they generally share the same general value system, including for some, religious values (based on forms of Christianity). English-born people with heritage from the Indian subcontinent have a rate of intermarriage with white European residents of only about three percent (ONS, 2014), perhaps because of religious differences, but according to the trends mapped by Heath et al. (2013), this rate will increase in future years.

Most of the research on identity, self-esteem and ethnicity in young children since 2000 now comes from American scholars, who examine how 'biracial' children of mixed marriages, and children adopted across cultural or ethnic lines develop identity and self-esteem. Good, recent examples of such research are Schmitt et al. (2015) on racial/ethnic identification of youth in foster care in America; and Yampolsky et al. (2016) on MULTIS, a multicultural identity scale for children and young people experiencing complex cultural environments, care or family situations. Garcia et al. (2015) develop the idea that "race" is a lived, dynamic and changing experience, with ethnic identity changing and developing, as the range and nature of the individual's interactions develop and change: this, in Archer's (2003) critical realist model, may be seen as the positive process of morphogenesis. Yap et al. (2014) develop a rather similar model.

GLOBAL SELF-ESTEEM IN ADOLESCENTS AND YOUNG ADULTS

Bachman and colleagues (2011) in a major overview of American data on adolescent self-esteem observed that:

> Global self-esteem', an individual's overall evaluation of self, is one of the most studied constructs in the social sciences. A wide and diverse literature that spans disciplines and theoretical perspectives suggests that high self-esteem is positively, though not necessarily causally, associated with goals, expectancies, coping mechanisms and behaviors, that facilitate productive achievement and work experiences; and it is negatively associated with mental and physical health problems, substance abuse, and antisocial behaviour. (p. 447)

Research available two decades earlier (e.g. Rosenberg, 1979) had already established this, and research on self-esteem since 1980 has taken a variety of directions.

Kaplan (1980) argued that individuals naturally seek out situations which maximise social support and praise for their actions – even if those giving positive feedback in are "deviant" sub-groups which they eventually join. In this model of "deviant behaviour in defense of the self", self-esteem levels should tend to rise with age as individuals seek to "maximise social returns", a thesis with some support from research studies (Rosenberg & Kaplan, 1982; Mason, 2001).

As William James advised, the child's developing body and sensory system is at the core of the changing, ongoing identity. When catastrophes do occur in the form of "non-voluntary deviance", such as an adult imposing himself sexually upon a child, that whole process of identity development for the child is disrupted and changed, and the long-term mental health of the child is imperilled (Bagley, 1996; Bagley & King, 2003). When physical and emotional abuse and neglect are added to sexual abuse, outcomes for children can be catastrophic (Bagley & Mallick, 2000). In the worst case, the child becomes the victim of what Schatzman (1973) called "soul murder" (Bagley, 1996).

That physical, emotional and sexual abuse may have profoundly negative effects on child and adolescent self-esteem has still not been fully absorbed in mainstream clinical and social psychology. In their major review of literature and concepts on the "social psychology of the self-concept" edited by Rosenberg and Kaplan in 1982, none of the 42 writers who contributed chapters, mentions child abuse as a factor influencing self-esteem. Some twenty years later in another major review of self-esteem research edited by Owens et al. (2001) none of the 18 contributors mentioned child abuse of any kind as having an impact on child, adolescent and adult self-esteem. The chapter by Rosenberg and Owens (2001) on "Low self-esteem people: a collective portrait" painted a picture of people (identified within a population of more than 7,000 high school and college students, and amounting to about five percent of those studied) who as a group who were frequently depressed, often anxious, fearful, afraid, underachieving, avoiding risk, isolated and lonely. But the authors failed entirely to elucidate *why* this group had such very low self-esteem.

The failure to link self-esteem research to measures and concepts of child sexual abuse in the often very large samples of high school students which were being accessed by these American researchers is puzzling. The idea that within-family sexual abuse could occur, and cause psychological devastation, had been introduced into the American 'social problems' literature by Bagley in 1969, and by the early 1980s the widespread prevalence of child sexual abuse, and the damage it could do to the developing child's identity was well established in the literature in American sociology and social work (Finkelhor, 1979, 1982), and psychiatry (Bagley, 1995).

This is an important theme in self-esteem research, to which we will return to in a later chapter, arguing from the English Northern Schools study, that it is sexual and physical abuse that is mainly responsible for "devastated self-esteem", particularly in adolescent women.

MEASURING SELF-ESTEEM IN DIFFERENT ETHNIC GROUPS: RESEARCH PAST AND PRESENT

The ethnic, religious or linguistic minority child has an added set of identity tasks, especially if the wider society stigmatises their identity in various ways. Sometimes the minority family can "pass", not mentioning their minority religious status, even denying that status when people call them 'Paki' or 'Yid'. Lewin (1936) famously advised Jewish parents to take pride in being Jewish, a manifest identity which they and their children should carry into society with pride rather than concealment.

The 'black pride' movement of America beginning in the 1960s has taken a similar stance, with some success when we consider the self-esteem profiles of different ethnic groups studied by Rosenberg and Simmons (1976). They found, contrary to hypothesis, that African-American children did *not* have 'poorer' self-esteem than European-Americans – rather, African-Americans had created their own reference groups so far as feelings of self-worth were concerned. In critical realist terms, African Americans have rewritten the script on "master-slave" relations: they have created a new ground of being, an ontology of freedom.

Today in Europe, Muslim children face a dilemma – to "pretend" to be part of the mainstream, trying to avoid Islamophobia: or to be a proud Muslim, bearing the message of peace of Prophet Muhammad (Ramadan, 2010). Wilkinson (2015), a critical realist scholar offers the model of "seriousness" in which Muslim adolescents in Britain "reimagine" themselves as true citizens of Europe, recreating themselves on the affective-cultural dimension of "success".

British and North American Research on Adolescent Self-Esteem

British and Canadian studies. Surprisingly, there has not been much research on self-esteem and ethnicity in Britain since 2000, with a few notable exceptions. Robinson (2000) for example, used the RSES with adolescents in a multi-ethnic population admitted to residential care, and found that *within* ethnic groups, significant variation in scores was related to adjustment, although there were no significant differences *between* ethnic groups. Thomas et al. (2002) used the RSES in a questionnaire study of 722 English secondary school students, finding that 'white' European and 'black' African-Caribbean students had equally high levels of self-esteem; but Asian females in particular were significantly more like to have eating disorders, and to have poorer self-esteem.

Bagley and Mallick (2001) sought to establish the reliability and validity of the 10-item Rosenberg Self Esteem Inventory (RSES) in 1,330 English adolescents, using measures validated in previous Canadian work with several thousand adolescents (Bagley, Bolitho & Bertrand, 1995, 1997). This Canadian research had established the factorial reliability of the RSES in all of the age and gender groups studied; and construct validity in terms of correlations with relevant scales from the Ontario Child Health Survey. Since this survey of Canadian high school students included a brief measure of sexual harassment and assault at, or on the journey to school, the research was able to show that females in particular had poorer mental health and self-esteem profiles if they reported such sexual assaults.

In the first English replication of this work (Bagley & Mallick, 2001) it was not possible to include a measure of sexual assault. But the study *did* show that the RSES was in psychometric terms, a reliable instrument when used with English adolescents. And face validity was established through correlations with Ontario Child Health Scales, which had been validated against an individually diagnosed population of English adolescents (Pace et al., 1999). Our second English replication of the Canadian work was able to utilise a more comprehensive measure of physical and sexual abuse, validated in previous Canadian work. This study is reported in a subsequent chapter of this book.

American and International Studies on Global Self-Esteem,
Particularly the RSES

Considerable research on self-esteem has been carried out in America, and internationally. Schmitt and Allik (2005) analysed data for the RSES in completed in English, and in various translations, for young people in 53 nations, and report that although there were differences in mean levels across countries, in terms of validity (correlation with tests of adjustment, and various kinds of behaviour) the test was remarkably robust.

The authors of this review point to Rosenberg's (1979) important results and theories which show that African-Americans had *higher* levels of self-esteem than did European-Americans, a difference attributed both to the high levels of segregation of ethnic groups in American cities (so that the normative reference groups in home, community and school were for African-Americans, the positive values of their family, community, church and peers). An additional factor has been the growing American movement to achieve structural equality for different ethnic groups, as was evidenced in Thomas-Hope's (1982) study, cited earlier. In Archer's Critical Realist account (2003), the recreation of black self-esteem and self-concept in the United States could be seen as both reflexive, and morphogenetic. As William James put it, "we become what we want to be". Thus, as Hughes and Demo (1989) showed, African Americans centred themselves on family, church, school, and community, and knowing that racial discrimination still existed, attributed failure to achieve goals not to themselves, but to a racist society.

Bachman et al. (2011) were able to access a national, cross-sectional data set of American adolescent sample at ages 14 (N=102,109), 16 (N=107,849) and 18 (N=107,421) (8th, 10th and 12th grades respectively) sampled each year from 1991 to 2008. Results using the Rosenberg Self-Esteem Scale (RSES) were identical, so far as ethnic groups were concerned, in each year. First of all, RSES scale means were invariant across the years 1991 to 2008. Within each year, rank ordering of RSES scores between ethnic groups was similar: African-Americans highest; Hispanics and European-Americans significantly lower; and Asian Americans lowest. The tendency for Asian-Americans to be self-effacing was judged to be a cultural trait, and was consistent with research from countries such as Japan and China. 'Despite' their somewhat lower self-esteem scores, Asians did better than the other two groups in terms of gaining entrance to college.[4]

Bachman et al. (2011) in reporting these results, observe the tendency for African-American parents to develop a special kind of self-consciousness as a group with a history of being oppressed, but who retain a coherent and aspirant identity. 'Whites' in contrast are a very heterogeneous group, with only pockets of a coherent consciousness or ethnic coherence (similar to our Canadian findings – Bagley et al., 2001). In all ethnic groups females had significantly poorer self-esteem than males, but the authors do not advance any particular theory to account for this gender difference.

Commenting on the emerging British situation in the 1990s, Osuwu-Bempah and Howitt (1999) point to the "irony" of White youth having poorer self-esteem than Black youth, basing their comments on qualitative findings, and the fact that a disadvantaged group could have high levels of self-esteem in a still mainly racist culture.

In an important American study Erol and Orth (2011) first of all review the literature on a variety of factors known to be associated with self-esteem levels. Amongst these was gender (in 21 studies) – females having significantly lower mean scores (i.e. poorer self-esteem) than males: but although statistically significant, there was considerable overlap in scores across the genders (correlations between RSES scores for male versus female groups usually being a correlation of 0.2, or less). Erol and Orth's data analysis was of a nationally representative sample of 7,100 young Americans systematically followed up from ages 14 to 30, at 14 data points (at 14, 16, 18 years and so on). Ethnic differences familiar in previous American work clearly emerged: but in each ethnic and gender group, self-esteem increased with age, levelling off by age 30. At each age, correlations of high self-esteem in each ethnic and gender group were remarkably similar: the 'high self-esteem' individuals were (according to other tests administered at the same time) extroverted, emotionally stable, and conscientious (from the Big Five Personality Test), low in risk taking, and in better health. The strongest predictor of self-esteem was a sense of satisfaction in reaching one's goals at any point in time. Differences in self-esteem by gender, pertained within all ethnic groups, when all other psychological variables were controlled for. But in this, as in the other large-scale American studies, abusive or traumatic events in childhood were not measured.

The authors do not offer any explanation for their findings on gender differences in self-esteem: but similar findings on self-esteem and gender continue to emerge in international research. Mokses and Espnes (2012) found, for instance, in a Swedish study of 1,208 adolescents aged 13 to 18, that females, compared to males, had higher levels of depression, and poorer self-esteem. The correlation of depression and lower self-esteem was also significantly higher in females.

Bleidorn et al. (2015) offer the results of massive international study on gender and self-esteem, which combined a huge sample size, "apparently" offsetting problems of validity and reliability of the data collected, and in logical problems in making inferences as to the meaning, if any, of their findings. They used an internet site aimed at young people's issues, inviting respondents to, anonymously, complete a brief self-esteem scale, and to give details of their situation and circumstances, and their home country. Notwithstanding the impossibility of establishing the validity or truthfulness of the responses, the researchers analysed data from 985,937 of those who responded from 48 countries (including only 10% of the American responders, in order to give the inter-country comparisons some balance). The selected respondents were said to be aged 16 to 45, and for statistical purposes were divided into five age groupings. 130,383 of the respondents (49% female) were said to come from a geographical region called "Great Britain" (which, in terms of UK's political geography, would exclude Northern Ireland).

The brief measure of self-esteem, derived from and validated against the RSES, was converted to a standardized score with a mean of 50 for all respondents. The GB group scored 47.22 on this measure, which meant that they had significantly poorer self-esteem than nationals from many other countries. For all respondents, males had a score that was 1.85 points higher (at 51.85) than that of females, on the score normed at 50 for the pooled data for both genders – a highly significant difference. However, the size of the gender RSES score differences varied significantly across the 48 nations selected. A variety of multivariate procedures were used to try and explain these differences. Problematically, all of the comparisons were subject to the "ecological fallacy" (a fact not acknowledged by the authors), meaning that correlating, say, RSES scores (and gender differences on scores) with a country's average GDP per head could be an artefactual correlation, with no implications for cause.

These methodological problems did not prevent the authors of this paper, lauded by the American Psychological Association,[5] from advancing two theories. The first concerned 'normative factors' built into cultural socialization (and here they cite Williams & Best, 1990, on acquired stereotypes concerning class, race and gender – noting that people can shake off the racial stereotypes). The second hypothesis concerned structural factors, in that women in countries where females do not have to compete with men in the world of work were less likely to have lower self-esteem scores, since their reference and comparison groups were, apparently, different from those of men. (Traumatic or abusive events in childhood were not measured, although the anonymity of an internet site might have been a good place to ask about such events.)

These hypotheses concerning gender differences did not seem to advance or verify the ideas put forward by the much-cited paper by Kling et al. (1999) who reviewed 216 US studies including 97,172 individuals showing small but consistent, and statistically significant differences in self-esteem levels at all ages from adolescence to adulthood, women having slightly "poorer" self-esteem, the largest differences occurring in late adolescence (ages 14 to 18). They speculated, without supporting data, that young women put a greater stress than men on "being attractive", and their subjective failure to achieve this was reflected in poorer self-esteem.

A different, and somewhat more productive meta-analysis was offered by Gentle et al. (2009) who analysed data from 428 studies on 32,486 young Americans who completed more complex measures of self-esteem (e.g. the Piers-Harris, the Coopersmith, and the Tennessee scales) which measured not only core self-evaluation (the RSES domain) but also various domains thought to influence core self-esteem. Overall, men had "better" self-esteem than did women, but in different domains, particular those relating to athletic prowess, physical appearance, and self-satisfaction. Women however appraised themselves more favourably in moral-ethnical domains, and in areas relating to good behaviour. The authors concluded that slightly poorer overall levels of self-esteem in females were "reflected appraisals" of how young American men and women were expected to behave. In this analysis women are not deficient in self-esteem, but rather are more thoughtful and helpful. Clearly, these thoughtful, moral women would make good wives for their macho husbands.

Experience of Sexual Abuse As a Cause of Impaired Self-Esteem in Adolescent Women?

It is surprising that none of those speculating about differences in self-esteem (particularly RSES scores) have, publicly at least, considered the possibility that these differences reflect the fact the child sexual abuse could be a *major* factor in differential levels of self-esteem between genders. This hypothesis assumes that (a) child sexual abuse (CSA) is likely to impair self-esteem in girls and adolescent women; and (b) this kind of abuse, and its likely effects is more likely to mar the lives of girls and adolescent women. Thus, differences in RSES scores between genders could be a function of (a) the differential incidence of CSA, females more likely to be victims; and (b) the greater negative impact that CSA has on female psychological development.

We have to concede that despite the fact that, with colleagues, we have published published a number of studies on the incidence and psychological impacts of CSA[6] – including, frequently, the negative impact which CSA had on self-esteem – but he had never articulated this seemingly straightforward thesis, that gender differences on RSES scores reflect the differential incidence and impact of sexual abuse. This was despite having published data from a survey of more than 1,000 female Canadian high school students which showed that sexual harassment, assault and abuse in school had a significant negative impact on self-esteem (measured by the RSES) in adolescent women (Bagley, Bertrand & Bolitho, 1995; Bagley, Bolitho & Bertrand, 1997). Bagley and Mallick (2001) partially replicated this Canadian work in 1,300 English adolescents, establishing the norms, factor structure, reliability, and face validity in terms of correlation with established mental health measures, of the Rosenberg Self-Esteem Scale, and recommended it for use in further clinical work. But in that study, data on ethnicity or on 'community sexual assault' were not collected.

However, variables on ethnicity, self-esteem and some types of sexual assault or abuse were included in a further follow-up study with 2,405 adolescents aged 11 to 18 attending English schools. These data, collected in the school year 2006 to 2007, were not analysed at that time because of the onset of Dr. Mallick's serious illness, and her subsequent death in 2007. We present, for the first time in any format, the results of the analysis of this data-set, in a later chapter.

Bagley and Mallick (2000a, 2000b) in their Canadian birth cohort followed up from birth to age 17 estimated (and from parallel studies carried out in Alberta, Canada) that about 12 percent of women prior to their 18th birthday, experience unwanted, physical sexual assault or intrusion: in about half of these the sexual abuse was be chronic and severely intrusive of the young person's body. They show that about a half of this severely assaulted group subsequently had 'devastated self-esteem' and chronic psychiatric problems which required psychiatric therapy, which could benefit from therapeutic group work aimed at enhancing self-esteem (Bagley & Young, 1998).

Antecedents in the Canadian longitudinal study, of becoming a chronic victim of sexual abuse were: prior events of physical and emotional abuse, early child health problems with some adverse neurological sequelae, and a family life marred by disruption, poverty and mother's multiple partners (who were often the sexual assailants of the child). The children were studied intensively at birth (since this was a perinatal sample, obtained through birth registrations) and at ages 5 and 17. The ethics of the longitudinal study meant that children considered to be at 'high risk' in terms of health and personal development had to be referred for intervention, but the long interval between collection of data (between age 5 and age 17) meant that the researchers failed to pick up many cases where the child's problems were not apparent at age five. Only when the cohort were aged 17 were the researchers able to ask the young people directly about abusive events in their lives.

The figures they give on the amount of sexual abuse endured by women in childhood and adolescents could well be an underestimate: Bagley and Mallick (2000b) acknowledge that sample loss was twice as great in the families known to be under stress when the child was born and at age 5, compared with children in stable family situations. Women with children whose lives were unstable are difficult to retain in this kind of longitudinal survey. What was remarkable, perhaps, was that a half of children experiencing multiple types of abuse and assault managed to survive to age 17 in a 'normal' psychological state: nevertheless, they gave moving and detailed accounts of how they retained their psychological and physical integrity despite the many difficult situations they had had to endure (Bagley & King, 2003). These are the "resilient survivors" identified in various research studies (Wyatt, Newcomb & Riederle, 1993).[7] Bagley and King (2003) advance the controversial hypothesis that the frequent sexual harassment and sexual assault of children and adolescent women in school, family and society is a kind of ritualised assault in which a sector of 'lower class' females learn to become subordinated in their social and sexual roles.

Across the world, studies continue to be published showing that severe and chronic sexual abuse (and other forms of maltreatment) of a child or adolescent can seriously disrupt her identity development, with resulting levels of very poor self-esteem, chronic depression, various anxiety and psychosomatic disorders, and impaired sexual adjustment. Moreover, these effects extend well into adulthood and seem likely to impair adjustment across the life span. Fergusson et al. (2013) report for example, in their longitudinal study of 900 New Zealand women up to age

30, that chronic and intrusive sexual abuse occurring before the age of 18 was (after statistically controlling for social class, and various family factors) associated to a statistically significant extent with the following: episodes of major depression, chronic anxiety disorder, low self-esteem levels, suicidal ideation, dependence on illicit drugs, dependence on alcohol, post-traumatic stress disorder, early 'voluntary' sexual behaviour, number of sexual partners, welfare dependency, and poorer physical health. Some ten percent of the women had endured prolonged and intrusive sexual abuse, although only half of these had devastated adjustment. The other half were, to a greater or lesser degree, "survivors".

The impact of CSA on the bases of self-esteem, and its recovery, is well-described by Krayer et al. (2015). In a qualitative, therapeutic study of 30 young adult women who had survived CSA, they identified three emergent themes concerning 'views of the self': The worthless self; the self as unknown; and the potential and developing self. They report:

> Ambivalence and tension were present in all narratives. Individuals were challenged to integrate the sexual abuse experience in a constructive way and develop a more coherent perception of the self. The narrative method highlighted the dynamic nature of people's experiences, at the same time recognizing that the narratives themselves are in progress. Reasons to disclose, social support and interpersonal connexions are crucial at every turn. (p. 148)

This, we think is an important quotation, since it illustrates how at the heart of every piece of research, on equality, gender, or ethnic identity is a unique set of individuals who have important, personal stories to tell. It is these stories which, like analytical accounts, lie at the heart of the critical realist research paradigm. According to Collier (1994), at the end of his lengthy discussion of critical realist methodology in the social sciences:

> ... psychoanalysis ... should be treated as the paradigm of good practice in this area. It derives all its theories from the analysis in depth of particular individuals. Insofar as it generalizes, it generalizes about mechanisms and tendencies discovered in such analyses. It generates no statistical predictions whatever; if it corrects and revises and supplements its discoveries, it does so not on the basis of any statistical data (which it can always explain away), but on the basis of more depth inquiries into more symptoms of more people. The 'more' adds not statistical confirmation, but new data: it is *different* phenomena, not more of the same, that refine and complexify this science. (p. 258)

In this fascinating model of social science research, individuals in a longitudinal study (for example) are not merely generating crunchable ciphers for the researcher's computer: they are recreating themselves in a reflexive way, explaining their life's morphogenesis.[8]

Our dilemma of course, is that much of the research we have been considering in this chapter is based on nuggets of data ripped from the lives of dehumanized individuals. Moreover, the research which we present in the chapter on the Northern Schools study suffers from the same positivist bias, the debasement of individuals as units of analysis in a statistical matrix. And we have no case material with which we can humanize this account. In mitigation, we note that Priscilla Alderson comments:

> Since learning about DCR [dialectical critical realism], I have revised some of my former ideas and discarded others, on the continuing journey of learning and change. (2013, p. 8)

But we am also comforted by the assertion that the "facts" of these statistical studies, are in Bhaskar's (1989, 2008) paradigm, 'value-saturated' in their assumptions, so that we can move from 'facts' to 'values' (and back) with ease. This, for us, makes social policy analysis much easier, and justifies the miscellany of "factual" studies (some of them virtually case studies) which we assemble in various sections of this book on Equality, in which we argue that an unequal society can bear oppressively on the lives of a sector of its children. In the DCR model, of course, the voices of children speaking against poverty, alienation and abuse must be heard in ways which are morphogenetic, and society-changing (Alderson, 2013, 2016).

The Social Self, and the Neglect and Abuse of Children

Finally, we move away from the existential self (or the 'spiritual self', as James 1892/1985 termed it) in which the ego appraises itself, albeit in comparison with others, to the 'social self' whose nature reflects (but is not determined by) an individual's position in social structure, reflecting a person's economic role, or what Marx described as "relationship to the means of production". Marx argued that the individual whose subordinate role was as a low-wage employee, whose terms of contract and conditions of work were subordinated to an organisation's profit, were *alienated* by the nature and exploitative conditions of labour, from his or her self. In the words of one of Brecht's stories, a couple had both reached 60. They were tired, exhausted, aged, ill, without hope, and now they faced death. 'Is this all there is?' they ask (Brecht, 2003).

This idea of alienation has been a concern for sociologists in the past 50 years (Churchich, 1990), who have described the state of powerlessness and normlessness which engulfs the exploited worker as one which engenders various forms of despair, mental illness, and unfocussed rebellion, as does Schmidt (2011). We argue in Appendix A on Equality that about a tenth of the English population form a permanent, alienated underclass, in which depression, mental illness, depressed aspirations, criminality and family breakdown co-occur (often in the same families, or individuals) in segregated areas of cities, awaiting the call from capital to enter the ranks of the employed, when capital's profit requires.

While the sexual abuse of children and adolescents occurs in all social classes and in all strata of society, it occurs much more frequently in the disorganised households of the sink estates, in which a woman's children from multiple partners are at elevated risk from sexual abuse by her new partners (Bagley & King, 2003). In this view, the ritual sexual subordination of young females in the underclass confirms them as sexual objects not only within the chronic underclass,[9] but also as recruits for the commercial sex industry (Bagley, 1995a).

CONCLUSIONS

There is a considerable literature on self-esteem, self-concept and identity and these concepts have been of major interests for psychologists and sociologists since the early part of the last century. Self-esteem involves the evaluation of characteristics of the self in various ways, and what self-characteristics are evaluated by oneself, and others, and becomes increasingly complex as the child grows older, interacts with a wider range of people and peers, and has an increasingly complex cognitive schema for organising aspects of the perceived self.

Minority group pre-schoolers are of particular concern, since in an institutionally racist society they may be socialised to accept and internalise the negative stereotypes which the wider society holds. This is a crucial issue for antiracist social and educational policies.

By about the age of seven, the child's set of self-evaluations become organized into a self-concept: that concept of who one is, how one behaves or should behave, how good and comely one is, how strong or weak, and so forth: this – becomes an enduring part of one's identity. A person's identity is both complex and unique, since the experiences of each human being are unique. Identity, in this theorisation, is the same as 'global self-concept'. Although facets of identity change with time and experience, and how the body (the 'me', the central part of identity) is regarded, is used, achieves, is injured, gives pleasure, gives pain, and ages – that central core of self-identity, the evaluating self, is both enduring and evolving.

Collier's (1994) account of Bhaskar's critical realism commends the model of research derived from psychoanalysis. This has led us back to Ernest Becker's (1971) psychodynamic sociology, and his weaving of threads from William James and Erving Goffman in the creation of an inner-outer world of self-hood and self-creation, and his use of Alfred Adler's psychoanalytic study of self-esteem: "The supreme law of life is this: the sense of worth of the self shall not be allowed to be diminished" (Adler, 1946, p. 356). When we add the Jungian paradigm of spiritual consciousness, we have a model of the child whose physical and emotional energy should be creatively expressed in ego tasks, in ways which are developmentally appropriate and which respect self and others, in seeking "the light" in oneself and in others, climbing, in morphogenic manner, to achieve the realisation of selfhood in a non-exploitive world.

NOTES

[1] Manchester may have been an exception: Tomlinson (2008) in her review of ethnicity and educational policies in England has observed " ...the minimal and grudging preparation of teachers to teach in a multi-ethnic society" (p. 179).

[2] For example, in the "Brexit" fugue of zenophobia in the UK Referendum of 2016.

[3] Structural factors may be influential as well, such as growing up in a mixed-race community, and sharing cross-ethnic friendships in school (Rutland et al., 2005).

[4] Greene and Way (2005) showed that in a "growth curve" analysis with US students, Asian Americans' self-esteem levels gained significantly in the post-college phase.

[5] APA (2016). *Self-esteem gender gap more pronounced in Western countries: basic trends in self-esteem appear universal but can be shaped by culture.* Washington, DC: American Psychological Association Press Statement, January 4, 2016.

[6] Bagley (1989, 1990, 1991b, 1995a, 1995b, 1996a, 1996b, 1997, 1991, 2002, 2003; Bagley, Bertrand & Bolitho, 1995; Bagley, Bolitho & Bertrand, 1997; Bagley & King, 2003; Bagley & LeChance, 2000; Bagley & Mallick, 2000, 2001; Bagley & McDonald, 1984; Bagley & Ramsay, 1986; Bagley & Young, 1990, 1998; Bagley et al., 1995, 1999).

[7] Males were, of course, researched in these Canadian samples. Boys experienced sexual abuse (almost always by males) at about half the frequency of females, and this appeared to have less impact on self-esteem levels. One problem identified however, was a statistically significant tendency for boys to become incipient adult offenders (Bagley, Wood & Young, 1994; Bagley, 2002).

8   Christopher Bagley has attempted to defend himself from this Critical Realist critique by pointing to the frequent "sexual stories" retold in his book on a humanist approach to child sexual abuse (Bagley, 1995). He cites Ken Plummer's book *Telling Sexual Stories* (1995): "No longer do people simply 'tell' their sexual stories to reveal the 'truth' of their own sexual lives; instead, they turn themselves into *socially organised biographical objects*" (p. 34). Perhaps these stories can be psychodynamically aware pieces of dialectical critical realism?

9   A 2015 English study which "polled" some 2,000 women aged 18-plus, reported that 10% had experienced frequent "sexual touching, groping, flashing, sexual assault or rape" in or around the schools they had attended. Some two-thirds of victims never reported these assaults to anyone who could have intervened. This survey was carried out for or by the charity Plan UK. Few details of methodology were given in the press release reporting these results (Smith, 2016).

A CRITICAL REALIST CASE STUDY OF A MULTI-ETHNIC, INNER CITY DAY NURSERY

Children, Workers, Management and Bureacracy in a Matrix of Change

My goal in writing this book was to present children's notions of racial and ethnic matters in their own terms, As an adult participant observer, however, I must confess that simply acting like a child does not give one the right to claim that one can learn exactly how a child conceives of such matters ... participating in the daily activities of a child allows one to experience and feel the elements of the child's complete universe – his or her social, cognitive, emotional, and physical spheres. Through these experiences, adults as participant observers in the culture of children is a pleasure and a privilege. It also offers the researcher the joy of revisiting the carefree, candid, and innocent times of childhood and conveying that journey to others.

(Robyn Holmes, 1995, p. 110)

INTRODUCTION

Critical realism is a philosophical model for social research, which may be applied using a variety of methodologies and case study methods. It has been used to analyse the results of studies with children as patients, and children in care (Alderson, 2013, 2016), in various educational settings (Shipway, 2011; Surra, 2011), and in case studies of industry and management (Easton, 2010).

We attempt, with mixed results, to apply this model later on, in this case study of an inner city nursery school: the study's original purpose was to examine how workers were transmitting learning goals established by central government, and how in the process they were addressing the development of ethnic identity in the children in their care. This study was begun in 2002–2003, but could not be continued, as the local authority closed, arbitrarily and without notice, the day care that Alice Sawyerr was studying. Later, analysing the materials that she had collected, we realised that in order to answer the basic research questions. the methodology would have to be modified (in order to meet the demands of the critical realist reflexive model), and the work carried out should be treated as a guide for fresh and more ambitious research in this field.

The nursery school we studied closed several years ago, and was located in a City in Southern England. In 2007 according to an overview of living conditions in the City, 27 percent of the population (total population about 215,000) came from ethnic minority groups (including 12% Asian, 7.5% African-Caribbean, 4% mixed race). Twelve percent of enumeration districts in the borough fell into the national English criteria for 'the highest level of deprivation' for England, measured by levels of material poverty and unemployment, poor health, low educational attainments, crime and delinquency, and a degraded living environment. About half of the African-Caribbean population lived in these areas of high deprivation.

At the city's periphery is a low-income housing estate which we call the Elgar Estate, after a famous musician. The Elgar Estate was (and remains) one of the most deprived urban area of an English city, according to various census indicators. Today, the press frequently focus on incidents of knife and gun crime, drug-dealing subcultures, dawn police raids etc. Despite this, there is a strong communal spirit on the estate, and for the visitor, no overt signs of violence, racial tension or inter-ethnic rivalry. Mixed black-white partnerships are common. Elgar turned out proudly with a street party to celebrate the Queen's 90th birthday, in June, 2016. Local residents claim that their area is falsely stigmatised by media.

At the time of the first phase of this research (2002–2004) Alice Sawyerr was working as a full time clinician in a NHS Mental Health Clinic concerned with the assessment and treatment of children adolescents, adults and families. AS received referrals from various agencies concerned with residents of the Elgar Estate. The City's Social work and Education departments were responsible for nursery placements according to the individual needs of children and families. The model was one of integrated care including health teams, social workers, educators, family centre workers and nursery practitioners.

These children were already placed in the focus nursery which we will call St. John's (St. J's). It was in this nursery that AS established her video-recorded, observational work in 2002. Three years earlier AS had published research which focussed on this same nursery, looking at the enhancement of ethnic identity and self-esteem in the minority group children in the centre (Sawyerr, 1999). As an introduction to the present Case Study, we reproduce an edited version of that book chapter here:

Working with Black Children and Adolescents in Need: Identity Project on 'Myself' with Pre-Schoolers At the Day Nursery (Sawyerr, 1999).

... Providing assessments and therapeutic sessions to referred children and their families on site at a local authority nursery (which offers services to paying and non-paying parents/carers) has been challenging, enjoyable and a good learning process. Over the past five years I have struggled to find imaginative, creative, flexible and pragmatic ways of engaging and working with adults and children inside and outside of the nursery system. The following is a narrative account of this experience which could provide pointers for professionals working with children in different settings.

The nursery was one of six nurseries run by the education department of [an inner city urban area]. Its large building was established as a day nursery during the second world war. It offered the equivalent of 45 full-time places, and had the equivalent of nine full-time qualified NNEB and Nursery Nursing 'B Tech' nursery officers. It is located in a multicultural and multiracial community, where black and white families have lived and intermarried for several decades. Many of their children have attended the nursery and now so too are their grandchildren. There were also British-born children from newly arrived immigrant families from Asia, North Africa, and Eastern European countries whose parents initially spoke little or no English.

The nursery was staffed by African/African Caribbean, White Middle Eastern and Asian nursery officers (which to some extent reflects the racial and cultural backgrounds of the children at the nursery). A key worker system operated within the nursery. The key worker's role was to ensure that the children and their parents/carers were offered stability and continuity. The key worker monitored each child's development and learning and set a series of personal goals. Parents were expected to work closely with their child's key worker, and together share information which could assist the child to develop to his/her full potential. Each child had a Care and Education Plan after three months of settling in; this was reviewed every six months or more often as appropriate. Parents/carers and children were encouraged to contribute to these plans.

The nursery's philosophy was to provide a stimulating and safe environment for all the children. It had a structured programme of activities, each designed to allow the children to learn through fun, imagination and thoughtful guidance. Access to the day nursery was by three routes:

- *A referral by the social services department for children who are assessed as children "in need" of a place.*

- *Via the Early Years Development Plan for three and four- year- olds whose often single parents wanted places for reasons of their own career and social development.*
- *Privately, if there were places available, but on a fee-paying basis (fees were not usually paid by children in the first two categories).*

Early Years Curriculum

The Early Years Curriculum programmes are, according to government claims, 'broad, balanced and differentiated to meet the age and development needs of each child'. Programmes were displayed in the nursery and planned around the six topics of the 'Desirable Learning Outcomes' and the Local Councils' Curriculum for the under-fives, namely: mathematics, language and literacy, personal and social development, knowledge and understanding of the world, physical development and creative development.

The nursery celebrates the various world and religious events as part of extending the children's knowledge and understanding of the world. Some of the events which I celebrated include Eid, Diwali, Chinese New Year, Easter, Christmas, and St. Patrick's Day. These involve story reading, entertainment, displays, meals and parties in which the parents/carers are often asked to participate, as well as to share their knowledge and experiences with the staff. The nursery also provides services for children with special needs as far as possible.

The need for the development of the identity project centring on Myself as a theme grew from an awareness within the staff team of the preschool age group (three to five-year-olds) that some children were either struggling with, or were unaware of their racial and cultural backgrounds, e.g. some children of "mixed – race" parentage were referring to themselves as white, and some black children were referring to themselves as "quarter caste".

- *There were ambivalent feelings among some of the parents and staff about when and how to introduce the concept of self, "race", culture and identity to the children.*
- *There were apparent difficulties for minority ethnic and, in particular, black and mixed parentage children in identifying their skin colour, and with heritage and cultural issues.*
- *Some children were receiving mixed messages from their parents/ grandparents/carers and from some nursery staff about their racial and cultural identity.*

- *Others were receiving no input from their parents/carers or staff about their racial and cultural identity.*

The availability and easy access to multicultural activities, group outings, celebrations of world and religious events, reading materials and other resources in the nursery, did not appear to have made any substantial difference to the level of understanding of the children's sense of self. For the most part, some white and some black staff members had assumed that, if the children were regularly exposed to relevant activities, resources and group discussions from workers of diverse ethnicities and cultures, they would "naturally" develop an awareness of the identity and concepts of self.

As the children's lack of awareness and seeming confusion about their identity increased, it became clear to one of the black key workers in the pre-school group that definite action was needed to address these issues, and that outside specialist help was necessary.

It is worth noting that three years earlier, I had identified some of these issues and had offered joint consultation sessions with a white colleague to the entire nursery staff team and management; I am black African. However, our efforts had been met with a lot of resistance. The consultation sessions were often cancelled on the scheduled days due to reported staff unavailability. In the event the consultation sessions had to end even though there had been approval and apparent commitment from senior management.

As my work with individual children and their families at the nursery continued (90 percent of which were referrals from the pre-school group), I began to encourage and engage with the key workers in joint sessions with the children on site as well as off-site. These involved observations of the parent-child sessions, family sessions (from behind the one-way screen with the families' consent), and in debriefing sessions. Over time the key workers began to develop a keener interest in the sessions, especially when they observed marked positive changes in the children's behaviour at nursery.

Following the identification of the issues by a key worker from the preschool group and the need for specialist help being recognized and agreed to from within the nursery system, a direct referral was made to myself by the concerned black key worker, with support from the white manager for consultation.

My assessment was that the identified children were not showing signs of "pathology", and therefore did not require individual therapy. They were, in my view, developing normally for children aged three to five years, showing curiosity about identity and self-concepts, as a normal part of socio-emotional development. Cognitively, they were demonstrating the beginnings of their acquisition of the ability to think, to notice small details and accurately observe discrepancies, and to make interesting associations. Part of children's normal language development involves asking "why" "when" and "how" questions of the significant adults in their lives, requiring simple answers and recounting the content of stories even though they may misinterpret facts or confused details.

In my professional view it was the nursery staff and some of the parents/carers who were 'feeling stuck' and needed support in understanding the issues and finding helpful ways of addressing them. Much clarity and collaborative work between the adults in the system when needed. Secondly, since these were normal development and identity stages that all children go through, it was important that both white and black children and their parents/carers be involved in the project.

Following a detailed referrals meeting with the three black key workers with their white manager and deputy manager, the schedule was developed for weekly two-hour consultation sessions. There was an agreement and commitment from the staff and management that:

- the three key workers from the preschool group in the management staff would I attend and actively participate in the weekly two-hour sessions;
- an identity project centring on the theme "Myself" would be developed to address the issues affecting the children's sense of self; and
- it was imperative to involve and engage all the parents/carers, children and staff in the preschool group in the project activities.

The main aims of the project were:

- to help the children develop a strong image of themselves;
- to help the children in the preschool group to look at themselves (including physical features) with their key workers and families and to feel more positive about themselves and their families;
- to help the children know and feel comfortable with their racial and cultural identity;
- to encourage awareness among the children about different racial and cultural backgrounds;
- to prepare the children for the challenges of the school environment, to feel confident and proud of themselves, their racial and cultural identities, and those of their families; and
- to raise awareness among the staff and parents within the whole nursery of the importance of the children's identity and development of pride and clarity in the children's sense of self.

The Consultation Process

Stage I.   This involved four weeks of training workshops for the three key workers and two managers, before the start of the project, in which the following areas were explored:

- *the meaning of "race," culture, religion, and spirituality for each nursery officer.*
- *Which communities were considered to be minority ethnic communities in Britain today.*
- *The meaning of the term black: who is considered to be black? Where do black people come from? As they a homogeneous group or not? And if not, why not?*
- *The knowledge, guiding principles, values, beliefs and assumptions that nursery offices bring with them in their negotiations with parents/carers.*
- *The needs, cultural beliefs, values, knowledge and childrearing experiences and practices that parents/carers bring with them in their negotiations with nursery offices.*
- *The expectations of parents/carers of the nursery offices in relation to the children.*
- *The negotiation process, the knowledge, skills, aptitudes and experience needed to work cross culturally and interculturally, i.e. how to join in with and engage families from diverse racial and cultural backgrounds in the identity project centring on Myself.*

Some exercises were given in the workshops to aid the understanding needed to accomplish the task.

Stage 2.   This involved a workshop in which the key concepts and materials to be used in the project were introduced:

Copies of Black Like Me, Workbook One by Dr Jocelyn Maxime were distributed to each worker. Some time was spent on adapting, redefining and elaborating on the activities on self and identity in the book to meet the specific needs of the children in the preschool group, given their age, multicultural backgrounds e.g. gathering information about grandparents, religion, dress worn on special occasions, languages spoken at home, favorite foods, foods eaten at home, etc.

In Black Like Me, Workbook One, Dr Maxime prescribes the child's identity as African. However, in this project a variety of identity categories were listed and the parents/carers were asked to choose a category with their child that best describes the child's identity. For parents/carers who did not see the child as exclusively black, Asian or white, etc. they were asked to choose from an additional category which listed a series of terms describing mixed parentage identities, the terminology that they and their children felt was appropriate. They were asked to indicate the identity of each parent.

Plain exercise books, plastic mirrors, skin tone crayons, skin tone papers, colour pencils for eyes and hair, envelopes containing the suggestions/ guidelines for 19 activities in a plastic case for storing the above materials were prepared for each parent/carer and the child.

Stage 3. In this stage, the key nursery offices used the consultation session to plan a step-by-step programme on how the activities would be implemented with the children at nursery and with the parents/carers at home. The starting and finishing dates for the project were decided and each worker was given the task of drafting a letter to parents/carers about the project, indicating the purpose and duration of the project, in preparation for the next consultation session.

Stage 4. Ideas from each staff member's draft letter to parents/carers about the project were incorporated into one letter, which was hand delivered to the parents/carers by the respective key workers on the Friday before the project was launched (the following Monday).

Some parents asked to spend some time at the nursery with their child and the key worker to complete each activity, because of language difficulties. Others requested individual sessions with me before commencing the activities with their child, because of sensitive emotional issues that they felt they needed to work through for themselves e.g. the child being adopted and not knowing about their own biological parents, and therefore feeling insecure about their own identity. For others it was the realization that they needed to deal with their own feelings of anger and hurt in relation to their absent partners, in order to help their child to make sense of their identity.

Each child was allocated their own tailor-made set of "identity" materials, according to individual circumstances, and their "identity book" was a unique resource for each individual child. The process is described below.

- The key workers pasted the suggestions/guidelines on the first page of each child's book.
- The parents/carers with their and child chose a photograph of their child and pasted it on the outer cover of the book at home.

- *Each activity was pasted on a new page in the book by the key workers in sequence, one at a time, once the previous activity had been completed by the parents/carers and children.*
- *The key workers were responsible for sending the books home with the pasted activity sheet in them each day. The parents/carers were responsible for completing the activities at home each day with their child, signing the page, and for ensuring that the books were taken back to the nursery every morning.*
- *The key workers met with respective parents/carers and key child each morning for feedback on the activity completed, as well as at the end of each day to explain how the newly pasted activity was to be completed.*
- *The first two activities were completed by the parents/carers and their children either at home all, with special arrangement, at the nursery.*
- *Three of the activities which covered facial features, skin colour, and hair were completed at the nursery with the key workers, as negotiated with the parents/carers during their initial planning meeting. The children were given mirrors and books specifically about "self " to look through. They were given time to discuss the facial features of the characters in the books which then led to them looking at their own facial features and issues about themselves. The colour of their skin, eyes, hair texture, etc. were talked about. The children worked in pairs all individually with their key nursery worker. The sessions took place either in the group room all in a separate room. The time spent with each child varied from 15 to 30 minutes depending on how much work the child was able to do at one time.*
- *The sessions which took place in the nursery with the parents/carers, their children and their key workers, were led by the parents/carers. The key workers' role was that of support and of giving guidance to the parents/carers when necessary, and not actually doing the activities with the children.*

Each parent/carer was given an evaluation form to fill in at home on completion of all the activities with your child. These were returned promptly.

Presentation of Achievement Certificates

With some of the children starting school at their fifth birthday, a party and presentation ceremony were organized at the nursery for all the children in parents/carers to mark their achievement. Each child was presented with a personalized, colourful certificate for completing all the activities to the identity project. Pictures were taken of each child receiving the certificate from the start. The parents/carers were called up alongside to the child, congratulated for completing all the activities with their child, and photographed with their child.

The certificate presentation ceremony was also videotaped. The ceremony ended with the key workers, management staff and the consultant joining in with the children and their parents/carers for an enjoyable Easter party celebration.

Stage 5. Involved a major review and evaluation of the entire project. The key workers, management staff and I met for half a day with our retainer assessment on the following areas of the project:

- *The children's completed activity workbooks.*
- *The parents/carers evaluation forms.*
- *The key workers', managers' and the consultant's evaluation forms.*
- *Feedback from the parents/carers and children on the certificate presentation day and ceremony.*

A discussion on the processes involved, lessons learnt and possible ways forward for future projects were carefully explored and noted.

A major presentation of the project was made to senior managers from the local authority's education department, social services and the NHS Trust. All the children's completed activity workbooks resource materials, completed evaluation forms, photographs and certificates were on display. They were also shown the video-tape of the certificate presentation ceremony.

The overall assessment was that the project had been successful in meeting the outlined aims and objectives: The following areas were highlighted:

- *Both written and verbal feedback from the parents/carers were very positive. All the parents/carers reported that the activities and processes involved had helped to them and their children to address key issues relating to who they were in a formalized way which they had previously been unable to deal with on their own.*
- *For some of the parents, issues around absent fathers which had been difficult for them to talk about with their children were addressed through the activities with much sensitivity and professional support.*
- *All the parents/carers requested more interactive activities ("homework") with the nursery staff for their children). They reported that the children*

were attentive and enjoyed completing the activities with them. It was meaningful and quality time was spent.

- There were also noticeable changes in the children's drawings of themselves and others at nursery e.g. particular attention being paid to skin tones, hair and eye colours and facial features in all the drawings subsequent to the project.

- The white children no longer left the drawings of themselves on white sheets of paper blank. They searched for the appropriate skin tone crayons for shading in the skin tone even though they were referred to by adults as "white".

- Similarly, the black, Asian and mixed parentage children shaded in drawings of themselves with the appropriate skin tone but not black it in though some of them were referred to as "black" by adults.

- All ten children were more able to describe themselves, their identity i.e. "race", culture, colour of their skin, nationality, language spoken at home, religion, clothes worn on special occasions and festivals where applicable, without any hesitation and with pride.

- They were also able, in group settings, to talk about observable similarities and differences in their skin tones, facial features, hair colours and textures in positive ways.

- The children took pride and great care in the handling of their Identity Activity Workbooks. There were no tone pages or marks in the books even though most of the books travelled daily between their homes and the nursery.

- The key workers and management staff acknowledged the value and importance of working jointly with parents/carers in addressing identity issues and concepts of self with preschool age children.

- The identity project provided the nursery officers and the consultant with vulnerable opportunities to learn first-hand from the parents and the children about their cultures, histories, values and beliefs. Most of the parents were very creative in the work that they did with their children. The process had the effect of bringing the parents/carers and professionals closer together to work in equal partnership.

- Both parents/carers and staff were unanimous in their recommendation that the identity project should become a formalized and integral part of the pre-school group curriculum at the nursery.

This recommendation was accepted [by St John's Nursery, subject of the case study focussed on in this Chapter] and it became an integral part of *the pre-school curriculum for this nursery. Plans were also underway for its implementation in the five other local authority nurseries in 1999* (the book chapter concluded).

THE VIDEO-RECORDED STUDY OF CHILDREN'S INTERACTIONS,
AND INTERVIEWS WITH KEY WORKERS

This work began in St. John's Nursery (St. J's), four years after the study reported above was completed at this nursery, and this earlier account of research on identity was included in Alice Sawyerr's chapter in the book edited by Barn (1999). The detailed account of interactions between staff and children, and between children themselves in St. J's are presented below.

The purposes of this further study in the focus therapeutic day nursery were several. First of all was the "official" reason, which allowed the researcher to access the nursery using videotaped interactions, was to assess how well the Qualifications and Curriculum Authority "early learning" goals were being implemented. Then there was the implicit goal of observing and drawing inferences on children's ethnic identity development, through analysing the interactions between nursery staff and children, and between the children themselves. Included in the observation matrix of video-recorded interactions were 11 staff members, and 22 children. Only one of the front-line workers was white, and the children themselves came from a variety of ethnic backgrounds including African-Caribbean and Middle Eastern, or were of mixed ethnicity.

The provision of preschool nursery care had been subcontracted, after competitive tender some years earlier to the company offering the service for the least cost. This company, 'Day Care Providers of DCP', was merged in 2011 with another commercial day care provider, and no longer exists by that title. St. J's was nearing the end of its 5-year contract with DCP, and I (AS) was informed that because of the possibility of a new competitive tendering process, only 27 of the 45 places were occupied. There was no intimation at any stage that St. J's would soon be closed, and there was every expectation that DCP would be awarded a continuation of the contract to run this therapeutic day nursery. DCP had declined to hire a trained kindergarten teacher, and so the task of delivering the Early Years curriculum was left to the NNEB-trained staff (whose hourly rates of pay were much less than those of a trained teacher). The staff suggested that they were focussing more on child care, rather than on child learning, since they had no specific training in delivering the latter. Because of frequent staff sickness (an occupational hazard for day care staff, who often acquire minor infections from the children), age groups in the three separate rooms often had to be merged.

But even before the ending of the formal ending of the DCP's contract, St. J's was suddenly and arbitrarily closed, with little consultation with front-line workers, or parents of the children attending.

The Multi-Ethnic Day Nursery Workers' Practice in Their Natural Work Setting, and the Children's Verbal and Social Interactions

The initial focus of the study was on the participant observation findings concerning (a) the practitioner to child interactions in their natural work setting; and (b) the interactions and responses between individual children and groups of children in this inner-city, multi-ethnic day nursery setting. This report provides a summary of the researcher's four-week videotaped participant observations of the daily interactions and activities of the 11 multi-ethnic day nursery practitioners and 22 under-five nursery children, who together are the focus of this study. This study used an exploratory methodology, supplemented by interviews with key practitioners and managers.

All the observations took place during the nursery practitioners' implementation (in theory at least) of *The Early Learning Goals of the Foundation Stage Curriculum* (QCA, 2000) to pre-school age children in the local authority day nursery. The initial aim was to explore how the 11 multi-ethnic nursery practitioners (Black African, Black Caribbean, White British, White Irish, White Eastern European, Filipino and Asian) perceived and tried to implement the Foundation Stage Curriculum (QCA, 2000): how their perceptions might have influenced the ways they planned and implemented six of the ten Early Learning Goals of the Foundation Stage Curriculum with 3 to 5 year-olds from multi-ethnic backgrounds (North African, Black African and Caribbean, White British and children of Mixed Parentage).

Alice Sawyerr (AS) had worked with this nursery staff and children four years earlier, in devising an ethnic identity enhancement programme, described in Sawyerr (1999) – part of the text of that study is reproduced above. The programme which AS had devised, using ethnically sensitive materials, attitudes, methods and concepts, survived to some extent in the practice of this day nursery. The manager who had been involved in the 1998 project retired the week before the study began. None of the workers I observed and interviewed had been in post at the time of my 1998 project, although I was confident that many of the concepts did survive in the current ethos of the nursery.

This research was guided by three investigative questions:

1. How do practitioners from multi-ethnic backgrounds working in a multi-ethnic local authority day nursery perceive the foundation stage curriculum for 3 to 5-year-olds children?
2. How are the practitioners' perceptions reflected in the way in which they plan and implement the Foundation Stage Curriculum which affects children's learning?
3. What are the potential implications of these interactions for children's learning and development including their self-esteem, self-concept and ethnic identity development in a multi-ethnic local authority day nursery?

This initial, qualitative, case study research approach in investigating these questions, reflected the uniqueness of the combination of the nursery practitioners, the mix of the children's ethnicity, and the location of the local authority day nursery in a multi-ethnic community. In order to explore these research questions, I had to come into close contact with the practitioners while they were working in the day nursery. The purpose was to learn what their work involved and to observe them while they were working with the children and implementing the Foundation Stage Curriculum (QCA, 2000), as I wanted to understand the nursery practitioners' feelings, spontaneous dialogues, discussions with each other, and their 'ideas' or rationales for their actions.

The participant observations were recorded by a video camera being placed safely either on top of book shelves in the three group rooms during activities, or on a tripod out-of-doors in the on-site fenced-in playground.[1] AS discovered that videotaping herself alongside the nursery practitioners, rather than being behind the video camera had an immediate, positive reaction from the practitioners. They were rather surprised that the researcher was videotaping herself. This meant of course that through "stepping into the frame" I had become a practitioner myself.

Observing, Processing and Analysing the Data

The videotaped participant observations took place continuously over a four-week period, including the practitioners' early shifts (7:45 AM to 4 PM) and late shifts (9:30 AM to 6:30 PM) indoors in each of the three group rooms (each catering to a different age group), and outdoors in the on-site playground.

This was followed by a day each of participant observation with the cook and her assistant in the kitchen who also served the meals to the children; and with the deputy manager, the administrator and the cleaner, all on site.

I became increasingly aware of the myriad of interactions that were going on all the time simultaneously in the preschool group room settings. The children were not static, they kept moving around the room, and also between activities. Roberts-Holmes, (2011, p. 115) highlighting the potential for unstructured observations of young children in group settings, observed:

In an early years setting there are literally hundreds of interactions going on all the time around you: practitioners talking with each other, and the children, the children talking and learning with each other, parents coming in and going, children moving around different activities, some children getting attention, whilst others are being ignored. For the first-time researcher it is all rather daunting. What are you going to focus on?

Keeping these suggestions in mind when AS reviewed her initial analysis of data some time later, she began by focusing on the methodological literature, in how to answer the initial three research questions, in order to guide her with selection of the relevant participant observation data, in order to develop relevant themes, as is customary in analysing qualitative data of this type (Heath, Hindmarsh & Luff, 2010).

The findings provided detailed accounts of the observed practices of all the practitioners in the entire day nursery setting who interacted with the children on a daily basis, and the ways in which their individual contributions through interactions with the children and the children's responses related to the three research questions. Obviously, what follows are selected highlights from more than 100 hours of videotaping in the nursery, as well as off-camera conversations and observations.

This was an exploratory, qualitative research study approach that was broadly looking at how the nursery practitioners (themselves from multi ethnic backgrounds) perceived and implemented the foundation stage curriculum in a unique multi-ethnic local authority day nursery in a major English city; the children's responses to the practitioners; and how the children interacted with their peers. The implicit theme of the research was to explore the concepts of ethnicity implicit in the various interactions observed.

The first research question was: How do practitioners from multi ethnic backgrounds working in a multi-ethnic local authority day nursery perceive the Six Early Learning Goals of the Foundation Stage Curriculum, set out by the Qualifications and Curriculum Authority (QCA, 2000) for 3–5 old children? The six Early Learning Goals[2] focussed on in this study are:

1. Personal social and emotional development.
2. Communication, language and literacy.
3. Mathematical development.
4. Knowledge and understanding of the world.
5. Physical development.
6. Creative development.

The second research question: How might the practitioners' perceptions influence the way in which they plan, and implement the Foundation Stage Curriculum of the QCA (Qualifications and Curriculum Authority) which affects children's learning?

The third research question: What were the possible implications for children's learning and development including their self-esteem, self-concept and ethnic identity development in a multi-ethnic London local authority day nursery? This last question focussed in particular on the First Learning Goal, in the words of the QCA document: "Personal, social and emotional well-being, in particular … supporting the transition to and between settings, promoting an inclusive ethos and provide opportunities for each child to become a valued member of that group and community so that a strong self-image and self-esteem are promoted" (QCA, 2000, p. 9). The QCA document urged that: "No child should be excluded or disadvantaged because of ethnicity, culture or religion, home language, family background, special educational needs, disability, gender or ability" (QCA, 2000, p. 12).

The day nursery was open for 48–50 weeks a year, Mondays to Fridays, from 7:45 AM to 6:30 PM. A maximum of five full-time places were allocated to fee-paying children who were resident outside the Elgar Estate. They attended from 7:45 AM to 6:30 PM Monday to Friday. Although there were 27 full-time places, the 22 assessed children with free places at nursery were generally given a half day nursery place from 9:30 AM to 12:30 PM, three days a week: only children with the highest priority needs (e.g. children whose names were on the child protection register, or cases in which a court order for day care provision had been made) were allocated full day places starting at 9:30 AM to 3:30 PM five days a week.

The free nursery places were allocated to children residing within the borough who with their families had been referred by health visitors, general practitioners, speech therapists or social workers, and had been assessed by the local authority Children's Services Department and the Education Department, and were judged to be 'Children in Need' as defined by Section 17 of the Children Act 1989, 'children in need'.

The nursery was staffed by key practitioners trained to NVQ Child Care level 3, NNEB (Nursery Nurses Education Board) or BTech, and one trainee at level 2 of the NVQ Child Care certificate. The nursery was managed by an NNEB trained manager and her deputy. Practitioners were all female.

Children's Ethnic Backgrounds

The practitioners reported a major change in the background of children attending the day nursery in the previous two years, from mainly Black African Caribbean origin children including those of mixed parentage, and White British heritage children – to a high intake of asylum-seeking or refugee children of North African and Arabic speaking (usually Muslim) children. The different ethnic profiles of the children are presented in Table 7.1.

Table 7.1. The nursery children's ethnic backgrounds

Number of children	Ethnic background	Religious background
3	Moroccan heritage	Muslim
2	Sudanese heritage	Muslim
2	Somalia heritage	Muslim
2	Lebanese heritage	Muslim
2	Egyptian heritage	Muslim
6	Black African Caribbean	Christian
5	White British	Christian
2	Mixed parentage (Black British fathers and White British mothers)	Christian
3	Mixed parentage (siblings with an Afghan father and White British mother)	Muslim

Description of the Observed Practitioners, Their Professional Roles and Their Ethnic Backgrounds

A total of 11 full-time female practitioners on site at the local authority day nursery were observed and videoed during four continuous weeks of the participant observation. Some of the practitioners had been permanent staff of the local authority before the day nursery was tendered to a private agency five years previously.

Table 7.2 lists the practitioners according to the order in which the group rooms and non-group room practitioners were observed. It also provides the practitioners' self-defined ethnic identity backgrounds.

Table 7.2. The ethnicity of the 11 practitioners observed

Practitioners and their location in the day nursery	Self-defined ethnic background
Practitioner 1: The sole key practitioner in the preschool group room	Black, African-Caribbean (Jamaican)
Practitioner 2: One of two practitioners in the blue group room	White British, (Irish origin)
Practitioner 3: The only unqualified practitioner (in training) who floats between the preschool group room and the blue group room	Caribbean Jamaican
Practitioner 4: One of two practitioners in the blue group room	Indian (Kerela)
Practitioner 5: One of two practitioners in the green group room	Black African (Kenyan)
Practitioner 6: One of two practitioners in the green group room	Black African-Caribbean (Jamaican)
Practitioner 7: The Deputy manager	White English (Celtic)
Practitioner 8: The cook	Black African (Sierra Leonean)
Practitioner 9: The Assistant cook	Black African (Nigerian)
Practitioner 10: The Domestic cleaner	Filipino
Practitioner 11: Office administrator	White (Eastern Europe)

In making, in addition to the videotaping and the individual interviews, AS made field notes each day, repeatedly reminded herself of the three research questions guiding the study:

How do practitioners from multi ethnic backgrounds working in a multi-ethnic local authority day nursery perceive the Six Early Learning Goals of the Foundation Stage Curriculum?

How might the practitioners' perceptions influence the way in which they plan and implement the Foundation Stage Curriculum which affects children's learning?

What are the possible implications for children's learning and development including their self-esteem, self-concept and ethnic identity development in a multi-ethnic local authority day nursery?

In order to answer these key questions, AS developed the following headings during this process that enabled her to streamline and focus observations on the relevant areas. In addition to the time of day, duration of the observation and the observation setting, the following headings were also useful in structuring the analysis of the videoed participant observation in this chapter. AS noted from her discussions with the practitioners as well as reading the children's files and case review reports, that there was significant emphasis placed on planning, activities and interactions. AS adopted these key concepts as headings, and added them to the questions concerning development of self-concept, self-esteem and ethnic identity, the third investigative research question.

Plan: Whether a published written plan (short-term, medium-term or long-term) was visible and available in the group room setting and whether or not it was being followed and referred to by the practitioners (e.g. daily, weekly, monthly, three monthly, six monthly or yearly plans).

Activities: A description of the content of the activities being implemented by the practitioners, the explanations, rationale and justification provided for implementing activities, whether the activities were structured or unstructured, and their relevance to the six Early Learning Goals of the foundation stage curriculum.

Interactions: The types of interactions taking place, whether generated as a result of the activities being implemented by the practitioners or not e.g. adult to child interactions, child to adult interactions, adult to adult interactions, individual child to child or group interactions, verbal as well us non-verbal interactions.

Development of Self-Esteem and Ethnic Identity in the Preschoolers

Activities that practitioners consider to be of importance, activities given to these ideas in a multi-ethnic day nursery located in a multi-ethnic community, and whether or not practitioners focused on these areas generally or specifically were evaluated, as were the overall implications for the children's learning and development in this multi-ethnic local authority day nursery. These activities are exemplified in excerpts from the researcher's records, given below.

Our initial observations were made in the blue group room, where the two practitioners responsible for the early shift that day are based. None of the other two group rooms were open at that time in the day nursery, as practitioners took it in turns to work on early and late shifts. The practitioners covered the early shift from 7:45 AM to 4 PM and late shifts from 9:30 AM to 6:30 PM in their own group rooms. The blue group room is for children aged 2.5 years – 3.5 years of age. There are 13 children out of the 27 children in the nursery in the blue group room.

Practitioners Observed: Both Female qualified NNEB trained.
Ethnicity: 1White Irish and 1 Indian

Activities and Types of Interactions

Child: 'She's wearing a blue jumper with white circles like my mummy today'.

Practitioner: 'Is she? How many white circles can you see in her jumper?'

Child: '1, 2, 3, lots and lots and lots'.

Practitioner: 'Good boy ..., very clever boy. Everybody clap for ...'

Children's reactions: All 5 children clapped their hands enthusiastically with the little boy who had made the observation beaming with smiles. Following breakfast, the children played in the home corner, 3 on their own and other two played together.

One of the practitioners was attentive to answering the intercom to let the parents and practitioners in and out of the day nursery. The other practitioner's attention was divided between supervising the children in the room as they arrived with their parents, and reminding the parents as they left the blue group room to shut the door behind them for the children's safety. When the practitioners from the Pre-school group room and the Green group room arrived at 9:30 AM, they greeted their colleagues and then had the following dialogue with the children.

Practitioner A: *'Good morning children, how was your weekend?'*

Children's group response: *'Very good thank you'*

Practitioner B: *'My weekend was very good, I wonder whether you all had a good weekend?'*

Children's group response: *'Yes we did'*

Practitioner C: *'I am interested in what you all did children, what was interesting and which one you was naughty at home? Who is going to start now?'*

Children: The children laughed heartily and responded individually.

Child 1: *'My mummy said I was good, cos I ate all my food and didn't give it to the dog so I didn't get into any trouble'.*

Child 2: *'I went to see my nan and she gave me sweeties',*

Child 3: *'My mummy took me and my sister to the movies and we had popcorn',*

Child 4: *'I helped my dad to cook spaghetti and my mum said it was yummy'*

Child 5: *'My mummy and daddy took me shopping and bought me this new shoes, I like them, see'.*

Practitioner C: *'It sounds like you've all been very good over the weekend at home, are you all going to be good at nursery this week?'*
Children: *'oh yes we are ...'*

Practitioners' reaction to the involvement of the researcher. The practitioners were very surprised to see me. They each asked what I was doing at the nursery. They were surprised to learn from me that it was my first day as a research student there, and informed me that although they were expecting me they had not been notified of my start date.

Parents and carers. The non-fee paying parents and their children started to arrive shortly after 9:30 AM. Each parent would stay on the corridor, open the blue group room door for their child to enter then hug each other and say goodbye. Some parents said hello and goodbye to me and the practitioners, others smiled and waved goodbye. This was however in contrast to the fee paying parents who on arrival at 7:45 AM walked into the blue group room with their children, said hello to me and engaged in conversations with the practitioners while helping their children to take off their coats, hang the coats up, kiss their children, tell them when they would be collected, before saying goodbye to the children, me and the practitioners. They seemed more at ease with the practitioners and myself than the non-fee paying parents and carers.

Session 9:30 AM–9:50 AM.   The practitioners from the preschool group room and green group room organised their respective group room children and escorted them to their group rooms. Details of the preschool group were:

Number of key practitioners based in the preschool group room: 1.

Ethnicity of preschool group room practitioner: Black African Caribbean, gender, female

Number of children in the preschool group room: 8, 2 boys and 6 girls.

Ethnicity of the preschool group children: Lebanese, Somalian, Sudanese, Egyptian, Black African Caribbean, Mixed ethnicity:(mother English and father from Afghanistan) and White British.

Age of children: Three and half (3.5) years of age to just before their fifth (5) birthday.

The published planned activities for the preschool group room.   A schedule of the planned foundation stage curriculum activities was clearly displayed: however, it had expired, covering only the previous week. I was later informed that the local authority's inspection of the day nursery had taken place during the previous week, and activities were posted for that reason only. The practitioners' published schedule of planned activities, activities implemented, types of interactions and whether or not these related to the foundation stage curriculum, I had to elicit through a special enquiry.

Development of self-concept, self-esteem and ethnic identity activities. There were no specific activities observed or reported by the practitioners aimed at or intended for developing the children's self-concept, self-esteem and ethnic identity, apart from general warmth, praise, and the creation of a caring environment in which the children felt confident in expressing their opinions to the worker, and to one another.

End of day reflections with the practitioner. The practitioner commented, at the researcher's request, that she had not planned activities for developing the children's self-esteem and ethnic identity as she felt they were too young, and that children at this age would not understand differences in ethnicity, or indeed experience racism at the nursery or at home. She thought that children only had these negative experiences when they entered primary schools in' bad' communities.

I asked the practitioner whether the identity project on 'myself' is still being implemented in the preschool group room. She replied:

> Not really, because a lot of changes have taken place in this nursery. The families have changed you know, most of the Black and Mixed-race families have moved out since the high-rise council estates was pulled down and replaced by townhouses. The local authority has been housing refugee and asylum-seeking, large Muslim families in this area now. Their issues are complex and involves major language difficulties too so the need for the 'Myself' work with the children on their identity is less relevant now.

Further Observational Findings

Preschool group room practitioner on early shift. On the second day of the participant observations, the preschool group room practitioner 1, and (the unqualified practitioner) practitioner 3, who worked as a floater between the preschool group room and the blue room were on the early shift in the preschool group room. By 9:30, 7 children out of the 8 were in attendance. There was a noticeable change in the setup from the previous day. The activities set out were distinctively, and were different from those of the previous day. There were brand-new musical instruments on display, with corresponding posters on the walls, special toys and reading materials on display that morning. The activities seemed focused on specific aspects of the Early Learning Goals, of the Foundation Stage Curriculum (2000).

The children were clearly excited but were told by both practitioners not to touch or play with the activities on display. Practitioner 3 asked the children to wait for her instructions. One of the children asked: ... *When can we play with these new toys please?'* Before either of the practitioners could respond to the child, the deputy manager entered the preschool

147

group room and informed them of a shortage of staff in the other two group rooms due to practitioners calling in sick that morning. The children just turning 3.5 years of age from the blue group room were brought into the preschool group room to enable the blue and green group room children to be combined into one group room to accommodate the staff shortage.

In addition she explained to me that although practitioner 3 in training on the NVQ level II course at college, and was being formally assessed by her college tutor that morning in the preschool group room, these changes were beyond her control and had to be accommodated. There were noticeable tense and anxious expressions on the faces of both practitioners in the preschool group room and unease in the body language and behaviour of both practitioners. especially practitioner 3 whose assessor was then present in the preschool group room and waiting to start a planned formal assessment.

Practitioner 1 was required to take a back seat in the preschool group room while practitioner 3 took the lead in the activities with the children in the preschool group room during her assessment. Practitioner 1 had to remain in the preschool group room throughout the assessment in a supervisory role. She explained to me that the children cannot be left on their own with an unqualified practitioner for any lengthy period of time, except to take children to the toilet.

I requested and was granted verbal permission by the NVQ College assessor and practitioner 3 to videotape the activities. The agreement was that I would not show the face of the NVQ assessor from the community college in any viewing of the video tape outside of the day nursery.

Practitioner 3 had put out specific planned activities for her assessment. These included musical instruments for the children to explore and play with in her assessment session. She also put out books and carried out a role-play activity involving shopping for books, as well as a painting session with the children.

The addition of children from the blue group room aged 3.5 years was clearly not planned for. It became necessary for practitioner 3 to accommodate and to simultaneously involve more children in other activities in the preschool group room. When the assessment came to an end, I asked clarifying questions of the assessor regarding the criteria and expectations of the assessment. The assessor explained: 'Although specific tasks and goals had been earmarked to be completed, given the unpredictable nature of working with preschool age children in day nurseries, the expectation is that the trainee practitioner being assessed would make reasonable adjustments *to the activities when the number of children increase or decrease during any assessment. This is part and parcel of working in day nurseries'.*

Practitioner 3 left the group room to get another practitioner from the blue group room to relieve her before leaving the preschool group room with her assessor for a private discussion in the staff room on the outcome of her assessment. It was later announced that she had passed the assessment.

As practitioner 1 left for her lunch break she turned to the children and said: 'Are you going to be nice for... now? Don't give her a rough time okay? I'm going for my lunch break when I come back if the weather is good we will go outside to play on the slides okay?'

Children: responded in unison: 'We are always good....'

Practitioner 1: Shook her head smiling and muttered: 'That's alright then, you cheeky lot.'

Activities and Interactions

The deputy manager did not look at the bulletin board for the scheduled planned activities. A second practitioner (temporary agency staff) in the preschool group room was busy attending to the children who were being collected by their parents as they only attend half-days. She however returned to the blue group room when the number of children remaining in the preschool group room returned to 8 as the ratio for practitioner to children aged 3 to 5 years is 8 children. The deputy manager was left on her own with the eight children in the preschool group (8 is the maximum number of children aged 3 to 5 years that can be supervised in a group room by one nursery practitioner). She encouraged the children to play in the home and book corners, in unstructured activities which she announced and described as *'this is your free play time, okay.'*

She then sat down behind a table in a central location in the group room where she could see all the children playing in different parts of the room. She went through her pile of paperwork, looking up intermittently to see what the children were doing. When they were being boisterous, she would ask them to slow down and be gentle with each other, or intervene by physically separating them.

Some of the children played by themselves, others did so in pairs concentrating on activities in the home corner, such as dressing up, role playing doctors and nurses, and being the teacher. Other children moved from activity to activity on their own, without exploring any of the activities for any length of time. A couple of the children wandered around aimlessly and were ignored by their peers when they tried to join them in their play activities. The deputy manager was in the preschool group room for a little over an hour: then practitioner 1 returned, after her lunch break. The deputy manager said goodbye to the children and left the preschool group room.

Return from the playground activities to the preschool group room activities. When the outside temperature began to drop and some of the children began to cough, sneeze and required their noses to be wiped by the practitioners, the preschool group practitioner announced that it was time for the preschool group children to return indoors to the warmth of the preschool group room. They were escorted upstairs, took off their jackets and coats and then made themselves comfortable in the home corner in the group room.

Practitioner 3 encouraged the children to make links to food items that they were familiar with which involved baking. The children named bread, cookies, pies and pasties. Practitioner 3 explained to them that while bread and the other food items would need to go into the oven to be baked, this particular type of play dough does not require any cooking. She also cautioned the children not to eat the play dough because it was not cooked, and would lead to them having upset stomachs. The children picked up the play dough to smell it, and the practitioner again reminded them not to eat it.

The children were asked by practitioner 3 to move to the mathematical corner in the room to look at the charts on the wall and to choose from the different shapes and colours the ones they would want to cut their play dough into. Each child was assisted with the cutting of their play dough using the shape cutters. These were placed on trays and put away for drying so that they would be painted the following day. At the end of the activity the children washed and dried their hands in a large bowl of water in the room. Practitioner 3 explained to me that this was necessary to prevent the children from eating the remnant uncooked play dough stuck on their fingers.

End of activity and interactions: reflections with practitioner 3. I asked practitioner 3 why she had moved the children to the mathematical corner and asked them to choose the different shapes and colours for their play dough. She told me the following:

Because these children know the different colours and shapes already. The colours they know very well but sometimes they get some of the shapes mixed up. For example they confuse rectangle and square, round and oblong and star and triangle. So if they are in front of the charts and have forgotten the name of the shape, they can point to the shape that they want and I can then call out the name of the shape which the child then repeats. This helps them to remember. Sometimes a child may not remember the name of the shape but the other children will say what the shape or colour is that is why I take them together as a group to explore the shapes and colours. These children know the difference between red and blue, black and white, round and square and so on. They recognise things that look the same and things that look different, including hair colour and skin colour. They will say black and white people but when you talk to them about the real colour they will talk about brown skin and pink skin. That's why I did it that way to help them out in case they have forgotten the names of the shapes or colours.

I noted from practitioner 3 who also self-identifies as Black Caribbean Jamaican that her explanations, perceptions and implementation of the foundation stage curriculum through her choice of activities and interactions with the children, were very different from that of practitioner 1. Practitioner 3 in fact acknowledged that children in the preschool group room have the knowledge and ability to recognise differences in colours and shapes, as well as skin colour. This was in line with Van Ausdale and Feagin's (2002) observations that nursery age children are aware of racial differences at that age.

Although both practitioners were Black and from the same ethnic and cultural background, their perceptions on child development and the Implementation of The Foundation Stage Curriculum (2000) appeared to be very different.

Making of clocks: activity and interactions. Practitioner 1 took the remaining five children to the 'mathematical and the telling the time' corner at the other side of the room where a table had been set up by practitioner 3 with white cardboard like paper, pairs of children's safety scissors for cutting, crayons and felt pens.

Practitioner 1 invited each child individually to sit opposite her at the table and to look at the clock on the wall behind her. She then gave the child the white cardboard-like paper and asked them to choose a pen or crayon and draw a round big circle on it. She then gave scissors to the child to cut around the circle. Each child was encouraged to draw a small circle in the middle of the large circle. Each wrote their name at the back of the clock drawing. All five children sat opposite the practitioner facing the clock on the wall with the practitioner going through the numbers on the face of the clock with the children starting from 1 to 12.

Reactions to a potential crisis. The deputy manager hurriedly returned to the preschool group room and informed the practitioners not to allow any of the children to enter the upstairs toilet area as it was flooded. The children must be sent to the downstairs toilet, but the downstairs staff must be told when a child was being sent downstairs so that they could keep an eye on the child for safety reasons.

She reported:

When I got back to the office downstairs after relieving another staff for her lunch break, I found water dripping from the office ceiling onto my desk. When I came upstairs and looked in the toilet which is directly over the office I found the sink stuffed with tissue paper and the taps left running. The children in the blue group room had done this. I now have to mop the upstairs children's toilet as everything is swimming in water. This is not the first time that this has happened either.

The deputy manager went on to narrate the following:

Some staff believe in pushing children into exploring and doing things for themselves. They believe that through exposure and experimenting on their own, children will acquire the necessary skills that they need to develop. I don't think that it works because they are underdeveloped physically, mentally, socially and emotionally and in need of guidance and support. They can turn the tap on but can't turn it off because they haven't developed the grip and strength to turn the taps off. So they wash their hands, wipe their hands, drop the tissue in the sink and leave the tap running. They don't see that they have done anything wrong so when they return to the group room they don't tell anyone that the tap needs to be turned off. We then have flooding and this is not the first time it has happened. It's part of the belief that some nursery officers generally have. You see some nursery officers strongly believe that children should be left to take the lead to explore things in the world. This includes some permanent staff and some agency staff too. It is difficult to get them to change their belief system, it's an on-going battle.

Snack time. The practitioners gathered the children around the table and served them fruits, biscuits, milk and cold drinks. Afterwards the cups and plates were returned to the trolley for collection from the preschool group room, by the kitchen assistant. When the parents started to arrive to take their children home shortly after 3 PM, the practitioners got the children to sit in a circle. They sang familiar songs e.g. twinkle twinkle little star, wind the bobbin up, while waiting for their parent.

Foundation stage curriculum & 6 Early Learning Goals implemented through activities:

All aspects of the early learning goals to a greater or less degrees were implemented through the observed practitioners' activities and interactions in terms of personal, social and emotional development; communication, language and literacy; mathematical development; knowledge and understanding of the world; physical development; creative development.

AS observed (in her notes) that there was a wide range of activities, which in turn generated interactions involving adult to child, child to adult, child to child, adult to group of children and adult to adult. But there were no observed or reported activities planned specifically for developing the children's ethnic self-concept, apart from affectionate feedback appropriate for each child, in ways which would likely bolster their personal self-confidence.

End of day reflections with practitioner 1. In discussion with practitioner 1, I asked whether the identity programme on 'myself' was still part of the foundation stage curriculum at the nursery. She told me:

> Yes we are supposed to be doing the identity work on "myself" with the preschool group children but as you can see I am the only staff in this group room with the children and I am the key nursery officer for all eight children. There is lot of staff shortage due to sickness, people taking time off to do their written work at home and managers leaving. I have to do a lot of report writing on each of the children and I don't get the time to do so here. It is very difficult to do the identity work with the children properly especially involving the parents because it takes a lot of time. It is especially difficult now because things have changed and a lot of the parents don't speak English or understand English properly so the work is extra hard, plus I don't have the time to do it with them. We don't have a teacher at the nursery or any input from a teacher either. The other thing is that I don't really think that these children experience racism at this age you know. Not when they are at this nursery anyway, may be when they are much older and attend big school and mix with the big kids. I think they are too young to understand these things, that's my experience you know.

I asked practitioner 1 whether the children at age 3 to 5 years understand whether they are boys or girls. Her answer was: *'Yes'.*

I then asked whether gender was part of their identity.

Her answer was: *'Yes, but I never thought of identity like that before you know.'*

Day 3 of week 1 in the preschool group room. There were 6 out of the 8 children in attendance in the preschool group room. 2 children were absent with no notice from the parents to the practitioner or the administrator for their absence.

The practitioner set up tables in a section of the group room facing a mirror (plastic safety mirror) on the wall. She organised the children at the next table with multicultural books and pictures to look at. She informed the children that they were going to draw pictures of themselves and that they would be called to sit beside her at another table to do the drawing of themselves. She announced: *'We will be doing "Myself"'.*

On her table she had a pile of blank skin-tone drawing papers, a round plastic open top container full of skin-tone crayons, and colouring crayons for the eyes in a separate container. The children were individually called by name and they took it in turns to sit on a chair opposite the practitioner at her table. She then gave the child the skin tone paper, asked the child to walk to the full-size mirror on the wall and asked the child to look closely in the mirror for the following. She ask each child;

'What is the colour of your hair?'
'What is the colour of your eyes?'
'How many eyes do you have?'
'How many noses do you have?'
'How many lips do you have?'
'How many ears do you have?'

If the child was able to answer the questions correctly she would move on to the next question. If they were unable to do so, she would repeat the same question and prompt the child by asking and gesturing with her fingers for example:

'Do you see one or two eyes? Do you see one or two noses on your face?'

When the child provided the correct answers she would ask the child to join her at the table and encourage the child to draw him or herself on the skin tone paper including those physical features.

She would then ask the child: *'What colour is your skin?'*

The darker complexioned children e.g. Black African: Somalian answered: 'Brown.'

The lighter complexioned children e.g. Lebanese, Sudanese, Egyptian, and children of Mixed parentage e.g. (mother English and father from Afghanistan) and the White British children answered: 'White'.

The practitioner did not clarify, explore or expand on the children's answers (which should be an important aspect of the identity programme e.g talking about the colour white and comparing it to skin tone colour which is not white, as also is talking about ethnicity and terminology used in describing individuals with different skin tones such as Black people and White people). She chose a number of skin tone crayons from the container, and put them next to the child's arm on the table and asked the child which skin tone crayon looked the same as their colour. The child would then point at the skin tone crayon that they see as similar to their skin colour. She would then ask the child the name of the crayon colour and the child would respond by describing the colour as either *pink, light brown*, or *brown*.

None of the children said *White* or *Black* when naming their skin tone crayons. The practitioner did not explore with any of the children why they had described themselves as Brown or White earlier. She then asked each child to draw themselves with that colour crayon, then shade their eyes with the choice of crayon, their hair with the appropriate colour and colour their lips with the appropriate colour crayon. Some children with brown eyes shaded their eyes blue.

Although practitioner 1 did not address the fact that child with brown eyes who had shaded her eyes blue, the group of children watching began to observe amongst themselves that the child did not have blue eyes. She continued by sending the child back to look in the mirror, asking the child the following questions:

'How many arms do you have?'
'How many fingers do you have on one hand?'
'How many hands do you have altogether?'
'How many fingers do you have on both hands?'
'How many legs do you have?'
'How many feet do you have?'
'How many toes do you have on each foot?'
'How many toes do you have on both feet?'

She would follow this repertoire until the child was able to provide the correct answer. The child would then join her at the table and continue with the drawing. Some children drew stick pictures of themselves with a round head, spiky hair, stick fingers and toes and she would help them by reminding them to count the number of fingers and toes physically before drawing those parts. Other children drew non-stick, rounded pictures of themselves with circular eyes, curved eyebrows, rounded arms, legs with rounded fingers and toes. These children would then shade in the colour of their various body parts appropriately with the necessary prompts from the practitioner. At the end of each child's activity, the practitioner would ask the child to write their name at the bottom of the picture. All the children were able to write their names with guidance except one boy. After several failed attempts, the practitioner wrote the child's name on the back of his drawing. The practitioner praised each child for completing the activity before taking the completed drawings from them.

The children's interactions with each other and the practitioner during the individualised activities. When the 6 preschool group children were waiting their turn to draw the picture of themselves, they were initially quite talkative amongst themselves. However as the practitioner began the individual activity with the first child at the table and invited the child to stand in front of the mirror and to respond to her questions, the remaining 5 children began to take keen interest in the activity and interaction between the practitioner and that child.

Some children became impatient and blurted out the correct answers to the questions when q child was either slow in providing the right answers, or made mistakes in answering the questions while looking in the mirror. A couple of the children spontaneously offered suggestions while others made derogatory remarks such as: *'Everybody has two eyes silly'*, *'Nobody has two noses stupid'*, *'You don't have blue eyes, your eyes are black, you silly billy'*.

Other children laughed aloud which sometimes had a negative effect on a child in front of the mirror, who appeared to be nervous and embarrassed. The practitioner's immediate response was to pause the activity with the child in front of the mirror, while she addressed the group of children at the next table by telling them *'be quiet'*. When they did not respond appropriately she raise the tone of her voice slightly and with a stern voice asked them by name: *'... Are you now the teacher?'* When the disruption continued, she singled out those individual children by name and said: *'Don't be rude or unkind to other children... It is not nice or polite, you know that don't you?'*

When two of the girls consistently interrupted and made fun of other individual children in front of the mirror, the practitioner told them: *'... One more comment like that from you and you will lose your turn. You will not be able to join in the activity if this disruption continues you know'.* This had the desired positive effect as both girls immediately altered their negative attitudes and disruptive behaviours. However observable issues such as the colour of eyes were not addressed by the practitioner with any of the children.

All 6 children in the preschool group room were asked at the end of the activities how they felt about their drawings, what they had learned and how they had felt when criticised by the group. They were encouraged to say sorry to each other for being impatient and disruptive and to shake hands with each other which they did spontaneously and willingly. Following this activity, the children were told it was time for them to use the toilet one at a time and to wash their hands and get ready for lunch.

Structured activities, individual, adult child interactions and group peer interactions. After lunch the practitioner informed the children that it was raining heavily outside so they would not be able to play in the playground. The time would be used to discuss their individual drawings completed that morning. She informed the children that she would be inviting them individually to sit at the table next to her while the rest of the children sat on the mat around the table. She reminded them it would be important for them to listen carefully to each other's story about their drawing.

During the individual presentations, some children were able to describe what they were doing in their picture. The observing group of children contributed with comments such as: *'You did not colour your eyes black, your eyes are not really Brown'* or *'You didn't draw your curly hair'*

Others laughed at their peers' pictures and commented on whether their pictures had any resemblance to the child who drew the picture. It became very noisy and competitive with some children claiming that their picture was the best. The practitioner continued to invite individual children to sit beside her and to tell her the story about the picture that they had drawn of themselves.

When it was the turn of an articulate Black Somalian boy, the practitioner had the following dialogue with him:

Practitioner: 'It's your turn now M... tell me about your picture and what you were doing in your picture this morning'.

Child: 'There's something in my big belly squashing me. That's why my belly is big'

157

Practitioner: 'So M... What is inside your belly? I don't understand you?'

Child: 'A baby is playing in my belly'.

Practitioner: 'Really? Did you say you have a baby inside your belly? Do boys have babies in their bellies? It is not making any sense to me. Does it make sense to anyone? You have a baby in your tummy?'

The other children mainly, the girls' spontaneous reaction and interjections were: 'Only girls have babies in their tummies.'

Child: 'Not girls, only mums.'

Practitioner: 'That's true, boys don't have babies in their tummy do they? How come you said you have a baby in your belly?'

Child: 'I don't know. Now I don't have a baby in my tummy. But look at my eyes they are very big'

Practitioner: 'How come your eyes are so big?'

Child: 'Because I am staring'.

Practitioner: 'Why you staring? Who are you staring at with your really big eyes?'

Child: 'Oh, oh.'

Reaction from the other children: Laughter and general discussion about babies in women's tummies and why boys cannot have babies in their tummies.

Practitioner: 'Okay M... You can take your picture now to show to your mum when you go home today okay, good boy'.

The practitioner went through each drawing with the child who drew it and each child was given the opportunity to describe their drawn picture of themselves, and to talk through what they were doing in the picture. The rest of the children looking on, took keen interest in each other's picture and added their own comments to that of the practitioner's such as: *'It doesn't look like you'; 'Your eyes are not blue they are black'; 'My picture is nicer than your picture'.*

To these comments the practitioner would respond by saying: 'Everybody's picture is nice and each of you has drawn them the way they see themselves or how they like to be seen. Is that Okay?' Some of the children who were still not in agreement with the practitioner's statement, and continued to disagree with her. She did not pursue this and moved on to another child's drawing.

As the activity was coming to a close the practitioner noticed that a very quiet boy who speaks very little English did not have his drawing and had not discussed his drawing. She searched the cupboard until she found his drawing. She invited the boy to sit beside her at the table and to talk about his drawing. The boy had scribbled small zigzag strokes and faint circle marks on his paper and could not verbally articulate what he had drawn. The other children became impatient with him and began to ask him a lot of questions, with some children laughing at his picture. The practitioner noticed that the boy had become very silent with his head hanging down. She immediately told the children that their behaviour was not nice and instructed them to leave the table and to start tidying up which they did. She went through the child's picture with him on his own without an audience.

At the end of the activity the practitioner informed me that the session had been an eye opener for her as she had never asked the children to specifically draw themselves in this way. She said that the children were used to drawing whatever objects they wanted and only discussed the drawings with their friends in the room. She reflected on how stimulating the discussions had been and the interest it had generated among the rest of the group of children.

End of day reflections with practitioner 1.   I asked practitioner 1 about the critical comments that some of the children had made about individual children's drawings, their disagreement with her when she had tried to correct them and why she had not followed through with further explanations but had ignored their argument and moved on with the activities.

She said that children at that age (3.5 – 5 year olds) are not yet able to or capable of understanding certain concepts. It is therefore a futile exercise to continue arguing or explaining these concepts to them and that as they get older and enter school, their brain would develop at the right time, and they would be able to naturally understand these concepts. She said it would be premature to force these children to grasp these concepts.

She also talked about needing to do more individual work with the boy whose understanding of the English language, as well as his verbal expressive skills appeared to be very limited. She repeated the fact that she is the sole key practitioner for all 8 children in the preschool group room (meaning that she has responsibility for their progress, reviews, their individual and group plans as well as their reports), therefore she had to find ways of building the boy's confidence in class. She told me it is important that plans for his preparation for school takes place in his next review to enable him to get the necessary support and input before his fifth birthday when he leaves the day nursery and starts school. She would begin by talking to the boy's parents about his presentation and performance in tasks, carry out further direct observations and record these in his file for planning purposes. She would discuss the observations with her line manager for her input and suggestion. A decision would be made regarding how soon a review would be necessary. This might involve a request for an assessment by the speech and language therapist as well as the health visitor to clarify whether it is a language-only issue, a mild learning difficulty, a physical developmental delay, a combination of any of these, or something else.

Observation Findings Week 1: Day 4

The day nursery manager who had been off sick all week, returned to work that day. There were however continued staffing issues in the blue and green group rooms in the day nursery. Arrangements were made for agency staff to cover for the absent practitioners in both group rooms. There were 6 out of the 8 children in attendance in the preschool group room and therefore the staff shortage in the blue and green group rooms did not have an immediate impact on the preschool group room.

Proposed plan for the Foundation Stage Curriculum (2000) to be implemented. There was no written or published plan of the structured activities to implement, on the bulletin board for the practitioner, or in her absence for other practitioners to implement for the week. The last published plan on the bulletin board remained, but was out-dated.

During the children's free play in the home corner, some of the children got into a role-play involving shopping at a department store in a big mall. During this children initiated unstructured play activity, and a girl who had been absent from day nursery the previous day informed the group: 'I had a nice time yesterday shopping with my mum and dad at IKEA. My mum said it was better to go yesterday because there aren't many people shopping and we can get parking but on the weekend it is very busy and it takes a long time to shop and pay. I got new cups and plates for myself.'

Structured activities and interactions. The practitioner set up 2 tables in the mathematics corner for the children and involved them in what she described to them as the 'Tell the time' and 'Working with shapes and textures' activities. This was a continuation of the previous day's structured activities that had been organised by the unqualified practitioner. Children who had cut out the play dough shapes were encouraged to paint them while the children who had cut out the cardboard paper circles for their clocks also added the numbers to the face of the clock plus the minute and hour hands to the face of their clocks. At the end of this activity the two groups of children swapped places and worked on the other activity they had previously not worked on.

Interactions between practitioners and children. The practitioner paid individual attention to each child's work. For the three children completing the play dough activity, she discussed with them individually what colour they liked the best, to select a fruit with the same colour from the plastic fruit bowl, and to point out the shape on the board in the mathematics corner. She did a similar individual activity with the children who were working on their clocks by asking them to individually count from 1 to 12, to write these on a separate sheet of paper, and to use the clock on the wall to guide their work. She helped each child to fold the clock into four and write the number 12 at the centre top, the number 6 at the bottom opposite to the number 12, and to do the same with the numbers 3 and 9.

At the end of the activities she asked the children to think of songs that involve counting and involved them in a sing along session before tidy up time, going to the toilet and the routine washing of hands time. This was followed by setting up the table for lunch and having lunch. After lunch a practitioner from the blue group room relieved the practitioner for her lunch break. There was the routine handover dialogue between the two practitioners.

The children were told it was free play time and that they could choose whatever activity or equipment they wanted in the room. The practitioner checked on the children in the different parts of the room and then sat on a chair and went through some paperwork that she had brought with her. On the practitioner's return from lunch, she informed the children it was raining outside, therefore playing on the slides in the playground was not going to be possible, so they should continue with their free play. Some of the children went to the window to watch the rain.

Two of the practitioners and children from the blue group room joined the preschool group and announced that they were joining the preschool group for the rest of the afternoon. They also informed the children that the next day would be the manager's last day at the nursery as she was leaving. The blue group room was being prepared for the manager' s leaving party.

The children were excited and hugged each other. The practitioners involved the children in drawing and cutting of shapes for posters for the manager' s party for the next day. This was followed by a rehearsal session in which the children chose the songs they would like to sing at the party. The preschool group children asked if they could play the musical instruments they had been introduced to earlier on in the week, at the party and this was agreed to. There was a musical rehearsal session in which the blue group room children also joined in.

Each of the 3 practitioners present in the preschool group room interacted with and responded affectionately to all the children, and did not make a distinction between the preschool group children and the blue group room children.

Interactions between children.　The interactions between all the children were welcoming and amicable. Some of the preschool group children had younger siblings among the blue group room children who had joined them. The preschool group children generally presented as more protective of the younger children who had joined them. They played alongside each other nicely and gently,and with them and allowed them to join in activities. The younger children reciprocated well to hugs and kisses from the preschool group children. The afternoon activities ended with all the children sitting together on the rug for a sing along and storytelling time, during which the parents arrived and collected their children.

Observational Findings Week 1: Day 5

All the children from the blue and green group rooms joined the children in the preschool group room in the morning with their practitioners. The practitioners explained to the children that the blue group room was being prepared for the manager's leaving party scheduled to start at 2 PM. Some of the practitioners from the two group rooms were helping with organising the room, the decorations, food and drink items. The parents, local authority office staff, other day nursery and clinic staff had also been invited as the manager had worked at the nursery for decades and was well-known and liked in the community.

One of the practitioners from the green group room pulled some tables and chairs together and covered the tables with newspaper. She mixed some paint, brought out some brushes and sheets of white paper and invited the children to sit around the table with her. The green group room practitioner

5 then announced: *'I am going to be painting hands to make some posters for… leaving party this afternoon. Who wants their hands painted? All those who wants their hands painted come and sit beside me at this table and I will paint your hands for you okay'.* All the preschool group children sat at the table and had their hands painted and printed on the poster. Then the blue group children did the same. However when she invited the green group room children they each in turn refused to have their hands painted.

I noticed this and asked the practitioner why the children from her group room were refusing to have their hands painted. She responded:

> My children from the … room don't like messy stuff, they don't like to get their hands dirty at all and don't consider this painting of hands to be fun – that is why each of them say no when I called them to come and sit beside me and to paint their hands. I don't argue with them or insist on them having their hands painted either because they will not sit still and it would only upset them. But I still ask them and give them the opportunity to say no to me. If I'd ask them to come and let me tickle their hands or kiss their hands they would gladly have done so because it's not messy it's not wet. When they move to the … room at age 2.5 years they will gradually learn to play with different textures, water, warm and cold, wet and dry objects and they will gradually find that wet things such as paint next to their skin or palm is not yucky any more. I believe in exposing the children to different experiences through listening, observing and discussion. It is also important to explore things with children, explain things to children and to give them opportunities to test things out, that is how children in my view learn not just by only exploring things on their own. Children need adult guidance, explanations, support and encouragement to make them feel confident in themselves and to explore and ask questions as well as for help. Then they begin to feel good about themselves and who they are. They are then able to take this attitude to primary school and do well. I must add that the children here are mostly children in need. Some have emotional, language, speech, learning or developmental delays and require stimulation.

Practitioner 5 announced: *Now it's the turn of the children to paint the adults' hands for the party posters. Who wants to paint my hand, children?'* One of the preschool group children offered to paint practitioner 5's hand and did so. Practitioner 5 involved all the children in a discussion about the posters, talking about sizes of hands and fingers, counting their fingers and clapping their hands.

163

Adult and children's activities and interactions. The rest of the practitioners in the room refused to have their hands painted so the children played a game of tag and managed to tag practitioner 3 who they then invited to the table with all the other children clapping their hands and laughing out loud as she had her hand painted for the poster. There was a lot of excitement and laughter in the room when this activity was going on. This was followed by the children having their hands washed and dried in the room. The posters were signed and hung up to dry on pegs before being taken to the blue group room to be added to the presents for the manager. The tables were cleared by practitioner 5 who took a lead role in the preschool group room. All the children were seated around the table and served their morning hot drinks. This was followed by the green and blue room group children being taken by the practitioners to use the upstairs and downstairs toilets. The preschool group children went to the toilet on their own unsupervised. When all the children returned to the group room, practitioner 5 suggested activities for the children to be involved in and asked them to make a choice between drawing, putting together puzzles or choosing books from the book corner for her to read to them. The children chose the latter.

She then asked them if they wanted to sit on the rug or on chairs. The children shouted: *'on the rug'*. She then asked three children one from each group room to select a story book for her to read out loud to the whole group which they did. She made the reading fun, by showing them the pictures and asking them to guess what happens next. This gave some of the children who were familiar with the story books the opportunity to tell the story. Sometimes she teased them by saying: *'Are you sure that's what happened or are you just making it up?'*

Week 2: Participant Observation Findings in the Blue Group Room

The researcher (AS) was welcomed to the blue group room by Practitioner 2 (British, Irish origin) and by Practitioner 4 (British, Indian origin). AS was introduced to the 10 out of the 13 children registered in the Blue group room (aged 2.5 to 3.5 years) who were in attendance and was informed that some of the children were away from nursery that week as it was half term for their older siblings, therefore some parents tended to keep their nursery age children at home.

The prescribed adult to child ratio for this age was one practitioner to four children. As with the preschool group room, the published 'lesson' or activities plan on the bulletin board was out of date, and had not been replaced since the previous inspection. This was another clear example and evidence of how the nursery practitioners perceived, rather negatively, the Foundation Stage Curriculum impact on their implementation of the learning stage goals.

Activities and interactions. The activities each day were part of a regular routine. The day starts with circle time during which the children are actively encouraged to each choose a nursery song for the whole group to sing. These are usually songs involving gestures e.g. twinkle twinkle little star, wind the bobbin up, five little ducks etc. This is followed by small group activities. The children have their hot drink, and this is followed by one of the practitioners taking the children to the toilet while the other practitioner sets up the room for such activities as counting and colouring with the whole group of children. This is usually followed by small group activities in which the group is divided into two or three small groups depending on the number of children in attendance on the day. One group gets involved at a table in a cutting activity with practitioner 2, while practitioner 4 involved the other half of the group in writing activity at the other table.

Practitioner 2 informed me during the videoed participant observation that the cutting activity is 'physical development' which is an aspect of the foundation stage curriculum. The aim is to help the children to use their hands and fingers and to learn how to cut and write in small groups, while learning to take turns. She explained that these are activities that had begun when the children were downstairs in the green group room where the same activities were started but were carried out on a one-to-one basis. These activities were then followed by lunch after which some of the children who had recently moved upstairs are taken back downstairs to the green group room to have their afternoon nap (their parents have insisted that they continue to have their routine naps in the afternoons). They are gradually weaned from taking these naps. This I was informed is negotiated by the key practitioner for the child with the parents during the review meetings, as the parents need to make the necessary adjustments at home which involves a change in the timing of the child's meals and bedtimes at home.

In the afternoons the children are taken to the playground to interact with the older and younger children, on the slides. The practitioners explained that this activity encourages and helps the children to develop their social skills and language development. When they return to the group room they are taken to the toilet again, to wash their hands. If it's raining or too cold outside, then they are introduced to dry or wet activities involving, for example, different textures. These activities are initially carried out individually and gradually extended to small group activities. As the children settle in the blue group room, they are introduced to the home corner, book corner, puzzle corner and mathematical corner, where they are initially supervised and gradually encouraged to play and explore the activities on their own or in pairs.

Later in the afternoons they have tea followed by another trip to the toilet, after which they have another circle time, waiting for parents to arrive. The various activities are deliberately structured and aimed at extending the children's attention span. However on days 3 to 5, practitioner 1 from the preschool group room and practitioner 3 (the floater) for the preschool group room and blue group rooms were both reported 'off sick'. Practitioner 2 from the blue group room was asked to cover the preschool group room taking with her two of the older children from the blue group room, as there were only six children in attendance in the preschool group room. Practitioner 5 from the green group room was also off sick, on days 4 and 5.

Given the low level of staffing. the children (aged 1.5 to 2.5 years) from the green group room downstairs were brought upstairs to join the blue group room children for the three days, with additional temporary agency staff. The merging of the two group rooms had the effect of disrupting the routines, e.g. the green group room children needed to have their nap between 12:20 PM to 1:30 PM. The staff have to make the beds for them and settle them which is time-consuming. Some of the younger children also had medication and inhalers administered which have to be signed for by two qualified practitioners. Accidental injuries such as scratches which tend to occur when the older and younger children are put together in one group room all day, also have to be noted in the incident book by a practitioner present and co-signed by another practitioner.

On day 3, three of the children refused to eat their lunch of curried chicken and rice, and said they did not like it. One of the practitioners went to the kitchen and brought sandwiches for three children.

Given that the manager had left the nursery the previous Friday and had not been replaced, the staff shortage and the merging of the two group rooms greatly affected the routines in the blue group room. The younger children from the green group room seemed to need a lot of physical comforting from the practitioners. This in turn appeared to be also unsettling for some of the older children who fluctuated between being bored and being boisterous and attention seeking. There was a general lack of structure and individual attention for the children

As a result of practitioners' absence due to sickness it became difficult to observe or explore which areas of the foundation stage curriculum, if any, they felt able to implement, or to explore with them their perceptions on children's development at this stage.

Week 3: Participant Observations of the Green Group Room

AS joined the two practitioners in the green group room downstairs on the early shift. They were: Practitioner 5, Black African, Kenyan; and Practitioner 6, Black African-Caribbean, Jamaican. There were a total of 5 to 6 children (aged 1.5 years to 2.5 years) in attendance at nursery most of the week. The adult to child ratio was one practitioner to three children. Planned activities were posted on the bulletin board, with a plan for the week and a breakdown of activities for each day.

The green group room had been set up by the practitioners with colourful train set and a tent. They explained that the activities set out to cover the following areas of the foundation stage curriculum: physical activity, creativity, mathematics, language and communication, social and emotional development, and knowledge and understanding of the world. The practitioners explained that the ships in the tent were the mathematical aspects of the Six Early Learning Goals of the Foundation Stage Curriculum. Learning about the Fire Brigade was the 'knowledge and understanding of the world' aspect. The children playing in there together and learning to take turns was the 'social and emotional' aspect. Exploring the various activities was the 'creative' aspect. The children running around and chasing each other was the 'physical development' aspect!

On day two practitioner 5 was asked to cover the blue group room with an agency practitioner as practitioners 2 and 4 were away on a training course. This meant that practitioners 6 had to also work in the green group room with an agency practitioner, as two agency nursery practitioners are not expected to work on their own together with children who are not familiar with them.

For most days, the routines for the five or six children in the green group room were no different to those of the preschool and blue room group rooms. The only difference was that these children had their lunch slightly earlier, since the practitioners had to prepare them for their afternoon nap time. This involved making the beds, having their nappies changed, having to settle each individual child (by rubbing their backs) until they fell asleep. There were times when two of the children threw tantrums because they did not want to go to sleep and became defiant and disruptive. Then deputy manager had to physically assist the practitioners in settling the children.

Because these infants are in the early developmental stages, the practitioner's interactions are intense, since they are more related to the children's physical and biological needs e.g. hunger, toileting, playfulness, crying when hungry or to show discomfort. The practitioners anticipate as well as respond to the children's physical and emotional needs appropriately, including cuddling and comforting them.

The practitioners also attend to the children's skin care needs.   Practitioner 6 explained:

> We have to work very closely with the parents at this stage and around the children's care needs because they are the experts on the children. We need to take on board their cultural practices, the children's skin care needs e.g. creaming their bodies, combing or brushing their hair etc. We have to be sensitive to ethnic differences, religious practices, allergies and sleeping patterns. Children at this stage understand a lot of what we say to them even though the speech may not be clear or well-developed. They know whether their clothes are blue or pink and whether they are boys or girls. Our work with them is on a one-to-one basis so we need to find ways of reinforcing what is appropriate for the children taking into account the parents' wishes and feelings too.

Both practitioners raised the issue about the pending inspection due to be carried out by the commercial agency responsible for running the day nursery. They discussed the need for them to prepare the plan from Monday in the charts, and the rota for the changing of the children's nappies.

The practitioners expressed some concerns about the green group room children being moved to the blue group room so frequently due to shortage of staff, and both practitioners said they found it to be unsettling for the children as they did not adapt well to the constant room changes. In their view it would be more helpful if the blue group room children who are older were brought downstairs to join the green group room children who have set routines including sleep times and feel more comfortable in their well set-up and familiar group room.

In their view practitioners tended to take the easy way out by not providing consistent structured activities based on the Foundation stage curriculum for the children. The consensus belief that the nursery practitioners held was that (in the words of a practitioner): *'Pre-school age children should be left to explore their environment and learn from it through experimentation, and not be forced to follow structured routines or curriculum from the government'*

Individual and Group Interactions Between the 22 Multi-Ethnic Children At the Local Authority Day Nursery

Each of the three group rooms had a mixture of children from the following ethnic backgrounds (ethnicity defined by practitioners and parents/carers). These included children of Moroccan, Sudanese, Somalian, Lebanese, Egyptian, African-Caribbean (including some 'mixed heritage' children), and White British heritage.

Indoor interactions between children.   None of the children was observed (in the videotaped material, or by AS in her participant observation) to be treated differently, based on their ethnicity, by their peers in the preschool group room, the blue group room or in the green group room, or when they were put together with other group room children.

The children's friendships were observed to be based on emotional needs and temperaments rather than on ethnicity e.g. whether they liked to be leaders or followers, whether they are naturally boisterous and spontaneous or quiet, shy and reserved, whether when feeling distressed they felt able to seek attention or comforting through crying aloud, or putting on a sad face and walking to another child with outstretched open arms and physically seeking a cuddle or a hug.

The children with speech and language delay presented as quiet, played on their own and moved out of the way of the talkative and articulate children who often sat together chatting in pairs or in a group in the home corner during unstructured play activity sessions.

When the children were put together in a large group e.g. the green room group children and the blue group room children, the older children who speak the same dialect would ask the younger children questions e.g. in patois: what is wrong with them, why they were crying or what they wanted: then they informed the nursery practitioners in standard English. Some practitioners would respond by saying:' X. *Are you an interpreter now?'* And then they would then turn to the younger child and encourage them to speak in standard English to express their needs.

During week two of my participant observation sessions in the blue group room when the children from the green group room had joined them, the older children (3–3.5 year olds) were given paper and crayons to draw a variety of vegetables and were shown pictures of the vegetables. Most of the children chose to draw pictures of tomatoes. The children were keen on getting the shapes of their vegetables to be the same shape. However one three-year-old girl repeatedly asked for the purple crayon which she used for colouring her tomato. The practitioners when discussing the children's drawings with them, did not ask the child why she had coloured her tomato purple. I asked the child whether her drawing was that of a purple eggplant or tomato. She quickly informed me that it was a purple tomato because she wanted her tomato to be purple. Although all the other children's tomatoes were red, green and yellow, the same as in the pictures, there was no negative value attached to her drawing of a purple tomato.

In a later discussion with her key practitioner (White Irish) in the blue group room, she explained that the children experiment with different colours when drawing, even though they can tell the difference between the colours that they see in the pictures, and they can describe them correctly. She said:

> It is the adults that teach children that dark colours have lower value or status than pale or lighter colours, the same as in skin colour. That is why I did not ask the child why she had coloured her tomato purple. Even when they talk about blue eyes, green eyes and brown eyes, they do not see one as being superior to the others. Children at this age do not discriminate, only the grown-ups do. That is why I don't believe it is necessary for children under five to be restricted to a pre-school curriculum like the Foundation Stage Curriculum. They should be allowed at this age to explore and experiment and discover things for themselves.

Outdoor interactions between all children. All the children knew each other even though they were usually interacting in three separate group rooms. This is because the children from the different group rooms are taken outside by their group room practitioners to the playground on site at the day nursery around the same time to allow all the children to play, and learn to take turns on the slides and different outdoor equipment, and to socialize with each other.

Some of the older children preferred to play with the younger children and seem to have their favourite younger or older friends. These were never on the lines of ethnicity but rather seemed to be based on the lines of personality e.g. some older children liked to give cuddles to the younger children. There were also boisterous energetic younger children who liked to play roughly with older children so they would run around in the playground, chase each other, go on the swings, slides and tunnels to see who is the fastest. Other children would seek the attention of each other by walking up to them quietly and asking *'would you like to be my friend'.* They would then build sand castles together, kick ball together, or play in the outside big dollhouse together.

There were also younger and older children who did not seem to get along and would often fight over balls and different equipment. This also did not seem to be based on ethnicity but rather seemed to be linked to temperament,/ or wanting to be the leader or not wanting to share activities.

Overall there was no evidence to suggest that any of the children interacted with their peers based on their ethnicity and language, colour of eyes, hair or skin tone.

Week 4, Day 1: Participant Observation Findings in Kitchen with the Cook and Assistant Cook

Practitioner 8 is the cook – Black African, Sierra Leonean. Practitioner 9 is an assistant cook – Black African, Nigerian. Practitioners 8 and 9 welcomed me to the kitchen and gave me a uniform package containing an overall and hat to wear in the kitchen. Practitioner 8 started off by informing me of the following routines:

> We provide a mid-morning drink for all the children at 10 am but there's no counting of heads for this Ovaltine drink. At 10:30 am my assistant goes to the rooms to find out how many children i.e. in each room for lunch plus how many would be eating halal and how many eating vegetarian meals. This is in preparation for lunch. Lunch is served at 11:30 am to the green group room and at 11:45 am to the preschool and blue group room. Now hot food has to be served at 63°C to the children and cold food has to be served at 5°C to the children, that is salads and cold puddings. But there is no hotplate for keeping the food warm so I keep it warm in the oven after the food is cooked to ensure that the temperature is maintained for serving. There is a set menu that I follow it is typed up and it is for five weeks which I plan with the manager with room for adaptation in recognition of different cultural and religious festivals. I have to order special items for delivery a day ahead but I have problems with freezer space. I am very aware of the mixed ethnicity of the children at this nursery. I used to work in a school in this area for 6 to 7 years and never had to prepare halal food for the children. All we made were regular English dishes plus vegetarian meals which the Muslim children ate. Some of the Muslim children attending eat regular non-halal foods anyway. Now things are different we have to cater to the needs of the ethnic groups in the community.

I asked whether she is able to meet the needs of all the children. I also asked about an incident two weeks earlier in the blue group room when three children refused to eat the curried chicken and rice dish and had to be served sandwiches instead.

Practitioner 8 observed.

'This is a difficult and sensitive area because the parents of these children are very sensitive about the food we give the children. Some children are very picky so the parents only give them what they like to eat at home. They tell the key workers at the nursery about it and they also tell me about it. Sometimes the manager and the key workers would tell me when they are trying to work on introducing new foods to the children who are fussy eaters at home so that I can prepare these dishes for them. But since all these changes started taking place with the manager leaving and the deputy manager also leaving soon, there has been a lot of turmoil in this nursery. When staff are off sick information is not passed on to me to make adjustments especially when they put two group rooms together and the key workers are not there and nobody has time to check the files or check with me. The parents too have really changed. It used to be a lot of Black, Mixed- race and White families mainly attending this day nursery for generations. These parents would drop by and have a chat with me and the manager about the children if they are fussy eaters but now all this has changed and we have a lot of Muslim North African families whose children attend this nursery. They don't seem to feel comfortable in telling us about their likes and dislikes beforehand. We only hear about things when they make complaints to the head office. Sometimes they listen to the children and get things wrong. What I try doing these days is to go up myself and say hello to the children and ask them in the rooms jokingly whether they like my food and whether they eat all their food. I encourage them to tell me the things they don't like. When I'm around and I see the parents going by I open the kitchen door and say hello to them on the corridor. I also ask them for suggestions and recipes so that I can make their children happy. My belief is that children cannot learn when their stomach is empty and they are hungry. So I have a key role to play in this nursery to make sure that the children eat well and the parents and staff here are all happy with the food that I serve. It is very, very important. You see some of the new staff don't realise how important this is when you are dealing with people from different parts of the world you know'.

In the researcher's observation in all the 3 group rooms, *planning* emerged as a central issue. AS observed workers to be overwhelmed with other practical duties and responsibilities, which made systematic, forward planning very difficult. Indeed, some staff members said that they did not believe there was any value in developing weekly, monthly, three monthly or six monthly plans – only yearly plans, and admitted to only providing these plans for inspection purposes.

The understanding practitioners have of their roles in children's learning. Practitioners held different beliefs and perceptions regarding how children learn and whether or not children are aware of differences in ethnicity and identities. Furthermore, there was no consensus as to whether or not all areas of the Foundation stage curriculum should be implemented at the preschool stage. These differences, expressed to me by practitioners and managers, did not reflect their varying ethnicities, but were unique expressions of opinion. However, the findings did indicate disagreements on how child development was conceptualised by the practitioners.

Some practitioners' interpretation and implementation of the pre-school curriculum appeared to be influenced by their subscription to a model of development which stresses a natural unfolding of behaviour according to age. This inner-directed development is thought to unfold according to what Piaget (1995) described as a fairly pre-set course according to the child's age, into a series of universal stages. The other practitioners' perceptions, interpretation, delivery and implementation of the pre-school curriculum on the other hand appeared to be influenced by their subscription to a model which viewed the individuals as passive recipients of environmental influences, a tabula rasa or blank slate to be written on by experience. Much behaviour was therefore thought to be learned, and each child was perceived as unique because each child's life experience is unique.

The significance of these diverging conceptualisations of children's development might have implications for how practitioners perceive, interpret, deliver and implement the pre-school curriculum in relation to constructs such as 'race', identity and ethnicity in a multi-cultural pre-school curriculum. These conclusions need to be explored further in further day care settings, using various methodologies.

Practitioner absenteeism and its impact on children's learning. There was a high level of sick leave and absence on short notice. This often resulted in the amalgamation of two age groups of children in one group room where their learning as well as physical needs, including attention and supervision were not always adequately met or addressed. The younger children needed their nappies changed which took time and attention from individual practitioners in the group room, and physically settling the younger children during afternoon nap time. It was during the merger of the blue group room and green group room children due to staff' shortage that the 2 to 2.5 year old children from the green group room were allowed to use the toilet unsupervised, and left the tap running which flooded the upstairs toilet and the manager's office below.

Conclusions from the Nursery School Observation Study

The above findings (reflecting an underfunded staffing situation in a for-profit child care centre, contracted by an inner-city London Borough, because thcommercial provider offered the cheapest tender) do have implications for the planning of children's activities in achieving the Early Learning Goals. In this nursery, at least, those government imposed curriculum goals were only partially met, since their implementation often clashed with alternative goals, of providing a comforting and therapeutic environment for children from families undergoing stressful change. Fostering self-esteem and pride in personal ethnicity was both explicit and implicit in the goals of the nursery. It was clear to the researcher than the children loved being in the nursery, and were delighted at the individual attention they received, and the affectionate and stimulating care they received from the trained staff.

The conclusions that the researcher reached, after analysing the video-taped interactions is that despite the underfunding and the frequent absences of staff, there was an overall atmosphere of friendliness and goodwill in the nursery, despite the often day-to-day chaos of groups doubling in size, overflowing toilets, puzzled parents, children speaking little English: despite all of this the children were manifesting spontaneous friendships across ethnic and racial lines. "Colour of skin" or particular physical appearance mattered little to them: their world really was a rainbow world, one full of wonder and things to discover. The government-imposed learning goals didn't seem to interfere with the joyful wonder of these young Britons.

It is interesting to compare these conclusions with those of Holmes (1995), from an American study by Robyn Holmes, whofor her doctoral research, joined in the interactions in several ethnically-mixed kindergarten classes (ages 5 to 6), asking children questions about "friendship". She concluded:

The children's ability and willingness to offer solutions for racial harmony reflect the general climate of racial attitudes and beliefs observed in all of the schools [i.e. they were conscious of inter-ethnic tensions and prejudice which prevailed in Los Angeles at that time] ... but the kindergarten children of this study exhibited little animosity or prejudice towards classmates from racial and ethnic outgroups. This finding appears to be in line with the developmental research suggesting that racial tensions increase generally with age ... Hence the racial cleavage that emerges in the latter elementary grades was not observed with these young children. (Holmes, 1995, p. 107)

It is salutary that very few intensive, observational studies of preschool childcare settings have been published, despite the potentially crucial importance of these centres in children's lives, and their cognitive, social and emotional development. We are reminded of Michael Rutter's *15,000 Hours* (the amount of time the average child spends in school from age five onwards) – and the mysterious phenomenon of the effective school. Our conclusions on the "5,000 hours" (the maximum time a child would spend in nursery schooling) are that nursery schooling can be highly effective, given the evidence from the observational study – despite the chronic underfunding of St. J's, and frequent, probably stress-related, staff absences. All of the workers we observed showed professional dedication and skill, warmth and love for the children, and fostered their emotional development (and implicitly, their self-esteem development). They were laying the groundwork for the development of secure ethnic identities.

On this theme, we note with fascination the results of the study by Blatchford, Baines and Pellegrini (2003) which observed children's play in a multi-ethnic junior school in London. Repeated observations of 7 to 8 year olds over a year found that over time, while boys and girls tended to play separately, there was no separation in play activities by ethnicities: black and white played happily together, leading Peter Blatchford (a noted social psychologist) to advocate more studies of this type – but we have not been able to locate any more British studies of this kind.

Conclusions from the Interview Study

Alice Sawyerr's conclusions from the interviews with 11 front-line workers, and managers (see Sawyerr, 2017 for detailed transcripts) are:

Looking back, with some awe and nostalgia, at the findings of 'the experiment' which involved myself as the interacting stranger, the provoker of perspective, the recording angel (sic), I recall that some of the practitioners I interviewed, when asked directly about their beliefs and perceptions on the purpose of the day nurseries, as well as the Foundation Stage Curriculum (2000) provided answers (to which I had somewhat arrogantly assumed was an appropriate question) in ways which did confront my curiosity with common sense:

1. From these practitioners' perspectives, there needed to be an acceptance that most children, especially those who had been assessed as 'children in need' in local authority day nurseries required more caring and less teaching between the ages of three to five years, in order to prepare them for school.
2. These practitioners believed that the change from a child developmental curriculum to an outcome curriculum (through the requirement for all registered day nurseries to implement the mandatory Foundation Stage Curriculum with its 'Early Learning Goals'), had meant that they had to plan, assess and teach children skills, which they judged was inappropriate for many children.
3. Despite practitioners' attendance at curriculum planning training sessions, they continued to adhere to "common-sense and humanity", and were reluctant in accepting the new manipulations of nursery provision. They continued to believe that they were not trained to teach reading and writing skills, or to teach anything other than basic numeracy. Moreover, they did not think that teaching those subjects to such young children was necessary.
4. The operations manager (the off-site manager for the DCP commercial chain which profited from keeping costs as low as possible, including the failure to ensure stable coverage during staff sickness), the on-site manager, and the deputy manager, all accepted as particularly challenging, the implementation of the Foundation Stage Curriculum. Their objections were grounded to a greater degree in their professional training, than were the "common-sense" objections of the front-line workers. Nevertheless, the group room practitioners were very clear that the training sessions they had attended were unfocused and unhelpful in the areas of curriculum planning, or in helping them to understand and implement the early learning goals of the Foundation Stage

Curriculum in areas that they had never had training in, and which involved teaching, planning and assessment.

5. Ethnic Minority and White practitioners, including the preschool group practitioner who is Black and works on her own in the preschool group room, said that they did not believe or perceive children under the age of five to be cognitively capable of understanding or experiencing (and indeed, expressing) racist, cultural or ethnic stereotypes at this age – this was certainly what their "common sense" view of childhood told them, and it had certainly not been contradicted in any of their training modules.

6. These practitioners also believed that discrimination and racist attitudes evolved either at home, or when children attended primary school.

Arbitrary Closure of St. John's, and the Ending of the Initial Research Project

Following the collection of a large amount of video-recorded and interview data, AS concentrated for two months on transcribing and analysing this material, according to established methodologies (Heath et al., 2010). During this time the researcher learned (from her professional role in the NHS child and adolescent mental health clinic) that both the manager and her deputy at St. J's had resigned within a month of one another. The reasons for this were unclear. A temporary manager was appointed from elsewhere in the day care company running St. J's. This temporary manager declined to give me access to undertake further research. A new permanent manager was appointed (one of the existing staff at St. J's, but she quickly resigned, apparently because of internal tensions). For the next eight months the nursery was administered by a series of temporary managers, which hindered the planning of further research.

Then, when AS attempted to visit St. J's in her clinical role, she was astonished to find the building closed, with workmen making internal refurbishments or changes. The researcher found that most of the clinic-referred children had been placed in other nurseries run by the commercial chain, which had also absorbed some of the front-line workers. The NHS clinic had not been informed of this closure. The City's social work department were informed of the changes only when they were about to occur, and had not been consulted about the impact these changes might have on the welfare and case-planning for the children involved. Alice Sawyerr subsequently talked to some of these workers, and to parents and carers of children: they all reported in various degrees, surprise, distress, bewilderment, and bitterness at the sudden and arbitrary nature of the changes.

Soon afterwards, AS learned that St. J's had been leased to the national agency delivering Sure Start child care centres, allowing considerable profit to the Local Authority (according to documents sh obtained through freedom of information methods – see Sawyerr, 2017).

The Local Authority Documents: An Exercise in 'New-Speak'

The full text of the confidential documents AS obtained from the Council's archive some years after the events in question through a freedom of information request, are appended to Sawyerr (2017), which gives much fuller information on the data generated in the St. J's study. These Appendices contains two documents considered by the 'Cabinet Members' of the Social Services and the Education committees of the Local Authority in 2004–2005.

The first document was a plan for the delivery of all nursery provision in the City in the light of the national government's Sure Start children's centre initiatives. The *second document* was concerned with the specific grounds for closing St. J's, moving the children elsewhere, and renting the premises to the national government for a Sure Start centre, for the sum of £375,000 for the next five years.

The announcement of a large budget by New Labour for its Sure Start child centres was rolled out, following pilot work in 1999, and expanded through the White Paper *Every Child Matters* (HMG, 2003) into Sure Start centres for *all* children in certain deprived areas. These centres could be accessed by parents for child care from birth onwards until aged 3, and later until aged 5. Up to the end of the New Labour government, nearly a billion pounds a year had been allocated to Sure Start in England and Wales. *Sure Start* implied a new way in which 'children at risk' could be addressed by local authority social work departments. Instead of a case plan based on detailed health, welfare and educational assessments, Sure Start centres, established in any area in which 10 percent of more of the population fell into an ecologically-defined area of economic and social deprivation, were open to *all* families in the area, regardless of the family's individual circumstances (Sawyerr & Bagley, 2016).

In some Sure Start centres, social work and health services were integrated into programming, but this was by no means guaranteed, so the services offered across England and Wales were uneven in quality and quantity. Offering social support on a group, rather than on an individual basis meant that social work services were often delivered in a new way. And since enrolment of a young child in the local Sure Start centre was not compulsory, some families would inevitably have "fallen through" the social safety net (Sawyerr & Bagley, 2016).

The two documents (appended to Sawyerr, 2017) which the City Council used to justify the closing of St. J's are skilfully written, and truth, half-truth, and deceit are neatly woven together by anonymous writers, who impress one as honorary graduates of Orwell's Ministry of Truth. The first false assertion of the document was that Sure Start child care (SSCC) "would be better" for children needing intensive support in the early years, rather than the traditional model of clinical identification of the child's needs, and an individual programme plan which included a nursery place. The second false assertion was that all interested parties in health, educational and social services, and the parents of children in the nursery (St. J's) to be closed, had been informed and consulted beforehand, and their views considered. The third false assertion was that in addition to group meetings, parents of affected children had been given individual consultation and counselling.

On the closure of St. J's, carrying out some minor refurbishments, and then allowing occupancy by the national government SSCC agency, the City obtained a payment of £375,500 for a 5-year occupancy by the Sure Start national programme (The City retained the lease of the building, and now that national government is closing Sure Start centres across England, it is now let lucratively, as commercial offices). The two Documents in Sawyerr (2017) were aimed at persuading the City Cabinet Members on Social Service and Education committees to vote for the SSCC contract (in the event, it was 'nodded through' the full council meeting, without the press, apparently, noticing this).

Document 1 (1.3) declared: *"The re-letting of this contract now provides an opportunity to take a further step in the direction of a more inclusive approach. It builds on the development of services for parents such as family centre services, Sure Start children's centres and other services directed at tackling the difficulties that parents experience in caring for the children. The new services will support a more family focussed approach so that parents will receive support in addition to the day care provision for their children."* The "weasel words" here are "builds on" and "support a more family focussed approach". Both of these statements were untrue: SSCC replaced the model of case-centred, family-focussed child care with one which was voluntary and contained no social work support (other than through referral to existing statutory services). Sure Start in itself was an excellent concept, but *only* if it ran parallel to and in co-operation with existing social and health services. As an alternative programme it was likely to spread scarce resources too thinly, offering day care to many families who did not need such care for any economic or therapeutic reasons.

Document 1 continued (1.6): *"There is good evidence that many children in need who previously received day nursery places are more appropriately placed in universal nursery school provision. All children benefit from educational input and this has informed government's policy to provide nursery school provision for all 2-year olds, and the government plans to extend this [to older children]."* The document fails to reference any studies providing this "good evidence" (probably because no such evidence existed, certainly in our reading of the clinical and research literature). No evaluative studies of Sure Start were available when this document was written. It is merely pseudo academic-speak to support political decisions, without any verifiable supporting evidence. This was a policy proposal pretending to be evidence-based, when in fact no such evidence existed.

Document 1 declared that:

> 4.3 ... for most children in need, the traditional day nursery place did not significantly impact on the child care issues which led to a child being identified as a child in need in the first place. 4.4 There is now considerable evidence to show that effective integrated early years service have a more positive and long term impact on the lives of children and families than 'stand alone' day nursery provision. This leads to necessary and significant changes in day nursery service that will be provided under a new contract.

Let's analyse this Ministry of Truth new-speak.   The document asserts that "the traditional day nursery place did not significantly impact on the child care issues ...". No academic research was cited to support this view, since none existed. Moreover, the document did not consult the integrated teams working with the children placed in the St. J's nursery, who would have explained how inter-professional assessment and case planning did in fact aim to address the problems of children and their families. The calumny of this document is the assertion that: "There is now considerable evidence to show that effective integrated early years service have more positive and long-term impact ... than 'stand alone' day nursery provision." First of all there was not "considerable evidence" from the research literature to support this assertion (and no supporting evidence or references were cited): in fact, there was no evidence at all in the professional literature. The statement was only true in a circular fashion i.e. "effective services are effective". To assert that the St. J's children were 'standing alone' without psychological or social support was a denial of the truth, but if accepted would certainly justify the Cabinet Members in voting for this lucrative closure.

"6.2 It is estimated that in the future the Social and Community Services Department will need to commission ... a significant reduction in the number of places in the Day Nursery Service Contract ... Children-in-Need places should be less than 10% of all places." The document assumes (without evidence) that far fewer children will be individually assessed as being in need of therapeutic day care placement, this function being taken on increasingly by Sure Start. This would represent an additional, but uncosted, benefit to the City.

"8.1 The City Council in partnership with DCP will ensure that the needs of individual service users are met as far as possible, through a clear information strategy and consultation about their individual needs ... Each child will have a planned transition to another appropriate resource." This supposed "information strategy and consultation" if it ever existed, did not involve the child care centres and their managers, or the parents of the children they served, or the children's social workers, or their mental health referral sources. There was, according to the nursery staff we interviewed later "no planned transition".

"9.1 Finance. The total cost of Day Nurseries on 2004–2005 is £1,569,309, including the saving of £375,000 through the leasing of St.J's to Sure Start." Clearly, money was the driver in this obfuscating policy document.

Document 2 (Appended to Sawyerr, 2017)

"4.1.4 A needs analysis has been undertaken to identify the numbers of children who will be provided with a fully funded day nursery place in future. The number takes into account all those children who are assessed as experiencing significant harm and those at risk of harm." Whoever carried out this mysterious "needs analysis", did not consult the City's Social Work department, or the health services involved, or the nursery managers. The cryptic "needs analysis" did not produce any kind of written report, so far as we can discover.

"9.1 DCP [Day Care Programming] began a consultation at St. J's nursery in December 2003. The outcome of this was that staff feel positive about the move and are anxious to complete the process as soon as possible." We could find no one who recalled any such consultation. The order for closure came "like a bolt from the blue."

"9.2 Officers from Social and Community Services, and Educational Services met with staff and parents of children attending St. J's nursery on 15 January 2004. At this meeting the parents were reassured that their child's allocated nursery place would continue at an alternative nursery of their choice. They were also offered the opportunity to talk with a DCP's senior manager about their own circumstances on an individual basis." We could find no social worker, nursery manager or staff member, or parent, who had any recollection of such a meeting ever having occurred. No parent attended, and none was offered individual consultation.

We have to conclude that the documents presented to the City council's Cabinet Members to vote upon were a skilful concoction of invented facts, half-truths, and non-truths, and that saving a considerable amount of money was the principle driver. The precious children of St. J's were sold for 375,000 pieces of silver. This would be a valuable lesson learned in their ongoing master-slave relationship.

The Agents in the Critical Realist Matrix in the Nursery School Case Study (NSCS)

These agents are several-fold in nature:

First are the *national government controllers* of policy concerning nursery education, who devise, Gradgrind-like, learning goals with which the playfulness of innocent children must be infected. These children are absorbing public money, so the brave new world of nursery education must prepare them for subjugation, to a life of school examinations and controlled achievement, being prepared to take their place in the ranks of productive workers, the precariat, or of 'workers-in-waiting'.

Then there are the *absentee managers* who at the stroke of a pen, following an obscure vote, close the nursery knowing that this would bring a large financial reward for the City: the children are not freed because of this closure, their bonds of friendship and relationship are merely broken as they are reallocated to different holding pens. This brave new world of nursery education gives them a lesson in being fired, just as later, being excluded from school will teach them the lesson that they are expendable, and must join the reserve army of pupils.

Then are the *local managers* who in a semi-privatised system of day care balance resources, programme delivery and profit, must ensure that the costs of 'nursery education' do not exceed the profits to be made.

Next are the *onsite managers*, making sure that the nursery is an ordered and productive institution, that the children are socialized for calmness and co-operation, with inklings of the world of examinations and trials to come.

Then there are the *onsite workers*, a mixed ethnic bunch like the children they lovingly tend and control, trying to fulfil the tasks given to them from above in controlling, feeding and educating their charges. They are underpaid, undertrained, insecure, frequently sick, overtaxed because of the low worker-child ratio, and liable to become redundant.

Then there are *the parents*, struggling with debt, mental illness, cultural alienation as refugees whose children have been marked as needing special help and supervision in learning to conform. For them, Bhaskar's master-slave struggle has already been lost.

The children: oh, the children, full of hope and fear, of bounce and playfulness, witty and enquiring, at the threshold of life … of life on the Elgar Estate and all its turmoils. Soon they too wil be stopped and searched, and will be excluded from school, will become unemployed, will become bewildered and impoverished parents. Only a few will escape.

The researcher: yes, she too is an actor in the research matrix, briefly entering the lives of children and workers, having unknown effects.

The Dialectical Critical Realist (DCR) Model

We have experienced two problems in applying, *post hoc*, the DCR model. The first concerned the choosing of what elements from Roy Bhaskar's original formulations to use in constructing the analytical model. The second, was in knowing what research "facts" to place into the model, at what level, and how to make inferences about the dialectical process. The researcher must also establish the ontological basis, the realism of the case study. And she must also decide on the epistemological and value basis for *underlabouring*, which metaphorically is a form of 'music in the base line' which provides the moral basis for the case study.

It will be clear from earlier chapters that our underlabouring ethic is that of Child-Centred Humanism (CCH). This value principle asserts that every human institution, and every human action should be evaluated by the principle of "children first". That is, all institutions and actions should be moulded to serve the needs, interests and rights of children.

Easton (2010) urges that every critical realist case study must 'stand on its own', and refer to a universe of events which may however, have implications for other universes, or nations. Thus Sarra's (2011) critical realist account of

Aboriginal identity in an Australian community school has implications for both identity development in ethnic minorities in other parts of the world, and also for the methodology of studies of identity and belonging in other spheres. Following Easton (2011) we have constructed the following matrix of the Agents in the case study, whose roles and functions interact with each other, at different levels in the MELD analysis, within the dialectical matrix.

Object	Causal Powers	Condition	Events
Children	Attendance (or 'made to attend')	Playing, Learning, growing	Observed, recorded, planned for, removed
Workers	Organise, play with, lead children	Meeting children's needs	Enact case plans, fired, hired
Managers	Admission of children, plan, control	Control of centre	Choosing children, meeting parents & case workers,
Parents	Obeying social workers	Obedience to social values	Centre's closure, removal of children
Researcher	Attendance	Observing & recording	Viewing, recording, writing reports, making models
Bureaucrats	(With)holding funds, ordering syllabus	Control at local and national level	Close centre, move children
Society	Symbolic approval of the rituals of control	Approves, through 'democracy' of the system of control	Agents of social control of children outside of the centre

The structure and capitalist organisation of society is the reality of "absence", defined by Norrie (2011) as meaning "absence of being" which is the basic level of ontology that dialectical critical realism addresses, "the elimination of constraints and ills." This is the first level 1M, in the MELD schema. "Thus, 1M is the initial critical realist ground of non-identity, meaning irreducible, real difference in the world ... This is then radicalised by the 2E account of negativity, related to the totality of 3L, and submitted to the importance of praxis at 4D. It is the move to 2E that most directly implicates absence, for the move is constituted by introducing negativity into critical realism. Absence is the underlying concept that unifies the second edge that dialectical thinking adds to critical realism" (Norrie, 2011, p. 28).

At level 1, although children should be the centres of concern, they are "absent" in a variety of ritualised ways. In the St John's case study they are the products of the nursery factory whom society wishes both to control and profit from. Their true worth is recognized only by the frontline nursery workers, who belong to the same age and ethnic groups as the children's mothers. These workers were only recently children themselves. Soon, like the children they would be transported into new settings of subordination. The children's consciousness is one of puzzled negativity, for they (like their parents) cannot understand the systems of capital, bureaucracy and power that manipulate them. Alderson (2013) paints a picture of about-to-be-deported unaccompanied teenage refugees from Afghanistan, imprisoned without trial, in Britain: "They were to be returned like parcels, non-persons, illustrating 2E in absence, leaving and loss, negative experiences and relationships. In their non-status as citizens, they were 'helplessly' thrown into specific time-space-cause contexts that are overwhelmed by negative Power2" (p. 76). In Bhaskarian sociology, Level 2E in the four-fold MELD paradigm should be the beginning of hope, of realisation of how oppressive forces can be unmasked, how the master-slave domination may be unseated. In St. John's nursery, as with these Afghan minors, hope was dashed at this second level.

Older children may form a group consciousness, a pride in themselves as "Strong and Smart" (Sarra, 2011); adults may join the dialectic of political movement and dissent. "Movement and process in MELD 2E" in Alderson's (2013) account of DCR and childhood "relate to research processes as they weave through the interpersonal child-adult-relationships. Hermeneutic research attends to performance: how children present and manage their bodies, learn and practice healthy behaviours, talk about normality and comparisons with their peers' bodies, respond to minor illness and injury and social events ... However, in some studies, children's real embodied ontology can then seem to be lost within social performance" (p. 80). The "seeds of hope" which the dialectical process has sown in 2E so often fail to germinate, as the brightness and bounce of childhood is flattened by the transportation of children into the grey and barren fields of secondary education, and adulthood. This, we fear will be the case with the St. J's children. Where are they now?

In constructing this DCR case study, and looking for case examples in the work of Alderson (2013, 2016) in the world of childhood, we realised how frequently very young, sick or marginalised children fail without firm advocacy and help from pioneering adults, to develop consciousness of themselves in a dialectical process. The best example of "success" in this regard that we can find is Wilkinson's (2015) account of adolescents' consciousness-releasing within the metaphysic of Islam. Other things are happening in the world of older children. Willis (2004) found that the lads were still 'learning to labour' 25 years after his original study, but with middle class aspirations, and electronic toys. And in terms of Bourdieu's habitus, "bright" working class boys deny that they are working class and enjoy a state of false consciousness which Stahl (2013) calls "habitus disjunctures".

The third level of the critical realist MELD model is 3L *totality*, which refers to the interlinked structures which are concerned with childhood, and childhood policy. This includes schools and their curricula, the forcing of children to take frequent tests and examinations, the success or failure of government agencies to end child poverty, the failure to provide vocational education, and the failure to provide decent paying jobs for all young adults. Alderson (2016) refers to Maslow's (1968) account of movement of the body 'from nature to culture', a culture which (in child-centred humanism) should provide a rich field for the flowering of the person, a self-actualization.

Alderson (2016) gives numerous illustrations of how social structures connive with powerful interests of state and capital to prevent this from happening: *"DCR drives towards resolving problems and contradictions of both epistemology (ignorance, error) and also of practical ontology (injustice, constraints). Yet if 1M began with misunderstanding and mis-identitiers, and if interviews at 2E increased problems instead of negating them, then 3L analysis shows more clearly how many totalities in and between the social and the natural worlds are split and incomplete. This affects progress at 4D"* (Alderson, 2016, pp. 46–47). The paper we have written, reviewing inequality and exclusion in British social structures in the period 1968 to 2008 (Sawyerr & Bagley, 2016, Appendix A) attempts to address these many aspects of social structure which prevent the self-actualization of British youth. And of course, these structures will block the self-actualization of most, and probably all, of the St. John's children we have studied.

The fourth level in the MELD model is termed 4D, *critical reflection*, and is concerned with the flourishing, the self-actualization, the morphogenesis of individuals in the matrices of social structure: *"Transformative agency's emancipation aims for the free society where each individual's flourishing depends on everyone's flourishing. 4D works to overcome the false sense of the self as separate and isolated. We relate to the world and to other people through recognising what we share in common (Bhaskar, 2002b). The key questions concern identity (who am I?) and agency (what am I to do)"* (Alderson, 2016, p. 46). These crucial questions of "who am I" and "what am

I to do" are facing "our" children from St. John's, who are now young adults. It frustrates and saddens us that we are not able to advise them, or to advise children like them. As we wrote in another context in 2002: "To develop intimacy, to develop closeness of whatever kind, one has to be prepared to take chances and risk vulnerability" (Mason & Sawyerr, 2002, p. xix).

Applying the Critical Realist Model to the St. John's Nursery School Case Study

Here is Baskhar's (2008) *MELD Framework* applied to our Day Care case study.

M: Level 1M

The first moment, of non-identity, and becoming 'conscious' of reality. The *Agents* at this level are: The children of St. John's; their parents; the front-line workers; the managers; the stranger (AS); the referring care systems, of social work and mental health; the faceless bureaucrats ordering who shall be admitted and on what grounds, and when the nursery shall be removed from the children; the absent power-holders who order a "curriculum" for young children, who must pay by their results; and the economic system of capital which controls the level of social service expenditures through the local and national government's budgetary system.

The Actions: The voices of the most powerless, children, parents, front-line workers puzzling their way through the day; the worried managers, sensing that the bureaucracy is up to no good, their only power being to move to another post; the bureaucrats planning and effecting closure of St.J's through "false rhetoric", falsifying the way things really were, creating a "false consciousness" which enabled the profitable closure of St. J's.

E: Level 2E The second edge 'negativity', moving from absence, and the transition into intervention (Bhaskar, 2008) involves: "… absenting of contradictions, constraints, ills and untruths … leading to emergence, change and transition" Alderson, 2013, p. 30. This ideal was not achieved at St. J's. Children, parents and front-line workers remained 'slaves', the managers remained 'overseers' and the absent controllers remained hidden. When the 'slaves' were sold off, they were unable to complain, or gather together any rhetoric of protest. What was apparent however was that the children themselves were, through natural morphogenesis of interaction and friendship, creating and recreating one another as social beings, unaffected in any negative way by ethnicity and colour. To paraphrase Orwell's (1949) character Winston in the novel *Ninety Eighty-Four*: "If there is morphogenesis, it lies with the proles" – the under-workers, the bearers of natural morality and friendship, these yet uncorrupted beings.

L: Level 3L is the totality of social structure. The events surrounding St. J's show that the social structure and its powerful sub-systems were unmoved by the plight of those below them. It was firm, intact, hard, manipulative, and controlling. In an about-to-be-transformed or modified system, the subordinated agents would "know" who their oppressors were. In St. J's, in Elgar Estate, we found no evidence of this. The oppressed agents might, in Brechtian terms, know that "there is more to life than this", that things need not be this way. That, we guess, was all they knew.

D: Level 4D concerns praxis, self-transformative agency, *Power1*, and the dialectic that is "the pulse of freedom": in the case of the Elgar Estate this would involve the recognition by the agents, of the nature of their exploitation, seeking ways to change that system, or at least to avoid its impositions of power. "4D can be part of a recurring process (Bhaskar, 2000, p. 8–9) rather than an ending, and it urges a return to 1M to restart the MELD process with the more accurate, deeper insights that have been gained" (Alderson, 2016, p. 48). Perhaps children who later on went to the idealistic Sure Start centres would, in this model, enter a self-transformative process. But powerful negative forces of social structure had closed Sure Start in the City by 2015.[3]

England's social structure in 2017 presents young people with "Malign MELD" (Alderson, 2016, p. 46). "MELD aims towards benign creative freedom. Yet the MELD schema can also clarify perverse processes (Bhaskar, 2000, p. 8–9) in what could be called malign MELD, just as negative, coercive power is the shadow side of creative, emancipating power" (Alderson, 2016, p. 46). Chief amongst the malign agencies preventing human morphogenesis at the 4E level is the ideology that binds together the self-interested bodies of state power, and global capitalism's interests.

This pervasive, alienating ideology is transmitted inter-generationally through a variety of institutions, including schools and colleges. The form of the "masking tape" changes with technology, and cultural change (Willis, 2004). Paradoxically perhaps, critical realism as a theory of social structure can in the present case study, take us no further than 2E of MELD, consciousness within certain groups of oppressive and alienating sub-systems. At the structural level (3L) a powerful social system is able to manipulate ideas and ideologies, and manipulate certain groups to its electoral advantage.

Archer's (2003) morphogenesis, in our English case study takes place mainly at level 2E, and could involve sub-groups (e.g. green activists, progressive educationists, anti-war factions, religious groups) while having little impact on the 3L power structures except in winning minor concessions on policy, but leaving the structures of international capitalism intact.

The ideal world of 4M remains a distant dream. In this regard, as Norrie (2011) observes, DCR does not replace or contend with Marx's theories of class oppression, alienation and false consciousness. Underlabouring this process, humanising the struggles of power, must be a humanism that puts children's interests first in all of human interests and actions, even when overtly at least, they appear only indirectly to affect children. We can however, following T.H. Green's ideology, tolerate capitalist enterprise so long as it is transparent, moderate and guarantees the rights and welfare of the world's children.

Elgar Estate: A New Study?

Learning lessons from this case study, we offer the outline of a new study which would employ a critical realist model, initiated and evaluated over several years. We take the model from Sarra (2011) who over several years from a position of relative power (principal of a community school) initiated changes which made all of his Aboriginal pupils "strong and smart".

Firstly, we have learned that a proper DCR case study cannot be a one-person enterprise. It needs to be well-funded and long-term in nature to enable the employment of several workers: first of all, a social geographer would map the patterns of disadvantage of "King's Ward" in which the Elgar estate is sited. This mapping would use traditional models of social and behavioural ecology in showing where particular types of disadvantage clustered, in what types of housing, correlated with what types of event, such as child care referrals, delinquency and adult crime, and mental illness (which may co-occur in the same families, or individuals). This kind of mapping can lead to focussed interventions. It is pertinent to observe that the eminent social geographer and educator Alice Coleman in her *Utopia on Trial* (1990) used the Elgar Estate and its (then) tower blocks as evidence of malign town planning.

A Family Service Unit model (Starkey, 2002) could put extra resources into supporting families experiencing "generations of trouble". An ethnographer would also act independently as a community organiser, mobilising consciousness of the causes of disadvantage, and the morphogenesis of disadvantaged children, adolescents and adults. A youth worker would focus on the development of young people, including the gaining of pride in their ethnicities, religious and national origins. The primary and secondary schools serving King's Ward would receive extra resources (more teachers, in-house counsellors and social workers) so that there would be integration between school, social work and clinical services, and community action, as advocated by Williams and Pritchard (2004).

Students at secondary school would be screened for self-reported events of physical and sexual abuse, and offered individual counselling for low self-esteem and identity confusion (which is the theme of the empirical research reported in the next chapter of this book).

The research team would also act as an advocacy group with local and national agencies, fostering neighbourhood action committees on issues of concern. A project such as this needs a tough and enduring leader. It's the kind of project whose long-term funding might come from one of the voluntary foundations (e.g. Rowntree, Cadbury, Nuffield, Leverhulme).

CONCLUSIONS

The original purpose of this study was to build on earlier research in St. John's nursery in a deprived urban zone, the Elgar Estate in an inner London borough. In this earlier research AS had explored and tried to enhance ideas of ethnicity and identity in the mixed ethnic population of the nursery, many of whom had been placed in the day nursery by the City's social services, following the recommendations of health visitors, general practitioners, paediatricians. Some of the children were subsequently referred to the NHS Mental Health Service in which Alice Sawyerr was working, for assessment and therapeutic work. AS developed materials for the enhancement of ethnic identity which could be used in nurseries with multi-ethnic populations, and one of these was St. John's, in which AS began a video-recorded, observational study of interactions between nursery staff and the children. The first aim of was to see how the Early Learning goals of the government-led curriculum were being implemented. The second goal was to evaluate how interactions between staff and students, and between children themselves, reflected ideas and evaluations concerning ethnicity. AS also added to this qualitative design, interviewing 11 staff members and managers on these issues.

This was intended to be the beginning of a longer-term study. Analysis of the interactions did not indicate negative concepts of ethnicity on the part of staff, many of whom were themselves from ethnic minority groups. Nor were negative feelings about colour and ethnicity expressed by children in their everyday interactions. This could have reflected several factors: the negative opinions of ethnic perceptions and evaluations in young children could have been declining, and later research particularly that from America, has shown this to be so. Furthermore, St. J's nursery had already engaged in the programme of education designed by AS, concerning positive aspects of ethnicity. And the presence of AS in the nursery as a Black African woman may have influenced responses.

Both interviews and recorded interactions revealed tensions concerning the implementation of the government-imposed 'Early Learning Goals'. Staff complained that these were largely irrelevant, since they interfered with the care plans for individual children which addressed their individual emotional, behavioural and affective need. Their cognitive development as "young learners" was seen as secondary to these goals. The nursery did not have a trained kindergarten teacher on staff, and nursery-trained staff had not been trained as teachers in their professional training.

When AS attempted to continue with work at St. J's, she found that the nursery had been suddenly closed, and very little notice of this had been given to parents, children, and staff. We later discovered that the reason for this was that the City Council had contracted with the national Sure Start child care centre programme to take over the nursery, for a significant financial reward, closing the nursery for several months and arbitrarily ending therapeutic programming for the children. Documents obtained from the archives of the City Council showed that there was obfuscation and deceit in the writing of these documents (and in their interpretation by the City council), which alleged that consultation had been undertaken with parents and staff: but none of those AS contacted could recall any such consultation. The council documents moreover, fudged academic evidence, claiming that the Sure Start model was superior to the existing model of clinical referral. We argue that the two models should be complementary, rather than Sure Start eclipsing existing social service models.

We have attempted to construct a Critical Realist model for analysing these findings, using Marxian and Child-Centred Humanist assumptions. Our attempts to apply the DCR model were challenging, in that we were unable to move beyond the first two levels of Roy Bhaskar's four-level MELD hierarchy of the path to the fourth level, emancipation. It was clear that forces of social structure which served the interests of a bureaucratic, capitalist-oriented system had masked the nature of the alienation of the 'ordinary' world imposed on the parents (minority groups, refugees, poor whites) and the under-regarded world of nursery care.

We conclude therefore that a Critical Realist model for the morphogenesis of the Elgar Estate must be long-term, well-staffed, and well-funded and should actively engage in "consciousness-raising" of the residents, and active lobbying for them and with them in the political arena, as a means of confronting the "false consciousness" imposed upon their alienated condition.

NOTES

1. Appropriate ethical approval was obtained for this study, and full confidentiality for the children, workers and parents was assured.

2. The Department for Education Qualifications and Curriculum Authority (QCA) document (2000) specifies 10 early learning goals. The additional four are: Social skills development; Positive attitudes towards learning; Attention skills, and task persistence; Reading and writing. It appears from this guidance document that a nursery could choose whether to implement six or ten goals, according to the nature of the children served. In the case of StJ's, the emphasis on support for children from families experiencing difficulty meant that "learning goals" were often not emphasised, especially as no trained kindergarten teacher was employed.

3. On the closure of Sure Start centres, and the negative effects of such closure on children and families, see Torjeson (2016) and Sammons et al. (2015).

CHILD MALTREATMENT AND MENTAL HEALTH

Ethnicity, Child Abuse and Self-Esteem in English Adolescents

INTRODUCTION

The data-set analysed below stemmed from the collaboration of Dr. Kanka Mallick of Manchester Metropolitan University, and Professor Christopher Bagley of the Manchester Educational Research Network. These researchers had previously collaborated on a number of studies of self-esteem, ethnicity, and child sexual abuse (CSA) (Bagley & Mallick, 1995; 2000a, 2000b; Bagley et al., 2000). The findings of data collected in the school year of 2006–2007 were not analysed or published at that time, because Dr. Mallick was taken ill in 2006, and tragically died in December, 2007.[1]

Students in some of the schools took part in a qualitative study reported by Al-Refai and Bagley (2008) on the citizenship education curriculum, and participation in RE and PSHE classes by Muslim and Non-Muslim students. None of these latter findings are relevant for the present data analysis, apart from the conclusion that Muslim students generally had excellent adaptation to school and community roles.

The aim of the study presented here was to extend the previous work of Mallick and Bagley in English schools on levels of self-esteem, using the Rosenberg Self-Esteem Scale (RSES) and exploring further its validation, including ethnicity and some data on prior sexual and physical abuse in the data matrix, in order to replicate and extend Canadian and international work (Bagley et al., 2000). The measures completed by students aged 11 to 18 included the RSES, the self-completion Ontario Child Health Scales validated in England with children and adolescents with known psychiatric diagnoses (Pace et al., 1999), and an adaption of a measure of physical and sexual abuse used in Canadian work (Bagley, 1996a), and developed further by Dr. Dan Offord and colleagues at McMaster University, Ontario (MacMillan et al., 2001).

*British Research on Child Maltreatment, School-Based Harassment and
Assault, and Child Sexual Abuse and Its Implications for Mental Health and
Adjustment*

> There has been little research carried out in the United Kingdom aimed
> at providing a holistic explanation of the victim experiences of young
> people within the school and community environments. (Jackson
> et al., 2016, p. 343)

One of the purposes of the research was to examine, through self-report
measures completed by secondary school students, to what extent they had
experienced episodes of physical and sexual assault and abuse in various
settings, and what the clinical correlates of such experiences might be, in
terms of self-completed measures of self-esteem, and mental health. The
initial purpose of asking questions about physical and sexual harassment
and assault was to replicate the Canadian high school studies of Bagley and
colleagues (1995, 1997), which had shown the link between such events
and poorer mental health in female high school students (but not in males).

In the English replication (reported below), Mallick and Bagley had
aimed to extend the questions about the location of physical and sexual
maltreatment from the school environment into the wider community,
including abuse which might be home or family-centred. But for ethical
reasons, the researchers felt unable to ask specific questions about who
was responsible for the abuse. If the researchers had learned about within-
family abuse, they would have been morally and legally obliged to follow
this up with a formal report to the authorities, which was not possible within
the context of a population of high school students who were assured of
anonymity in the completion of group-administered questionnaires.

*Earlier British Research on Forms of Child Abuse, Its Incidence and Its
Long-Term Effects*

Compared with North America, the British literature on child maltreatment,
its nature, effects, treatment and prevention is relatively small. But the
published work is of good quality, and offers several avenues for further
research and intervention strategies. The first located study is that of Baker
and Duncan (1985) who reported findings from a brief question about sexual
assaults in childhood, included within a questionnaire enquiring about a
range of public opinion matters and private issues, in a national random
sample of 2,019 individuals: 12 per cent of women, and 8 percent of men

recalled such abusive events, but no further details were available. The next study of note comes from Scotland (Gillham et al., 1998). This research team examined a large data set of referrals for child maltreatment (physical abuse and neglect, and sexual abuse) in Glasgow in the early-1990s, measured against a backdrop of a sudden rise in unemployment. They found a clear link between a rise in abuse referrals, and a rise in unemployment, especially in traditionally low-income areas. This research is important, since it links to the ecological accounts of social and educational deprivation discussed in previous chapters. This "sub-cultural" effect also emerged in the English work of Coid et al. (2001) who in research with 1,207 women registered with general medical practices in London, found that those who in childhood had experienced combinations of physical and sexual abuse, were four times more likely than other women of similar age and social class background, to have been subject, as adults, to domestic violence, and/or rape in various settings.

In contrast, Oaksford and Frude (2001) studied 213 English female undergraduates, using questionnaires, and found that 28 (13%) had experienced various types of sexual abuse in their childhood or teenage years. They comment on the generally good mental health of this group, and the fact that they were successfully coping with tertiary education. This and other research shows that there can be "survivors" of even the grossest forms of abuse, provided that it is not combined with other forms of maltreatment. Thus in the large-scale follow-up of a large cohort of identified child victims of child sexual abuse (CSA) probably combined with other forms of abuse, in Britain, 12.4 percent had diagnosable psychiatric disorders, compared with 3.2 per cent of individually matched, non-abused controls (Spataro et al., 2004).

One disturbing feature of children and adolescents experiencing chronic chaos at home and witnessing family violence, substance abuse, and the physical and sexual assaults of others – as well as experiencing such assaults themselves, is that of *running from home* (Meltzer et al., 2012). These researchers examined the life-histories of a subsample of 2,247 individuals in the English Psychiatric Morbidity Survey, and reported that seven percent of this group had run from home before the age of 16 – the rate in girls was double that in boys. In this population of runaways, 45 percent had been physically maltreated prior to running, 25 per cent witnessed frequent family violence, and nine percent were subjected to sexual penetration. After running, both males and females were at high risk for suicidal behaviours, and of being drawn into the worlds of commercial sex, drug use, and drug-dealing.

The NSPCC Studies

The studies commissioned by the National Society for the Prevention of Cruelty to Children (NSPCC) between 1998 and 2009 are the most comprehensive available studies on the prevalence of child maltreatment, and the social contexts in which it takes place (May-Chahal & Cawson, 2005; Radford et al., 2011; Radford, 2013; Radford et al., 2013). The first NSPCC survey was of a random sample of 1,998 British adults aged 18–24. The second survey in 2009 was more ambitious and asked questions about prior events of abuse not only of young adults, but also of the parents and caretakers of some 4,000 children.

The comparison of the young adult samples of 1998 and 2008–2009 is instructive, since the same set of questions applied to large random samples of the British population at both points in time, clearly showed that the prevalence of various forms of physical abuse, physical and emotional neglect and sexual violence was *declining*, and this welcome movement was clear statistically significant. I reproduce some of these results below:

	Any physical violence		Any coercive sexual abuse	
	1998	2009	1998	2009
Males	13.4%	10.9%	3.7%	1.6%
Females	13.1%	9.0%	9.9%	8.5%
'Middle class'	11.5%	9.0%	5.7%	4.3%
'Working class'	18.2%	13.1%	10.2%	7.2%
2-parent family	10.2%	7.9%	5.3%	3.2%
Other/in care	15.7%	15.7%	12.7%	9.7%

Source: Radford et al. (2011)

This research shows that there is indeed a class bias in the experience of physical and sexual abuse, which also occurs with greater frequency in disorganized family settings. The small but statistically significant *decline* in the amount of sexual abuse between 1998 and 2009 might be due to greater media publicity about high-profile abusers (children knowing more about, and being able to avoid CSA), and greater awareness of teachers and other professionals, as well as the introduction of relevant teaching in schools about avoiding CSA. But that is speculation, and difficult to prove without more detailed questioning of respondents. According to NSPCC data, reports to police of child sexual abuse and exploitation had increased by a third from 2015 to 2016 (Bulman, 2017). This could reflect a greater awareness of the problem, with the increased ability of victims to report this exploitation being associated with a fall in the actual incidence. This requires further study, however.

Lorraine Radford and her team included a number of mental health measures in their 2009 survey of young adults, and reported, for example, a six-fold increase in suicidal ideas and self-harm in prior victims of CSA and other forms of abuse:

> There were strong associations between maltreatment, sexual abuse and physical violence with poorer emotional well-being, including self-harm and suicidal thoughts, demonstrating the need for prevention and earlier intervention to protect young people from harm. (p. 122)

'Poly-Victims' and the Possibility of Enduring Neurological Changes Caused by Child Maltreatment

The idea of children being victims of multiple types of abuse, and as a result are at much greater risk of adverse mental health problems was identified in the review by Finkelhor et al. (2007) who coined the term poly-victimization. This idea had also been developed by Bagley and Mallick (2000a, 2000b) in their Canadian longitudinal study of a cohort studied from birth to age 17. They identified several interacting predictors of poor mental health at age 17: developmental problems identified at birth (including CNS problems), emotional abuse of the child and/or physical abuse and/or sexual abuse. According to their developmental model the marginal child is often emotionally neglected and abused in the preschool period, with overlapping physical punishments and abuse, with sexual abuse occurring from about eight years through to adolescence.

Such children already had very low self-esteem before the sexual abuse began, and they lacked feelings of competence and self-worth which would have enabled them to seek help. Children with good self-esteem, and no prior history of emotional and physical abuse, were usually able to report, and/or put a stop to, initial attempts at sexual exploitation. That was why, Bagley and Mallick (2000b) argued, brief episodes of sexual abuse did not usually impair the child's mental health and self-esteem. These and similar findings were confirmed in the review by Anda et al. (2006) which showed: "... the enduring effects of abuse and related adverse experiences in childhood ... from studies of neurobiology and epidemiology."

According to Radford et al. (2011) in their English national survey, there is *an overlap between types of abuse, emotional, physical and sexual*: "Children and young people who are poly-victims are an extremely vulnerable group. Early identification of, and intervention with these young people is needed to prevent both immediate and long-term problems" (p. 122). In commenting further on these results, and reviewing more recent studies, Radford (2013) observed that: "Self-blame, self-harm and suicide are commonly mentioned as consequences of sexual abuse." She cites the challenging American research of Alexander (2011) that prolonged and severe sexual abuse in childhood creates a "neurological syndrome" in which epigenetic pathways may be biochemically triggered in the nervous system causing brain changes, which lead to a prolonged sadness, incipient terrors, chronic guilt, and self-debasing activities which may be lifelong in nature.[2]

Chou (2012) confirmed the enduring, negative effects of child sexual abuse on *older people* in an English community sample of 3,493 individuals aged over 50, including many who were 70 or older. CSA (defined as sexual touching or penetration over a relatively long period in childhood and adolescence, occurring in 8%) was significantly linked across the lifespan to anxiety and depression (which were often comorbid), PTSD, suicidal ideas and self-harm, and periods of psychiatric hospitalization. The combination of different types of abuse was particularly likely to predict lifelong psychiatric morbidity.

Bebbington et al. (2011b) found that in the 7,353 adults in an English survey of psychiatric morbidity based on general population screening, the development of psychosis was *ten times* the expected rate in those experiencing prolonged and intrusive sexual abuse up to age 16. The development of chronic and severe depression and anxiety was a predictor of the development of this psychosis. The prior abuse is causally implicated in the development of this most serious form of mental illness, the authors conclude, and epigenetic factors may be involved in that the chronically abused child has developed a chronic neurological disorder, in which the psyche "withdraws" from everyday interactions and information processing.

The neurological problems imposed on the CNS of the developing child who is subjected to prolonged, severe and multiple forms of abuse have been identified in the American work of Teicher et al. (2012) who studied 183 young adults, using MRI brain scans:16 percent had been subjected to three or more kinds of abuse (sexual, physical emotional, experiencing parental violence) for prolonged periods. Teicher et al. observe that "The exquisite vulnerability of the hippocampus to the ravages of stress is one of the key translational neuroscience discoveries of the twentieth century." Their work showed "reduced volume in the hippocampal subfields CA3, dentate gyrus, and subiculum" in these poly-victims.

The Physical and Sexual Abuse of Children Is an International Public Health Problem

That child physical and sexual abuse is an international problem of public health is shown by Gilbert et al. (2009) who examined studies using comparable methodology in "high income countries" (including the UK), and concluded that about 8 percent of children will suffer physical abuse, 10 percent will experience physical and/or emotional neglect and abuse, and 7 percent of females and 3 percent of males will experience prolonged, often penetrative, sexual abuse. Moreover, these events have mental health sequels in adulthood which are very costly for the individuals, and for health and social care systems. Yet these events, they point out, are hardly recognised as major public health problems, and systems of prevention, and the identification and treatment of child victims are not well-developed in any country.

The extent of these problems in Britain has been emphasised by the research of Bebbington et al. (2011) whose team surveyed British 7,353 adults who completed a laptop questionnaire, on unwanted sexual contacts up to age 16: 11.1 percent of women, and 5.3 percent in males recalled such abuse. These figures included brief and non-recurring sexual assaults: nevertheless, the mental health burden upon some victims in adult life made this, clearly, "a public health problem". The authors note too that the rate of sexual abuse doubled when the child was not in a conventional two-parent family. As Radford et al. (2011) showed, sexual assaults of the classic incestuous type are actually quite rare: when CSA did occur within families, it was usually older brothers, or "mother's boyfriend" who were the perpetrators.

Child Sexual Abuse Takes Place in Community Settings, Rather Than in the Family

The epidemiological work reviewed above suggests that most sexual assault of children and adolescents takes place outside of conventional family settings, or is by unrelated adults who have access to women and children in disorganised families. Victims may be physically and sexually abused and emotionally neglected within disorganised one-parent families under stress (e.g. Gillham et al., 1998), but sexual victimisation is most likely to take place in community, school, or other settings. It is clear from the literature in forensic psychiatry (e.g. Pritchard & Bagley, 2001, 2002; Bagley & Pritchard, 2000) that persistent sex offenders and paedophiles prey on vulnerable children in various settings, and may become very adept at doing so, with multiple victims. Such men adapt skilfully to new forms of sexual exploitation, such as online grooming, which is now a growing problem (Kloess et al., 2014), and may account for the increasing number of reports of child sexual exploitation in England (Bulman, 2017).

The risks to vulnerable children is emphasised in the important research of Lereva et al. (2015) in their report of the 4,026 individuals retained in the UK Avon Birth Cohort study, followed up to age 24. Parents gave information of their social situations, and their relationships with the focus child at ages 8, 10 and 13 in terms of their child's experience of physical, emotional and sexual harm. While parents often admitted to their imperfections as carers in terms of physical and emotional care, it was rare for them to admit to any within-family sexual exploitation of the child, although they did report this when it was perpetrated outside of the family. Interviewed as young adults, the children in this birth cohort largely corroborated parental reports.

This study showed that single events of sexual assault were not usually harmful for the child's mental health (perhaps because the ethical procedures of the research required adequate therapy or referral when abuse was detected in one of the earlier data sweeps). Parental reports of events of physical abuse (e.g. parentally inflicted "punishments") were not associated with lasting mental health problems. However, the researchers found a *synergistic effect* for maltreatment at home combined with bullying and physical and sexual assaults carried out in or around the school. Many children and adolescents could, seemingly, survive within-family abuse and neglect: but when this was combined with bullying, harassment and assault in school settings there was a significant mental health burden in terms of depression (8%), anxiety (10%) and suicidality (9%).

The authors comment on these results:

The insufficiency of resources for bullying compared with those for family maltreatment requires attention. It is important for schools, health services and other agencies to co-ordinate their responses to bullying, and research is needed to assess such interagency policies and procedures. (Lereva et al., 2015, p. 525)

One implication of this research is that schools as institutions (e.g. through teacher, counsellor and social work resources) can help these vulnerable and often marginalised students to have a supportive peer network, which is clearly a crucial part of their psychological recovery. Instead, the abused child is often a loner, a misfit, a suitable person to be excluded from peer networks, a person to be sneered at, bullied, hit, sexually molested and even raped. From Lereva et al.'s (2015) research, this is clearly a particular problem for female victims. Finkelhor and Tucker (2015) who edited the special issue of the journal in which Lereva's research was published, comment on both American, and this British research:

> Molestation, rape, exposure to domestic violence, corporal punishment, physical abuse, bullying, sexual molestation ... all overlap. 'Peer violence' is part of this 'maltreatment syndrome.' (p. 481)

In important epidemiological work from the UK, Catone et al. (2015) report findings from two national surveys of randomly selected populations aged 16-plus (total numbers in the samples more than 19,000). They found a statistically significant link between being a chronic victim of bullying (usually during and after the period of school attendance), and the emergences of auditory and visual hallucinations, and incipient or probable psychosis. Controlling for a variety of potentially intervening factors, only a history of child sexual abuse appeared to have any causal significance. A picture emerges of the victimised child or adolescence whose depression (often reflecting prior CSA) and social alienation in school makes him or her a frequent target for bullying: the adolescent victim is "scared stiff", not knowing where the next blow will come from, fearing threats from every quarter, which builds for the victim, into a paranoid state. The psychiatric team carrying out this research advocate more vigorous, school-based programmes to intervene on behalf of bullied victims in ways "... which might ameliorate the course of psychosis."[3]

Peer Settings, Support, and Abuse

How *peers can help or impair mental health* is illustrated by Connell and Dishion's (2006) American research, which focussed on 176 vulnerable parents and their 10–14 years old children, interviewing both parent and child(ren) at monthly intervals, about personal stresses, and peer group relations, over a 9-month period. Stressed children tended to have poor peer relationships, often became depressed as a result, and also sometimes moved into delinquency. *"As expected depressed mood was higher for girls, and more prevalent for older adolescents. The results suggest that peer processes may be linked in time to the development of depression, especially among high-risk adolescents"* (p. 150). These authors also note that "best friend" nominations often changed several times over a school year. Social relationships in the high school are fragile, ephemeral, but crucially important. Yet the depressed adolescent is all too often marginalized and even rejected in such peer contacts.

That the young person's social world outside the family can be of crucial importance is emphasised by the English study by Jackson et al. (2016) of 730 13 to 16 year olds, the study reflecting that fact that "There has been little research carried out in the United Kingdom aimed at providing a holistic exploration of the victim experiences of young people within the school and community environments" (p. 343). The study found that many of the adolescents had experienced some form of victimization outside the family, within the past year. One in three had property vandalised or stolen; one in two had experienced verbal harassment or physical bullying; one in 28 experienced "dating violence" including rape and sexual assault, and one in seven had been victims of sexual assault or harassment in school settings. Moreover, these types of assault on person or property tended to overlap. Bagley and King (2003) reflecting on their Canadian research suggest that it is likely that the female victims of multiple assaults were marginal to peer networks, and thus became marked for victimisation in school: once sexually assaulted the adolescent girl gains the reputation of being "an easy lay" or a "slag", subject to verbal and physical assaults from both males and females.

Girls themselves may be involved in the bullying and sexual harassment of other girls, according to the interesting work in two London secondary schools by Jamal et al. (2015) which used a qualitative design in examining the social ecology of "bullying spaces", which often involved sexual rivalries, and sexual denigration of peers. While this may seem depressing, Farah Jamal (2015) adopts the logic of empowerment for change in the girls she worked with, using "empowerment" models derived from Bourdieu and Giddens.

Male Victims

Male victims of sexual and physical assault in childhood and adolescence have been less intensively studied, but several studies suggest that they may be better able to "shrug off" physical assaults, and the attempts at sexual assault by older males. Only when the boy's sexuality is put in doubt (e.g. 'enjoying' imposed gay sex) are there likely to be early reactions in terms of suicidality and self harm (Bagley & D'Augelli, 2000; Bagley & Tremblay, 2000a, 2000b). Young transgender males who are seduced by unscrupulous, older males, gay or otherwise, have greatly increased rates of self-harm, drug-use, and school absences.

The English work by Salter et al. (2003) which followed up 224 male victims of sexual assault in childhood and adolescence, found that in a 7 to 19 year follow-up after the original referral for psychiatric treatment at a paediatric hospital, 26 (11.6%) had become sexual abusers themselves (of both male and female children). Statistically significant predictors of this "victim-to-abuser" cycle were material and emotional neglect in childhood, and being sexually assaulted by a female. A psychodynamic explanation might invoke the idea of oedipal guilt in the young boy, and his inability to have sexual relations with adult women.[4]

MacMillan et al. (2001) in their Ontario research with 7,016 individuals aged 15 to 64 found that a history of "physical abuse" in the childhood of males was much less likely to have adverse, long-term effects on mental health than was such abuse imposed on females. For women who had experienced both physical and sexual abuse in childhood, psychological outcomes were particularly poor.

Several major *British longitudinal studies* have yielded information which confirms North American and other epidemiological work on the long-term negative effects of child abuse of various kinds. The National Child Development Study of more than 10,000 individuals born in a single week, in March, 1958 has yielded numerous reports of the adult sequels of early antecedents in child and adult development. Clark et al. (2011) reported that by the time the cohort was aged 45, there were clear links between earlier sexual and physical abuse, and adult psychopathology, especially when the two types of abuse were combined. Michael Rutter's longitudinal cohort of children born in 1968 found that by 2009 "harsh parenting", and CSA in various settings were linked to adult neuroticism and suicidality, especially when the two types of abuse were combined (Pickles et al., 2010).

The first notable British longitudinal study of a birth cohort was of several thousand children born in 1946. No adult recall studies of abusive events in childhood have been published, but one study of the cohort (Hatch & Wadsworth, 2008) gives us cause for concern. This study followed up into middle age adolescents (within the total cohort of 4,600 individuals studied) who were "very anxious" or "very sad", without enquiring into possible reasons, although socioeconomic factors did not explain any of the variance. Around five per cent of the cohort were identified as having lifelong problems of "social integration", reflecting the depression and anxiety of their childhood years. This group appeared to have very low self-esteem, lacked social confidence, had poor educational outcomes (despite their generally average social class backgrounds), did not often enter higher education or obtain professional qualifications, or follow rewarding careers. Of the very depressed and/or anxious adolescents 70 percent had poor mental health at age 53. We would hypothesise that this group had experienced severe and prolonged sexual and/or physical abuse in their childhood years.

Colman et al. (2014) examined perinatal factors in this cohort, and later economic and social deprivations in childhood, including stressful events such as parental loss – but physical and sexual abuse were not studied. They found that a combined equation including low birth weight, childhood poverty, and various childhood stressors was highly predictive of clinical depression at ages 46 or 53. Again, we would suggest that physical and sexual abuse could have a major role in these mental health outcomes.

Ethnic Minorities and Abuse Histories in Britain

Sexual and physical assaults experienced by *ethnic minorities* have not received much attention in British research. The national studies reported by Radford et al. (2011, 2013) report that the category "Ethnic not white" was 8.1 percent in 1998, and 15.2 percent in the 2009 national survey. However, separate data on experience of physical and sexual assault within this minority population was not presented in their analyses. This raises the intriguing possibility that the decline in the prevalence of such assaults between 1998 and 2009 might be due to newly-accessed groups such as those of Asian heritage having low rates of abuse. Moghal et al. (1995) did comment on the possible reasons for lower rate of child sexual abuse in Asian populations in Northern cities in England. Cultural factors and religious norms could protect children in such communities; or there could be an extreme reluctance to report abuse, for a variety of reasons. Bebbington et al. (2011a) reported "no association" between ethnicity and experience of child sexual abuse in their national sample. Their definition of "ethnicity" seems to be very broad, however.

Large scale English surveys of random samples of the population face the problem that unless the 'stratified random' model is used, certain ethnic minorities (who tend to live in urban clusters) will be missed, or will be underrepresented. This was not the case in Bellis et al.'s (2014) English sample of 3,885 adults, which showed that "adverse childhood events" (ACES) when occurring in combination in an individual (which they usually did), were strong predictors of later psychopathology, substance misuse, and poor personal health care. They were able to recruit a sufficient number of "Asians" (7.9%) to allow for statistical analysis. This heterogeneous ethnic group experienced, in childhood, parental separation, family violence, and physical and sexual abuse at much *lower* rates than the "white" population, social class controlled. The rate of child sexual abuse recalled by Asians was 3.2%, compared with 6.2% in whites, for example.

However, Bellis et al. (2013) who randomly selected 11,500 adults in the North West region of England were unable to obtain enough ethnic minorities for meaningful statistical analysis, due to their failure to use stratified methods (i.e. oversampling in areas of known ethnic density). Their research is relevant for this review however, since it was conducted in the same geographical area as that in which the Northern Schools (reported on below) were situated. Bellis et al. showed that "child sexual abuse" was associated with a three-fold *reduction* in adult levels of "trust, confidence, optimism and safety".

In the Northern Schools data set reported on below, we have had the opportunity to examine self-reported abuse, and its correlations in an 'Asian heritage' population, whose cultural antecedents were mainly in the Indian sub-continent.

Further English Epidemiological Studies of the Long-Term Sequels of Child Maltreatment

Methodologically sophisticated English studies using large samples continue to appear, and emphasise that childhood victimization is a major, but still unaddressed, public health problem. Bellis et al. (2014b) used a specifically public health model in designing and analysing the results of a national English survey of 3,885 adults aged 18 to 69, focussing on "adverse childhood events" (ACES) which included parental quarrelling and violence, parental absence, family violence directed towards child, verbal abuse of child, sexual assaults on the child, mental illness and/or drug and alcohol misuse in a caretaker, criminal conviction, and imprisonment of a caretaker or sibling: 8.3% of those surveyed had experienced four or more of these adverse events in childhood.

Such a history was associated with a greatly elevated risk of poor adult mental health, substance abuse, and behavioural problems including criminality in the adult lives of those who had experienced highly stressed childhoods. These problems were manifested in particular individuals living in deprived urban areas. In reading yet another depressing English national survey, one is prompted to pose the unanswered questions: What of the children of these now adult victims? What is this new generation's history of abuse, in the "cycle of deprivation" described by Rutter and Madge (1976)? What kinds of schools were the children in this cycle of deprivation attending, and how could these schools identify and address their problems, and break the 'cycle of alienation' described by Williams and Pritchard (2006)?

Using their public health model, Bellis et al. (2014b) show that ACES explained: 11.9% of adult binge drinking; 5% of heroin use; 38% of unwanted teenaged pregnancy; and 14% of poor diet and poor personal health care. Reducing the incidence of adverse childhood events they argue, would be a highly productive public health strategy. On adverse mental health outcomes, they argue that:

> Links between such behaviours and childhood circumstances are likely to operate through the impact of ACES on the developing brain and its stress regulatory systems, which affect factors such as emotional regulation and fear response, and this may predispose individuals to health-harming behaviours. (p. 90)

Problems of Questionnaires on Child Maltreatment

It is important to comment on the difficulties of asking questions about sexual abuse that have occurred in studies which ask adolescents and adults to report on such abuse occurring previously, in childhood and adolescence (Hardt & Rutter, 2002). The most frequent method employed is that of "adult recall", asking adults (and adolescents) to give details of such events in either face-to-face interviews, or in anonymised questionnaires[5]. Such methods are (presumably) likely to underestimate the actual incidence of such abuse if respondents find the questions embarrassing or troubling, and fail to report abuse when it did in fact occur (it seems unlikely that respondents would fabricate such accounts – Hardt & Rutter, 2002). This is an artefact working "against significance", since in the language of epidemiology, an unknown number of probands would be included in the control or contrast group.

Brown et al. (2007) addressed these issues in validation work with the "Childhood Experiences of Care and Abuse" (CECA) scale which they had devised for their English (London-based) epidemiological work with women with serious, chronic depression compared with non-depressed controls.

The CECA was completed by 118 pairs of sisters who had grown up together, and their accounts of any family maltreatment were compared. Probands (depressed women) tended to underestimate parental maltreatment (another artefact working against significance). Nevertheless, Brown et al. (2007) conclude that their instrument is probably one of the best available for epidemiological purposes.

Ontario-based researchers also justified the ethics of approaching children using direct, verbal questioning in gathering data on child maltreatment, seeing the children and young persons in the light of an "active agency" model, as human beings capable of reviewing and commenting on events in their lives, and who may be set on particular paths of healing and resistance to further abusive events (Tonmyr et al., 2014).

In its Canadian development, the measure of physical and sexual maltreatment and abuse used in the Northern Schools study has had to face many of the problems familiar to those trying to develop measures in this field, including the ethical one of how to offer advice and help to those who do reveal past abuse, and currently have poor mental health (Bagley, 1990 to 1999; Bagley & King, 2003; Bagley & McDonald, 1984; Bagley & Mallick, 1999; Bagley & Ramsay, 1986; Bagley & Young, 1998). English researchers have tended to ask about physical and sexual assaults up to age 16, although it seems more appropriate to screen for the whole time that most spend in school, up to age 18. Differently worded questions may elicit different kinds of response, and there is some debate about distinguishing between "unwanted" sexual contact (e.g. the rape of a 17-year-old), and the "consenting" but illegal sexual intercourse of a 13-year-old.

Asking about who the abuser was may create a reluctance to reveal abuse if the victim had been threatened, or wishes to protect someone. In the study reported below, two short questions were asked, which did not ask "victims" to be specific about who the other person(s) might be. This short, non-complex questionnaire was, according to development work and a cross-validation study with established clinical profiles, at least 90 percent valid in eliciting "true" events of physical and sexual maltreatment (Walsh et al., 2008). Tanaka et al. (2012) found that their CEVQ (Childhood Experience of Violence Questionnaire) short- form had excellent reliability when individuals were retested two weeks later. In the longitudinal Ontario Child Health Study. Tanaka et al. report that the scale had validation through its correlation with adult measures of mental health in a large population of adults – and combinations of physical and sexual maltreatment were particularly likely to have adverse psychiatric sequels.

We have to accept that there will always be inaccuracy of measurement in a sensitive field such as this, but note that recent Canadian work with the short-form of the CEVQ did obtain acceptable concordance in accounts of their childhood's family life, when adult sibling accounts were compared (MacMillan et al., 2013).

The "true identity" of an individual is the personal property of a unique person, and we must respect an individual's right to reveal or conceal aspects of that identity, according to their personal choice. In the Northern Schools study some three percent of respondents completed only part of the Maltreatment section (none revealing abuse) or left all of it blank. The original researchers had assumed that in those cases no abuse had occurred, and coded the questionnaire that way. This could have been a mistake, but the original questionnaires were destroyed immediately coding had taken place.

Conclusions from the Literature Review on Child and Adolescent Maltreatment

It is clear that in Britain, as elsewhere in the developed world, the maltreatment and neglect of children, physically, sexually, emotionally, is an important public health problem with lifelong negative consequences in terms of depression, anxiety, suicidality, psychosomatic disorders, posttraumatic stress disorder, psychosis, substance misuse, and self-defeating lifestyles. While up to a half of child and adolescent victims survive without manifesting overt psychological symptoms, a half do not. Combinations of abuse, physical and sexual are particularly likely to have adverse mental health outcomes: about four percent of females, and about two percent of males will have experienced chronic, intrusive (penetrative) sexual abuse combined with either physical abuse, emotional abuse, or both of these. British research confirms the results of the Canadian longitudinal work of Bagley and Mallick (2000a, 2000b).

While the British researchers, who are mainly child and adult psychiatrists, focus on diagnosable mental health conditions, there are grounds for assuming that an individual with depression, anxiety and self-harm falling into the clinical domain, would also have very low self-esteem. In terms of William James' (1890) model of the body being at the centre of self-concept and self-esteem: the violation of the child's body through physical and sexual abuse interferes profoundly with core developments of the self-concept, and the evaluative construct of self-esteem, the innate feelings of 'goodness' or 'badness' by which the child develops a self-schema. The abused child acquires an identity which moves on a particular trajectory, one of watchfulness, fear, nightmare, nervousness, a pattern "burned into the brain", even causing permanent structural brain changes which last a lifetime.

At school other children "know" that this child is different: this child has been dominated, and in school they are once again dominated. School should be a haven, but too often it is an arena of fear in which the child is again bullied, sneered at, hit, sexually handled, lewdly suggested, forced unwillingly in her state of learned helplessness into further dominated and sexualized relationships. Her very *will* is raped. In the worst case, her body belongs not to her but to others, to kick around and prod as they please. In the worst case, they attempt to murder this kid's soul, and the psychotic core of her being is the only respite, the only safety she has. She is like the American Indian whose culture the British raped and enslaved, and psychosis, self-harm or addiction is her only way out. But Black kids, we assert, have *juk* in their cultural soul. They hit back, they survive.[6]

The *dramatis persona* of the victim which we have sketched may seem exaggerated and over-dramatized. But is it? For one in twenty five children in England (and in many other countries) it seems a frightful reality, as the evidence we have reviewed seems to show: and school cultures can make things worse rather than better. Will the Northern Schools study yield any different results?

THE NORTHERN SCHOOLS STUDY

All of the ten schools participating were in urban areas of the North West of England: Greater Manchester, Liverpool, Warrington and Lancashire. A quarter of the secondary schools approached agreed to participate, allowing access to some (but not all) classes in each school for group testing. It was easier to gain access to older students, especially in post-exam time slots. The final sample was 'over-weighted' by older students, although the researchers had not aimed at obtaining a random sample of students: rather, given the difficulties in persuading schools to participate in an era of increasing curriculum rigidity and examination pressures, the number of students participating (2,025) was considered adequate both for representativeness of a sector of Northern schools in England, and for multivariate data analyses.

Since one of the original purposes of the questionnaire was to examine attitudes and adjustment of students with origins in the Indian sub-continent, and Muslim students in particular, schools containing a relatively high proportion of these students were approached. This survey of English schools then, is not nationally representative, but pertains to a multicultural sector of education in North Western England. It should be borne in mind too that the sample of older students would be biased to an unknown extent by the fact that students whose attendance at school is intermittent, or who had dropped out altogether, or who had been transferred to special educational units, would be under-represented. If (as we fear) frequently absent or excluded students contain a disproportionate number with abuse histories, we will have actually *underestimated* both the prevalence of abuse, and its negative behavioural sequels.

Questionnaire Administration

The questionnaire was kept as brief as possible, and was completed by the average student within 20 minutes or less. It contained the 10-item Rosenberg Self-Esteem Scale (RSES), three scales from the Ontario Child Health Study measuring Anxiety, Depression, and Conduct Problems (4 questions in each scale, 12 in total); a measure of self-described ethnicity; and a brief measure of physical and sexual abuse. Only two questions on abuse were used, which were the main questions in an instrument subsequently validated in terms of known clinical and personal interview data (Walsh et al., 2008).

There were clearly ethical problems in asking young people to reveal abuse when there was no direct plan to intervene. In order to partially address this, a brief and easy to remember website was included in the questionnaire, which directed users to local and national sources of help, including the telephone resource of Child Line. School counsellors were also alerted in case the questions had stimulated help-seeking behaviour. In addition, a number of the schools planned to address abuse issues in Personal, Social and Health Education (PSHE) classes. The questions on physical and sexual assault and abuse focussed on the school and on the school environment and the journey to school, but also asked about "any other place" where abuse might have occurred. It was thus intended to elicit information on incidents of school-based abuse, but also took into account serious abuse occurring elsewhere, including domestic settings.

Students were instructed not to write their names on the questionnaire, and were assured that no individual could be identified, although they could talk to teachers about the questionnaire if they wanted. Only age, gender, ethnicity and religious affiliation were asked for.[7] Information on ethnicity was sought by means of a specially devised questionnaire. Following the statement: "People today often say they come from different *ethnic* groups.

Which of the following (if any) applies to you?" Options were "white British, Irish or European", "black British – heritage African or Caribbean", "Asian – heritage Pakistan, India or Bangladesh", "Other", or "Mixed". Students who ticked more than one category were placed in the final grouping, which for analytic purposes was described as "Other/Mixed". Pilot work with the questionnaire indicated that only about four percent of students were likely to place themselves in "mixed" categories: but if a White pupil wanted to identify as Black, we accepted that as a valid, subjective choice.

The full self-esteem measure (Rosenberg Self-Esteem Scale, or RSES) and the three Ontario Child Health (OCH) Scales (measuring depression, conduct problems, and anxiety problems) are not reproduced here for copyright reasons. These OCH scales were known from previous work in North America and England, to have reasonable validity for psychometric purposes. One of the purposes of the research in the Northern Schools study was to establish the face validity of the RSES in terms of its correlation with other measures, and its internal structure and reliability as a coherent scale.

A subsidiary purpose of the research was to explore some of the mental health profiles of contrasted ethnic groups in English secondary schools.

Results from the Northern Schools Study

Tables 8.1 and 8.2 show that the 10-item Rosenberg scale (RSES) has excellent internal reliability and scale coherence, across the four age and gender groups within which it was analysed. A strong 'general factor' emerged, with all items (regardless of direction of scoring) loading on a general factor explaining more than 50 percent of the scale's variance, in each age and gender analysis. The 'gender gap', with males having rather 'better' self-esteem levels than females is clearly present, and is concordant with findings from previous studies in America, Canada and Britain.

Table 8.3 shows that the difference in RSES scale means, when compared between males and females, reaches a high level of statistical significance. Ethnic groups within males also tend to have higher RSES scores than females from similar ethnic groups. Within males, there is no statistically significant variation in RSES scores across ethnic groups. However, within the female sample, there *is* a statistically significant variation of RSES scores by ethnic groups. The 'black' ethnic group (with cultural origins in Africa and the Caribbean) have the *highest* levels of self-esteem compared with other females, and this is statistically significant when they are compared with the 'white' group (those with cultural origins in Britain, Ireland or Europe). The reasons for this are not clear, but are of some ethnographic research interest.

Table 8.1. General factor (item means) of Rosenberg self-esteem scale items in 1,021 males in English secondary schools

Scale items (abbreviated)		All 1,021 Males	522 males 15–18	499 males 11–14
1.	Satisfied with self	3.07	3.17	2.99
2.	No good at all	3.01	3.08	2.96
3.	Have good qualities	3.01	3.04	2.96
4.	Can do things as well as others	2.90	2.95	2.87
5.	Not much to be proud of	3.00	3.03	2.99
6.	I feel useless	2.94	2.99	2.92
7.	I'm a person of worth	3.01	3.05	2.95
8.	Don't respect myself	3.04	3.06	3.00
9.	I'm a failure	3.06	3.08	3.04
10.	Positive self-regard	3.53	3.57	3.48
Scale mean		30.57	31.02	30.16
Standard deviation		5.27	5.12	5.40
Alpha (scale consistency)		0.83	0.83	0.80
Percent with 'very poor' SE (score <21)		3.62%	3.26%	3.83%

Note: RSES scale items in this table paraphrased and shortened, for copyright reasons Items scored on a 4-point scale from 'very unlike me' (scored 1) to 'very like me' (scored 4). Scores for negatively worded items were reversed, so the higher the scale total, the better the self-esteem. Minimum possible score 10, maximum possible score 40.

What is clear (Table 8.7) is that girls who do *not* report sexual assault or abuse in their lives have generally *similar levels of self-esteem to their male peers.* Although males have slightly higher self-esteem scores, the differences are no longer statistically significant, when sexual abuse history is taken into account. This is an important finding, and should be considered by future researchers using the RSES to explore differential levels of self-esteem in various groups, including both gender and ethnic groups.

Table 8.2. General factor (item means) of Rosenberg self-esteem scale items in 1,004 females in 10 English secondary schools

Scale items (abbreviated)	All 1,004 Females	522 females 15–18	482 females 11–14
1. Satisfied with self	2.90	2.96	2.84
2. No good at all	2.81	2.85	2.76
3. Have good qualities	2.86	2.87	2.85
4. Can do things as well as others	2.88	2.89	2.87
5. Not much to be proud of	2.83	2.85	2.81
6. I feel useless	2.81	2.86	2.75
7. I'm a person of worth	2.80	2.86	2.74
8. Don't respect myself	2.86	2.88	2.82
9. I'm a failure	2.85	3.02	2.69
10. Positive self-regard	2.94	2.95	2.92
Scale mean	28.54	28.99	28.05
Standard deviation	5.47	5.12	5.48
Alpha (scale consistency)	0.85	0.86	0.81
Percent with 'very poor' SE (score <21)	7.57%	6.89%	8.37%

Note: RSES scale items paraphrased and shortened in the above Table. Items were scored on a 4-point scale from 'very like me' to 'very unlike me'. Scores for negatively worded items were reversed, so the higher the scale total, the better the self-esteem. Minimum possible score 10, maximum possible score 40.

In the present study, boys' reports of sexual abuse were less in frequency than such reports from girls (Tables 8.5 to 8.7), and they also seemed more likely to survive such abuse psychologically. Boys likewise seemed "tough" enough to survive forms of physical assault and abuse, even though they reacted with elements of conduct disorder. The amount of physical assault and abuse endured by girls in this survey is alarming, and such physical assault has statistically significant negative associations with self-esteem levels in females. Girls who had been both physically and sexually abused were particularly likely to have "devastated self-esteem", as well as clinical profiles on the measures of depression and anxiety.[8] Some girls in this 'devastated'

Table 8.3. The Ontario child health scales completed by English school students

Scale Mean (SD)	Males	Males	Females	Females
	11–14	15–18	11–14	15–18
	499	522	482	522
Anxiety	3.0 (.69)	2.9 (.66)	5.3 (1.8)	5.1 (1.9)
r with RSES	0.44	0.39	0.49	0.46
Depression	2.4 (.80)	2.2 (.69)	3.7 (1.25)	3.9 (2.0)
r with RSES	0.36	0.38	0.43	0.47
Conduct Disorder	3.7 (.90)	3.6 (.97)	1.8 (.82)	2.0 (0.97)
r with RSES	0.23	0.19	0.25	0.22

Notes: (1) Example of Anxiety Scale item "I am too fearful or anxious." Example of Depression Scale item "I am unhappy, sad, or depressed." Example of Conduct Disorder Scale item "I get in many fights." Each scale contains four items, and was scored: 0 = "Never/Not True"; 1 = "Sometimes or somewhat true"; 2 = "Often or Very True" (minimum score 0, maximum score 12, for each scale). (2) Because of direction of scoring, correlations in this table are negative e.g. high self-esteem individuals tend not to be anxious or depressed. Correlations of 0.20 and beyond are significant at the 1 percent level.

category had zero scores on the RSES, and scores of more than two standard deviations above the depression and anxiety disorder scale means.

Although experiencing sexual abuse was associated with diminished self-esteem, and increased levels of depression and anxiety to a significant degree in females (but not in males), it was the combination of sexual and physical abuse that was particularly damaging for self-esteem in females in both of the age groups (11–14 and 15–18) considered (Tables 8.7 to 8.8) – this assumes a causal relationship between CSA and diminished self-esteem, although alternative models are possible, including vulnerability (reflecting earlier types of abuse) resulting in lowered self-esteem, which makes any further forms of abuse such as CSA particularly traumatic.

Ethnicity clearly made a difference in the proportions of females who were experiencing (or reporting) sexual and physical abuse, and rates of physical abuse or assault were very much lower in Black and Asian females. Combined sexual and physical abuse was markedly different across ethnic groups: 9% of white females had such a history of combined types of abuse, compared with less than 2% in minority ethnic groups. These were highly significant differences, but they applied only to the

Table 8.4. RSES scores by self-described ethnicity of 2,025 English students

Gender Group	All 1,021 Males	All 1,004 Females
RSES (SD)	30.57 (5.27)	28.54 (SD 5.47)
"White", English or European Born	Males 552 (54.1%)	Females 554 (54.2%)
RSES (SD)	30.80 (5.31)	28.47 (5.39)
"Black", English/Caribbean/ African Born	Males 99 (9.7%)	Females 99 (9.9%)
RSES (SD)	30.76 (5.96)	30.07 (5.71)
"Asian", Parental Heritage Indian Sub-Continent	Males 291 (28.4%)	Females 281 (28.0%)
RSES	30.24(6.19)	29.90 (5.90)
Other/ Unknown/Mixed Ethnicity	Males 79 (7.7%)	Females 70 (6.9%)
RSES (SD)	29.94 (6.59)	21.47 (7.31)

Notes: (1) Ethnicity was not stated by 1.8% of respondents; these are included in the 'Other' category. The higher the RSES score, the better the self-esteem level. (2) Statistical significance of comparisons: For all males versus all females, comparison of the two RSES means: T=8.59, P<.00001. Males have significantly higher self-esteem scores than females. (3) Within males, no ethnic group differed significantly in self-esteem level compared to any other male ethnic group, by ANOVA across groups, or in any post hoc T-test comparison of pairs of groups (1-way ANOVA, F=0.681, P=0.564, not significant). (4) Within females, self-esteem varied significantly by ANOVA across ethnic groups (1-way ANOVA, F=3.266, P=.011). "Blacks" had significantly better self-esteem than "whites" (T=3.42, P=.001). "Black" versus "Asian" T=1.85, P=.065, just outside the 5% value. No other post hoc comparison between pairs of ethnic groups reached statistical significance. (5) ANOVA is an acronym for Analysis of Variance.

female population of Northern Schools, and not to males, for reasons which are not clear.

Although the trend for females to experience greater amounts of child maltreatment, and to react to it more adversely than males is in line with other research, the general lack of statistical significance in the results from comparisons within the male group is somewhat puzzling.

DISCUSSION OF RESULTS

First of all, the original idea of Mallick and Bagley to replicate their work (Bagley & Mallick, 2001) on the widely used Rosenberg Self-Esteem Scale

Table 8.5. *Physical assault and abuse in English school students*

Before you were 18, how many times did someone slap you on the face, head or ears; or hit or spank you with something like a hard object or a belt?

	Never	One or Two times	Three to Four times	More than Five Times
Males 11–14	80.94%	5.01%	6.01%	8.04%
Males 15–18	74.91%	6.90%	8.04%	10.15%
Females 11–14	80.08%	4.98%	6.02%	8.92%
Females 15–18	75.12%	5.93%	5.93%	13.02%

"Physical assault" 5+ times: All males 9.1% (N=93) compared to All Females, 10.9% (N=110) (P>.1, NS).

(RSES) in a new sample of English high school students has been fulfilled. The scale has clear factorial reliability in terms of all ten items loading strongly on a single factor, and internal statistical consistency in age and gender groups. The RSES has face validity too, in terms of its correlation with validated mental health measures, in particular the Anxiety and Depression scales developed in the Ontario Child Health Study, and validated through self-completion by an English clinical group with known diagnoses.

Research reviewed in the previous chapter on self-esteem shows that in most world cultures, males regard themselves more favourably than females, and

Table 8.6. *Sexual assault and abuse in English school students*

Before you were 18, did anyone ever do any of the following things when you didn't want them to:
Touch the private parts of your body, or make you touch their private parts, or threaten to have sex with you, or force themselves sexually on you?

	Never	One or Two Times	Three to Four Times	More than Five Times
Males 11–14	91.99%	4.01%	1.00%	3.00%
Males 15–18	91.02%	4.02%	1.91%	3.06%
Females 11–14	80.92%	7.05%	4.98%	7.05%
Females 15–18	75.09%	9.96%	7.85%	7.09%

"Sexual assault" 3+ times: All Males, 4.5% (N=46); All Females. 13.6% (N=136) (P<.0001, statistically significant).

Table 8.7. RSES scores by sexual and physical abuse incidence in females in the English secondary schools study: comparison with male RSES scores

	RSES (SD)	Depression	Anxiety	Conduct problems
'Sexually abused' Females (N 136)	17.88 (5.91)	4.66 (1.71)	7.21 (1.8)	2.19 (0.73)
'Not sexually abused' Females (N 868)	30.21 (5.57)	3.67 (1.90)	4.88 (1.12)	1.86 (0.54)
'Physically abused' Females (N 88)	10.64 (6.74)	3.88 (0.8)	7.06 (1.60)	2.46 (1.81)
'Not physically abused Females (N 916)	30.26 (5.79)	3.70 (0.9)	4.92 (0.93)	1.85 (0.53)
All Males (N 1,021)	30.57 (5.27)	2.29 (0.49)	2.95 (0.70)	3.65 (0.93)
Males 'not sexually Abused' (N 980)	30.55 (5.49)	2.15 (0.70)	2.90 (0.71)	3.61 (0.92)

Notes: (1) Definitions of 'Abuse': Three or more events of unwanted sexual contact; and 5 or more events physical abuse up to age of 18. Cut-off points chosen since they maximise differences between the abused and the non-abused groups in terms of RSES scores, and Ontario Child Health Scale means, in females. In males, experience of physical and sexual assault had no significant association with the RSES, or with clinical profiles. (2) Females, RSES: Statistical significance: "Sexually abused" versus "Non sexually abused" females T=22.89, p<.000 "Physically abused" versus "Non physically abused" females T=21.07, p<.000 "Non sexually abused females" versus "All males" T=1.21, p<.227, NS Separate analysis by age groupings gave similar results. (3) Depression in females : Statistical Significance "Sexually abused" versus "Non sexually abused" females: T=6.58, p<.000 "Physically abused" versus "Not physically abused" females: T=1.99, p=.051 Anxiety Disorder in females: Statistical Significance "Sexually abused" versus "Non sexually abused" females: T=22.29, p<.000 "Physically abused" versus "Non physically abused" females: T=12.36. p<.000 (4) Statistical Significance – further comparisons, in none of the comparisons did differences on Conduct Disorder score reach statistical significance, when the various abuse groups were compared, in females or in males. Likewise, male RSES scores, and Depression and Anxiety Disorder Scores had no statistically significant variation across the sexual and physical abuse categories. Comparing RSES scores in males and females by combined physical and sexual abuse histories, did not add to the significance of the analysis, substantively or in statistical terms. (5) RSES indicates Rosenberg Self-Esteem Scale.

Table 8.8. Sexual and physical assaults by ethnicity in the secondary school students

---

Sexual Abuse/Assault Experienced by Females:

All: 130/954 (13.6%)	*White*: 88/554 (15.2%)	*Black*: 8/99 (8.1%)	*Asian* 29/281 (11.9%).

Other/Mixed/Unknown: 5/60 (8.3%).

Chi-squared (3 d.f.) across the four ethnic sub-groups: 9.08, p=.0282.

Physical Abuse/Assault Experienced by Females:

All: 87/954 (9.1%)	*White*: 80/554 (14.4%)	*Black*: 2/99 (2.0%)	*Asian*: 4/281 (1.4%)

Other/Mixed/Unknown: 1/60 (1.7%).

Chi-squared (3 d.f.) across four ethnic sub-groups: 49.64, p=.0000.

Both Physical and Sexual Assault Experienced by Females:

All: 56/954 (5.5%)	*White*: 50/554 (9.02%)	*Black*: 2/99 (2.0%)	*Asian*: 4/281 (1.4%).

Other/Mixed/Unknown: 0/60 (0.0%).

Chi-squared (3 d.f.) across four ethnic sub-groups: 27.36, p=.0000.

Sexual, Physical and Combined Assaults had no statistically significant variation across Ethnicity in Males in any age group. For Females, analysis by age categories (11–14/15–18) yielded no additionally significant findings.

have 'higher' scores on the RSES. A variety of cultural, social and psychological reasons have been advanced to explain this, but none has been proved, or tested in any definitive way. In the Northern Schools studied, reported above, males did have significantly higher RSES scores than females. But why?

In looking at past findings on the effects of child maltreatment (physical and sexual abuse and exploitation) it was clear that such maltreatment was frequently linked to "depressed self-esteem", which has formed the basis for emerging clinical conditions such as depression, anxiety, PTSD, suicidality, and even psychosis. Yet no research which we can locate has actually "controlled for" the potential effects of maltreatment in explaining gender differences in self-esteem. The Northern Schools data set has given us the opportunity to explore this idea. This study used a measure developed in Canada, the Childhood Experiences of Violence Questionnaire Short Form (CEVQ), an instrument of established reliability and validity.

A comparison of results from Canadian work (MacMillan et al., 2013) and the Northern Schools Study is instructive:

	Severe physical abuse	Sexual abuse	Both types of abuse
Canadian females (969 adults)	18.3%	22.1%	11.6%
English Schools Females (954, 11–18)	13.6%	9.1%	5.5%

The main reason for the lower rate of reported abuse in the English sample, compared with the Canadian normative group, is presumably because the average age is much lower (about 15.3 years, and did not include older students absent from or excluded from school), compared with the adult Canadian cohort who were recalling childhood events. We speculate on the dismal possibility that these girls would in their remaining years before becoming adults (at age 19), have had to endure many more abusive events in their lives. It's a further possibility that the absent students were particularly likely to have been abuse victims, so this English study will have underestimated both prevalence of CSA, and its negative sequels.

It was clear from inspecting the tabulated data that some schools were salient in terms of their ethnic profiles, as well as being salient on scores of measures of adjustment, and in females' experience of sexual and physical abuse. We were struck by two schools (described in Table 8.9 as 'City School' and 'United School') a few miles distant from each other, in the same urban conurbation. City School served a mainly white student population who lived in relatively poor quality council housing, built to house families resettled from slum redevelopment, mostly in the 1930s. United School had a majority of students whose ethnic heritage was from the Indian sub-continent. The students mainly lived in pre-war terraced housing, or in pockets of relatively new houses and flats. Most of the Asian-heritage students were Muslim.

Statistical profiles of the two schools were markedly different: 40 per cent of all City School students were eligible for free meals, compared with 12 percent of those attending the United School. In the year previous to the research, more than half of students at this latter school obtained five or more 'good' GCSEs, compared with only 23 percent of those attending City School. On all of the indicators of adjustment, girls at City School scored less favourably, and significantly more had been sexually or physically

Table 8.9. Exploring the profiles of two schools marked by different levels of sexual and physical abuse of females, achievement, poverty, and female adjustment

Variables compared	City school (250 girls)	United school (297 girls)
% Free School Meals*	40%	12%
GCSE 5 'C+ Grades'*	23%	54%
% 'White'*	84%	31%
% 'Black'	5%	10%
% 'Asian'	8%	55%
% 'Mixed/Other/Unknown'	3%	4%
RSES Mean Score	25.10	30.09
Depression mean	3.95	3.18
Anxiety disorder mean	5.56	4.60
Conduct disorder mean	1.81	0.50
Sexually abused	18.8%	10.8%
Physically abused	17.2%	2.3%
Abused sexually and physically	11.6%	1.7%
"Ego Devastated" (very low Self-Esteem, high Depression & Anxiety)	12.8%	0.8%

*Data on free school meals and GCSE passes relate to whole school, information given by the school and not by pupils, and refer to the previous school year. Percent falling into different ethnic groups derived from information given in the student self-completion questionnaires by the girls themselves. High score on RSES indicates better self-esteem. High score on Depression & Anxiety scales indicates poorer adjustment. 'Devastated' group had RSES scores of 21 or less, and Depression and Anxiety scores at least one standard deviation above the mean for all females.

Note: Statistical significance: Using the non-parametric Sign Test (Siegel & Castellan, 1988), on nine items indicating disadvantage, poor adjustment or abuse, City School pupils scored worse than those in United School, p<.002. 'City' and 'United' are names derived from famous soccer teams; neither school was connected with, or was actually close to the soccer stadia in question.

abused. The combination of physical and sexual abuse (as in all of the other Northern Schools) was reflected in very poor self-esteem, and in markedly higher scores on the measures of depression and anxiety. Particularly striking was the number in City School whom we have described as being "ego devastated" with very low self-esteem, and markedly elevated scores on depression and anxiety. We fear for the future of these girls, who without help, intervention and support (which they would have been unlikely to obtain) would drift into futures marked by the negative adjustments which the review of literature earlier in this chapter has identified.

Although the data did not extend to neighbourhood variables, we would speculate that City School is serving an urban subculture, probably marked by chronic patterns of intergenerational maladaptation, mental illness and crime in adults, dysfunctional parenting, and abused girls become marginally-adjusted adults.

We have been struck by the large scale epidemiological and public health research on child maltreatment that has been published in Britain in the past 15 years. This research is costly and difficult to undertake when national sampling is involved. Yet there is a dearth of neighbourhood and community studies, and studies of the schools that serve deprived neighbourhoods as possible centres of support and welfare (or its converse, when chronic patterns of bullying and victimisation occur), in "breaking the cycle" of deprivation, abuse, and adults' dysfunctional behaviour (Williams & Pritchard, 2006). Ecological, ethnographic and neighbourhood research should be a major priority in future work.

CRITICAL REALIST CONCLUSIONS: THE 'ABSENT' CHILDREN

The above study was undertaken, and the data (or 'things') were generated before we had been influenced by the critical realist research paradigm of studies of childhood (Archer, 2008; Alderson, 2013, 2016). It should be instructive to focus on these findings through a critical realist lens. First of all, the original research was framed within an implicit positivist paradigm, assuming that the research "instruments" were valid, and the results falsifiable in terms of implicit null hypotheses. But such a research model fails to address the basic humanity of the actors in their struggle for identity in achieving fulfilled, meaningful lives.

"The missing children" are like the ones described by Alderson (2013, 2016) in her critical realist accounts of "absence" in childhood: the vulnerable and wounded children whom research ignores, and who are not dignified with an identity. Alderson (2013) is scathing in her critique of research on child victims "when epistemology predominates over ontology" (p. 80). In contrast, hermeneutic research in the critical research model "... attends to performance: how children present and manage their bodies, learn

221

and practise healthy behaviour" (p. 80). Winter's (2011) text on helping children to become 'themselves', following child abuse involving what CR theorists call "absence" (meaning reflexive change, based on denying the "nothingness" or objectification of the abused child) is a model of enabling children to expand their lives. In the case studies that Winter's research presents, young people in care review their "life histories", and plan with social workers what their future may be.

Further research and practice must begin with a clear value base, such as that of *child-centred humanism*, which seeks to address alienation at the very beginning of the research. The research process itself should be a dialectical process which seeks to unmask alienation, through case studies which enable the actors (both researchers, and their engaged audience) to *understand* (*Ich verstehe*, as Weber would put it) the wrap of alienation.

Consider "Margaret", a 15-year-old student at "City High School", in the study of students in secondary schools, described above. She had endured maximum levels of physical and sexual abuse: she had 'devastated' self-esteem (a virtual absence of any feelings of self-worth), and was very depressed and extremely anxious. Yet we know her as a cipher, knowing only her gender and her ethnic background (white English). A critical realist approach would have focussed on City High School as an intensively researched case study, with the ethnographic researcher conducting extensive interviews with students about their lives, acting over a period of a year as a teacher and a counsellor whom students could approach. Students like Margaret need to begin a dialectic questioning of their fate, accusing their abusers, and the oppressive systems which mask and allow abuse, and permit the negation of women's aspirations, their natural state of their being as fulfilled, self-actualizing humans.

Ideas about "cause" do not, ultimately, come from the statistical manipulation of variables in a matrix, but from an ontological understanding of "reality", and the totality of the interactions of the lives of Margaret and her fellow students not merely in school, but in the entire community, or ecology, in which they live. The lives and the community of these students were, and almost certainly still are, masked in the alienation of silence, cloaked in *non-being* (Bhaskar, 2008; Archer, 2014). 'Self-esteem' is a cipher, a mysterious marker, but is collectivised by researchers into a description of reality (like "gender", "ethnicity", "systems of abuse"). We wish to release individuals who, in dialectical terms, can interrogate their past and their present, to become, morphogenetically, new people (Archer, 2003); that is, *becoming* new beings in the final level of Bhaskar's (2008) application of dialectical realism to his initial model of critical realism (Norrie, 2010). Priscilla Alderson (2013, p. 126) calls this escape from child abuse an escape from alienation, *the flourishing of the child's inner being.*

Individuals 'present themselves' in everyday life (Goffman, 1969; Shulman, 2016) as individuals who are variously: joyful, defeated, bad, insane, winners, losers or as Margaret Archer would prefer it, sometimes as newly self-created individuals, the increasing number who are 'coming out' from the legacies of child abuse, and mental illness (Bagley & King, 2003, 2005).

NOTES

[1] See www.kanka-gajendra.org for details of the "giving back" activities carried out in Britain and India, in memory of Kanka.

[2] When one of us was undergoing my nurse training in Britain, we experienced an old lady who had carried the guilt of child sexual abuse all her life, and now very ill, could only die peacefully if she could be "forgiven" for the sin of her childhood victimization.

[3] Another form of bullying, that using various kinds of electronic media, also impacts negatively on young victims (Slonje et al., 2016).

[4] For case examples, and possible psychodynamic explanations of the relatively rare phenomenon of consummated incest, see Bagley (1969) and Pincus and Dare (1980).

[5] Requesting informants to use a laptop to answer sensitive questions was first used by Bagley and Ramsay (1986) in their random sample studying suicidality and childhood abusive events recalled by Alberta adults aged 18 to 27. Such technology is now widely used in such studies.

[6] We have a theory that the excess of black adolescents who are excluded from school results from their revolt against the "master-slave" relationship (elaborated by Bhaskar, 2008) in British secondary schools. The black child is not "just another brick in the wall". Wright et al. (2000) in writing about 'race, class and gender in exclusion from school' do address these possibilities, in a valuable qualitative study.

[7] The questionnaire did not address "citizenship education" issues. That part of the study (Al-Refai & Bagley, 2008) used different methods to access Muslim and Non-Muslim students.

[8] The RSES cut-off point for measuring "devastated self-esteem" was chosen as the level which was most predictive of "high" (scores in the highest quintile) on the measures of depression and anxiety: i.e. had fewest false negatives and positives. All students in this category had depression and anxiety scores at least one standard deviation above the female population mean.

CHAPTER 9

CONCLUSIONS

Unmasking the Alienation of Childhood

INTRODUCTION

It is becoming increasingly common for social scientists to give an account of their personal biography, for this may allow insight into their choice of research topic, their selection of methodology, their use and selection of evidence, and the conclusions they draw. The individual is part of the research matrix that she or he studies, and inevitably has influence upon it, or at least on how it is interpreted, and written about. The Aboriginal researcher Chris Sarra (2011) in his critical realist account of reform in the community school of which he was principal, informs us that telling one's life story, one's history of "walk about" is essential in Aboriginal interactions, and he devotes 12 pages of his book in telling this story (and published an autobiography two years later). The Black British researcher Chris Mullard (1973) published his autobiography (of being a 'mixed-race' kid in racist Britain) before going on to publish major scholarly works on race in Britain (Mullard, 1985). Chris Searle (2001) in writing about the inclusive school, also gives an autobiographical account of his life as a head teacher. In reading these works we understand Searle, Sarra and Mullard more fully, and understand and appreciate both intellectually and morally their research, in a critical, humanist mode.

Our intellectual concerns developed in this book (reflecting our African, Jewish, and 'Mixed Race' journeys), began for Alice Sawyerr in the 1990s when, working in an urban all age NHS Mental Health clinic she experienced black and ethnic minority children manifesting identity issues, children who were confused about or denigrated their ethnicity, as well as demonstrating other 'problem' behaviours. AS devised a programme of identity enhancement, which was pioneered in "St. John's" day nursery in which through the combined recommendations of the clinical, educational and social services, children who were placed, with various specialised goals for their improved mental health and identity formation. The publication of this programme (Sawyerr, 1999) was well received, and was adopted by all six of the local authority's nurseries. In 2002 AS formulated an action research programme at StJ's, in which she video-recorded herself, the children, the workers, as well as the managers over a 4-week period. The purpose of this research was to examine how government-prescribed "early learning goals" were being implemented, and how the nursery workers' interactions in this regard were relevant to the development of positive identities in the children.

HISTORICAL REVIEW

Returning to the video-recorded material more than a decade later, AS decided to frame the results within the context of a review of Equality issues – social class, ethnicity and gender – in Britain over a 40-year period, 1968 to 2008, taking into account numerous governmental policy changes in the fields of ethnicity, education, and self-esteem development in minority children, as well as exploring some of the reasons why girls appear to have lower self-esteem levels than boys, and why Black and Ethnic Minority children and adolescents in Britain no longer seem to have issues with self-concept and self-esteem.

Thus we have broadened the focus to take a perspective on *equality issues* affecting children and adolescents, which impinge on the lives of a variety of groups: ethnic and religious minorities, economically disadvantaged groups, and gender groups. Although this book is historical in focus, we began by a review of recent research on social class in Britain, examining, in Chapter 2, Savage's (2015) seven-fold classification, based on a group's access to economic, social and cultural resources. At the lowest level in these seven strata are the *Precariat*, some 15 percent of the British population whose access to economic resources is precarious, whose social capital is minimal, and whose cultural capital is severely restricted by factors such as their low educational levels. Further recent studies point to sectors of the minimally-qualified precariat youth who are variously termed NEETS (not in education, employment or training), Chavs, or Yobs. We deploy a Marxist model of global capitalism to theorise the "usefulness" of this marginalised group for the capitalist system: they are useful as a 'reserve army of labour', available when in times of boom, capitalism needs a supply of cheap labour whose very insecurity ensures that their wages shall be kept low, and their tenure shall be made short.

Our argument, further, is that "poor whites" are identity-disadvantaged, unlike ethnic and religious minorities in Britain many of whom have a strong and ethnic and religious heritage, and a desire and a feeling of duty to be upwardly mobile, or at least to create those chances for their children. At the present time ethnic and religious minorities are underrepresented in the precariat: we predict that in a couple of generations very few will remain in this lowest stratum, as Heath (2014) has proposed for Muslim minorities in Britain. Of course, disadvantaged white youth have a right to nurture, dignity and respect, and this may come from social policy action interventions, such as the universal, citizen's basic income, advocated by Standing (2014) in his writing on this group.

CRITICAL REALISM: AN INTELLECTUAL ADVENTURE

Our intellectual adventures in the complex and challenging intellectual world of Roy Bhaskar's critical realism are explored in Chapter 3. Critical realism is an integrative philosophy of social research, and offers the possibility of integrating Marxist and spiritual assumptions in qualitative and quantitative research, in humanistic ways, based on identifying aspects of a social structure that are "real", and not socially or linguistically constructed.

This value-based account of what is real in society allows the researcher to construct models of dialectical critical realism, which enable individuals not only to personally reflect on social situations and possibilities for change, but also through social interactions, to build a consciousness which is liberating, and can expose the false ideologies which blame the stigmatised underclasses, or ethnic minority groups, for their perceived faults. Critical realism is commended as an ideal model for studying (and changing) schools. Within critical realism is the idea of "underlabouring" the process of subjecting social institutions and social interactions to critical scrutiny by evaluation using an ontologically grounded value system. The model chosen for that process in this thesis is termed *Child-Centred Humanism* (CCH).

Child-Centred Humanism, and Child and Adolescent Self-Esteem and Self-Actualisation

The psychological well-being of the child needs to be carefully nurtured, and Alice Sawyerr has approached this obligation as a developmental psychologist and systemic and family psychotherapist throughout her practice with children and adolescents. During her work with referred children in nursery education in the 1990s, Alice was aware of the challenges which a broader system of institutional racism could impose on the developing child's ethnic identity. The literature on the development of ethnic identity in children, and their later development of 'global' self-esteem has been reviewed. Pleasingly, the research literature suggests that far from African-American (and by inference, African-Caribbean) children having low self-esteem, they

227

had developed, as ethnic and cultural groups, a self-esteem that is *more* favourable than that of their white peers (Bergner, 2009; Gibson et al., 2015). The reasons for this are several: the Black Pride movement was influential in America, and at the same time African Americans took support from their traditional reference groups in family, community and peers.

Studies on black children attributing negative characteristics to black dolls and figures in standardised tests are now rarely published, either for political reasons, or because replications are failing to yield significance results. Our (online) literature search yielded only one recent study according to the identifiers "color" and "dolls", and other relevant search terms. This study by Wong and Hines (2015) found that preschool boys liked all colours except pink; girls liked the colour pink most; boys chose as their favourite toy anything with wheels; and girls chose dolls. Racism in children's symbolic play may be disappearing, but genderism is alive and well.[1]

The most widely used scale measuring global self-esteem is the Rosenberg Self-Esteem Scale (RSES), which has been translated into many languages, and has been validated cross-culturally in terms of its ability to predict various behaviours, and its correlation with psychiatric diagnoses, and with other validated measures of personal distress. In America, African-Americans now have the *highest* levels of self-esteem as measured by the RSES, but persistent gender differences in all cultural and ethnic groups in America, Canada, England and other countries remain. Why females have significantly poorer RSES scores than males has not been satisfactorily explained in any research study.

However, examining evidence on child maltreatment, and sexual abuse in particular, we observe a number of studies showing that such events in childhood and adolescence are reflected in depressed levels of self-esteem. This, we argue, is a causal connection: child sexual abuse diminishes personal feelings of self-worth. Since girls and adolescent women are those most likely to suffer sexual abuse (and are also those, compared to males, who are most negatively affected by it), we argue that when prior events of abuse and its effects are taken into account, gender differences in levels of self-esteem should diminish – a hypothesis that was sustained in the Northern Schools study, summarised below.

The Multicultural Nursery

We have attempted to apply a critical realist model to the case study of an urban, multicultural local authority day nursery in London. The original study was not conceived within a CR framework, but aimed to focus through observations, and interviews with staff and managers, on how staff were implementing some of the Early Learning Goals imposed on nurseries by government. Implicit in these observations was an enquiry into how well a programme for identity enhancement that AS had initiated in the nursery (St. John's or StJ's) four years earlier, was now working. That earlier work had prepared multicultural materials for use by staff in order to enhance ethnic identity, and create a positive sense of their cultural heritage in the children. StJ's served the Elgar Estate, a socially and economically deprived inner city area in London.

The results from the initial period of fieldwork indicated that staff noticed apparent tension between the learning goals they were supposed to follow, and the individualised care-plan devised for each child, in collaboration with the educational and social services involved with the child and his or her family. As for the interactions between staff and children, and between children themselves we could find no evidence of the formal or informal transmission of negative views concerning colour or ethnicity. The children freely and affectionately interacted, regardless of their ethnic origins.

The happy state of StJ's was brutally terminated, without notice, when the Council decided to close the nursery, refurbish it, and lease it to the national government's Sure Start children's centre programme, which was beginning to unroll across England and Wales. The city earned a considerable fee from Sure Start for allowing this to happen, and justified the closure of StJ's in a document which was clouded in obfuscation, deceit and half-truths. We interpreted this as part of the process of alienation which oppressed the lives of many of the population of the "Elgar Estate".

We have tried to fit these findings within a Critical Realist framework. We found, as had Alderson (2013) that it is challenging to fit one's previous research into a CR framework when the original research was carried out before the researcher was familiar with a dialectical critical realist perspective. Critical realism is a model built on *ontology* (the 'real' nature of being and of social structure) and then analyses the actions of 'agents' in that framework in leaving behind 'absence', a form of concealed being or alienation, through a social and intellectual reflexivity founded in dialectical critical realism, which leads to self-actualization, morphogenesis, and upward social mobility. We were unable to describe such a process of liberation or the unmasking of alienation in this case study, because the structures of oppression and false ideology were too powerful, too strong.

Instead, we have argued for the construction of an ideal study which would be long-term and well-funded, with a variety of professionals, researchers, community workers and social activists who from the outset will proceed on a critical realist model of social regeneration on the Elgar Estate, one of Britain's most depressed urban areas, on a path of political challenge which unmasks the alienating forces which keep its population in check.

Adolescent Self-Esteem, Gender, Ethnicity: Recipes for Failure and Success

On the Elgar Estate there are doubtless many child and adolescent victims of emotional, physical and sexual abuse. We can make this assertion with some confidence, from a review of the epidemiological literature on child maltreatment in Britain, which shows (a) about 12 per cent of female children and adolescents experience unwanted sexual assaults, and for half this abuse will be intrusive of the child's body, and long-term; (b) for up to five per cent of childhood and adolescents, their lives will be marred by a combination of physical, emotional and sexual abuse – a combination of events which will likely have negative long-term consequences for self-esteem, mental health, and social adjustments. "Poly-victimisation" is particularly likely to occur in disrupted families who are part of the cycle of deprivation, and live in low-income housing of the type that exists on the Elgar Estate (and in many other parts of Britain).

Because of the increased prevalence of negative adult outcomes in victims of multiple abuses (severe depression, suicidal behaviour, anxiety, PTSD, psychosis, alcoholism and addiction, unwanted pregnancies, instability of relationships, educational and occupational behaviour) public health advocates argue that a nation which prevents such early abuse, or offers prompt and effective treatment when abuse does occur, would earn considerable moral and fiscal credibility. In Britain today there is no sign of any such preventive or therapeutic programmes; rather, in times of economic constraint, mental health programmes for adolescents and adults are being pared, not improved.

Schools can be important agencies for the abused child to find support from a teacher or counsellor, who can then organise supportive programmes for the child or adolescent – including guided peer support. But, as we have argued elsewhere (Sawyerr & Bagley, 2016) in an age of underfunding, school class sizes are increasing, and teacher's lives are increasingly stressed by a variety of factors, which means that they are less able to respond to the individual needs of their pupils. The informal culture of the school, its system of friendships, interactions, social controls, informal punishments, persecution and bullying can, several studies show, make the psychological situation of the abused child worse, and she becomes the chronic victim of harassment, bullying and sexual assault, often with very negative consequences for her long term social and psychological adjustment.

At the family level, research seems to show that for some children, there is a progression of events which undermine self-esteem: at first she is physically and or emotionally neglected and abused, which undermines the development of adequate self-esteem. The low self-esteem child who is approached by a sexually predatory adult will already have developed feelings of worthlessness, and will have poor ego defences, and no trusted adult to whom she can turn to, for help to have the abuse stopped. A skilled abuser may alienate her further from conventional social relationships; this may be a repeated pattern for adolescents recruited into commercialise sexual exploitation. Certain areas of cities (typically on "sink estates"), as well as children removed into "care" are prey to these predatory sexual abusers.

We are writing here on the evidence which in the main, focuses on "white girls". What of ethnic minority children in Britain, from African-Caribbean, and Asian-heritage families? British research to the present time has not offered much information on this, although it is clear that the incidence of child abuse in minority families may be significantly lower than in mainstream (white, indigenous) families: nevertheless the sexual abuse and exploitation outlined above do occur to some extent in the lives of ethnic minority children.

Some of these issues are explored in the analysis of data from the Northern Schools study. The results from 2,025 students aged 11 to 18 in ten schools, show that the Rosenberg Self-Esteem Scale (RSES) is a factorially valid and internally reliable measure across age and gender groups. It has face validity in terms of its correlation with measures of child and adolescent adjustment. The results confirmed American and Canadian research, in that males had significantly "higher" levels of self-esteem than females. However, within females (but not in males) RSES scores had statistically significant variation across ethnic groups, black females in particular having higher self-esteem than white females. Reasons for this emerged when findings on child maltreatment were analysed. White females had significantly higher levels of such maltreatment, which correlated with depressed levels of self-esteem. When RSES data for all males and females in the Northern Schools study were compared, taking account of histories of child maltreatment, differences in self-esteem between genders *failed* to reach statistical significance.

Identifying students who had "devastated self-esteem" (extremely low levels of self-esteem, often associated with high levels of depression and anxiety) the study found that such adolescent women often had a history of chronic abuse, both physical and sexual, imposed on their childhoods. Some five per cent of females fell into this category, but they were unevenly distributed across the schools studied. We identified two schools within the same urban conurbation which had differing profiles of self-esteem, and much higher levels of devastated self-esteem, anxiety and depression, as well as high levels of sexual and physical abuse of females, which were significant predictors of very low self-esteem. One school, whose pupils were mainly White had salient profiles on these indicators of abuse, disadvantage and poor self-esteem. The contrasted school, which had many Black and Asian students, had relatively good levels of self-esteem, and significantly lower levels of abuse history, and adverse psychological profiles. We argue that disadvantaged schools identified by questionnaire screening linked to neighbourhood surveillance of social disadvantage, should be the focus of ethnographic case studies, which could be moulded within the critical realist framework of knowledge generation, and social change.

FINAL CONCLUSIONS: AN INCLUSIVE SOCIETY?

Our conclusions concern the advocacy of an *inclusive society*. At the present time, England stands out amongst affluent nations as having high levels of income inequality, a high proportion of the population who are in poverty, with low rates of upward social mobility. In such a society immigrants and ethnic minorities will struggle to be upwardly mobile, and they may face discrimination in employment and promotion (as do women) (Bagley & Abubaker, 2017). High levels of inequality are dynamically linked to high levels of racism, xenophobia and Islamophobia. Blaming victims for their lack of success is, we argue, one of the functions through which the holders of wealth and power retain their status and position in society.

The review of recent history (1968 to 2008) on selected studies and episodes of history concerning ethnicity, equality and identity show that some aspects of British social structure are changing quite rapidly, while others maintain their basic character, in which for example, high levels of child morbidity and mortality are embedded in the class system.

African Caribbean ethnic groups are rising above the lowest sector of employment, achieving some upward mobility, but still have many rungs to rise. Mixed Black-White marriages are increasingly common, and a "liberal" sector of whites are interacting on terms of equality with black minorities. Black children and adolescents, according to various projective and self-completion measures, no longer devalue their identity or their self-esteem. Our work in the period of 1998 to 2003 on identity enhancement may have been part of that process of social change.

A strong racist or xenophobic element remains in British society however, although its venom has been somewhat diverted from attacking African-Caribbeans (and their black and mixed-race children) as a cultural group, into a new kind of ethnicism which attacks (figuratively and literally) Asian, African and Middle Eastern English communities and individuals who are Muslim, or simply "foreign".

Schools have been passive rather than active in the anti-racist movement. Schools as institutions have been under stress because of changing curricula, frequency of government imposed examinations, and underfunding. Class sizes are becoming larger, and this can undermine effective teaching. In the child-centred humanist philosophy, which "underlabours" the critical realist appraisal of social institutions concerned with equality, teachers should be able to know the children they teach as individuals, with unique sets of potentials and needs. When class sizes exceed 25, this is hardly possible. Britain's entrenched social class system, which ritualises the folkways of class membership, debases the possibilities for child-centred humanism.

Ethnic and religious minorities in Britain are in many cases, helping themselves by enhancing their life's path through the conscious memory of the deprivation of earlier generations, and the desire to advance socially and occupationally through education, with cultural support for their minority group status. The 'poor whites' have fewer such "ethnic identities" on which to draw, in seeking to be upwardly mobile. It is these 'poor whites' who are variously described as "chavs", "yobs", "NEETS", "the precariat" – "the reserve army of labour" who frequently fail to rise from the alienation imposed upon them by the British class system. Ethnic minorities are (other factors being equal, such as fairness in employment practices) likely to rise occupationally, year by year, since it may be useful for a class-based economy to have "ethnic pockets" of labour who become increasingly skilled, and specialised in their work.

A persistent problem in British society is that of child maltreatment, which occurs in all social classes but certainly occurs most frequently amongst the poorest groups of society, whose family disorganisation is transmitted across generations, in certain sub-zones of cities. The girl who is both sexually and physically abused (and emotionally abused as well, although this could not be measured in the Northern Schools study) will also be failed by her school's peer culture and her teachers, and she is likely to go on to parent a new generation of victims. Research has shown that this cycle can be broken, and that doing so is highly cost effective. In 2017, this message has not been absorbed by national government, and seems unlikely to be acted upon.

DCR analysis level	The reality
Level 1M 'Moral realism': harms and benefits are real and all-pervasive. These are experienced by individuals and sub-groups in varying ways ' … because humans are vulnerable, sensitive, social beings, able to suffer and to flourish, moral realism is part of daily life.' (Archer, 2003; Bhaskar, 1986)	Class-dominated Britain serves the interests of Capital imposing alienation and absence upon sub-cultures, and maltreatment upon its precariat, who suffer in various ways, attempting to be 'socially mobile', but on capitalism's terms
Level 2E is the edge of transition, actively negating absences, aspiring to 'a transformational model of social activity', unmasking the 'master-slave' relationship (Bhaskar, 1993)	Child-centred humanism exposes the numerous absences imposed by class oppression, and in research tries to avoid 'moving the deck-chairs on the Titanic': rather 'planting' seeds of hope' (Archer, 2016)
Level 3L is the totality of change, including new totalities resulting from 2E change activism: 'connects past, present and future to illuminate how … the younger generation all matter now.' (Archer, 2016)	Social structure is in flux, changing, adapting, resocialising alienated youth, with its own "urban" philosophy. Powerful class interests counteract change strategies through false media, and material bribery ('the toys' or cultural capital of the Class above)
Level 4D involves critical reflexive analysis or morphogenesis by individuals. This process leads to 'transformative praxis', in which individual flourishing depends on everyone flourishing. 'Malign Meld' (Bhaskar, 2008) occurs when 'capitalism strikes back' and imposes new forms of masked alienation	"Breakthroughs" come piecemeal through pressure groups who are part of the class struggle on behalf of children's values e.g. ethnic minority consciousness, some schools, religious groups, Green value groups, "Fabian" scholar-activists. Progress is fragmented, since Capital's counter agents offer powerful trinkets to divert the proles

We turn, last of all, to the critical realist model of social research. The CR literature mostly addresses theoretical domains, which is appropriate for a newly emerging philosophy of social research. Applied studies using the model of dialectical critical realism (DCR) are relatively few. After our research has been completed, we found it difficult (as have others) to apply the DCR model *post hoc* to our completed research, so we have proposed an ideal study which is community and school based, long-term and well-funded, and has active DCR goals of reaching for praxis, and the morphogenetic model of social change. Looking at the alienation which is imposed on the lives of the lowest social class group, the precariat, we offer a DCR framework for the whole of British society, using the four levels of analysis which make up Baskhar's (2008) MELD framework of analysis.

The nursery school children, within their degraded urban community in Inner London, and the secondary school students in the Northern Schools whose questionnaire data we analysed, fit into the above table, of course. But we have been unable to speak for them, to act for them, to offer them any kind of way forward to escape from the hard hand of capitalism. Their alienation remains unmasked.

NOTE

[1] Doll studies are still being used occasionally, by those working in the field of self-esteem enhancement of groups other than African Americans eg. Stokes-Guinan (2011).

REFERENCES

Abbott, A. (1999). *Department and discipline: Chicago sociology at one hundred.* Chicago, IL: University of Chicago Press.

Abubaker, M., & Bagley, C. (2016). Work-Life Balance and the needs of female employees in the telecommunications industry: A critical realist approach to issue in industrial and organisational social psychology. *SAGE OPEN: Comprehensive Psychology, 5,* 1–12.

Adams, G. R. (1978). Racial membership and physical attractiveness effects on pre-school teachers' expectation. *Child Study Journal, 8,* 29–41.

Adler, A. (1946). *Understanding human nature: The psychology of personality.* New York, NY: Greenberg.

Ahmed, S. (2004). *The cultural politics of emotion.* Edinburgh: Edinburgh University Press.

Aitken, S. C. (2001). *Geographies of young people: The morally contested spaces of identity.* London: Routledge.

Akram, S., & Hogan, A. (2015). On reflexivity and conduct of the self in everyday life: Reflections on Bourdieu and Archer. *British Journal of Sociology, 66,* 606–625.

Alderson, P. (2013). *Childhoods real and imagined: An introduction to critical realism and childhood studies.* Abingdon: Routledge.

Alderson, P. (2016). *The politics of childhoods real and imagined: Practical application of critical realism and childhood studies.* Abingdon: Routledge.

Alexander, R. (2011). Introduction to special section: Medical advances in child sexual abuse. Part 2. *Journal of Child Sexual Abuse, 20,* 607–611.

Allport, G. (1954/1979). *The nature of prejudice.* New York, NY: Doubleday; and Addison-Wesley.

Allport, G. (1968). *The person in psychology.* Boston, MA: Beacon Press.

Al-Refai, N., & Bagley, C. (2008). *Citizenship education: The British muslim perspective.* Rotterdam: Sense Educational Books.

Anda, R. F., Felitti, V. J., Bremner, J. D., Walker, J. D., Whitfield, C., Perry, B. D., Dube, S. R., Giles, W. H. (2006). The enduring effects of abuse and related adverse experiences in childhood: A convergence of evidence from neurobiology and epidemiology. *European Archives of Psychiatry and Clinical Neuroscience, 256,* 174–180.

Ansari, D., Fugelsang, J., Dhital, B., & Ventatramen, V. (2006). Dissociating response conflict from numerical magnitude processing in the brain: An event-related fMRI study. *Neuroimage, 15,* 799–805.

Archer, M. A. (1979). *The social origins of educational systems.* London: Sage.

Archer, M. A. (1995). *Realist social theory: The morphogenetic approach.* Cambridge: Cambridge University Press.

Archer, M. A. (2000). *Being human: The problematic agency.* Cambridge: Cambridge University Press.

Archer, M. A. (2003). *Structure, agency and the internal conversation.* Cambridge: Cambridge University Press.

Archer, M. A. (2007). *Making our way through the world: Human reflexivity and social mobility.* Abingdon: Routledge.

Archer, M. A. (2010). *Conversations about reflexivity.* Abingdon: Routledge.

Archer, M. A. (2012). *The reflexive imperative in late modernity.* Cambridge: Cambridge University Press.

Archer, M. A. (2014). *Late modernity: Trajectories towards morphogenetic society.* New York, NY: Springer.

Archer, M. A., & Giner, S. (1971). Social stratification in Europe. In M. A. Archer & S. Giner (Eds.), *Contemporary Europe: Class, status and power* (pp. 1–59). London: Weidenfeld and Nicolson.

Archer, M. A., Collier, A., & Porpora, D. V. (2004). *Transcendence: Critical realism and god.* Abingdon: Routledge.

Arestis, P., & Sawyer, M. (2005). The neoliberal experience of the United Kingdom. In A. Saad-Filho & D. Johnston (Eds.), *Neoliberalism: A critical reader* (pp. 199–207). London: Pluto Press.

Arnold. J. H. (2000). *History: A very short introduction.* London: Oxford University Press.

Avineri, S. (1970). *The social and political thought of Karl Marx.* Cambridge: University of Cambridge Press.

Bachman, J., O'Malley, P., Freedman-Doan, P., Trzesniewski, K., & Donnallan, M. B. (2011). Adolescent self-esteem: Differences by race/ethnicity, gender and age. *Self-Identity, 10,* 445–473.

Badgley, R. (1984). *Sexual offences against children.* Ottawa: Ministry of Justice, Government of Canada.

Bagci, S., Kumashiro, M., Smith, P., Blumberg, H., & Rutland, A. (2014). Cross-ethnic friendships: Are they really rare? Evidence from secondary schools around London. *International Journal of Intercultural Relations, 41,* 125–137.

Bagley, C (1969). Incest behavior and incest taboo. *Social Problems, 16,* 505–519. (Reprinted in B. Armour (Ed.) *Treatment of family sexual abuse.* University of Minnesota Press. 1975.)

Bagley, C. (1965). Juvenile delinquency in Exeter: An ecological and comparative study. *Urban Studies, 2,* 39–50. (Reprinted in J.B. Mays (Ed.) (1972) *Juvenile Delinquency, the Family and Social Groups* (pp. 121–150).)

Bagley, C. (1972). *The social psychology of the child with epilepsy.* London: Routledge.

Bagley, C. (1973). The welfare of the child: An examination of judicial opinion about medical and social work evidence in adoption cases. *British Journal of Social Work, 3,* 79–90. (Reprinted in S. Curtis (Ed.) (1977) *Child adoption.* London: Association of British Adoption and Fostering Agencies.)

Bagley, C. (1983). Alienation and identity in young West Indians in Britain and The Netherlands. In C. Bagley & G. Verma (Eds.), *Multicultural childhood: Education, ethnicity and cognitive styles* (pp. 180–193). Aldershot: Aldershot.

Bagley, C. (1984). Urban delinquency: Ecological and educational perspectives. In T. Freeman (Ed.), *Mental health and the environment* (pp. 204–259). London: Churchill-Livingston.

Bagley, C. (1987). Child sexual abuse and juvenile prostitution. *Canadian Journal of Public Health, 76*, 65–66.

Bagley, C. (1989). Prevalence and correlates of unwanted sexual acts in childhood. *Canadian Journal of Public Health, 80*, 295–296.

Bagley, C. (1990). Development and validity of a measure of unwanted sexual contact in childhood in childhood, for use in community mental health surveys. *Psychological Reports, 66*, 401–402 & 449–450.

Bagley, C. (1991a). Transracial adoption in Britain: A follow-up study with policy considerations. *Child Welfare, 74*, 286–299.

Bagley, C. (1991b). The prevalence and mental health sequels of child sexual abuse in a community sample of women aged 18 to 27. *Canadian Journal of Community Mental Health, 10*, 103–116.

Bagley, C. (1991c). Sexual abuse recalled: Evaluation of a computerised questionnaire in young adult males. *Perceptual and Motor Skills, 72*, 287–288.

Bagley, C. (1991d). The prevalence and mental health sequels of child sexual abuse in a community sample of women aged 18 to 27. *Canadian Journal of Community Mental Health, 10*, 103–116.

Bagley, C. (1992). The urban environment and child pedestrian and bicycle injuries: Interaction of ecological and personality characteristics. *Journal of Community and Applied Social Psychology, 2*, 1–9.

Bagley, C. (1993a). The urban setting of juvenile pedestrian injuries: A study of behavioral ecology and social disadvantage. *Accident Analysis and Prevention, 24*, 673–678.

Bagley, C. (1993b). Psychological and social adjustment in racially-mixed marriages. *International Journal of Marriage and the Family, 1*, 53–59.

Bagley, C. (1995a). *Child sexual abuse and mental health in adolescents and adults.* Aldershot: Ashgate.

Bagley, C. (1995b). Early sexual experience and sexual victimization of children and adolescents. In G. Rekers (Eds.), *Handbook of child and adolescents sexual problems* (pp. 135–163). New York, NY: Lexington Books.

Bagley, C. (1996a). Development and validity of a measure of unwanted sexual contact in childhood, for use in community mental health surveys. In *Child maltreatment: Data collection and related issues* (pp. 50–58). Ottawa: Centre for Disease Control.

Bagley, C. (1996b). A typology of sexual abuse: The interaction of emotional, physical and sexual abuse as predictors of adult psychiatric sequelae in women. *Canadian Journal of Human Sexuality, 5*, 101–112.

Bagley, C. (1997). *Children, sex and social policy: Humanistic solutions for problems of child sexual abuse*. Aldershot: Ashgate.

Bagley, C. (1999a). Adolescent prostitution in Canada and The Philippines: Statistical comparisons, an ethnographic account and policy options. *International Social Work, 42*, 445–454.

Bagley, C. (1999b). Children first: Challenges and dilemmas for social workers investigating and treating child sexual abuse. In C. Bagley & K. Mallick (Eds.), *Child sexual abuse and adult offenders: New theory and research* (pp. 103–142). Aldershot: Ashgate.

Bagley, C. (1999c). Child and adolescent prostitution in Canada and The Philippines: Comparative case studies and policy proposals. In C. Bagley & K. Mallick (Eds.), *Child sexual abuse and adult offenders* (pp. 192–210). Aldershot: Ashgate.

Bagley, C. (2002). *Child abusers: Research and therapy*. Miami, FL: Universal Publishers.

Bagley, C. (2008). The logic and morality of educational inclusion. In C. Bagley & G. Verma (Eds.), *Challenges for inclusion: Educational and social studies in Britain and the Indian Sub-Continent*. Rotterdam: Sense Publishers.

Bagley, C. (2011). From sure start to children's centres: Capturing the erosion of social capital. *British Journal of Educational Psychology, 37*, 95–113.

Bagley, C. (2015). *Islam today: A Muslim Quaker's view*. London: The Quaker Universalist Group.

Bagley, C. (2016, March 17). Becoming a non-violent extremist. *The Friend: Quaker Weekly Journal*, p. 14.

Bagley, C., & Abubaker, M. (2017). Muslim woman seeking work: An English case study of discrimination and achievement, with a Dutch comparison. *Social Sciences, 6*, 1–13.

Bagley, C., & Al-Refai (2015/2017). *Religious and ethnic integration in British and Dutch cultures: Historical and contemporary review of citizenship, education and prejudice*. Paper given to SOAS-Nohoudh Muslim Integration Conference, University of London *Engaging with the Integration Discourse*, November, 2015; and in revised form in *Journal for Multicultural Education*, Vol 12, part 2.

Bagley, C., & Coard, B. (1975). Cultural knowledge and rejection of ethnic identity in West Indian children in London. In C. Bagley & G. Verma (Eds.), *Race and education across cultures* (Vol. 11, pp. 82–100). London: Heinemann.

Bagley, C., & D'Augelli, A. (2000, June 17). Gay, lesbian and bisexual youth have elevated rates of suicidal behaviour: An international problem associated with homophobia and homophobic legislation. *British Medical Journal, 320*, 1617–1618.

Bagley, C., & King, K. (2003). *Child sexual abuse: The search for healing*. London & New York, NY: Routledge-Taylor and Francis.

Bagley, C., & King, M. (2005). Exploration of three stigma scales in 83 users of mental health services: Implications for campaigns to reduce stigma. *Journal of Mental Health, 14*, 343–356.

Bagley, C., & LeChance, M. (2000). Evaluation of a family-based programme for the treatment of child sexual abuse. *Child and Family Social Work, 5*, 205–213.

Bagley, C., & Mallick, K. (1999). Introduction: Child sexual abuse and adult offenders. In C. Bagley & K. Mallick (Eds.), *Child sexual abuse and adult offenders: New theory and research* (pp. 1–8) Aldershot: Ashgate.

Bagley, C., & Mallick, K. (2000a). Spiralling up and spiralling down: Implications of a long-term study of temperament and conduct disorder for social work with children. *Child and Family Social Work, 5*, 291–301.

Bagley, C., & Mallick, K. (2000b). Prediction of sexual, emotional and physical maltreatment and mental health outcomes in a longitudinal cohort of 290 adolescent women. *Child Maltreatment, 5*, 218–226.

Bagley, C., & Mallick, K. (2001). Normative data and mental health construct validity for the Rosenberg Self-Esteem scale in British adolescents. *International Journal of Adolescence and Youth, 9*, 117–126.

Bagley, C., & McDonald, M. (1984). Adult mental health sequels of child sexual abuse, physical abuse and neglect in maternally separated children. *Canadian Journal of Community Mental Health, 3*, 15–26.

Bagley, C., & Pritchard, C. (1998a). The reduction of problem behaviours and school exclusion in at-risk youth: An experimental study of school social work with cost-benefit analyses. *Child and Family Social Work, 3*, 219–226.

Bagley, C., & Pritchard, C. (1998b). The billion dollar cost of troubled youth: Prospects for cost-effective prevention and treatment. *International Journal of Adolescent and Youth, 7*, 211–225.

Bagley, C., & Pritchard, C. (1999). Completed suicide in men accused of sexual crimes involving children: Implications for a humanistic approach. In C. Bagley & K. Mallick (Eds.), *Child sexual abuse and adult offenders: New theory and research* (pp. 295–290). Aldershot: Ashgate.

Bagley, C., & Pritchard, C. (2000). Criminality and violence in intra- and extra-familial child sexual abusers in a 2-year cohort of convicted perpetrators. *Child Abuse Review, 9*, 264–274.

Bagley, C., & Ramsay, R. (1986). Sexual abuse in childhood: Psychosocial outcomes and implications for social work practice. *Journal of Social Work and Human Sexuality, 4*, 33–47.

Bagley, C., & Thurston, W. (1996). *Understanding and preventing child sexual abuse volume II: Male victims, adolescents, adult outcomes and offender treatment.* Aldershot: Ashgate.

Bagley, C., & Tremblay, P. (2000a, June 10–14). Special report: Repeal of Section 28. *Professional Social Work.*

Bagley, C., & Tremblay, P. (2000b). Elevated rates of suicidal behavior in gay, lesbian and bisexual youth: Estimates of prevalence and an account of causes. *Crisis: Journal of Crisis Intervention and Suicide Prevention, 21*, 111–117.

Bagley, C., & Verma, G. (1979). *Racial prejudice, the individual and society.* Aldershot: Ashgate.

Bagley, C., & Verma, G. (1983). *Multicultural childhood: Education, ethnicity and cognitive styles*. Aldershot: Ashgate.

Bagley, C., & Young, L. (1979). The identity, adjustment and achievement of transracially adopted children: A review and empirical report. In G. Verma & C. Bagley (Eds.), *Race, identity and education* (pp. 192–219). London: MacMillan.

Bagley, C., & Young, L. (1980). The long-term adjustment and identity of a sample of inter-country adopted children. *International Social Work, 23*, 16–22.

Bagley, C., & Young, L. (1984). The welfare, adaptation and identity of children from intercultural marriage. In G. Verma & C. Bagley (Eds.), *Race relations and cultural differences: Educational and interpersonal perspectives* (pp. 247–258). London: Croom Helm.

Bagley, C., & Young, L. (1990). Depression, self-esteem and suicidal behavior as sequels of sexual abuse in childhood: Research and therapy. In M. Rothery & G. Cameron (Eds.), *Child maltreatment expanding our concepts of helping* (pp. 183–219). Hillsdale, NJ: Lawrence Erlbaum.

Bagley, C., & Young, L. (1993). Chinese adoptees in Britain: A 20-year follow up of adjustment and social identity. *International Social Work, 36*, 141–155.

Bagley, C., & Young, L. (1997). Multi-ethnic marriage and interculturalism in Britain and The Netherlands. In D. Woodrow, G. Verma, M. Rocha-Trinidade, G. Campani, & C. Bagley (Eds.), *Intercultural education* (pp. 317–328). Aldershot: Avebury.

Bagley, C., & Young, L. (1998). Long-term evaluation of group counselling for women with a history of child sexual abuse: Focus on depression, self-esteem, suicidal behaviors and social support. *Social Work with Groups, 21*, 63–73.

Bagley, C., Bart, M., & Wong, J. (1978). Cognition and scholastic success in West Indian 10-year-olds in London: A comparative study. *Educational Studies, 4*, 7–17.

Bagley, C., Bertrand, L., & Bolitho, F. (1995). Mental health profiles, suicidal behavior, and community sexual assault in 2112 Canadian adolescents. *Crisis: Journal of Crisis Intervention and Suicide Prevention, 16*, 126–131.

Bagley, C., Bolitho, F., & Bertrand, L. (1997). Sexual assault in school, mental health and suicidal behaviors in adolescent women in Canada. *Adolescence, 32*, 361–366.

Bagley, C., Bolitho, F., & Bertrand, L. (2001). Ethnicities and social adjustment in Canadian adolescents. *Journal of International Migration and Integration, 2*, 99–120.

Bagley, C., Kadri, S, Shanaz, A., Simkhada, P., & King, K. (2017). Commercialised sexual exploitation of children, adolescents and women, and sexually transmitted infections: A case study of Bangladesh. *Advances in Applied Sociology, 7*, 137–150.

Bagley, C., Madrid, S., Simkhada, P., & King, K. (2017). Adolescent girls growing beyond commercialised sexual exploitation: Case study from The Philippines of voluntary action for income support. *Submitted for publication, under review.*

Bagley, C., Mallick, K., Verma, G., Bolitho, F., Tse, J., Bertrand, L., & Madrid, S. (1999). Adjustment, stress and family life in adolescents in Canada, Britain, Pakistan, India, Hong Kong and The Philippines. *International Journal of Adolescence and Youth, 7*, 263–278.

Bagley, C., Rodberg, G., Wellings, D., Moosa-Mitha, M., & Young, L. (1995). Sexual and physical child abuse and the development of dissociative personality traits. *Child Abuse Review, 4*, 99–113.

Bagley, C., Thurston, W., & Tutty, L. (1996). *Understanding and preventing child sexual abuse volume I: Children – Assessment, social work and clinical issues, and prevention education*. Aldershot: Ashgate.

Bagley, C., Verma, G., Mallick, K., & Young, L. (1979). *Personality, self-esteem and prejudice*. Aldershot: Ashgate.

Bagley, C., Wood, M., & Young, L. (1994). Victim to abuser: Mental health and behavioral sequels of child sexual abuse in males in a community survey of young adults. *Child Abuse and Neglect, 18*, 683–697.

Bagley, C., Young, L., & Scully, A. (1993). *Transracial and international adoption: Mental health perspectives*. Aldershot: Avebury.

Baker, A., & Duncan, S. (1985). Child sexual abuse: A study of prevalence in Great Britain. *Child Abuse and Neglect, 31*, 961–969.

Baker, D., Taylor, H., & Henderson, J. (1998). Inequality in infant morbidity: Causes and consequences in England in the 1990s. *Journal of Epidemiology and Community Health, 52*, 451–458.

Banfield, G. (2016). *Critical realism for a Marxist sociology of education*. Abingdon: Routledge.

Bannister, D., & Fransella, F. (1971). *Inquiring man: The theory of personal constructs*. London: Penguin Books.

Barn, R. (1993). *Black children in the public care system*. London: Batsford Books.

Barn, R. (Ed.). (1999). *Working with Black children and adolescents in need*. London: British Agencies for Adoption and Fostering.

Barn, R., Sinclair, R., & Ferdinand, D. (1997). *Acting on principle: An examination of race and ethnicity in social services provision for children and families*. London: British Association for Adoption and Fostering.

Barnes, J., Belsky, J., Broomfield, K., Dave, S., Frost, M., & Melhuish, E. (2005). Disadvantaged but different: Variation among deprived communities in relation to child and family well-being. *Journal of Child Psychology and Psychiatry, 40*, 952–968.

Batsheer, J. (2016). Precarity, food and accompaniment in community and youth work. *Ethnography and Education, 11*, 189–203.

Bebbington, P., Jonas, S., Brugha, T., Meltzer, H., Jenkins, R., Cooper, C., King, M., & McManus, S. (2011a). Child sexual abuse reported by an English national sample: Characteristics and demography. *Social Psychiatry and Psychiatric Epidemiology, 46*, 255–262.

Bebbington, P., Jonas, S., Kuipers, E., King, M., Cooper, C., Brugha, T., Meltzer, H., McManus, S., & Jenkins, R. (2011b). Childhood sexual abuse and psychosis: Data from a cross-sectional psychiatric survey in England. *British Journal of Psychiatry, 199*, 29–37.

Becker, E. (1971). *The birth and death of meaning*. London: Penguin.

Bellis, M. A., Hughes, K., Jones, A., Perkins, C., & McHale, P. (2013). Childhood happiness and violence: A study of their impacts on adult well-being. *BMJ Open, 3*(9). doi:10.1136/bmjopen-2013-003427

Bellis, M. A., Hughes, K., Leckenby, N., Perkins, C., & Lowey, M. (2014b). National household survey of adverse childhood experiences and their relationship with resilience to health-harming behaviour in England. *BMC Medicine, 12*, 72–100.

Bellis, M., Lowey, H., & Leckenby, N. (2014a). Adverse childhood experiences: Retrospective study to determine their impact on adult health. *Journal of Public Health, 36*, 81–91.

Belsky, J., & Melhuish, E. (2007). Impact of Sure Start local programmes on children and families. In J. Belsky, J. Barnes, & E. Melhuish (Eds.), *The national evaluation of Sure Start: Does area-based early intervention work?* Bristol: The Policy Press.

Belsky, J., Melhuish, E., Barnes, J., Leyland, A., & Romaniuk, H. (2006). Effects of Sure Start local programmes on children and families: Early findings from a quasi-experimental, cross-sectional study. *British Medical Journal, 332*, 1476.

Bennett, M., & Sani, S. (2004). *The development of the social self*. London & New York, NY: Taylor and Francis, Psychologists Press.

Bergner, G. (2009). Black child, white preferences: Brown v. Board, the doll tests, and the politics of self-esteem. *American Quarterly, 61*, 299–332.

Beveridge, W. (1968). *Social insurance and allied services, 1942*. London: Her Majesty's Stationery Office.

Bhaskar, R. A. (1986). *Scientific realism and human emancipation*. London: Verso.

Bhaskar, R. A. (1993/2008). *Dialectic: The pulse of freedom* (1st & 2nd editions). Abingdon, Routledge.

Bhaskar, R. A. (2000). *From East to West: Odyssey of a soul*. Abingdon: Routledge.

Bhaskar, R. A. (2002a). *From science to emancipation: Alienation and enlightenment*. Abingdon: Routledge.

Bhaskar, R. A. (2002b). *Meta-reality*. London: Sage.

Bhaskar, R. A., & Danermark, B. (2006). Metatheory, interdisciplinarity and disability research: A critical realist approach. *Scandinavian Journal of Disability Research, 8*, 278–297.

Blatchford, P. (2003). *The class size debate – Is smaller better?* Maidenhead: Open University Press.

Blatchford, P., Baines, E., & Pellegrini, A. (2003). The social context of school playground games: Sex and ethnic differences, and changes over time after entry to junior school. *British Journal of Developmental Psychology, 21*, 481–505.

Blatchford, P., Edmonds, S., & Martin, C. (2003). Class size, pupil attentiveness and peer relations. *British Journal of Educational Psychology, 73*, 15–36.

Blatchford, P., Russell, A., Brown, P., & Martin, C. (2007). *The effects of class size on the teaching of pupils aged 7–11 years*. London: Institute of Education, University of London.

Bleidorn, W., Arslan, R., Denisson, J., Rentfrow, J., Gedover, J., Potter, J., & Gosling, S. (2015). Age and gender differences in self-esteem: A cross-cultural window. *Journal of Personality and Social Psychology, 111*(3), 396–410.

Boucher, D., & Vincent, A. (2006). T.H. Green: Citizenship as political and metaphysical. In D. Boucher & A. Vincent (Eds.), *British idealism*. London: Continuum.

Bourdieu, P. (1984). *Distinction: A social critique of the judgement of taste*. London: Routledge.

Braun, C. (1976). Teacher expectation: Socio-psychological dynamics. *Review of Educational Research, 46*, 185–213.

Brecht, B. (2003). *Bertold Brecht: Poetry and prose*. London: Continuum International.

Brighouse, T. (2004). *Policy statement*. London: Office of The Commissioner for London Schools.

Brighouse, T., & Tomlinson, J. (1991). *Successful schools*. London: Institute of Public Policy Research.

Brooks, T. (Ed.). (2014). *Ethical citizenship: British idealism and the politics of recognition*. London: MacMillan.

Brophy, J. (1980). Research on the self-fulfilling prophecy and teacher expectations. *Journal of Educational Psychology, 75*, 631–661.

Brown, D., Andi, R., Edwards, V., & Felitti, V. (2007). Adverse child experiences and childhood autobiographical memory. *Child Abuse and Neglect, 31*, 961–969.

Brown, G. W., Craig, T. K., Harris, T. O., Handley, R. V., & Harvey, A. L. (2007). Development of a retrospective interview measure of parental maltreatment using the Childhood Experience of Care and Abuse (CELA) instrument. *Journal of Affective Disorders, 103*, 205–215.

Brown, W. (2005). The future before us. In B. Richardson (Ed.), *Tell it like it is: How our schools fail Black children*. Stoke: Trentham Books.

Bruner, J. (1980). *Under five in Britain. Oxford pre-school research project*. London: Grant McIntyre.

Bulman, M. (2017, March 23). Child sex offenders recorded across UK hits all time high among growing concerns over online grooming. *The Independent Online*.

Campbell, A. (2005). The birth of neoliberalism in the United States: A reorganisation of capitalism. In A. Saad-Filiho & D. Johnston (Eds.), *Neoliberalism: A critical reader* (pp. 187–198). London: Pluto Press.

Carlile, A. (2011). *Permanent exclusion from school and institutional prejudice*. Rotterdam: Sense Publishers.

Catone, G., Marwaha, S., Kuipers, E., Lennox, B., Freeman, D., Bebbington, P., & Broome, M. (2015, July 2). Bullying victimisation and risk of psychotic phenomena: analysis of British survey data. *Lancet Psychiatry, 2*, 618–624.

Chamorro-Premuzic, T. (2007). *Personality and individual differences*. Oxford: Blackwell, for the British Psychological Society

Chess, S., & Thomas, S. (1999). *Goodness of fit: Clinical applications from infancy through adult life*. Philadelphia, PA: Brunner Mazel.

Children Act. (1989). Section 17 of the Children Act 1989. Retrieved May 14, 1989, from http://www.devon.gov.uk/cp-sec-6-1.htmChou, K. L. (2012). Childhood sexual abuse and psychiatric disorders in middle-aged and older adults: Evidence from the 2007 adult psychiatric morbidity survey. *Journal of Clinical Psychology, 73*, 1365–1367.

Churchich, N. (1990). *Marxism and alienation*. Toronto: Farleigh Dickinson University Press.

Clark, K. B. (1966). *Prejudice and your child*. Boston, MA: Beacon Books.

Clark. C., Caldwell, T., Power, C., & Stansfield, C. (2010). Does the influence of childhood adversity on psychopathology persist across the life-course? A 45-year prospective epidemiological study. *Annals of Epidemiology, 20*, 385–394.

Clarke, S. (2005). The neoliberal theory of society. In A. Saad-Filho & D. Johnston (Eds.), *Neoliberalism: A critical reader* (pp. 50–59). London: The Pluto Press.

Coard, B. (1971/2005). How the West Indian child is made educationally subnormal in the British school system: The scandal of the Black child in schools in Britain. In B. Richardson (Ed.), *Tell it like it is: How our schools fail Black children*. Stoke: Trentham Books (also published in 1971 by New Beacon books).

Coard, B. (2005). Thirty years on – where do we go from here. In B. Richardson (Ed.), *Tell it like it is: How our schools fail Black children*. Stoke: Trentham Books.

Coid, J., Petruckevitch, A., Feler, G., Chung, W. S., & Richardson, J. (2001). Relation between childhood sexual and physical abuse and risk of revictimisation in women. *Lancet, 358*, 450–454.

Coleman. A. (1990). *Utopia on trial: Vison and reality in planned housing*. London: Shipman.

Collier, A. (1994). *Critical realism: An introduction to Roy Bhaskar's philosophy*. London: Verso.

Collier, A. (1998). Explanation and emancipation. In M. Archer, R. Bhaskar, A. Collier, T. Lawson, & A. Norrie (Eds.), *Critical reality: Essential readings* (pp. 444–463). Abingdon: Routledge.

Collier, A. (1999). *Being and worth*. Abingdon: Routledge.

Collier, A. (2002). Dialectic in Marxism and critical realism. In A. Brown, S. Fleetwood, & J. M. Roberts (Eds.), *Critical realism and marxism* (pp. 168–186). Abingdon: Routledge.

Collison, D., Dey, C., Hannah, G., & Stevenson, L. (2007). Income inequality and child mortality in wealthy nations. *Journal of Public Health, 13*, 1093 (March, preprint).

Colman, I., Jones, P. B., Kuh, D., Weeks, M., Naicker, K., Richards, M., & Croudace, T. J. (2014). Early development, stress and depression across the life course: pathways to depression in a national British birth cohort. *Psychological Medicine, 44*, 2845–2854.

Connell, A., & Dishion, T. (2006). The contribution of peers to monthly variation in adolescent depressed mood: A short-term longitudinal study with time-varying predictors. *Development and Psychopathology, 19*, 139–154.

Connelly, F. M., & Clandinin, D. J. (1994). Narrative inquiry. In T. Husen & N. Postlethwaite (Eds.), *International encyclopaedia of education* (Vol. 7). Oxford: Pergamon Press.

Connolly, P. (1998). *Racism gender identity and young children: Social relations in a multi-ethnic, inner city primary school.* London: Routledge.

Coopersmith, S. (1975). Self-concept, race and education. In G. K. Verma & C. Bagley (Eds.), *Race and education across cultures.* London: Heinemann.

Craig, G. (2007). *Sure Start and Black and minority populations.* London: Department for Children, Schools and Families.

Craig, G. (2009). *Institutional racism is still alive and thriving in Britain.* Hull: Centre for Social Justice and Social Inclusion, University of Hull.

Creaven, S. (2007). *Emergentist Marxism: Dialectical philosophy and social theory.* Abingdon: Routledge.

Creaven, S. (2015). The 'Two Marxisms' revisited: Humanism, structuralism and realism in Marxist social theory. *Journal of Critical Realism, 14*, 7–53.

Croxford, L., & Raffe, D. (2007). Young people's experience of compulsory schooling in England and Scotland during two decades of educational reforms. In G. Bhatti (Ed.), *Social justice and intercultural education: An open-ended dialogue.* Stoke: Trentham Books.

Currie, C., Gablainn, S., Godeau, G., Roberts, C., Smith, R., Currie, D, Pickett, W., Richter, M., Morgan, A., & Barnekow, B. (2008). *Inequalities in young people's health: Health behaviour in school-aged children – international report from the 2005–2006 Survey.* Copenhagen: WHO Regional Office; and Edinburgh: Adolescent Health Research Unit, University of Edinburgh. Retrieved from www.euro.who.int/Document/E91416.pdf

Currie, J., & Thomas, D. (1993). Does head start make a difference? Cambridge, MA: National Bureau of Economic Research.

Dale, R., Esland, G., & MacDonald, M. (Eds.), (1976). *Schooling and capitalism: A sociological reader.* London: Routledge.

Davey, A. (1982). Ethnic identification, preference and sociometric choice. In G. Verma & C. Bagley (Eds.), *Self-concept, achievement and multicultural education* (pp. 60–69). London: MacMillan.

Davison, K., & Bagley, C. (1969). Schizophrenia-like psychoses associated with organic disorders of the central nervous system: A review of the literature. In R. Hetherington (Ed.), *Current problems in neuropsychiatry* (*British Journal of Psychiatry* supplement, pp. 113–184). London: Royal Medico-Psychological Association.

Douglas, J. W. B. (1964). *The home and the school: A study of achievement and attainment in primary schools.* London: MacGibbon and Kee.

Dovermark, M., & Beach, D. (2016). From learning to labour to learning for precarity. *Ethnography and Education, 11,* 174–188.

Easton, G. (2010). Critical realism in case study research. *Industrial Marketing and Management, 39,* 118–128.

Edwards, P., O'Mahoney, J., & Vincent, S. (Eds.). (2014). *Studying organization using critical realism.* London: Oxford University Press.

Ellis, C., Adams, T., & Bochner, A. (2011, January). Autoethnography: An overview. *Forum: Qualitative Social Research,* 12.

Engels, F. (1845/1978). *The condition of the working class in England.* London: Penguin Books.

Epstein, D. (1993). *Changing classroom cultures: Anti-racism, politics and schools.* Stoke-on-Trent: Trentham Books.

Erikson, E. (1965). The concept of identity in race relations. *Daedalus,* 56–58.

Erikson, E. (1968). *Identity, youth and crisis.* London: Faber.

Erol, R. Y., & Orth, V. (2011). Self-esteem development from age 14 to 30 years: A longitudinal study. *Journal of Personality and Social Psychology, 101,* 607–619.

Evans, L. (1998). *Early years teachers: Their lives, work and careers* (Doctoral Thesis). Coventry: University of Warwick, Institute of Education.

Farah, M., Shera, D. M., Savage, J. H., Betancourt, L., Giannetta, J. M., Brodsky, N. L., Malmud, E. K., & Hurt. H. (2006). Childhood poverty: Specific associations with neurocognitive development. *Brain Research, 1110,* 166–174.

Fekete, L. (2008). *Integration, Islamophobia and civil rights in Europe.* London: Institute of Race Relations.

Fekete, L. (2009). *A suitable enemy: Racism, migration and Islamophobia in Europe.* London: Pluto Press.

Ferguson, D. M., McLeod, G. F., & Howard, L. J. (2013). Childhood sexual abuse and adult development outcomes: Findings from a 30-year longitudinal study in New Zealand. *Child Abuse and Neglect, 37,* 664–674.

Fine, M. (1994). Working the hyphens: Reinventing the self and other in qualitative research. In N. Denzin & Y. Lincoln (Eds.), *The handbook of qualitative research.* London: Sage.

Finkelhor, D. (1979). *Sexually victimized children.* New York, NY: The Free Press.

Finkelhor, D. (1982). *Child sexual abuse: New theory and research.* New York, NY: MacMillan.

Finkelhor, D., & Tucker, C. J. (2015). A holistic approach to child maltreatment. *Lancet Psychiatry, 6,* 480–481.

Finkelhor, D., Ormrod, K., & Turner, H. A. (2007). Poly-victimization: A neglected component in child maltreatment. *Child Abuse and Neglect, 31,* 7–26.

Flaschel, P. (2009). *The macrodynamics of capitalism: Elements for a synthesis of Marx, Keynes and Schumpeter.* Berlin: Springer-Verlag.

Flaschel, P., Griener, A., & Luchtenberg, S. (2012). Flexisecurity societies. Educational formation and the role of elites. *Review of Political Economy, 24,* 85–111.

Foner, N. (1977). *Between two cultures*. Oxford: Blackwell.

Foucault, M. (1976). *The birth of the clinic*. London: Tavistock Publications.

Fox, D., & Jordan, V. (1973). Racial preference and identity of Black American children, Chinese children, and White American children. *Genetic Psychology Monographs*, *88*, 229–286.

Friedli, L. (2009). *Inequality is bad for your health*. Geneva: The World Health Organization.

Gaine, C., & George, R. (1999). *Gender, 'Race' and class in schooling*. London: Falmer Press.

Garcia, J., Sanchez, G., Sanchez-Youngman, S., Vargas, E., & Ybarra, V. (2015). Race as a lived experience: The impact of multidimensional measures of race/ethnicity on the self-reported health status of Latinos. *Du Bois Review*, *12*, 349–373.

Gay-Little, B., & Hafdahl, A. R. (2000). Factors influencing racial comparisons of self-esteem: A quantitative review. *Psychological Bulletin*, *126*, 126–154.

Gentle, B., Grabe, S., Dolan-Pascoe, B., Twenge, J., Wells, B., & Maitino, A. (2009). Gender differences in domain-specific self-esteem: A meta-analysis. *Review of General Psychology*, *13*, 34–45.

George, R., & Clay, J. (2013, May 31). Challenging pedagogy: Emotional disruptions, young girls, parents and schools. *Sociological Research Online, 18*(2).

Giarretto. H. (1981). A comprehensive child sexual abuse treatment program. In C. Mrazek & P. Kempe (Eds.), *Sexually abused children and their families* (pp. 179–198). Oxford: Pergamon Press.

Gibson, B., Robbins, E., & Rochat, P. (2015). White bias in 7-year-old children across cultures. *Journal of Cognition and Culture*, *15*, 344–373.

Gilbert, R., Widom, C. S., Browne, K., Fergusson, D., Webb, E., & Janson, S. (2009). Burden and consequences of child maltreatment in high income countries. *Lancet*, *373*, 68–81.

Gillham, B., Tanner, G., Cheyne, B., Freeman, I., Rooney, M., & Lambie, A. (1998). Unemployment rates, single parent density and indices of child poverty: Their relationship to different categories of child abuse and neglect. *Child Abuse and Neglect*, *22*, 79–90.

Glass, P. G. (2016). Using history to explain the present: The past as born and performed. *Ethnography*, *17*, 92–110.

Glynn, S. (2005). East End immigrants and the battle for housing: A comparative study of political mobilization in the Jewish and Bengali communities. *Journal of Historical Geography*, *31*, 528–545.

Goetz, J. P., & LeCompe, M. D. (1984). *Ethnography and qualitative design in educational research*. London: Academic Press.

Goetz, J. P., & LeCompe, M. D. (1984). *Ethnography and qualitative research in education*. London: Academic Press.

Goff, J., Hall, J., Sylva, K., Smith, T., Smith, G., Eisenstadt, N., Sammons, P., Evangelou, M., Smees, R., & Chu, K. (2013). *Evaluation of children's centres in England – Strand 3: Delivery of family services*. London: Department for Education.

Goffman, E. (1969). *The presentation of the self in everyday life*. London: PenguinBooks.

Good, T. L. (1987). Two decades of research on teacher expectations: Findings and future directions. *Journal of Teacher Education, 38,* 32–47.

Goodwin, M., & Heath, O. (2016). The 2016 referendum, Brexit and the left behind: An aggregate-level analysis of the result. *Political Quarterly, 87,* 323–332.

Gorski. P. (2013). What is critical realism? And why should you care? *Contemporary Sociology, 42,* 658–670.

Green, T. H. (1999). *Lectures on the principles of political obligation*. Kitchener, ON: Baloche Books (McMaster University Series of Books Online).

Greene, M., & Way, N. (2005). Self-esteem trajectories among ethnic minority adolescents. *Journal of Research on Adolescence, 15,* 151–178.

Greengarten, J. (1981). *Thomas Hill Green and the development of liberal-democratic thought*. Toronto: University of Toronto Press.

Greenway, C. (2011). *The "Quality" of nursery provision: An exploration of the relationship between inspection and the development of education and care* (PhD Thesis). Birmingham University, England.

Hall, J., Sammons, P., Sylva, K., Evangelou, M., Eisenstadt, N., Smith, T., & Smith, G. (2016). Disadvantaged families are at greatest risk from austerity cuts to Children's Centres. *British Medical Journal, 352,* i897.

Hardt, J., & Rutter, M. (2002). Validity of adult retrospective reports of adverse childhood experiences: A review of the evidence. *Journal of Child Psychology and Psychiatry, 45,* 260–273.

Hatch, S., & Wadsworth, M. (2008). Does adolescent affect impact adult social integration? Evidence from the British 1946 birth cohort. *Sociology, 42,* 155–177.

Hayler, M. (2011). *Autoethnography*. Rotterdam: Sense Publications.

Heath, A. (2014). *Migrants and their children in Britain: Patterns of ethnic minority integration*. London: Routledge.

Heath, A., Fisher, S., Rosenblatt, G., Sanders, D., & Sobolewska, M. (2013). *The political integration of ethnic minorities in Britain*. London: Oxford University Press.

Heath, C., Hindmarsh, J., & Luff, P. (2010). *Video in qualitative research*. London: Sage.

Henriques, F. (1967). *Family and color in Jamaica*. Atlanta, GA: Clark Atlanta University Press.

Henriques, F. (1974). *Children of Caliban: Miscegenation*. London: Secker and Warburg.

Hertzig, T. (2004). Rags, riches and race: The intergenerational economic mobility of Black and White families in the United States. In S. Bowles, H. Gintis, & M. Osborne (Eds.), *Unequal chances: Family background and economic success*. New York, NY: Russell Sage and Princeton University Press.

Hewitt, J. (1976). *Self and society*. London: Allyn and Bacon.

Hines, V. (1998). *How Black people overcame fifty years of repression in Britain 1945–1995.* London: Zulu Books.

Hinton, E. (2016). *From the war on poverty to the war on crime: The making of mass incarceration in America.* Boston, MA: Harvard University Press.

HMG. (1991). *Children Act 1989 guidance and regulations: Volume 2, family support, day care and educational provision for young children.* London: Her Majesty's Government.

HMG. (1995). *Child protection: Messages from research.* London: Her Majesty's Government, Department of Health.

HMG. (2003). *Every child matters.* Norwich: Her Majesty's Government.

Holmes, R. (1995). *How young children perceive race.* London: Sage.

Hughes, B. (2005, October 15). *Sure Start.* Statement by the Minister for Families and Children.

Hughes, M., & Demo, D. H. (1989). Self-perception of Black Americans: Self-esteem and personal efficacy. *American Journal of Sociology, 95,* 132–159.

Ingram, E. (1982). British and West Indian children in day nurseries: A comparative study. *New Community, 9,* 423–430.

Jackson, V., Browne, K., & Joseph, S. (2016). The prevalence of childhood victimization experienced outside of the family: Findings from an English prevalence study. *Child Abuse and Neglect, 41,* 343–357.

Jacob, S., & Nieder, A. (2009). Notation-independent representation of the fractions in the human parietal cortex. *Journal of Neuroscience, 8,* 4652–4657.

Jamal, F. (2015). *A sociological imagination in public health: Systematic review, qualitative studies and young people's health in schools* (Doctoral Thesis). University of East London, London.

Jamal, F., Bonell, C., Harden, A., & Lorenc, T. (2015). The social ecology of girls' bullying practices: Exploratory research in two London schools. *Sociology of Health International, 37,* 731–744.

James, H. (1920). *The letters of William James* (Vol. I). Boston, MA: Houghton.

James, W. (1890). Selections from the principles of psychology. In H. Thayer (Ed.), *Pragmatism: The classic writings* (pp. 135–179). New York, NY: New American Library.

Jha, M. M. (2008). From special to inclusive education. In C. Bagley & G. Verma (Eds.), *Challenges for inclusion: Educational and social studies from Britain and the Indian Sub-Continent* (pp. 21–42). Rotterdam: Sense Educational Publishers.

Johnston, D. (2005). Poverty and income distribution: Back on the neoliberal agenda. In A. Saad-Filho & D. Johnston (Eds.), *Neoliberalism: A critical reader* (pp. 135–141). London: Pluto Press.

Jones, O. (2013). *Chavs: The demonization of the working class* (2nd ed.). London: Verso.

Joshi, M. (2008). *The millennium cohort study children at age six.* London: Centre for Longitudinal Studies, Institute of Education, University of London.

Kaplan, H. B. (1980). *Deviant behavior in defense of the self.* San Diego, CA: University of California Press.

Kelly, G. (1955). *The theory of personal constructs.* New York, NY: Norton.

Kevne, E. (2014). *Deconstructing flexisecurity: Towards new concepts and approaches for employment and social policy.* London & New York, NY: Routledge.

Kling, C., Hyde, J., Showers, C., & Buswell, B. (1999). Gender differences in self-esteem: A meta-analysis. *Psychological Bulletin, 125,* 470–500.

Kloess, J., Beech, A., & Harkins, L. (2014). Online child sexual exploitation: Prevalence, process and offender characteristics. *Trauma, Violence and Abuse, 15,* 126–139.

Krayer, A., Seddon, D., Robinson, C., & Gwilym, H. (2015). The influence of child sexual abuse on the self from adult narrative perspectives. *Journal of Child Sexual Abuse, 24,* 135–151.

Kundari, A. (2007). *The end of tolerance: Racism in twenty-first century Britain.* London: Pluto Press.

Lam, V., Guerrero, S., Damree, N., & Enesco, I. (2010). Young children's racial awareness and affect, and their perceptions about mothers' racial affect in a multiracial context. *British Journal of Developmental Psychology, 29,* 842–854.

Lampen, J. (2015). The Quaker peace testimony in twentieth century education. *Quaker Studies, 19,* 295–304.

Leland, A. P. (Ed.). (2011). *The educational theory and practice of T.H. Green (Collected Papers).* Leopold Classic Library, online resource.

Lereva, S. T., Copeland, W. E., Costello, I. J., & Wolke, D. (2015). Adult mental health consequences of peer bullying and maltreatment in childhood. *Lancet Psychiatry, 6,* 524–531.

Lewin, K. (1936). Social psychological differences between the United States and Germany. *Character and Personality, 4,* 265–293.

Little, D. (2012). *Varieties of social explanation: An introduction to the philosophy of social science.* Boulder, CO: Westview Press.

Lovelock, J. (1979). *Gaia: A new look at life on earth.* London: Oxford University Press.

Lowenthal, D. (1967). Race and color in the West Indies. *Daedalus, 96,* 580–626.

MacMillan, H. L., Fleming, J. E., Streiner, D. L., Lin, E., Boyle, M. H., Jamieson, E., Duku, E. K., Walsh, C. A., Wong, M. Y., & Beardslee, W. R. (2001). Childhood abuse and lifetime psychopathology in a community sample. *American Journal of Psychiatry, 158,* 1878–1883.

MacMillan, H. L., Tanaka, M., Duku, E., Vaillancourt, T., & Boyle, M. (2013). Child physical and sexual abuse in a community sample of young adults: Results from the Ontario Child Health Study. *Child Abuse and Neglect, 37,* 14–21.

MacPherson, W. (1999). *The Stephen Lawrence inquiry.* London: HMSO.

Mahamdallie, H. (2005). Is this as good as it gets? In B. Richardson (Ed.), *Tell it like it is: How our schools fail Black children.* Stoke: Trentham Books.

Majors, R. (Ed.). (2001). *Educating our Black children: New directions and radical approaches.* London: Routledge.

Marmot, M. (2008). *Report of the commission on social determinants of health.* Geneva: World Health Organisation.

Marmot, M. (2010). *Fair society, healthy lives: Strategic review of health inequalities.* London: Institute of Health Inequalities, University College, London.

Marmot, M. (2015). *The health gap: The challenge of an unequal world.* London: Bloomsbury.

Marx, K., & Engels, F. (1948/2008). *The communist manifesto.* London: Oxford World Classics.

Maslow, A. (1964/2014). *Religions, values and peak experiences.* Columbus, OH: Ohio State University Press; and New York, NY: Stellar Classics.

Maslow, A. (1968). *Towards a psychology of being.* Princeton, NJ: Van Norstrand.

Maslow, A. (1970). *Motivation and personality.* New York, NY: Harper and Row.

Mason, B., & Sawyerr, A. (Eds.). (2002). Introduction. In *Exploring the unsaid: Creativity, risks and dilemmas in working cross-culturally.* London: KARNAK Family Therapy Publishers.

Mason, W. A. (2001). Self-esteem and delinquency revisited. *Journal of Youth and Adolescence, 30,* 83–102.

Maxime, J. (1986). Some psychological models of black self-concept. In J. Cheetham (Ed.), *Social work with children and their families.* London: Batsford Books.

Maxime, J. (1987). *Black like me – Workbook one: Black identity.* Beckenham Kent: Emani Publications.

Maxime, J. (1991). *Black like Me – Workbook two: Black pioneers.* Beckenham Kent: Emani Publications.

Mayall. B. (2013). *A history of the sociology of childhood.* London: Institute of Education Press.

May-Chahal, C., & Cawson, P. (2005). Measuring child maltreatment in the United Kingdom: A study of the prevalence of child abuse and neglect. *Child Abuse and Neglect, 29,* 969–984.

McGowen, R. (1998). Power and humanity: Foucault among the historians. In R. Porter & C. Jones (Eds.), *Reassessing Foucault: Medicine and the body* (pp. 91–112). London: Routledge.

Mead, G. (1934/1964). Mind, self and society. In A. Strauss (Ed.), *George Herbert mead: On social psychology.* Chicago, IL: University of Chicago Press.

Meltzer, H., Ford, T., Bebbington, P., & Vostanis, P. (2012). Children who run away from home: Risks for suicidal behaviour and substance misuses. *Journal of Adolescent Health, 51,* 415–422.

Meltzer, H., Gatward, R., Corbin, T., Goodman, R., & Ford, T. (2003). *The mental health of young people looked after by local authorities in England.* London: Department of Health.

Meltzer, H., Gatward, R., Goodman, R., & Ford, T. (2000). *Mental health in children and adolescents in Great Britain.* London: HMSO for the Office of National Statistics.

Milner, D. (1973). *Children and race*. London: Penguin Books.

Milner, D. (1983). *Children and race: Ten years on*. London: Penguin Books.

Milner, D. (1996). Children and racism: Beyond the valley of the dolls. In W. P. Robinson (Ed.), *Social groups and identities*. Oxford: Butterworth-Heinemann.

Milner, D. (1997). Racism and childhood identity. *The Psychologist, 10*, 123–125.

Mirza, H. S. (1992). *Young, female and Black*. London: Routledge.

Moghal, N. E., Nota, I. K., & Hobbs, C. J. (1995). A study of sexual abuse in an Asian community. *Archives of Diseases in Children, 72*, 346–347.

Moksnos, U. K. (2012). Self-esteem and emotional health in adolescents: Gender and age as potential moderators. *Scandinavian Journal of Psychology, 53*, 48–57.

Morland, J. K. (1966). A comparison of race awareness in northern and southern children. *American Journal of Orthopsychiatry, 36*, 22–31.

Morris, T. (1957). *The criminal area*. London: Routledge.

Mortimore, P., Sammons, P., Stoll, L., Lewis, P., & Ecol, R. (1988). *School matters: The junior years*. London: Open Books.

Morton, A. L. (1938). *A people's history of England*. London: Victor Gollancz.

Mullard, C. (1973). *Black Britain*. London: Allen and Unwin.

Mullard, C. (1985). *Race, power and resistance*. London: Routledge.

Muttarak, R., & Heath, A. (2010). Who intermarries in Britain? Explaining diversity in intermarriage patterns. *British Journal of Sociology, 61*, 275–305.

Newton, N., & Broadfoot, P. (2016). *Summary report of quaker schools research project*. Bristol: University of Bristol School of Education.

Norrie, A. (2010). *Dialectic and difference: Dialectical critical realism and the grounds of justice*. Abingdon: Routledge.

Oaksford, K., & Frude, N. (2001). The prevalence and nature of child sexual abuse: Evidence from a female university sample in the UK. *Child Abuse Review, 10*, 49–59.

Ogilvy, C. M., Boath, E. H., Cheyne, W. M., Jahoda, G., & Schaffer, H. R. (1990) Staff attitudes and perceptions in multicultural nursery schools. *Early Child Development and Care, 64*, 1–13.

ONS. (2014). *What does the 2011 census tell us about inter-ethnic relationships?* London: Office for National Statistics.

Orwell, G. (1949). *Nineteen eighty-four*. London: Penguin Books.

Owens, T., Stryker, S., & Goodman, N. (2001). *Extending self-esteem theory and research: Sociological and psychological currents*. New York, NY: Cambridge University Press.

Owusu-Bempah, K. (1994). Race, self-identity and social work. *British Journal of Social Work, 24*, 123–136.

Owusu-Bempah, K. (1998). Race, culture, and the child. In J. Tunstill (Ed.), *Children and state: The challenge of children*. London: Cassell.

Owusu-Bempah, K., & Howitt, M. (1999). Even their soul is defective. *The Psychologist, 12*, 126–130.

Pace, M., Martin, E., Wilson, H. A., & Huismeier, J. (1999). Validating the Ontario child health scales in a U.K. population. *European Journal of Child and Adolescent Psychiatry, 8*, 255–259.

Pauker, K., Williams, A., & Steele, J. (2015). Children's racial categorization in context. *Child Development Perspectives, 10*, 33–38.

Pettigrew, T. F. (1998). Intergroup contact theory. *Annual Review of Psychology, 49*, 65–85.

Pettigrew, T. F. (2011). *When groups meet: The dynamics of intergroup contact.* Philadelphia, PA: The Psychological Press.

Philips, N. (2001). *London crossings: A biography of Black Britain.* London: Continuum Books.

Phillips, C. (2011). Institutional racism and ethnic inequalities: An expanded, multilevel framework. *Journal of Social Policy, 40*, 173–192.

Piaget, J. (1995). *Sociological studies.* London: Routledge.

Pickett, K., & Wilkinson, R. (2007). Child well-being and income inequality in rich societies; ecological cross-sectional study. *British Medical Journal, 335*, 1080.

Pickles, A., Aglan, A., Collishaw, S., Messer, J., Rutter, M., & Maughan, B. (2010). Predictors of suicidality across the lifespan: The Isle of Wight study. *Psychological Medicine, 40*, 1453–1460.

Pidgeon, D. A. (1970). *Expectation and pupil performance.* London: National Foundation for Educational Research.

Piers-Harris, E. V., & Smith, D. B. (1991). *The Piers-Harris children's self-concept scale.* New York, NY & London: MHS Psychological Assessment.

Pillay, D., Naicker, I., & Pithouse-Morgan, K. (Eds.). (2016). *Academic autoethnographies: Inside teaching in higher education.* Rotterdam: Sense Publications.

Pincus, L., & Dare, C. (1978). *Secrets in the family.* London: Faber.

Platt, L. (2009). *Ethnicity and family relationships within and between ethnic groups: An analysis using the labour force survey.* Colchester: Institute of Social and Economic Research, University of Essex.

Plummer, K. (1995). *Telling sexual stories: Power, change and social worlds.* London: Routledge.

Popper, K. (1945/2013). *The open society and its enemies.* London & Princeton, NJ: Routledge, and Princeton University Press.

Popper, K. (1957). *The poverty of historicism.* London: Routledge.

Popper, K. (1974). *Unended quest: An intellectual biography.* London: Routledge.

Popper, K., & Eccles, J. (1977). *The self and its brain: An argument for interactionism.* London: Routledge.

Porter, R. (1971). *Black child, White child: The development of racial attitudes.* Boston, MA: Harvard University Press.

Porter, R. (1997). *The greatest benefit to mankind: A medical history of humanity from antiquity to the present.* London: Harper-Collins.

Porter, R., & Jones, C. (Eds.). (1999). *Reassessing Foucault: Medicine and the body*. London: Routledge.

Pritchard, C. (2001). *A family-teacher-social work alliance to reduce truancy and delinquency: The Dorset healthy alliance project* (RDS Occasional Paper No. 78). London: The Home Office.

Pritchard, C., & Bagley, C. (2000). Multi-criminal and violent groups among child sex offenders: A heuristic typology in a 2-year cohort of men in two English counties. *Child Abuse and Neglect, 24*, 579–586.

Pritchard, C., & Bagley, C. (2001). Suicide in child murderers and child sexual abusers. *Journal of Forensic Psychiatry, 12*, 579–586.

Pujo, B. (1998). *Vincent de Paul: The Trail-Blazer*. Notre Dame, IN: University of Notre Dame Press.

QCA. (2000). *Investing in the future: Curriculum guidance for the foundation stage*. London: Department for Education and Employment, for the Qualifications and Curriculum Authority.

Radford, L. (2013). *Child sexual abuse: An NSPCC research briefing*. London: National Society for the Prevention of Cruelty to Children.

Radford, L., &Seven Others. (2011). *Child abuse and neglect in the United Kingdom today*. London: National Society for the Prevention of Cruelty to Children.

Radford, L., Corral, S., Bradley, C., & Fisher, H.L. (2013). The prevalence and impact of child maltreatment in the United Kingdom. *Child Abuse and Neglect, 37*, 801–813.

Ramadan, T. (2010). *What I believe*. London: Oxford University Press.

Richardson, B. (Ed.). (2005). *Tell it like it is: How our schools fail Black children*. Stoke: Trentham Books.

Rist, R. C. (1970). Student social class and teacher expectations: The self-fulfilling prophecy in ghetto education. *Harvard Educational Review, 40*, 411–451.

Roberts-Holmes, G. (2011). *Doing your early years research project*. London: Sage.

Robins, R., Tracy, J., Trzesniewski, K., Potter, J., & Gosling, S. (2001). Personality correlates of self-esteem. *Journal of Personality, 35*, 463–482.

Robinson, L. (1995). *Psychology for social workers: Black perspectives in human development and behaviour*. London: Routledge.

Robinson, L. (2000). Racial identity attitudes and self-esteem of Black adolescents in residential care: An exploratory study. *British Journal of Social Work, 30*, 3–24.

Rogers, C. (1982). *A social psychology of schooling*. London: Routledge & Kegan Paul.

Rogers, C., & Stevens, B. (1967). *Person to person: The problem of being human*. London: Condor Books.

Rollock, N., Gillborn, D., Vincent, C., & Ball, S. (2015). *The colour of class*. London: Routledge.

Rose, E. J. B., & Deakin, N. (1969). *Colour and citizenship: A report of British race relations*. London: Oxford University Press.

Rosenberg, M. (1965). *Society and the adolescent self-image*. Princeton, NJ: Princeton University Press.

Rosenberg, M. (1979). *Conceiving the self*. New York, NY: Basic Books.

Rosenberg, M., & Kaplan, H. B. (Eds.). (1982). *Social psychology of the self-concept*. Arlington, IL: Harlan Davidson.

Rosenberg, M., & Owens, T. J. (2001). Low self-esteem people: A collective portrait. In T. Owens, S. Stryker, & N. Goodmanm (Eds.), *Extending self-esteem theory and research* (pp. 400–436). New York, NY: Cambridge University Press.

Rosenberg, M., & Simmons, R. G. (1972). *Black and White self-esteem: The urban school child*. Washington, DC: American Sociological Association.

Rosenzweig, J. E. (1998). *I have a new friend in me: The effect of a multicultural/anti-bias curriculum, in the development of social cognition in pre-schoolers* (Doctoral Dissertation). University of Arizona, Tucson, AZ.

Runnymede Trust. (2016). *Islamophobia – 20 Years on, Still a Challenge*. London: Runnymede Trust.

Rutland, A., Cameron, L., Bennett, L., & Ferrell, J. (2005). Interracial contact and racial constancy: a multi-site study of racial intergroup bias in 3–5-year-old Anglo-British children. *Journal of Applied Developmental Psychology*, 25, 699–713.

Rutland, A., Cameron, L., Milne, A., & McGeorge, P. (2015). Social norms and self-presentation: Children's implicit intergroup attitudes. *Child Development, 76*, 451–466.

Rutter, M. (2007). Sure Start local programmes: An outsider's perspective. In J. Belsky, J. Barnes, & E. Melhuish (Eds.), *The national evaluation of Sure Start*. Bristol: The Policy Press.

Rutter, M., & Madge, N. (1976). *Cycles of disadvantage*. London: Heinemann.

Rutter, M., Maughan, B., Mortimore, P., & Ouston, J. (1979). *Fifteen thousand hours: Secondary schools and their effects on children*. London: Open Books.

Rutter, M., Yule, B., & Bagley, C. (1975). Children of West Indian immigrants. III Home circumstances and family patterns. *Journal of Child Psychology and Psychiatry, 16*, 105–123.

Saad-Filhu, A., & Johnston, D. (Eds.). (2005). *Neoliberalism: A critical reader*. London: Pluto Press.

Salter, D., McMillan, D., Richards, M., Talbot, T., Hodges, J., Bentovim, A., Hastings, R., Stevenson, J., & Skuse, D. (2003). Development of sexually abusive behaviour in sexually victimised males: A longitudinal study. *Lancet, 361*, 471–476.

Sammons, P., Hall, J., Smees, R., Goff, J., & Four Co-Authors and Consultants. (2015). *Children's centres: Their importance for children and families: Evaluation of Children's Centres in England (ECCE, Strand 4)*. London: Department for Education. Retrieved froom www.gov.uk/government/publications

Sarra, C. (2011). *Strong and smart – Towards a pedagogy of emancipation: Education for the first people*. London: Routledge.

Sarra, C. (2013). *Good morning, Mr. Sarra: My life working for a stronger, smarter future for our children*. St. Lucia: University of Queensland Press.

Savage, M. (2015). *Social class in the twenty first century*. London: Pelican.

Sawyer, A., & Bagley, C. (2017b). England's *Sure Start* pre-school child care centres: Public policy, progress and political change. *Open Journal of Political Science, 7,* 116–132.

Sawyerr, A. (1999). Identity project on 'Myself' with pre-schoolers at a day nursery. In R. Barn (Ed.), *Working with Black children and adolescents in need* (pp. 34–47). London: British Agencies for Adoption and Fostering.

Sawyerr, A. (2017). *Ethnic identity and equality issues in urban children: Historical case studies in the context of a review of British policy and practice 1968–2008* (Doctoral dissertation). Royal Holloway, University of London, London.

Sawyerr, A., & Bagley, C. (2016). *Excluded youth in Britain: Historical review of research and policy on inequality, education, health, family support and community development 1968–2008*. Manchester: Manchester Educational Research Network.

Sawyerr, A., & Bagley, C. (2017a). Child sexual abuse and adolescent and adult adjustment: A review of British and world evidence, with implications for social work, and mental health and school counselling. *Advances in Applied Sociology, 7,* 1–15.

Scambler, G. (2012). Resistance in unjust times: Archer, structured agency and the sociology of health inequalities. *Sociology, 33,* 275–296.

Scambler, G. (2012–2016). *Critical realism, Archer and Bhaskar.* Web Commentaries. Retrieved from www.grahamscambler.com

Schaffer, H. R. (1984). *The child's entry into a social world*. London: Academic Press.

Schatzman, M. (1973). *Soul murder: Persecution in the family*. London: Allen Lane.

Schmidt, K. (2011). Alienation, powerlessness and meaningless: A Neo-Thomist approach. *Journal for the Sociological Integration of Religion and Society, 1,* 100–120.

Schmitt, D., & Allik, J. (2005). Simultaneous administration of the Rosenberg-Self Esteem Scale in 53 nations: Explaining the universal and culture-specific features of global self-esteem. *Journal of Personality and Social Psychology, 89,* 628–641.

Schmitt, S., Dubey, S., Dalton, L., Nelson, M., Lee, J., Kennedy, M. O., Kim-Gervey, C., Powers, L., Geenen, S., & Research Consortium to Increase the Success of Youth in Foster Care. (2015). Who am I? Who do you think I am? Stability of racial/ethnic self-identification among youth in foster care. *Children and Youth Services Review, 56,* 61–67.

Searle, C. (1973). *The Forsaken lover: White words and Black people*. London: Penguin Books.

Searle, C. (2001). *An exclusive education: Race, class and education in British schools*. London: Lawrence and Wishart.

Shepherd, J., & Farrington, D. (2003). The impact of antisocial lifestyle on health. *British Medical Journal, 326,* 834–835.

Shipway, B. (2013). *A critical realist perspective of education*. Abingdon: Routledge.

Short, N., Turner, L., & Grant, A. (Eds.). (2013). *Contemporary British autoethnography*. Rotterdam: Sense Publications.

Shulman, D. (2016). *The presentation of the self in contemporary social life*. London: Sage.

Sidebotham, P., Herson, J., & ALSPAC Study Team. (2006). Child maltreatment in the "Child of the Nineties": A cohort study of risk. *Child Abuse and Neglect, 30*, 497–522.

Siegel, S., & Castellan, N. (1988). *Nonparametric statistics for the behavioral sciences*. New York, NY: McGraw-Hill.

Simon, B. (1991). *Education and the social order 1940–1990*. London: Lawrence and Wishart.

Sinclair, S., Blais, M., Gansler, D., Sandberg, E., & Bistis, K. (2010). Psychometric properties of Rosenberg self-esteem scale: Scores across demographic groups living with the United States. *Evaluation and the Health Professions, 33*, 56–80.

Singer, P. (1996). *Marx: A very short introduction*. London: Oxford University Press.

Singh, D. (2007). *Our shared future*. London: The Commission on Integration and Cohesion, Communities and Local Government Publications.

Siraj-Blatchford, I. (1994). *The early years*. Stoke on Trent: Trentham Books

Sivandandan, A. (1975). *Race and resistance: The institute of race relations story*. London: Race Today Publications.

Sivandandan, A. (2005, October 16). Why Muslims reject British values. *The Guardian*.

Skeggs, B. (1997). *Formations of class and gender*. London: Sage.

Slee, R., Wiener, G., & Tomlinson, S. (Eds.). (1998). *School effectiveness for whom?* London: Falmer.

Slonje, R., Smith, P., & Frisen, A. (2016, June). Perceived reasons for the negative impact of cyberbullying and traditional bullying. *European Journal of Developmental Psychology, 14*, 295–310. doi:10.1080/17405629.2016.1200461

Smith, D. J., Tomlinson, S., Bonnerjea, L., Hogarth, T., & Tomes, H. (1989). *The school effect: A study of multi-racial comprehensives*. London. Policy Studies Institute.

Spataro, J., Mullen, P., Burgess, P., Wells, D., & Moss, A. (2004). Impact of child sexual abuse on mental health. *British Journal of Psychiatry, 184*, 416–421.

Stahl, G. (2013, August 31). Habitus disjunctures, reflexivity and the white working-class boys' conceptions of status in learner and social identities. *Sociological Research Online, 18*(3).

Stahl, G. (2015). *Identity, neoliberalism and aspiration: Educating White working class boys*. Abingdon: Routledge.

Standing, G. (2011 & 2014). *The precariat: The new dangerous class* (1st and 2nd ed.). London: Bloomsbury Academic.

Standing, G. (2014). *A precariat charter: From Denizens to Citizens*. London: Bloomsbury Academic.

Starkey, P. (2002). Innovation and experiment with deprived families in Britain, 1940s to 1980s: The work of the family service units. *British Journal of Social Work, 32*, 573–587.

Steger, M., & Roy, R. (2010). *Neoliberalism: A very short introduction*. London: Oxford University Press.

Stokes-Guinan, K. (2011). Age and skin tone as predictors of positive and negative attitudes in Hispanic children. *Hispanic Journal of Behavioral Sciences, 33*, 3–21.

Stone, M. (1981). *The education of the Black child in Britain: The myth of multicultural education*. London: Fontana.

Strand, S. (2008). *SEN and ethnicity: What we know*. Warwick: Institute of Education, University of Warwick.

Sure Start Research Team. (2008). *The impact of Sure Start local programmes on three year olds and their families*. Nottingham: DfES Publications.

Tanaka, M., Wekerle, C., Leung, E., Waechter, R., Gonzalez, A., Jamieson, E., & MacMillan, H. L. (2012). Preliminary evaluation of the childhood experience of violence short form. *Journal of Interpersonal Violence, 27*, 396–407.

Taylor, C. (2006). *Quality of secondary schools*. London: Report to House of Commons Public Accounts Committee.

Taylor, E., Gillborn, D., & Ladson-Billings, G. (2016). *Foundations of critical race theory*. London: Routledge.

Teicher, M., Anderson, C., & Polcari, P. (2012). Childhood maltreatment is associated with reduced volume in the hippocampal subfields, CA3, dental gyrus, and subiculum. *Proceedings of the National Academy of Sciences, 109*(9), E563–E572. doi: 10.1073/pnas.1115396109Thomas, B., & Dorling, D. (2007). *Identity in Britain: A cradle-to-grave analysis*. Bristol: The Policy Press.

Thomas, G., & Vaughan, M. (2004). *Inclusive education: Readings and reflections*. Buckingham: Open University Press with McGraw-Hill.

Thomas-Hope, E. M. (1982). Identity of migrants from the English-speaking Caribbean in Britain and North America. In G. Verma & C. Bagley (Eds.), *Self-concept, achievement and multicultural education* (pp. 227–239). London: MacMillan.

Tizard, B., & Phoenix, A. (1993/2003). *Black White or mixed race? Race and racism in the lives of young people of mixed parentage* (Revised Edition, 2003). London: Routledge.

Tizard, B., Cooperman, O., Joseph, A., & Tizard, J. (1972). Environmental effects on language development: A study of children in long-stay residential nurseries. *Child Development, 43*, 337–358.

Tizard, B., Philips, J., & Plewis, I. (1976). Staff behaviour in pre-school centres. *Journal of Child Psychology and Psychiatry, 17*, 21–33.

Tomlinson, S. (1998). A tale of one school in one city: Hackney Downs. In R. Slee, G. Weiner, & S. Tomlinson (Eds.), *School effectiveness for whom? Challenges for the school effectiveness and school improvement movement*. London: The Falmer Press.

Tomlinson, S. (2008). *Race and education: Policy and politics in Britain*. Maidenhead: Open University Press and McGraw Hill.

Tomlinson, S. (2013). *Ignorant yobs? Low attainers in a global knowledge economy*. London: Routledge and Taylor & Francis.

Tomlinson, S. (2014). *The politics of race, class and special education: The selected works of Sally Tomlinson*. London: Routledge & Taylor and Francis.

Tonmyr, L., Houdestad, W. L., & Draca, J. (2014). Commentary on Canadian child maltreatment data. *Journal of Interpersonal Violence, 29*, 186–197.

Torjesen, I. (2016, January). Austerity cuts eroding benefits of Sure Start. *British Medical Journal, 19*, 352.

Tosh, J. (2002). *The pursuit of history*. London: Longman.

Toynbee, P., & Walker, D. (2008). *Unjust rewards: Exposing greed and inequality in Britain*. London: Granta Publications.

Troyna, B., & Hatcher, R. (1992). *Racism in children's lives: A study of mainly White primary schools*. London: Routledge.

Troyna, B., & William, J. (1986). *Racism, education and the state*. London: Croom Helm.

Tse, J., & Bagley, C. (2002). *Suicidal behaviour, bereavement and death education in Chinese adolescents: Hong Kong studies*. Aldershot: Ashgate.

Unwin, J. (2011, September 8). Reading the riots. *The Guardian Online*.

Unwin, J. (2013). *Why fight poverty?* London: London Publishers' Foundation.

Van Ausdale, D., & Feagin, J. (2002). *The first R: How children learn race and racism*. Plymouth: Rowman and Littlefield.

Verma, G., & Bagley, C. (1982). *Self concept, achievement and multicultural education*. London: Macmillan.

Verma, G., Woodrow, D., Bagley, C., Darby D., Shum, S., Chan, D., & Skinner, G. (1999). *Chinese adolescents in Hong Kong and Britain: Identity and aspirations*. Aldershot: Ashgate.

Walsh, C., MacMillan, H., Trocme, N., Jamieson, E., & Boyle, M. (2008). Measurement of victimization in adolescence: Development and validation of the childhood experience of violence questionnaire. *Child Abuse and Neglect, 32*, 1037–1057.

Warmington, P. (2014). *Black British intellectuals and education: Multiculturalism's hidden history*. Abingdon: Routledge.

Weinreich, P (1979). Cross-ethnic identification and self-rejection in a Black adolescent. In G. K. Verma & C. Bagley (Eds.), *Race, education and identity*. London: Heinemann.

Wells, G. (1986). *The meaning maker: Children learning language and using language to learn*. New Hampshire, NH: Heinemann Educational Books.

Wilkinson, M. (2013). Introducing Islamic critical realism: A philosophy underlabouring contemporary Islam. *Journal of Critical Realism, 12*, 419–442.

Wilkinson, M. (2015). *A fresh look at Islam in a multi-faith world: A philosophy for success through education*. Abingdon: Routledge.

Wilkinson, R., & Pickett, K. (2009). *The spirit level: Why more equal societies almost always do better*. London: Allen Lane Penguin Books.

Williams, J. E., & Best, D. L. (1990). *Sex and psyche: Gender and self viewed cross-culturally*. Newbury Park, CA: Sage.

Williams, J. E., & Morland, K. (1976). *Race, color and the young child*. Chapel Hill, NC: University of North Carolina Press.

Williams, R., & Pritchard, C. (2006). *Breaking the cycle of educational alienation: A multi-professional approach*. Maidenhead: McGraw-Hill Educational.

Willis, P (2004). Twenty five years on – old book, new times. In N. Dolby, P. Dimitriadis, & P. Willis (Eds.), *Learning to labour in new times*. London: Routledge-Falmer.

Willis, P. (1977). *Learning to labour: How working class lads get working class jobs*. Aldershot: Ashgate.

Wilson, A. (1987). *Mixed race children: A study of identity*. London: Allen and Unwin.

Wilson, A. (1987). *Mixed race children: A study of identity*. London: Allan and Unwin.

Wilson, A. N. (1978). *The developmental psychology of the Black child*. New York, NY: Africana Publications.

Wilson, T (2015). *Hospitality and translation: An exploration of how Muslim pupils translate their faith in the context of an Anglican primary school*. Newcastle: Cambridge Scholars Press.

Winter, K. (2011). *Building relationships and communicating with young children: A practical guide for social workers*. Abingdon: Routledge.

Wong, W., & Hines, M. (2015). Effects of gender color-coding on toddlers' gender-typical toy play. *Archives of Sexual Behavior, 151*, 1233–1142.

Woods, P. (1986). *Inside schools: Ethnography in educational research*. London: Routledge.

World Bank. (2008). *World development indicators database*. Washington, DC: The World Bank.

Wragg, E. (2004a). *Education, education, education*. London & New York, NY: Routledge-Falmer.

Wragg, E. (2004b). Introduction. In *Teaching and learning*. London: Routledge.

Wright, B. (2015). Perceptions of mixed race: A study using an implicit index. *Journal of Black Psychology, 41*, 513–539.

Wright, C., Weekes, D., & McGlaughlin, A. (2000). *'Race'. Class and gender in exclusion from school*. London: Falmer Press.

Yampolsky, M., Amiot, C., & de la Sablonniere, R. (2016). The Multicultural Identity Scale (MULTIS): Developing a comprehensive measure for configuring one's multiple cultural identities with the self. *Journal of Cultural and Ethnic Minority Psychiatry, 22*, 166–184.

Yap, S., & Ten Others. (2014). Investigating the structure and measurement invariance of the multigroup ethnic identity measure in a multi-ethnic sample of college students. *Journal of Counselling Psychology, 61*, 437–446.

Young, L. (1982). Identity, self-esteem and evaluation of colour and ethnicity in young children in Jamaica and London. In G. Verma & C. Bagley (Eds.), *Self-concept, achievement and multicultural education* (pp. 191–213). London: MacMillan.

Young, L. (2005). Accentuate the positive. In B. Richardson (Ed.), *Tell it like it is: How our schools fail Black children* (pp. 148–151). London: Trentham Books.

Young, L., & Bagley, C. (1982). Self-esteem, self-concept and the development of Black identity: A theoretical overview. In G. Verma & C. Bagley (Eds.), *Self-concept, achievement and multicultural education* (pp. 41–59). London: MacMillan.

Young, L., & Bagley, C. (1988). Evaluation of color and ethnicity in young children in Jamaica, Ghana, England, and Canada. *International Journal of Intercultural Relations, 12*, 45–60.

Zacharialis, M., Scott, S., & Barrett, M. (2010). *Exploring critical realism as the theoretical foundation of mixed-method research: Evidence from the economics of IS innovations*. Cambridge: Cambridge Judge Business School.

Ziller, R. C. (1973). *The social self*. New York, NY & Oxford: Pergamon Press.

EXCLUDED YOUTH IN BRITAIN

Historical Review of Research on Inequality, Education, Health, Family Support for Excluded Youth, 1968–2008[1]

ONE: OVERVIEW

Britain offers the promise of a quality education from preschool to university, but currently youth in the population who formed a more or less permanent underclass (at least ten percent of the population) rarely took full advantage of these educational opportunities, due to a variety of negative pressures in their lives. Up to 2008, Britain was one of the world's wealthiest countries, both in terms of gross national income, and average income per head – but this wealth was distributed much more unequally than in most countries of the developed world, with the exception of the United States, in which the grossest forms if inequality prevail. In Britain, health indicators – rates of illness and death from various diseases and "accidents" in the first two decades of life – illustrate the chronic disadvantages experienced by the poorest income quintile of the population. Differences between rich and poor families in this regard were actually increasing. The poor remained poor and in poorer health, decade upon decade, while the incomes and good health of the richest quintile improved year by year. The rich were becoming richer, but the poor remained poor (Goldthorpe & Jackson, 2007; Blanden et al., 2007; Wilkinson & Pickett, 2009).

There were powerful structural problems within British society which created enduring economic poverty, and which persisted between generations, with its associated educational poverty: at least half of children from families in the poorest income quintile endured second-rate conditions of living, second-rate educational provision, and restricted occupational opportunities. These were "the excluded youth" of Britain. This sector of the population also suffered disproportionately from chronically poor health, maladaptive behaviour, exclusions from school because of their "special educational needs", and various long-term neurological disorders.

Children from the underclass were much more likely to live in areas of large cities in Britain marked by social or poor housing, high levels of criminality, intergenerational family problems, and psychiatric illness in adults. The schools which served their "sink" estates were often of poor quality, "crumbling schools" with high rates of teacher turnover, and the lack of specialist teachers in maths, science and languages in secondary schools. Classes in these schools were often too large for effective teaching, and teacher morale was often low. 'Troublesome' pupils from these schools were often subject to temporary or permanent exclusion from the educational system, and if they completed schooling they only atypically gained examination successes which enabled them to proceed to college or university. They were likely to become a chronically unemployed underclass, leading disorganized lifestyles marked by petty criminality, as well the drift into begetting the next generation of the underclass.

Britain could offer focussed school-based educational and social work intervention services for families and children otherwise destined for school exclusion and educational failure. These demonstration projects have shown that although such interventions are costly in the short term they are nevertheless frequently successful in diverting young people from depressed and self-defeating lifestyles. Because of the criminal justice and social service costs saved, in the long-run these interventions have profound psychological and fiscal benefits.

The 'poverty of education' in Britain in the period under review is illustrated by international comparisons which highlight Britain's comparative failure on a number of indicators of achievement, health and well-being in children and adolescents. Two groups were identified as having especially high levels of stress and failure within the educational system: children growing up in (or having recently left) residential child care; and children with 'special educational needs'. High levels of permanent and temporary school exclusions identified an educational system which practised *exclusion* rather than inclusion. Children were particularly likely to be excluded from mainstream schools on grounds of alleged disruption, poor academic performance, disability of various kinds, or the simple fact of being bullied. Britain, although a signatory to the UN Commission on the Rights of Disabled Children (2006), in practice violated this convention through its high levels of educational exclusion of children because of their cognitive, emotional or behavioural challenges. The plight of children with autistic spectrum disorders was particularly dire in this regard. Children labelled as gay, lesbian, bisexual and transgendered suffered severe harm from bullying and assaults, and consequent threats to their mental health (Bagley & D'Augelli, 2000).

International literature on school class sizes has been reviewed, showing clearly that in smaller classes teachers could focus on the learning, emotional and behavioural needs of each pupil, without the need for forced exclusions. However, in Britain many school classes contained 30 or more pupils, and in secondary schools, classes could be up to 60 in size, because of lack of specialist teachers in mathematics and science. It was argued on the basis of American, British and international evidence that one of the crucial investments needed in a rich nation is one that of halving school class sizes.

We commended the government's Sure Start initiatives for under-fives in families in deprived areas, but almost certainly these programmes although successful in some applications, were underfunded and not comprehensive enough in scope to be fully effective. We describe an alternative type of intervention in which social workers and specialist teachers are attached to primary and secondary schools serving deprived areas. Such interventions can be highly cost-effective in reducing school exclusions, problem behaviours in school and community, school drop-out and later problems such as unwanted pregnancy, drug use, unemployment and criminality. Here, we argue, is a way of preventing children of the poorest families becoming the next generation of the underclass.

TWO: THEORETICAL PERSPECTIVES

This historical overview takes a Marxian perspective on the sociology of education, and our position is similar to that of Collier (2002) who saw a fruitful marriage of Marxian concepts with those of Dialectical Critical Realism, in Roy Bhaskar's (1992/2008) development of Hegel and Marx's ideas of alienation and its unmasking. We follow critical realists (e.g. Bhaskar, 2008; Archer, 2007; Alderson, 2013, 2016) on the sociology of Emile Durkheim, seeing societies and cultures as organic wholes, in which values and actions occur within integrated social groupings in which the tendency to accept a central set of values may be accepted uncritically, even by those for whom such value systems offer profound disadvantages. As Marx for example. observed, the oppressions and dysfunctions of capitalism remain "unmasked" (Avineri, 1970). We follow too Bhaskar's (2008) extension of Marx's ideas of alienation into dialectical critical realism, whose ultimate aim is to remove the layers of "false consciousness" which cloud effective action for positive social change. In Marxian critical realism, the sociological theories of Weber and Durkheim are integrated within the liberating model of dialectical critical realism (Creaven, 2007)

Britain is a society in which an unequal social order, one based on class exploitation, is melded by a set of values both explicit and implicit, and by many rituals, religious observances, folkways and forms of speech, which make fractures, pressures and hierarchies between social class groups and their "masked alienation" difficult to understand or act upon.

Our vision of an ideal society is one which both maximises personal freedom through state intervention – an idea derived from the philosophy of T.H. Green – but also enhances that freedom through welfare reform (Greengarten, 1981). Translated into the modern era, this is the post-socialist philosophy of New Labour, in which the state's role is that of addressing not only individual liberty, but also in the ending of curbs on freedom imposed by lack of income, poor housing, poor health, and inferior education. The origin of this idea of *freedom from want* (in addition to J.S. Mill's idea of freedom to engage in a wide variety of actions) lies in the Beveridge Report of 1942, which proposed a programme for "social insurance and allied services", which has still been only partly realised. This is, of course, a liberal (and liberating) version of the Marxist analysis of social class.

The sociologist Peter Townsend has explored extensively in his empirical work the idea of *relative poverty*. While absolute poverty in countries such as India and Nepal has profoundly deleterious effects on child welfare (Bagley, 2008a; Simkhada & Bagley, 2008), even having basic needs met is not a formula for good child and family welfare when families in the poorest sector of society of a capitalist society are profoundly disadvantaged, relative not only to the richest and most powerful classes; but relative also to the majority of the population as well.

It is the politics of despair, not of envy, which are likely to blight the lives of the relatively poor (Townsend, 1970, 1979). Systems of welfare, far from lifting the lot of the poor to that of the average citizen, often served to depress the lives of families with children through the humiliating rituals of means tested benefits, and the stigma for some, in being welfare dependent.

Townsend and Davidson (1992) drew on their previous work undertaken with medical colleagues (in "The Black Report") showing that economic deprivation and poor health are intimately and directly linked: poverty causes depressed and despairing lifestyles, conditions of work leading to higher injury and death rates, and environmental conditions which cause premature deaths at all ages. We review evidence showing that even in

2008 lower income and associated social class groupings were associated with significantly poorer health and higher death rates in children – and, moreover, the differences between socioeconomic classes were increasing. The well-off were becoming more prosperous, and more healthy. The poor stayed the same.

Another strand in the arguments about poverty and social exclusion of British youth derives from our interest in urban sociology derived from the pioneering work of Robert Park and his colleagues in Chicago (Abbott, 1999). We are fascinated by the mapping and correlation of different aspects of social adaptation and social conditions within urban areas (usually, city wards and the smaller enumeration districts they contain), examining data to see if rates of poverty and childhood accidents, and delinquency for example, occur within the same neighbourhoods, probably fuelled by the same social forces. While these correlations do not imply direct cause, they invite fuller case studies.

In Britain in the decade 1996 to 2005, the sector of youth with the highest failure rates in secondary schools were the poor whites, who saw many of the hard-working and ambitious children of immigrants overtaking them in schools, and in economic settings. These "poor white" individuals were likely to be those who were most hostile to their ethnic minority peers. Their racism emerged from a form of status deprivation (Runciman & Bagley, 1971; Bagley et al., 1979). This idea of reactionary ideas emerging from the relative deprivation of the precariat is also observed by Standing (2014) and Goodwin and Heath (2016).

The reason why relative deprivation in an affluent society creates both resentment, anger and despair is intriguing, and we must probably look to social psychological theory, such as that advanced by Wilkinson and Pickett (2009) in their important book *The Spirit Level: Why More Equal Societies Almost Always Do Better*. We note however Alderson's (2013) critique: that explaining the ills engendered by relative poverty can in fact be victim-blaming rather than system-blaming. Alderson implies that we should consider a Marxian approach, examining who gains from inequality in society, rather than engaging in a psychological analysis of the impact on 'the losers'. Indeed, Alderson (2013, p. 108) is critical of Wilkinson's apparent attempt to pathologize the poor.

The fact that the segregated, underclass is the *victim in being pathologised* should not lead us into the semantic slippage of assuming that because "the poor" are often "mad or bad", that they are also blameworthy, and need to be controlled or oppressed. This underclass is caused by, is a function of, the capitalist system of exploitation (Standing, 2014).

While we strive hard not to blame the poor, we do throughout this document advocate support and help for the poor and their children, to protect them from the worst of the ills imposed by the capitalist state. We frequently stray into the language of accountancy, dwelling on cost-benefit analysis. Spending a small amount of money on social service and educational support, will yield great financial reward in the medium to long run. Why is this message so hard for governments to accept? Perhaps they do not, in the final analysis, wish to radically interfere with the system of capital and class privilege which Britain, more than any other European nation, enjoys.

THREE: SOCIAL CLASS, INEQUALITY AND THE CRISIS IN BRITISH EDUCATION

For those struggling to provide universal, inclusive, free quality education at primary and secondary levels worldwide, the British case was (in 2008) paradoxical. Pupils were allowed to stay in school and take public examinations until the age of 18, and were encouraged to apply for college and university entrance (Dutton et al., 2005). For the large majority of students from the disadvantaged social classes, comprising about a fifth of the nation, the possibility of entering tertiary education was hardly possible (HEFCE, 2005).

In addition an important minority of pupils at secondary level were temporarily or permanently excluded from school (or permanently excluded themselves) because of their alienation from school and learning, or because of problems of behaviour and underachievement which made them unacceptable to their schools, who in consequence suspended or permanently expelled them. Cumulatively since 1996 at least 200,000 (more than two per cent) of students under age 17 had been permanently or temporarily excluded from school by the end of 2007 (ONS, 2009).[2]

The rate of these exclusions was significantly higher in areas of Britain marked by much poor quality or social-tenancy housing, areas in which a high proportion of parents were living in poverty, marked by various indicators of social deprivation (NLT, 1998; Reed, 2004). For youth of Afro-Caribbean descent, permanent exclusion rates were three times those in other ethnic minorities, a practice described as reflecting a school culture of 'institutional racism' (Wanless, 2006; Strand, 2008; Craig, 2009).

The number of rejected, dispirited or discouraged pupils who never took any public examinations at age 16 had by late 2005 reached a record level in Britain, with 12.6 percent of adolescents leaving school without any public examination successes. These young people either became permanently unemployed, or took unskilled jobs (Bekhradnia, 2006). According to OECD figures (2006, 2007) Britain ranked poorly (rank 27 out of 30 OECD industrialized nations) in terms of young people staying in school or further education beyond the age of 16. GCSE failure rates, disproportionately high in children from poverty backgrounds and from schools serving depressed neighbourhoods "expose the increasing gap between rich and poor" (Garner, 2008a).

Fimister (2001) in a review of Britain's "wasted youth" undertaken for the Child Poverty Action Group pulled together evidence showing the health and educational disadvantages of being born into a family marked by economic poverty. Such families were particularly likely to live in 'blighted' neighbourhoods, marked by an excess of poor housing. The collection of research papers edited by Fimister (2001) was offered to the New Labour government as a blueprint for change in crucial areas of social policy. Writing several years later, we noted that New Labour had taken up very few of these challenges.

FOUR: THE PARADOX: EDUCATION INEQUALITY IN A WEALTHY COUNTRY

Britain was one of richest countries in the world according to average GNP per citizen (Brewer et al., 2005; OECD, 2006), and by 2007 ranked fifth among the world's top seven richest nations (World Bank, 2008; ONS, 2009).

However, the distribution of this wealth in Britain was more unequal than in most European nations (Hobson, 2001; Bradshaw & Chen, 2002). Britain ranked 51st on the inequality index (i.e. had a high score on the Gini Coefficient, which measures unequal distribution of wealth) in the 124 countries included in international comparisons (UN, 2005). Nordic and some former Communist countries as well as Japan had the most equal distributions of national wealth. Britain's distribution of national wealth had been becoming *more* unequal: in 1976 the poorest 50 percent of the British population owned only eight percent of national wealth; by 2003 this had fallen to seven percent (HM Revenue & Customs, 2006). OECD data for 2006–2007 also indicated that Britain was becoming more unequal, with the richest 10 percent possessing nine times more wealth than the poorest 10 percent of the population (Booth, 2008a).

There was a strong correlation in 21 major industrialized countries between higher Gini scores (indicating a greater income gap between rich and poor) and diminished life expectancy (De Vogli et al., 2005). This correlation

(0.87) was unaffected by the availability of a universal, free health service in any particular country, including Britain which ranked strongly in terms of inequality of income distribution. In part a high Gini score is due to the failure of social security and welfare payments in Britain to have had very much influence on patterns of income inequality (Bradshaw & Chen, 2002). Britain's Minister for Social Inclusion [sic] (Armstrong, 2006) conceded that 3.66 million adults (some nine percent of the population) had five or more chronic disadvantages, including high rates of relative poverty, poor housing, chronic unemployment, poor health, and living in an environmentally deprived neighbourhood. In international measurements, the link between infant mortality and income inequality in Britain was actually increasing, relative to other developed nations (Collison et al., 2007).

FIVE: POVERTY, SOCIAL DEPRIVATION AND INEQUALITY IN BRITAIN

Although there is high average wealth per head in Britain, such wealth is more unequally distributed than in many comparable countries (Shaw, 2004). This is reflected in a persistent, self-perpetuating underclass whose poor educational and occupational achievements was frequently transmitted from generation to generation – Bagley (2002) summarized some of this evidence in a book on 'the child abusers', and argued that adults who had grown up in poverty-laden, neglectful and abusing homes were particularly likely to become abusive or neglecting parents themselves.

Economic poverty in Britain is relative rather than absolute (Townsend, 1979). Few individuals starve, although the number of homeless families appeared to be growing. British government data indicated that by June, 2004 the number of homeless families seeking emergency accommodation had reached an all time high at 97,280 in the previous quarter, an overall increase of 135 per cent since 1997 (ODPM, 2004).

Neustatter (2004) reviewed a variety of statistical resources on poverty and deprivation affecting young people in Britain. UNICEF figures indicated that although Britain in terms of total wealth stood near the top in world rankings, Britain stood nineteenth in the world league of proportion of families with children in marked poverty, a higher percentage in relative poverty than in countries such as Turkey, Poland and Hungary. Britain imprisoned more young people (population adjusted rates) than any other European country except Russia, and there was, Neustatter argued, a direct link between poverty and deprivation, and delinquent behaviour in young people. These young delinquents were particularly likely to have failed at all levels of schooling, and to be permanently excluded from regular schooling.

Narey (2008) reported data showing that there has been a five-fold increase in the locking up of children aged 10 to 14 since 1997, many being incarcerated for trivial offences. Only Russia, of developed nations, held a greater proportion of this age group in jail at any one time. The cost of incarcerating a child for one year was more than £100,000, and if this sum had been used on behavioural support, counselling, family support and diversion programmes, the drift into more serious criminality could well have been avoided (RESET, 2007). Many children in the system of child detention were "written off" at age 12, the implicit assumption being that they could never be reformed because of their disorganised or abusive family backgrounds (Narey, 2008).

Together with the young delinquents in these child detention centres were numbers of children who had committed no crime, but who had mental health problems, were suicidal or were considered to be sexually promiscuous (Brogi & Bagley, 1998). Very often these were children from poverty backgrounds, victimized because of behaviours associated with coming from economically poor or disorganized families. Later many were likely to drift through the child care system, into young offender jails, through to the adult jail system. Narey's (2008) figures indicated that only some five percent of the £445 millions spent in the previous year by the Youth Justice Board went to preventive programmes, the bulk being spent on incarceration.

A United Nations report (Bowcott, 2008) criticized Britain as a nation that was intolerant of children, marked by a set of public attitudes which caused rather than reflected youth alienation, and imprisoned youth for whom rehabilitation and diversion programmes would be much more efficient.

SIX: INEQUALITY AND RELATIVE POVERTY IN BRITAIN

Increasing affluence in British society has not been associated with a 'trickle down' of wealth, and income inequalities in Britain have increased rather than diminished (Glennerster, Hills, Piachaud & Webb, 2005). In their major study of poverty in the United Kingdom, replicating Rowntree's work of a hundred years earlier Glennerster et al. (2005) found pockets of extreme poverty all over Britain, associated with low wages, unemployment, and other indicators of social deprivation including underachievement of school pupils. In assessing social policy alternatives they noted the continued failure of government initiatives to end poverty, and offer the following "pessimistic" outcome if government initiatives continued to fail:

On a bleaker, pessimistic view, any success in tackling underlying inequalities would come too slowly to counter continuing polarisation of economic opportunities. Those without access to capital, home ownership and good education for their children, would fall further behind – widening wealth inequalities would continue to reinforce intergenerational links, for instance those with most wealth purchase houses near good schools. Even if policy succeeded in raising the skills of some young people, the lowest wages would still be set by an increasingly cut-throat global market.

It is salutary that proportionately, more families in Britain lived in relative poverty than in any other country in the unenlarged European Union (Policy Action Team, 2000). Brewer and Gregg (2003) reviewed the British evidence, and looking at various definitions of poverty and concluded that: "Over the past 20 years the incidence of relative poverty among Britain's children has tripled." The relative poverty measure which is now generally accepted is that a family in poverty had an income of less than 60 per cent of the median income for the country as a whole. A family in which a parent relied on state benefits or on minimum-wage earnings would inevitably have fallen into this band of poverty. Struggling with this low level of income was likely to put a significant strain on a family's psychological coping resources. At least ten per cent of British families fell within this poverty sector (Glennerster et al., 2005). Despite a number of policy initiatives by the national government, relative child poverty had diminished less than politicians had hoped, for a variety of fiscal reasons (Brewer, Goodman, Shaw & Shepherd, 2005).

Data for 2005–2006 indicated that relative poverty (incomes less than 60 percent of the national median income) had *increased* from the previous year, with 12.7 million adults and 3.8 million children being in such relative poverty. According to the Institute of Fiscal Studies research, the causes of this rise were the failure of 'family credits' and of the minimum wage to keep pace with the rise in the general cost of living (Adam, Brewer & Shepherd, 2006; Adam, 2007; Brewer et al., 2009). For the fiscal year 2006–2007 the numbers of children living in families with incomes below the poverty line had again increased, this time by some 100,000, meaning that the official goal of halving the amount of child poverty by 2010 could not be realised (Booth, 2008b). It should be mentioned that the criterion for a child to be eligible for free school meals is a family income which was at least £2000 a year *below* the official poverty line (Curtis, 2008d). This meant that in many schools there were pupils (more than a million in the UK as a whole) from economically poor families who did not receive a free school lunch.

Government goals in 2008 were to significantly reduce child poverty by 2020, but this goal would not be met if current economic trends prevailed (Hirsch & Sutherland, 2009). There was an unexpected rise in child poverty in the period 2004–2007, largely due to the failure of tax-based measures supposed to help working parents (Gentleman, 2009). Effectively, a missing £2.2 billion needed to be transferred to economically poor families in the period 2004–2007 by welfare and fiscal systems if child and family poverty were to be reduced in line with earlier government proposals (Hirsch & Sutherland, 2009). Using 2007–2008 figures for estimated levels of unemployment for the next decade, these authors calculated that the proportion of children in poverty in 2020 would be about the same as the percentage in 2010. However, if there were higher levels of unemployment, families that remained within this intergenerational cycle of poverty would be *deeper* in poverty. These effects were thought likely to have multiple. negative effects on family welfare and adjustment.

Hirsch and Sutherland (2009) advocated therefore vigorous programmes of skill training which, with free child care, could enable adults and adolescents to enter the work force productively. Given an economic recession that began in 2008 however, it is likely that by 2020 the numbers who are "deeply in poverty" because of their chronic unemployment and inadequate welfare payments would have increased significantly (Hirsch & Sutherland, 2009). In 2009 the numbers who were unemployed and therefore in relative poverty, had increased by more than a million over two years. The job-seekers allowance (£64.30 a week, or £50.95 a week for the under 25s) was only 10.5 percent of the average wage, compared with such allowances which were 21 percent of the average wage in 1979, and 22 percent in 1912 when the unemployment insurance system was introduced in Britain (Bradshaw & Lynes, 2009).

The evidence indicated that by 2008 in each British city there were areas of 'social exclusion' where lived a high proportion of economically poor people living in low-quality housing (of the type described Bagley, 1984). There appeared to be both a policy allocation of stressed families into low-rent public housing, and a movement into poor quality, low-rent housing in the private sector by the marginally coping. In 2005 in Greater Manchester for example, there were large areas of public housing with many boarded-up buildings, in which truanting or excluded youth squatted or pursued recreations which included drug-using and dealing. One-third of children in Britain's North West region (which includes Greater Manchester) lived below the official poverty line (Carter, 2005). In five boroughs of Greater

Manchester the proportion living at or below the official 'relative poverty' line was over fifty percent (Osuh, 2005). It is not coincidental that in these areas marked by poor housing and much family poverty, elementary school class sizes were often very large – 18.1 percent of classes had 30 or more children, and more than 5,000 children across Greater Manchester were in elementary school classes of 35 or more (Haile, 2005). Adolescents in these areas of Manchester had particularly low levels of GCSE (General Certificate of Secondary Education) passes at age 16 (Leeming, 2007).

Bennett (2005) reviewed evidence claiming that: "Labour … failed to transform the life chances of Britain's poorest children, despite a succession of initiatives costing billions of pounds. By the age of six, clever children from poor homes have already fallen behind less-able pupils in the classroom, according to a progress report on Labour's eight years in power" (Bennett, 2005). Numbers of children in families living in "relative poverty" (family income less than 60% of the national median income) had increased to 12.7 millions in the accounting year 2005–2006, compared to 12.1 million in the previous accounting year (Seager, 2007). The number of children in these economically poor families had risen in the same period by 3.8 percent. The official goal of halving the rate of child poverty by 2010 appeared to have no possibility of achievement (Booth, 2008).

When we translate these dismal indicators of economic deprivation for families with children into rates of physical and emotional maltreatment of children in Britain, we can see how crucial economic deprivation may be in undermining family life. Sidebotham et al. (2006), for example, followed up 14,256 children in a longitudinal cohort, and identified two per cent who were maltreated in the first five years of life, to an extent requiring social service interventions. Significant factors predicting maltreatment were having a single parent, or having two youthful parents; low educational achievement in parents; psychiatric illness in a parent; high levels of material deprivation; residence in public housing or frequent moves of residence; and lack of supportive social networks. These findings replicate those made in several previous studies (Bagley, 2002).

In studying children in primary and secondary schools in deprived urban areas, we noticed a marked tendency for poverty, child maltreatment and neglect, and social disorganization to be transmitted across several generations in stressed families living in particular sectors in urban areas (Bagley and Pritchard, 1998a, 1998b). Given the number of teenaged mothers in these deprived groups, it was not uncommon for schools to remember the parents and even the grandparents of these children as "problem pupils" in their own time at school.

Ballard (2008) the incoming president of the Association of Teachers and Lecturers observed this trend in rural as well as in urban settings. According to the evidence he reviewed, at least a tenth of children in modern Britain continued to live in "near-Third World conditions, short of basics such as food, clothing and proper housing". He observed further: "Poverty is the scourge of our society. It is unacceptable to me that children from poor families are treated as if they were feckless and idle, as if poverty was their fault ... These children must become our collective responsibility." He observed that in his 30 years of teaching in rural Somerset he had seen grandchildren of earlier pupils pass through the same schools, trapped in the same levels of poverty. "There still remain children living in systemically poor families, and I mean really poor, not just a bit short of the readies, poorly housed, poorly clothed, culturally isolated and deprived. In rural communities, the lack of aspiration and opportunity is more acute. The lack of affordable housing and lack of well-paid work forces young people and families to find homes and jobs away from rural areas, ultimately leading to the closure of playgroups, schools and youth services."

The statistics on relative poverty showed a marked north-south division in Britain, with families and children in midland, Welsh, northern and Scottish regions much more likely to experience poverty than families in the South East of Britain – a gap which was widening and was now more marked than at any time in the past sixty years (Martin & Kitson, 2008).

An important study by Noden and West (2009a) followed up 550,000 pupils whose abilities were assessed at age 11, in order to examine the potential impact of poverty (measured by a child receiving free school meals) on GCSE success at age 16. Despite having high scores on the SAT test at age 11, the top ten percent of pupils from poverty backgrounds did significantly poorer in terms of obtaining five GCSEs at grade 3 or better (including English and mathematics) at age 16, than did their "less bright but economically better off peers". Overall, 22 percent of the "ever in receipt of free school meal group" achieved five good GCSEs, compared with 52 percent of the remainder. This research reinforces the findings from many other British studies: belonging to families in the poorest social classes in Britain has a profoundly negative effect on children's life chances.

SEVEN: HEALTH, INCOME AND SOCIAL CLASS

Health indicators measured according to income, or social and occupational class groupings are a useful and telling way of measuring social deprivation. In Britain in 2006 some 3,000 annual deaths of children aged 0 to 14 were associated with economic poverty, reflected in poor perinatal care, sudden infant death syndrome, other infant deaths associated with infectious disease, and deaths from 'accidents' – dying in fires, and being struck by motor vehicles (Bagley, 1992; Baker et al., 1998; Smith, 2003; Kyffin et al., 2004; Sethi et al., 2007). This evidence also indicated that poorer quality, older housing, overcrowding and degraded environments were associated with a greater incidence of accidents and fires, infectious illnesses in children and young people, as well as with poorer use of preventive health services. Children of the unskilled manual social classes in Britain were twice as likely to die in an 'accident' compared to those in middle class families (Rahman et al., 2000).

A comprehensive UK study by Mitchell et al. (2000) confirmed the strong link between poverty and increased rates of child morbidity and mortality: "Redistribution of wealth would have the greatest absolute effect because it could improve the lives of the largest number of people. Eradication of child poverty would have the greatest relative effect (in terms of the proportion of lives saved)." That the potential for intervention can be highly cost-effective is illustrated by the experimental studies of Howden-Chapman et al. (2007), which provided insulation to the houses of 2,200 individuals, compared with a similar number of comparable individuals who did not receive such insulation. After a year the 'insulated housing' individuals had significantly fewer cases of respiratory disorder, fewer days off school and work for respiratory illness, fewer GP consultations, and fewer hospital admissions. In a subsequent study Howden-Chapman et al. (2008) provided additional heating to families with 409 asthmatic children, and controls with similar medical problems. Children in the heated houses had significantly fewer days off school, better general health, fewer respiratory tract infections, and fewer episodes of night coughing.

Government figures cited by Elliott (2005) indicated that between 1997 and 2005 the child mortality gap between rich and poor families in Britain had widened. By 2005 parents in the lowest income quintile were 19 per cent more likely to have a child die from any cause in the first five years of life than were parents in the highest income quintile. Infant mortality rates had a strong statistical link to earlier mortality at any age in surviving members of low income families. A report from Scotland (Scottish Office, 2005) indicated that in the most deprived urban areas, childhood (0–14) 'accidents' were three times the rate in the most advantaged areas. Just over half of these 'accidents' involved a child pedestrian.

An English study (Heyderman et al., 2004) showed that meningitis deaths in children (0–4) were three times higher in the lowest income quintile families, compared with children from the wealthiest fifth of the population. In Scotland too the "poverty gap" had, in terms of child health, widened: in a review of more than one million low birth weight babies born in Scotland it was found that women from economically poor families were 2.4 times more likely than women from the wealthiest quintile to have a child with birth weight less than 2,500 grams, a known factor in adverse child development (Scottish Office, 2006).

Child mortality and morbidity were linked to many indicators of social deprivation and social disorganisation, including the incidence of one-parent families, educational under-achievement, school exclusions, and secondary schools which had high staff turnover and class-sizes which were too large for effective teaching. Deprived children become deprived parents, and the cycle of poverty and disadvantage affects each subsequent generation (DoH, 1998; Boateng, 2000). Just as lack of wealth and educational under-achievement are often socially inherited, so was the tendency to commit crime, to be a single mother in the teenaged years, the tendency to have poorer pre- and post-natal care, and to be homeless, spurring the cycle of child deprivation into the next generation (SEU, 2000a, 2000b, 2000c).

A report from the British Medical Association (BMA, 1999) found that the income and health gap between the highest and lowest social classes in Britain had increased significantly in the previous decade. In Britain's poorest social classes the proportion of underweight babies and associated perinatal morbidity and mortality was the highest in any developed country, higher than in countries such as Slovenia and Albania. Observing that children born in the poorest sector of the British population were 70 per cent more likely to die or suffer serious disease, or life-threatening accidents in the first five years of life than children in other social classes, the report comments: "The first five years of life are absolutely critical to the development of children's bodies, minds and personalities. Deprivation early in life causes life-long damage, delinquency and despair ... Poorer children are more prone to accident and injury because they often have nowhere to play but the street or a dangerous room such as the kitchen. They live on estates where there are broken glass, needles and other dangerous objects." The report estimates that each £1 spent on improving the conditions of child health in the early years would ultimately save £8 in later health care costs.

Dyer (2005) using government data, indicated that the social class differentiation in 'disease free years' remained unchanged over a decade – in other words, children and young people in the poorest social classes have chronic illness rates which continued to be significantly greater, compared with children of the wealthier social classes. Although differences in death rates had diminished somewhat over time when social classes were compared, those in the poorest social classes died, on average 6.0 years earlier than those in the most advantaged social classes. Put another way, children of the well off were becoming healthier, but yet in 2002 children of the very poor had not increased their chances of surviving or avoiding serious accident and disease in their early years.

Data from the 2001 census indicated that the most economically deprived quintile of the British population had an incidence of very low birth-weight deliveries (<1500 grams), and long-term childhood illnesses that was twice the incidence of such conditions in the most advantaged fifth of the population (McFarlane, Stafford & Moser, 2004). Life expectancy in the most disadvantaged wards in parts of Greater Manchester, for example was ten years lower than in the most advantaged (Woodhouse, 2005).

A study by Petrou et al. (2006) showed that British children under 10 in the poorest segment of families (Class V) had death rates which are 40 percent higher than those of children from the richest group of families (in Social Classes I and II). This longitudinal study of 117,212 individuals showed that non-fatal respiratory disease, poisoning and accidents had the same social class bias.

In a comparison of "external" causes of mortality in children aged 0 to 15 for the census years 1981 and 2001, Edwards et al. (2006) showed that although deaths from fires, poisoning, pedestrian and cycle "accidents" and from unexplained causes (e.g. SIDS) had more than halved over twenty years, in the poorest class (in which a male parent was absent, had never worked, or was long-term unemployed) child death rates had *not* declined over 20 years. Compared with Professional and Managerial Classes I and II, this "underclass" of the unemployed Class V group experienced pedestrian deaths in children at 20.6 times the upper class rate; child cyclist deaths at 27.5 times the upper class rate; deaths in fires at 37.7 times the upper class rate; and 'undetermined' (including SIDS) deaths 32.6 times the upper class rate.

Further work by Edwards et al. (2008) studied all hospital admissions for serious injury involving children 0 to 15 in the period 1999 to 2004. This study found that children from the most deprived areas (according to census indicators) were 4.1 times as likely to be seriously injured as pedestrians, and 4.7 times as likely to be injured as cyclists, compared to children living in the most advantaged areas.

Blair et al. (2006) identified 369 SIDS deaths in their longitudinal study, comparing cohorts between 1984 and 2003, compared with 1,300 controls with non-fatal illness gathered from hospital records. While the rate of SIDS had reduced markedly over 20 years in middle class and stable working-class families (probably due to public health messages and perinatal advice given to new mothers) the causes of SIDS amenable to parent education were increasingly relevant in the poorest socio-economic groups living in the most disorganized families. Thus the proportion of SIDS caused by parent co-sleeping with a child had risen from 12 to 50 percent, and the number of mothers with a SIDS infant who smoked during and after pregnancy had increased from 57 to 86 percent in the poorest group of mothers. Both co-sleeping and parental smoking were causally related to the tragedy of sudden infant death, and had a much higher incidence in the poorest social classes.

A review by the British Medical Association (BMA, 2006) on diagnosable and treatable *mental health conditions* in children and adolescents under 16 suggested an overall prevalence rate of about ten percent, ranging from internalizing disorders involving anxiety, depression and self-harm, through to externalizing disorders involving extreme aggression, destructiveness and hyperactivity. Some major causes of these disorders identified wee high levels of economic deprivation, poor perinatal care, inadequate parenting in adults who themselves often had mental illness of various kinds, chronic family poverty, and welfare dependency (Wilkinson, 2005). All too often these young people would become adults with a variety of dysfunctional behaviours which reflected their disorganized childhood, their movements into and out of alternative care, and their experience of abuse and neglect of various kinds (Bagley & King, 2003; Bagley, 2002).

Goodman et al. (2002) in a major interview study with several thousand British children found that some eight percent had a serious psychiatric disorder, a rate which had doubled over three decades. These tended to be chronic illnesses, particularly with regard to conduct disorder. The higher rates of psychiatric disorders in childhood were associated with the development of addiction, alcoholism, poor sexual health, and suicidal behaviours in adolescence and beyond. The "usual suspects" were identified as aetiological factors – poverty, low birth weight, neighbourhood deprivation, youthful parents, and disorganized family life. The Avon longitudinal study of some 6,300 children indicated that by their early teens, up to ten percent had one or more indicators of psychotic illness (Horwood et al., 2008). Significant background factors in this symptom pattern were the child's poor intellectual achievements, being bullied at school, birth to a younger mother, and a family history of depression.

Scott and Maughan (2008) in a major inquiry on the psychological well-being of children in Britain gathered together a wide range of evidence, including that from several specially commissioned surveys. They confirmed that rates of emotional and conduct disorder in children aged 16 or less had at least doubled in the past 25 years, and at least a million children in Britain had a diagnosable psychiatric disorder, which tended to be chronic in nature (Goodman et al., 2002). The major reason they adduced was the increasing amount of income inequality in Britain, and the pressures this brings to bear on young parents. Poor mental health is associated with both poverty and deprivation in parents (especially mothers), family disorganization, and drug and alcohol use in older siblings and parents (Meltzer et al., 2000; ONS, 2009). Poor parental mental health was transmitted to their children, which was in turn transmitted in many cases, to the next generation when those children became adults.

The official review of *Social Trends* issued by the Office for National Statistics (ONS, 2009) charted the continuation of child poverty, poor housing linked (almost certainly in causal terms) with the risk of being injured or killed in pedestrian or cycling accidents in children and adolescents. While the number of children living in a high degree of relative poverty had fallen to 22 percent in 2007, from a peak of 28 percent in 1999 these poverty rates (associated with childhood illnesses and maladjustments) were well above government policy targets (ONS, 2009). No less than 31 percent of British children according to the ONS survey of Britain for 2006–2007 continued to live in 'non-decent' homes, marked by problems of decayed fabric, poor insulation, and heating problems

Friedli's (2009) research on increasing rates of self-harm and attempted suicide in young people in Britain meshed with this research to paint a dismal picture of a generation, a significant minority of whom were growing up in Britain poor, angry and sad. The number of calls to crisis help lines by adolescents had increased by more than a quarter in one decade, the increase being greatest amongst boys (ONS, 2009).

This section offers the conclusion that chronic poverty occurs in frequently occurring subcultures, mostly urban but sometimes rural, and is causally associated with elevated rates of illness (both physical and psychological), and death in children and adolescents, relative to those in stable working class, middle class and upper working class families. Moreover, it is argued, scholastic failure is also linked to the conditions of family life which undermine health. Indeed, poor health in children and their "intellectual disability" are closely linked.

EIGHT: POOR HEALTH AND INTELLECTUAL DISABILITY

In an important study, Emerson and Hatton (2007) examined data for a representative sample of 12,160 British children under 17 located within the Department of Work and Pensions' 'families with children' study. They found that children with intellectual disability (defined as chronic scholastic failure due to a number of causes) were significantly more likely to have poor health on many different measures: 31 percent of these "poor health" pictures were attributed to the socio-economic disadvantages endured by their parents.

A possible explanation of findings such as these comes from the American research of Farah et al. (2006) which showed that "being poor can damage your brain". Growing up in poverty was associated with a variety of cognitive disadvantages and differential brain functions (often associated with learning difficulties and other conditions such as ADHD – attention-deficit hyperactive disorder). The disadvantages of the poor which made them experience schooling (in behavioural and learning terms) differentially were *not* attributable to genetic factors, but to adverse conditions of pregnancy and birth, poor diet, early illness of various kinds, abuse and neglect, and environmental toxins.

NINE: THE INCREASE OF RELATIVE POVERTY AND PERSISTENCE OF POOR HEALTH: PUBLIC HEALTH AND SOCIAL SYSTEM INTERVENTIONS

Analysis of Census and Household Survey data on deprived families and communities in Britain by Meen et al. (2005) shows that cycles of deprivation are very difficult to break; virtually every local authority in the Britain contains persistently enduring zones of extreme deprivation in terms of housing type and individual characteristics marked by poverty, chronic unemployment, and personal disorganisation (associated with high levels of crime, delinquency, drug use, and mental illness). Any young adults who can, move out of such areas, but few want to move *into* such areas marked by vandalism and frequent community violence, and even in an era of housing shortage many houses on these 'sink estates' remain abandoned, and are often vandalised.

A comprehensive overview of available data on income inequality and health indicators in Britain up to 2004 concluded that despite the stated policy intentions of government, income inequalities had *increased* steadily in the previous two decades, and the gap in life expectancy between the highest and lowest social classes had actually grown, just as differences in scholastic achievement between social class and income groups were, in parallel, growing larger (Shaw, Davey-Smith & Dorling, 2005).

A study from the National Audit Office (NAO, 2007a) found that 16 percent of Britons lived in a household where no-one was working or seeking work, a group in danger of "... drifting into a spiral of joblessness, poverty, ill-health and crime" which was often transmitted to children of such families. Permanently jobless households were found in particular, in depressed urban areas of London, Birmingham, Liverpool and Manchester. Dorling (2007) in an analysis of 40 years of British census data showed that the poverty gap between low and high income groups was by 2005 greater than at any time since 1968, the largest increase occurring in the previous fifteen years. Moreover, this research showed, there are pockets containing families with very low incomes in most British cities, and it was likely that the schools which serve these areas would have to grapple with problems of high teacher turnover, and a higher than average proportion of truanting, rebellious and poorly achieving pupils (Lawlor, 2007).

Toynbee and Walker (2008) pointed to figures showing that the wealthiest ten percent of Britons owned 47 percent of national wealth in 2002, a figure that had risen to 54 percent in 2006. The poorest ten percent owned about three percent of national wealth at these two points in time. Thus, the rich were becoming richer, but the poor remained poor. "Subcultural" economic and social poverty is strongly linked to this picture of enduring economic inequality. Addressing this issue, the Wanless Report (2004) analysed in particular the nature of health inequalities in Britain, and proposed the achievement of a number of goals which included: halving the rate of child poverty by 2010, eradicating it by 2020; reducing inequalities in health by reducing measured infant mortality by 10 percent, and increasing life expectancy at birth by the same margin, by 2010; improving life chances of children by reducing the conception rate in under-18s by 50 percent, by 2010; and reducing the number of children killed or seriously injured in road traffic accidents by 50 percent by 2010. However, research by the National Audit Office (NAO, 2009) indicated that death rates in child pedestrians and cyclists were actually increasing, especially in deprived urban areas. By the time this review ended in 2008–2009, there was no indication whatever, that any of the Wanless goals would be achieved.[3]

Godlee (2007) cited available international data which showed that "the healthiest and happiest societies are those with the most equal distribution of income". According to her data Britain was not amongst these "healthy societies", and none of the goals set by Wanless had any possibility of achievement within the time frames he advocated. Indeed, the rate of relative child poverty had *increased* rather than diminished (Seager, 2007), reflected in high levels of child mortality (in those aged 0 to 4) compared with other developed nations (Collison et al., 2007).

Professor Sir Ian Kennedy, Chair of the British Health Care Commission, in February, 2007 issued a report on "unintentional injuries to children" in Britain, through the Audit Commission. The cost of such admissions to Accident and Emergency Departments in hospitals was around £146 millions a year. Deaths from such serious injuries (burns, poisoning, severe child abuse, falling down stairs, road traffic accidents were a major cause of death in childhood, and were 13 times as frequent in the poorer social classes, than in families from other social classes. Kennedy found that national and local governments and health care systems had no plans in place to prevent such deaths. None of the initiatives which he advocated in February 2007 had, at the time that this review ended (May, 2009) been undertaken.

By 2007 more than 75,000 pedestrians and cyclists of all ages had been killed or seriously injured on British roads, the *increase* in fatalities over two years being 11 percent (NAO, 2009). Britain ranked seventeenth out of 24 OECD countries on the population-adjusted measure of the high number of child pedestrians killed. "There is a disproportionately high level of pedestrian and cycle casualties in deprived areas," this report concluded. Similar findings have been made in studies in Canada and Britain (Bagley, 1992, 1993a).

O'Dowd and Coombes (2008) in a review of a decade of government data on death rates by income group, showed that poorer people were now significantly *more* likely to die prematurely than the average English person. Babies born to the poorest quintile of families were 17 percent more likely to die at or soon after birth than the English average. Ten years previously this figure had been 13 percent, indicating that in relative terms the chances of dying early in children in the poorest classes was *increasing*.

The WHO Commission on Social Determinants of Health (Marmot, 2008) presented data which showed the profound gap in mortality and morbidity between social classes in Britain. For example, a male child born in the poorest part of Glasgow had a life expectancy of 54 years, compared with a child born a few miles away in Glasgow's wealthiest area who had a life expectancy of 82 years. Similar differences existed in many British cities. Causes of curtailed life expectancy were deaths in the first year of life due to adverse perinatal events, and deaths of children due to poisoning, accidents, falls, and being struck by motor vehicles; in adolescence and beyond the poorer were at greater risk of deaths from smoking and its consequences, poor diet, diabetes, suicide and drug overdoses. The WHO commission pointed out that a number of countries – Australia, Sweden, Canada and Italy – had markedly reduced these causes of premature deaths in the previous two decades, by means of social and public health interventions. Clearly, Britain could do better. This Report made the forthright comment that In Britain there was a "toxic combination of low income, poor education, bad housing and unhealthy diets." These social injustices, particularly those involving child poverty, were according to Marmot's analysis, systemically linked to class inequalities, housing deprivation and insecurity, poorer mental health, poor education and deprivation across the lifespan, disadvantages transmitted between generations.

This section concluded with a bleak summary: in Britain up to 2008 some 10 per cent of families with children suffered chronic poverty which placed great strain on a family's social and psychological resources. Within such families, who tended to live in poorer housing in 'socially excluded' zones of the city, there were disproportionate numbers of children who suffered poorer health, higher death rates from various causes, higher rates of physical neglect and abuse, delinquency, and underachievement in school associated with poorer quality education in crowded classes.

These pupils, not surprisingly often achieved at a level which the pressurised schools found unacceptable, and such students were more often excluded because of challenging behaviour, underachievement, or 'special needs' of various kinds. Children from these economically poor families were significantly more likely to enter a cycle of poverty, in which family life was marked by disruption of parental bonds, addiction to drugs and alcohol, child abuse (physical and sexual), children removed into care, and juvenile and adult criminality. Social policies to prevent this were either meagre, or effective for only a minority of the targeted populations.

TEN: EXPENDITURES ON EDUCATION IN BRITAIN: THE POVERTY OF EDUCATION

Primary and secondary education in Britain was (like welfare services) significantly under-funded in comparison with other wealthy countries, and the number of pupils per teacher in publicly-funded schools in Britain was actually rising in the period under review (Haile, 2005; Paton, 2008c). Amongst the 30 OECD nations, Britain had one of the highest number of pupils per teacher amongst the leading industrialised nations (OECD, 2006, 2008; Civitas, 2008).

Those countries spending the highest proportion of national wealth on publicly-funded education were the Nordic countries. Significant increases in spending on education in Britain were however promised (Brown, 2006), and further OECD and international comparisons (OECD, 2007; ONS, 2009) showed that Britain's proportion of GNP apportioned to education (at 5.6 percent) was now closer to that of her OECD partners (average 6.2 percent). However, Britain was unusual in enrolling children into full time education at aged five (most nations enrol children at age six) and when this factor is adjusted for, Britain's expenditure on education for older pupils was appreciably worse than in many of her OECD partners.

A report from the British Centre for Economic Performance in 2004 (Chevalier & Dolton, 2004) found that the drift of teachers from the profession was outstripping the number of new recruits. Main reasons given by departing teachers were low pay, stress, and problems of teaching large classes which contained too many disruptive students. The problem was a circular one: as more teachers left the profession, classes became larger, and stress levels became worse, and in consequence more teachers left the profession.

Curtis et al. (2008) in a study of state secondary schools in which a high proportion went on to the Russell Group of universities (Britain's 'Ivy League') found that large sixth forms were one of the factors associated with success in this regard. Such schools were, apparently, able to recruit and retain well-qualified maths, physics and other specialist teachers with good degrees, for sixth form courses which could lead to university success for students. Giving written answers to Parliamentary Questions, the Secretary of State for Education conceded that only three percent of pupils from the poorest sector (qualifying for free school meals) obtained GCSE Advanced Level passes at a sufficient level which would make them eligible for entry to a Russell Group university. Only one in 16 of these economically poor students stayed in school beyond the age of 16, so they frequently failed to take any of the examinations which would qualify them for entry to any type of tertiary education (Hansard, 2008).

The Parliamentary Answer also conceded that in three of Britain's poorest boroughs in 2007, not a single pupil was entered for the externally moderated, advanced level GCSE physics examination (GCSE), open to all pupils at the age of 16. In the country as a whole 7 percent of students were not entered for any kind of external examination in mathematics, and when the population who had dropped out permanently before age 16 is counted, the estimate of "innumerate" students is about 10 percent of pupils in their mid-teens (Garner, 2008c). At least 6,000 pupils "disappear" from school rolls each year, leaving school at age 14 or earlier (Skidmore, 2008) – often following episodes of exclusion because of difficult behaviour, academic failure, or diagnosis of 'special needs'. Cumulatively, these 'disappeared' students total more than 100,000 of those aged 18 or less. Some will be drawing benefits, some will graduate to a life of crime, and some teenaged girls will have become pregnant. Schools lack the social work resources which would enable them to follow up these pupils who are particularly likely to live in deprived areas (Tomlinson, 2009). But their numbers serve to remind us that if they had been counted in the educational achievements of deprived schools, the average achievements of these schools would have been even lower.

ELEVEN: THE CRISIS IN TEACHING MATHEMATICS AND PHYSICS

While the shortage of teachers was greatest at primary level according to a CEP (2004) report, parallel work had highlighted a crisis in science teaching at the secondary level in Britain (Williams, 2004). The Engineering and Technology Board indicated that although graduates in science, engineering and technology had in the past contributed 27 per cent of Gross Domestic Product, there was now a significant shortage of specialist science teachers. In consequence fewer secondary school students took advanced public examinations in these subjects, and some university departments of physics, chemistry, engineering and mathematics appeared to be threatened with down-sizing or closure as a result, with an estimated closure of one third of science departments in British universities.

This in turn fed into the recruitment crisis of science and mathematics teachers in British schools, to the point where many secondary schools in less privileged areas did not have teachers with a degree in physics or mathematics, and in consequence they could not offer these subjects in the advanced level examinations for university entrance (Smithers & Robinson, 2006). Summarizing research by Alan Smithers, Curtis (2008) indicated that by June, 2008, 26 percent more physics teachers were leaving the profession than were entering teacher training courses with a degree in physics. Physics teachers probably choose the most rewarding schools in which to teach, and not surprisingly they were opting most often for independent schools, and high achieving state schools. Under-performing state secondary schools (in terms of low levels of examination successes at ages 16-plus) were those most likely to have no qualified physics teacher (Curtis, 2008).

By February 2007 because of a national shortage of mathematics teachers in secondary schools, it was becoming increasingly common for class sizes to 'double up' into groups of 60 or more for lecture type instruction, which appeared to work for the brightest pupils, but not for the least able (Hackett, 2007). The same report indicated that a quarter of maths classes for 11 to 14-year-olds in British schools were taken by teachers who had no degree level qualifications in mathematics, and not even an advanced sub-degree course take as part of B.Ed preparation. Those training as primary school teachers are required to take an examination in the first year of their B.Ed in basic mathematics, achieving 60 percent on the equivalent of the GCSE ordinary-level school leaving examination in mathematics. According to answers to Parliamentary questions, the failure rate of trainee teachers on this examination had increased steadily since 2001, and by 2006 56 percent of teachers failed the examination on their first sitting. Resits are permitted, and one trainee teacher finally obtained the required mark after 27 resits (Khan, 2008).

A government programme called *Learn Direct* which aimed to help adults achieve acceptable goals in literacy and mathematics found in a survey of 1,000 British adults, that one in ten had not even basic mathematical skills, which when generalised to the population as a whole was estimated to cost about £820 millions per annum in lost productivity, and inability to acquire vocational skills (Smithers, 2007). Similar problems were expected to beset the teaching of modern languages and history in secondary schools (Smithers & Bowden, 2005). In Greater Manchester the number of pupils aged 14+ studying a foreign language fell from 50 to 33 percent in a single year (Warden, 2005). In Scotland, the number of pupils opting for German in the intermediate school certificate has fallen by 40 percent in ten years, although those taking French had fallen by only six percent (Mackinnon, 2009).

In 2007 the government announced the development of 14 new diploma courses, which could be organised through the integration of existing GCSE and Advanced-level courses (taken at ages 15 to 18), but with additional academic and vocational components. Considerable dismay was expressed by the educational and vocational community at the fact that the proposed Diploma in Science has been abandoned or delayed (Garner, 2007e). As the *New Scientist* (2007) commented in an editorial:

> The proportion of teenagers choosing to study physics at ages 16 and 18 is in free fall. The situation in engineering and maths is little better

and in chemistry things are beginning to decline too. (By 2017 these diploma programmes had all been abandoned)

Figures for those completing teacher training courses and entering the teaching profession (Smithers & Robinson, 2008) indicated that only 68.9% of those training as mathematics teachers finally entered the profession, and only 63% of those training to teach modern languages finally chose teaching as a profession. It appears that many teacher trainees drop out during their initial course, while many others choose alternative professions. The reasons for this were not entirely clear, but it might be that after their initial, lengthy 'teaching practice' these individuals became disillusioned at the prospect of a lifetime of work in pressurized or unrewarding careers.

University applications for the one-year postgraduate certificate in education (PGCE) from graduates in mathematics and physics fell once again in 2008 by a record 22 percent, meaning that schools would find even greater difficulty in recruiting teachers qualified to teach these subjects in Autumn, 2009 (Lipsett, 2008). Whether, at a time of reduced job opportunities for graduates in other sectors more would turn (or return) to teaching was not clear.

One outcome of the lack of teachers with degrees in mathematics capable of teaching GCSE examinations at Ordinary and Advanced level has been to "double up" classes in the school assembly hall, teaching 60 or 70 pupils at a time – an acceptable practice according to the Minister for Schools (Lipsett & Curtis, 2008). Given these practices it was not difficult to understand why many able students might "fail" mathematics at GCSE levels, through puzzlement, boredom or alienation.

Another solution to the problem of the lack of well-qualified mathematics teachers is to make the public examinations which students must take easier – the process which cynics term "dumbing down". Marks (2008) showed definitively how this has could happen by analysing public examination papers in mathematics for the period 1951 to 2006. He found that the curriculum had become "broader and shallower", and a definite fail in 1960 (with a mark of 20%) would yield a C-grade pass in 2006.

The crisis of quality in maths and science teaching was reflected in the knowledge in these areas manifested by B.Ed and PGCE students at university, where around half of trainee teachers had to resit their initial college examination in basic numeracy (Khan, 2008). Cassidy (2008) reported research by Christine Gilbert, Chief Inspector of Schools showing that less than half of secondary school teachers who taught GCSE classes up to A-level standard actually had a degree in mathematics. This presented schools with the dilemma of asking minimally qualified teachers to instruct smaller classes, or doubling up classes which could be instructed by a well-qualified teacher. Gilbert suggested that about half of all school classes in maths "are not good enough". Instruction is confined to drills and rote learning for the narrow purpose of passing examinations. The "excitement" of discovering numerical and spatial relationships and their applications in the real world was missing (Gilbert, 2008). In an international study of mathematics ability in final year B.Ed students Burghes (2008) found that the British students scored least on the standardised tests, while students in China scored highest.

A colleague who is head of undergraduate mathematics degrees at a northern university informed us that an advanced level GCSE in Mathematics is no longer the equivalent of the old Advanced Level examination, and students now spend their first term of instruction in bringing them up to the old A-Level standard.

According to a report from OFQUAL (Office for Quality Assurance in Education) secondary school science too is "dumbed down", with multiple choice questions inviting responses based on rote learning rather than on experimentally based reasoning. As a result, many independent schools were opting for the IGCSE, the international general certificate of secondary education with much higher standards than the GCSE examination.

The new Academies were by 2008, being advanced as offering a solution, through their specialisms, to the problems of low achievements in particular subjects. But research by Alan Smithers of Buckingham University, reported by Garner (2009c) indicated that a quarter of the 310 British schools purportedly specialising in science and technology failed to enter a single candidate for the GCSE in physics, chemistry or biology in 2008. The pupils were however, often entered for the 'general science' GCSE, which was, apparently, an easier option than a specialist examination such as physics. These schools entered only 4.8 percent of their pupils for a modern language GCSE in that year. Of the 350 specialist schools focussing on foreign language teaching, only 4.3 per cent entered pupils for the relatively easy general science GCSE.

TWELVE: THE CRISIS IN TEACHING

One reason why teaching school pupils is becoming an increasingly unattractive profession in Britain is the chaotic raft of policies which beset schools at all levels, leading to confusion of roles and increased pressure to achieve in passing narrowly assessed achievement tests, at the expense of an educational programme in which teachers could commit themselves to offering broader programmes of education which could engage both teacher and pupil (Pring, 2006).

There appeared for example, to be confusion in the organisation of the history syllabus in primary and secondary schools, leaving many pupils without a clear sense of the continuity of historical events. In secondary schools 70 percent of students give up the study of history by the age of 14 (Garner, 2007c).

A study of teachers in officially designated "failing schools" (in terms of low academic achievements, and exclusions of "difficult" pupils) found that 80 percent of these teachers had "drifted into their posts", and many were not qualified in the subjects they were designated to teach (Lawlor, 2007). Nine percent of teachers in these schools left each year, a much higher proportion than in 'successful' schools. These so-called failing schools with high teacher turnover served pupils from the poorest economic areas. Lawlor (2007) advocated special payments for well-qualified and dedicated teachers in these schools, which might then attract the best, and not the worst teachers in the profession. This idea, of paying teachers a £10,000 enticement fee (the so–called 'golden handcuffs' bonus) appears to have been adopted by government as part of its Narrowing the Gap programme (Morgan, 2009). How many schools would be included in this programme was unclear, but responses from teachers to The Times Educational Supplement (TES, 2009d) were not encouraging – as one teacher said, no amount of money would encourage him to go back to a school where he was abused and threatened by pupils and parents alike, with his car parked at school being vandalised.

THIRTEEN: FAILING SCHOOLS AND WORKING CLASS YOUTH

A study for the Rowntree Foundation (Cassen & Kingdon, 2007) of pupils who failed to achieve any GCSE passes in the A to C range, the traditional matriculation level (174,000 of all 16-year-olds) found that 80 percent of these young people were white males – their GCSE achievements were about a third less than females from similar social class backgrounds. While Bangladeshi and Afro-Caribbean youth also tended to under-perform in GCSE examinations, this was a function of their social class disadvantage, rather than of problems of motivation, and compared to white youth, Afro-Caribbean boys from economically depressed backgrounds were performing well. Pupils from Indian and Chinese backgrounds outperformed all other groups on the GCSE examinations. Further research (Cabinet Office, 2008) suggested that pupils of Bangladeshi origin, though initially handicapped in their language skills at age 7, were above average performers on numeracy and literacy tests at age 14.

It is white males from the poorest backgrounds, served by the least well-equipped, smaller state secondary schools, who were likely to form the core of the small army of economically depressed youth, many dependent on state support and minor crime for their continued income. Fifteen urban centres had particularly poor achievements in GCSE examinations, and in Manchester 15 percent of all pupils failed completely in public examinations, compared with five percent in the country as a whole. In Manchester, children whose first language was not English had depressed performance in English language tests at age eight; but by age 16 they were outperforming their monolingual peers (Leeming, 2007).

In her Annual Report, the Director of OFSTED, the government Office for Standards in Education (Gilbert, 2007b) found that although the number of "inadequate" or failing secondary schools had fallen from 13 to 10 percent of all schools, these 10 percent were nevertheless institutions which year on year, produced a high number of underachieving pupils, many of whom had failed to reach the required reading and arithmetic standards in their primary schools, and went on to leave secondary school with few or no GCSE passes, failing in turn to enter the world of work, further education or training. These 'failing' schools typically served areas of high social and economic deprivation in urban areas. Many of these 200,000 teenagers leaving school each year with minimum academic or vocational skills belonged to white working class groups, and it was notable that ethnic minorities who attended these schools did *not* usually leave school without examination successes. Rather, they carried into education strong motivation to succeed given by their families, as research on pupils from Muslim backgrounds who were educated in state secondary schools has shown (Al-Refai & Bagley, 2008).

One indicator of the problem of British schools was the reluctance of senior teachers to take on the role of head teacher, despite the sometimes high salaries offered. The National Audit Office reported in 2006 that a fifth of all secondary schools in England and Wales did not have a permanent head teacher. An important reason for this was the very high levels of stress involved in managing an underachieving school containing many rebellious and underachieving pupils, particularly in areas of high poverty (Blair, 2006a).

A comparison of 30 industrialised countries (OECD, 2006) indicated that Britain, despite its national wealth, was near the bottom of this league in retaining students in education or training after age 16. OECD reported that these largely unqualified school-leavers faced considerable penalties in the labour market, which was one factor in the unequal distribution of earnings in Britain. There was a significant weakness, according to OECD, in apprenticeship education in Britain, and a dearth of technically skilled workers. Many skilled posts had to be filled by migrant workers from Europe and elsewhere.

Browne (2006) drew on government data to show that the number of unemployed adolescents aged 16 to 19, had increased from 665,000 in 1997 to 702,000 in 2005. For those aged 16 to 17, one in four were unemployed (43% in London) – these were youth who had few if any examination passes, and had often truanted from, or been excluded from schooling.

On average, educational achievements in Britain were slipping behind other nations to a greater extent, year by year. Smithers (2007) examined data from the Programme for International Student Achievement (PISA) and showed that between 2000 and 2003, the achievements of British 15-year olds on standardized scholastic tests had deteriorated relative to many other countries, and Britain ranked an overall fifteenth amongst the nations participating in PISA. The decline in performance on mathematical skills was particularly marked, Britain's ranking fell from ninth to nineteenth amongst the 33 participating nations, over a three year period. Moreover, these figures for Britain were likely to *underestimate* levels of achievement, because of the high rates of truancy and drop-out amongst British youth (Micklewright & Schnepf, 2006). The PISA data showed that pupils in private, fee-paying schools had very good mean achievements when compared to other nations, and another reason for Britain's poor overall performance in state schools was likely to be that the brightest pupils were 'creamed off' by the private sector.

In addition, since aware, middle class parents were often able to obtain admission for their children into the highest quality state and voluntary-aided faith schools, the poorest quality secondary schools were likely to receive a disproportionate number of the most disadvantaged students (Clark, 2008a).

Students with the poorest health profiles were also often those with the poorest achievement, coming disproportionately from areas of urban blight marked by disorganized behaviours, poorly performing schools and poor life chances in terms of health, adjustment, achievement and behaviour.

FOURTEEN: BRITAIN'S CRUMBLING SCHOOLS AND UNDERFUNDED COLLEGES

Britain's 'crumbling schools' were another cause of teacher alienation in Britain (NASUWT, 2008). Browne (2008) cites government data which showed in January, 2008 that a promised £45 Billion programme to refurbish or rebuild 3,500 British schools by 2020 has been abandoned. Only 14 of the 100 promised new-build schools had any prospect of completion within the next two years. This was despite the fact that many schools, were in structural terms, "not fit for purpose" (DfES, 2004b). In Wales a survey of members by a teachers' union found that the fabric in nearly a half was "poor" or "very poor" (Mourant, 2007).

What this means in practice came from a survey of its 250,000 members by a leading teachers' union (NASUWT, 2008). Some schools had chronically leaking roofs, and unrepaired broken windows: in one fifth of schools water dripped from walls and ceilings when it rained heavily. In a third of schools floors were frequently slippery. One fifth of classrooms were poorly lit. One third had no access to fresh drinking water for pupils; many schools were poorly ventilated, 'baking hot' in summer, and freezing in winter. The comprehensive Cambridge Primary Education Review (Noden & West, 2009b) found that poor quality building structures were common, and resulted in problems of temperature control, ventilation and acoustics. Teachers would leave these schools as soon as they were able, and these buildings were certainly not conducive to productive learning. It is likely, although there is no direct evidence from the Cambridge Review, that the only teachers who would remain employed in conditions such as these would be either the most dedicated, or the least able, unable to find unemployment elsewhere. A national survey indicated that a half of state schools in Britain had "unsatisfactory" toilet facilities (Frankel, 2009). The situation was particularly bad for female pupils, with toilet doors that did not lock, not enough toilets for pupils to use during breaks, and overflowing sanitary bins.

In Stockport in Greater Manchester some schools were actually in danger of being closed because of their poor structural condition, according to a local authority report (Dawson, 2008). Funding for immediate maintenance work costing £800,000 was unavailable from central government; nor was the £31 millions promised, but not now available for more long-term maintenance and building projects. In Greater Manchester at least 86 percent (903 of 1,043 state and voluntary aided schools) still had asbestos in walls and roofs; in Stockport the proportion was 123 out of 135 schools – 91 percent (Keegan, 2009).

Given the widespread nature of the "crumbling schools" phenomenon, the existence of such schools may not play any causal role in pupil disaffection. It may account however, for the desire of so many teachers to leave the profession, or for the best teachers to seek employment in the private education sector. Asbestos residues exist in the majority of British schools, and one local authority hit upon the ingenious solution of prosecuting a head teacher because he had violated Health and Safety Regulations by allowing asbestos to remain in his school. Although the court held that the teacher should not be punished for this crime, it was held that he was legally responsible (Barker, 2008). A teacher who had taught in such a school for 30 years, and was now dying of asbestosis, successfully sued her local authority for the damage caused to her lungs (Marley, 2009).

Apparently, during the "credit crunch" the PFI (Private Funding Initiative) for school refurbishment had sometimes failed because potential contractors were unable to obtain loan capital in the wider market which they could then redeploy (at profit with fees and interest paid by government) for school rebuilding. Schools had been told by the national government "to plan for an austere future" in building, and in the hiring of teachers, since the national education budget could not be increased (Paton, 2009a). The only new funding available for school building was now directed to the new Academies, which were meant to demonstrate the government's progressive new educational policy (Garner, 2008d).

One solution which local authorities were attempting was to meet the challenge of decaying school fabric by closing primary schools that were in a severe state of disrepair, requiring the excluded students to attend schools with better fabric some distance away. This had the negative effect of requiring young children to make long journeys to the new school, which sometimes accommodated the influx by means of increasing the number of children per teacher. This had its own negative consequences, as we shall see in the section on class-teacher ratio below. However, some schools were in such bad repair that parents and teachers had actively petitioned their local authority to relocate pupils in a nearby school (Madden, 2009). But in Glasgow 25 schools in Glasgow were scheduled to close, the majority of these closures being strongly opposed by parents (Buie, 2009).

Further education and sixth form colleges had experienced their own building programme crises, in the withdrawal of promised funding for college expansion. Sir Andrew Foster chaired a government review of funding increases for FE colleges and as a result the colleges in England and Wales were offered funding of more than a billion pounds. Plans were drawn, architects commissioned, and building work begun. But then in January 2009 (in a new era of economic malaise) funding was suddenly withdrawn, since potential partners withdrew from PFI arrangements, and the government was unwilling to make up this funding with direct grants.

A case study of a single FE college (TES, 2009a) showed that the Learning and Skills Foundation (LSF) had provided £86 millions of initial funding for this college, which set in train a variety of planning and building preparation projects, leaving £15.1 millions to be raised by the college through commercial arrangements underwritten by a PFI to complete the final building phase. But the PFIs were now without funds, meaning that the college had to recruit 850 fewer students than planned for 2011–2012, as well as 2,600 fewer adult learners, the majority on government "high priority learner" programmes for the young unemployed. The consequences for the local economy were the loss of 167 FTE teaching posts within the community, and the loss of 630 jobs in the wider community including those which would have been taken by trained and educated students, as well as the loss of 400 temporary construction jobs (TES, 2009b, 2009c). Many colleges were apparently facing bankruptcy, since they had borrowed or drawn on reserves heavily in order to meet start-up costs for programmes now which seem to have little possibility of realisation.

FIFTEEN: SOME CONSEQUENCES OF UNDER-EDUCATION AND SOCIAL EXCLUSION

Hales et al. (2006) in a sociological study of unemployed teenagers found that in some urban areas many were drawn into gang culture, in which drug marketing and even firearm use played a significant role, as well as street crime and other robberies to provide a means of livelihood more attractive than the government's "New Deal" programme. Cultures of illegal drug marketing were found to be well-established in London, Manchester and Liverpool. Many of these youths were likely to graduate into the prison system, and a government report (Cabinet Office, 2006) anticipated that the prison population in all age groups in Britain would increase by 15 percent in five years, this increase being largely the result of increasing numbers of unemployed young men for whom crime has become the best form of livelihood, despite the occasional incarcerations involved.

Britain already had the highest rate of imprisonment (142 of all ages per 1000) of all EU countries (the EU average was 90 per 1000 – BBC, 2005). Between 2005 and 2007 the number of young people (aged less than 18) in prison in Britain increased by 26 percent, with the rate of imprisonment for the young (less than 18) being 23 per 100,000 compared with 6 per 100,000 in France, 2 per 100,000 in Spain and 0.2 per 100,000 in Finland (Cambell & Travis, 2007). The problems of these incarcerated adolescents and young men and women, frequently begin in economically poor homes, homes stressed by social and interpersonal breakdown, and in their poor schools serving economically poor neighbourhoods (Neustatter, 2004).

A report by the government's Social Exclusion Unit (SEU, 2006) examined existing studies as well as official data to show that:

Firstly: Imprisoning adolescents and young adults does not deter them from reoffending – within two years 75 percent who had served short sentences for burglary and theft will have reoffended.

Secondly: Prison could often make things worse – youngsters diverted into community service and further education programmes rather than prison, had lower reoffending rates than youngsters who were locked up.

Thirdly: Programmes which did work addressed homelessness, unemployment, drug and alcohol use, poor literacy and lack of skills, and mental health problems.

As Meen et al. (2006) show, members of this soon-to-be-imprisoned underclass tended to live in the most deprived areas of the city, and community regeneration programmes in these areas were both very expensive, and prone to fail. Economic forecasting estimated that by 2020 the 3.4 million unskilled jobs in Britain would have shrunk to 600,000, while the economy required an increase in the number of skilled personnel from 14 million to 20 million (McLeod, 2007). The outlook for unskilled school leavers who had few if any examination successes at age 16 was likely to become bleaker year by year, and unless they were offered new and successful programmes of vocational education, it was likely that Britain's only way of meeting skill shortages was through further recruitment from overseas.

A report from the Centre for Social Justice (CSJ, 2006) used data from the Office of National Statistics to focus on these issues. The report showed that there were 1.24 millions in the age group 15 to 24 who had few educational qualifications, and who had received no occupational or vocational training, the numbers in this "unschooled and unemployed" group of 15 to 17-year-olds having risen by one-third since 1997. Many of these young people, according to this report, formed 'a white underclass' with lifestyles marred by chronic unemployment, delinquency, drug use, begetting fatherless children, and eventual imprisonment. This underclass, according to the report, tended to be self-perpetuating with children from these marginal and disorganised families forming the underclass of the next generation.

Despite protests by the New Labour Government, it could hardly be denied that educational policy and practice were failing in Britain, and this formed the platform of a policy proposal of the Conservative Opposition, the encouragement of Swedish-style 'quality' schools, new academies which would be sponsored in the poorest areas, in view of the fact that some 45 percent of persistent truants come from poverty backgrounds, although they made up only about 14 percent of all pupils (Curtis, 2008).

These pupils were chronic underachievers, bored, alienated, and dropped out of school early, lacking the confidence to take public examinations or attend technical colleges post-16. There were (and remain) major structural problems here, which would need political and economic assaults on many fronts if the lot of this permanent underclass were to be changed. No one political party is to blame for these educational failures, which stem from policies going back many years, which had ensured that Britain remained a class-dominated culture.

SIXTEEN: CHILDREN IN CARE – A SPECIAL GROUP WITH SPECIAL NEEDS

There is strong evidence that public policies had significantly failed to address the educational and mental health needs of children removed from disrupted, abusive or neglecting families into alternative care. A Children's Act of 2000 placed stronger obligations on local authorities to support children leaving care at the then statutory age of 16, but this had according to the research reviewed by Sergeant (2006) made little difference. According to Sergeant, each year up to 2005 some 6,000 young people left (or ran from) the formal care system: 87 percent had experienced physical, sexual or emotional abuse or neglect within their family of origin. Of children in care, 45 percent had a definable and treatable mental health disorder (BMA, 2007).

The residential children's homes into which such children were removed were too often 'centres of chaos' staffed by untrained workers who often remained in such employment for a relatively brief time. Foster homes were a better alternative, but these were in short supply and if foster parents and child do not get along, the child would be returned to the residential system. Only five percent of foster parents had full professional training which would enable them to cope with the needs of traumatised children; only 20 percent of staff in children's homes had relevant professional qualifications (Bennett, 2006; Sergeant, 2006). It was not unusual for a child in care to have at least five different placements from infancy to mid-teens. When they left formal care at age 16, a quarter of girls were pregnant, and a half would be unsupported single mothers by age 18 (Sergeant, 2006). One quarter of men under 25 who were in prison had been in care; one third of young, homeless people were graduates of the care system. They had left care for a world in which social and family supports were few, and these care leavers were vulnerable to multiple new stresses.

The educational achievements of care leavers at age 16 were low: only 12 percent obtained five 'good' GCSE passes (at grades A to C, including English and Mathematics), compared with 56 percent of children growing up in more stable homes (Gilbert, 2007b). More than a third of the care group were not entered for *any* public examinations, and were probably semi-literate, having experienced frequent changes of schooling, as well as enforced school exclusions (DfES, 2006). Only 60 (1%) of the some 6000 care leavers in any one year would go on to college or university, compared with at least a quarter of the mainstream population (Sergeant, 2006). Children in care and those leaving care needed extra educational help, support and counselling at all ages; but they received much less than the average child. Leaving care at age 16 without a supportive family network was often linked to recruitment into urban gangs, being pimped, and drug-using subcultures, who offered a kind of alternative family (DfES, 2006; Harker, 2007).

The government response to Sergeant's *Centre for Policy Studies Report* (2006) was to some extent promising (DfES, 2006). While the grosser deficiencies of the care system would remain, professional foster families providing care children up to the age of 21 were promised, as well as grants for books and equipment when attending college, free transport for college attendance, and a £2000 bursary towards university costs (Bennett, 2006). The number of professional foster homes for children in care up to age 21 was still very small however, relative to the large numbers in care and could serve less than a quarter of the more than 6000 16-year-olds who "graduated" from care each year (Bennett, 2008). The professional foster parent was likely to lose a payment of more than £20,000 a year as a professional foster parent, receiving instead a much smaller lodging allowance on behalf of the foster child if the 16-year-old remained living with their foster family. Many foster parents would, it seems under these circumstances turn to new foster children, and the former foster child would have to make their own way in the world of work and independent lodging, largely unsupported by any professional social care facilities. Their drift into maladjustment or crime is one result of this.

Many children in the care system exhibit profound mental health problems, reflecting not only the original abuse and/or neglect which led to them being removed to care, but also in many cases their drift through the care system – becoming bonded to a set of carers, only to have that bond broken when the foster carers were unable or unwilling to continue with the care arrangements (Bagley 1992, 2002). A survey by Meltzer et al. (2003) of the mental health needs of 2,500 English children in various foster and child care settings found that 45 percent had a diagnosable psychiatric condition: the overlapping diagnoses were conduct disorder (37%), emotional disorder (12%); and hyperactivity or ADHD (7%). Of those with a psychiatric disorder 87 percent were struggling with school subjects, and 30 percent had been "statemented" – that is, they were flagged for special inputs by their schools. The prevalence of 45 percent of foster children with a diagnosable mental health condition should be compared with the prevalence of about 9 percent in the general population of children and adolescents, established by the same research team (Goodman et al., 2002).

The Mubarek Report (Riddell, 2006) on a vulnerable young offenders cites data showing that seven out of ten of the 19,000 young people aged 18 to 20 who left prison in one year, were back in prison within two years. It seems that the young offender system, like the child care system, offered little in the way of education, therapy and reform. Former children in care receive no special education and support when they entered prison.

The government announced a further programme for children in care called *Care Matters*, in November, 2008. However, according to a report from the Parliamentary Select Committee on Children, Schools and Families in April, 2009 (Sheerman, 2009) the problems of children in care might be worse than previously thought, in that local authority children's homes (containing 29% of all children in care) were often themselves neglectful and even sexually abusive of the children they housed. Staff turnover was high, salaries for care workers were low, and workers were poorly qualified or trained. More than 1,000 children of the approximately 59,500 currently in care had had at least 10 different foster placements, and ten children were identified who had experienced at least 50 foster home and residential centre placings. It is rare for a child to have a single foster care placing once he or she has been taken into care. Foster parents were often not qualified for their difficult task, and were able to reject any child whom they perceive as "difficult". The foster care system for this vulnerable group, concluded the Select Committee, was making things worse rather than better. "We have to go further and faster and be more radical" the Committee concluded.

Since a well-publicised case in 2008 of a child ('Baby P') murdered after social workers declined to move him from abusive parents into care, the number of children moved into local authority care had increased by 38 percent in one year (CAFCASS, 2009). By March, 2009 more than 700 children a month (a record number) were being removed into the care system. There was some evidence that some of these were panicked reactions by social workers, anxious to avoid charges of professional neglect. The weakness of the foster care model has been illustrated by the fact that in Wales (and presumably elsewhere in Britain) more than two-thirds of foster carers were aged 50-plus, while only eight per cent were in their thirties (Lewis, 2009). There is an acknowledged shortage of several hundred foster carers across Britain. While permanent adoption of some children moved into temporary care can have excellent outcomes (Bagley, Young & Scully, 1993), the movement of children in and out of care situations, according to the caprice of both biological parents and of social workers, can be very harmful to a child's development. The task of caring for 'looked after' children in care is challenging and calls for the highest levels of professional competence (Golding et al., 2006). These professional inputs were in the period under review, atypical.

There has been some British interest in the "social pedagogy" model of child care practised in much of Europe. In Germany for example, around 80 percent of 'looked after' children lived in highly professional group homes in which the child's needs are assessed and catered for through continuing professional effort (with a high staff-child ratio). In this model the child is treated holistically as an individual with multiple psychological, learning and relationship needs; the group home is also supported by a holistic model in which children's relationships with each other and with staff receive skilled support (Cameron & Moss, 2011).

The final, crucial question remained unanswered: why were a quarter of young men in prison, graduates of the British care system? Why did so many drift into chaotic lifestyles through which the next generation of children in care is generated? Why has the care experience so frequently not helped them to overcome the effects of earlier separations, neglect and abuse, and their consequent mental health problems? These were crucially important research and policy questions, which we posed in 2008: by 2017 no adequate government response had been forthcoming.

SEVENTEEN: CHILDREN WITH SPECIAL EDUCATIONAL NEEDS: AN EDUCATIONAL SYSTEM IN DISARRAY

The 1972 Education Act gave all children in Britain a right to education, regardless of the severity of any disability (Warnock, 2008). The concept of the ineducable child was abolished, and new principles of universal education were debated. A *Committee of Inquiry into the Education of Handicapped Children* was formed in 1974, guided by Dame Mary Warnock, its chair and chief author. The committee's report was finally published in 1979. One of the crucial recommendations was that a 'statement' should be made of the need that any child had for special educational measures. Such 'statements' were to be based on a comprehensive assessment of the child's needs and potentialities:

> The statement of special educational need was seen in contrast to the medical model, according to which some children are 'normal', others are 'handicapped'. Our idea was that there are common educational goals – independence, enjoyment, and understanding – towards which all children, irrespective of their abilities or disabilities, should aim. We suggested that for some children the path towards these goals was smooth and easy, whereas for others it was beset by obstacles. They encountered special difficulties on the path towards the common goals. Every human being has certain needs and difficulties, so this approach was inclusive rather than exclusive. (Warnock, 2008)

'Statements' were intended to confer a right to special provision on the children according to the child's needs, and imposed a corresponding duty on their local authorities to provide for those needs. While it was clear that severely disabled children needed special help, this was less clear for some of the children with milder disabilities. Warnock (1979) had estimated that about two percent of children would need to be supported by 'statemented' assessments, a dossier which would follow the child, enabling education authorities to offer the best form of individualized educational programme., and to assess and add to further statements of special educational need. Warnock's proposals were accepted by the government in passing the Education Act of 1981. However, the original aims of the 1981 Act had not been fulfilled, and by 2006 a significantly higher proportion of children were classified as having a 'special educational need' than the original estimate of two percent (Warnock, 2008; ONS, 2009).

For many children the process of statementing was a quasi-disciplinary procedure, an early warning of the possibility of temporary or permanent exclusion from school of a child whom teachers had difficulty with, or whose poor examination results might detract from the school's publicly declared examination successes. Children with dyslexia, and with autism had become particularly vulnerable to the dual process of being first statemented, and then excluded.

Dyson (2001) points to the paradox of statementing policy – there was a fundamental contradiction in the British educational system between "an intention to treat all learners as essentially the same and an equal but opposite intention to treat them as different." One way to overcome these tensions, Warnock (2008) argued, was the setting up of 'specialist schools' under the same roof as regular schools. The problem with this policy might be that such special schools would have lower status, and parents would resist the transfer of their child to a such an 'inner school'.

An alternative considered by Warnock (2008) were specialist schools on separate campuses in which children with more severe learning problems could focus on subjects such as IT and Performing Arts. Warnock suggested that such well-endowed schools should be open to the community at evenings and weekends:

> Indeed small specialist schools of the kind described would be inclusive in an important sense of the word for children who currently suffer from feelings of exclusion within mainstream schools ... I believe that small specialist schools could engender this feeling [of belonging] ... for many children who now lack it. (Warnock, 2008)

Lady Warnock's plea for specialized school units – separate from mainstream schools, or contained within regular schools – were controversial. A group of policy advocates within the Centre for Studies on Inclusive Education had cogently argued the case for the complete integration of children with special needs (Booth & Ainscow, 2002; Rustemier, 2008a, 2008b; Thomas & Vaughan, 2004). Following systematic reviews of the evidence on inclusion of children with special educational needs, these researchers argued that segregated children had poorer academic outcomes, impaired self-confidence and fewer social skills, fewer occupational choices, and negative labelling as a result of segregation.

In an ideal educational system, classes would be small (less than 15), teachers would be highly trained in instruction and management techniques, and would be assisted by classroom assistants within the integrated classroom. Each child would be carefully assessed, and would have individualized learning goals with access to an individual computer, programmed to assist the achievement of these goals. British schools are however grossly under-funded, and at the present time only a small number of private schools can offer this ideal model which can optimise the education for the child with special need.

A report to House of Commons Education and Skills Select Committee (Halpin, 2006) described an educational system for the 1.23 million children with special educational needs (including sensory and cognitive challenges; autistic spectrum diagnoses; and emotional and behavioural problems often reflecting abusive and disorganised families) as "not fit for purpose". Neither efforts at mainstreaming, nor efforts to provide separate, specialist schools in the public sector were in overall terms, successful. While the number of specialist schools for SEN (Special Educational Needs) children had fallen dramatically following an Act of 2001 which aimed to establish a fully inclusive educational system, in practice chronic under-funding has meant that the inclusive educational system in Britain had effectively failed (Bagley, 2008b).

The only way a parent with a child with autism or severe dyslexia can obtain adequate educational provision from the state system is through litigation; many who can afford to, sue their local authority or instead opt for private education (Bagley, 2008b). A few local authorities do provide a good service; but most do not (Halpin, 2006; Clarke, 2008b). A single statistic on pupil exclusion illustrates the profound injustice of Britain's SEN system: 87 per cent of children excluded from primary school had special educational needs prior to that exclusion; the comparable figure for secondary schools was 60 per cent, according to the Commons Select Committee. Less than one per cent of pupils who do not have prior special educational needs are ever excluded from school.

A survey by the National Union of Teachers (Garner, 2007a) of its members found that only nine percent were fully trained and confident in accepting children with learning difficulties in their main-streamed classroom; and 74 percent said that they had no classroom aides who could help them in addressing the needs of SEN pupils. The NUT indicated that government had failed to provide funds for both adequate teacher training, and classroom provision which could enable SEN pupils to be successfully main-streamed.

The profound irony of this British failure to offer an adequate inclusive education for all children, without discriminating against their needs and aspirations is that Britain is a signatory to the UN Disability Convention on the Rights of Disabled Persons, adopted in December, 2006. Article 24 of this agreement confirms the right of *all* children to the following:

1. No exclusion from the general educational system for any pupil;
2. Access to inclusive education within the pupil's local community;
3. Reasonable accommodation of individual needs;
4. Support should be given within general educational systems to facilitate effective education, including individualized support measures.

Britain, one of the world's richest economies, had singularly failed to meet these UN guidelines. Britain's signature on the UN agreement is nothing more than tokenism. Only when no child is excluded from mainstream schooling because of their special educational needs could Britain be said to begin to fulfil its obligations to children beset with cognitive, behavioural, emotional and sensory challenges.

Aynsley-Green (2006) the Children's Commissioner for England observed for example, that the educational system served the country's 90,000 children with 'autistic spectrum' disorders particularly poorly: 60 percent of children in this category were not in the type of educational setting which adequately served their needs. He observed: "It is ... appalling and shameful for our country, one of the richest economies in the world, to have so many children that are not being looked after and given the resources they needed." The Commons Select Committee on Education found (2006) that although many special schools had been closed by local authorities, the policies for inclusion of autistic children, and others with cognitive challenges in mainstream schools were very variable between local authorities, in quality and scope.

The failure of policies for the integration of children with special needs in mainstream education is reflected in a dismal indicator: the prevalence of bullying (verbal and physical persecution and discrimination) experienced by 'special needs' children at the hands of their so-called normal peers (Bagley, 2008b). According to Office for Standards in Education's surveys of 150,000 pupils, 48 percent had been verbally or physically bullied in the previous year (Paton, 2009b).

A House of Commons Select Committee enquiry found that 38 percent of children with autism-spectrum conditions had been severely bullied within the previous six months (Meikle, 2007). One way in which schools reportedly dealt with 'the problem' of such bulled children was to exclude them from school 'on health and safety grounds', leaving the culture of bullying intact. Verbal harassment of main-streamed children with learning difficulties seems to be universal, and according to a MENCAP survey, sixty percent of such children were also physically hurt by bullies (Garner, 2007d).

The dismal conclusion was that currently, British schools do not have the resources to protect or properly integrate main-streamed children with learning problems, and autistic spectrum disorders (Bagley, 2008b). In the school year 2006–2007, 55 percent of children excluded from school had been previously statemented as having special needs, an increase of 45 percent over four years (Garner, 2007g).

EIGHTEEN: PROBLEMS OF DYSLEXIA AND NUMBER DIFFICULTY

While there is likely to be an overlap between formally diagnosed dyslexia and failure to achieve reading standards, the officially diagnosed population with dyslexia numbered only about 76,000, far too small to explain the 10 percent or more of 11-year-olds who appeared to be reading "failures", in relative or absolute terms. One explanation came from a study funded by the British Dyslexia Association which commissioned research by a Hull University Team (Singleton, 2008). This research tested 1,341 seven and eleven-year-olds who had recently undergone the National Curriculum reading tests. Generalising from these findings to the national population, the research suggests that the numbers with some kind of "problem" in their neurologically-based perceptual and information processing strategies which make the acquisition of reading skills difficult when exposed to conventional methods of teaching, was nearer two million than 76,000.

This is an extremely important finding, since if replicated it would suggest that rather than suffering some kind of neurological pathology, the large majority of these two million children have ways of perceiving and processing symbolic data which although entirely normal as a basis for learning, are nevertheless ignored by conventional modes of teaching. Strategies in reading require at least seven different kinds of assessment and teaching strategy (Abisgold, 2008), but in large classes, under-prepared or under-trained teachers are simply unable to cope with the learning needs of important subgroups who required a more individualised type of instruction. This suggestion should be borne in mind which we consider the section on problems of large class sizes in the sections below.

The work by Gross (2006) is relevant and important here. She has shown that more than five percent of children may never acquire the ability to read unless they are offered careful diagnostic assessment, and individualized tutoring. The cost of this individualized programme is about £2,500 per child, but is likely to be highly cost effective when set against the costs of servicing children and adults who have never acquired the skills of basic literacy.

It is acknowledged that English is a particularly difficult language in which to learn to read and spell, because of its irregular phonic system, compared to more regular systems in a number of European languages (Bell, 2002, 2004). Bell (2008) argues that English schoolchildren have to learn 800 "unspellable" words by the age of 11, an argument for the form of spelling as advocated, for example, by George Bernard Shaw, who made the case for an alphabet consisting of 48 letters, which are easy to memorize, and would cope with the now expanded English word spellings.

Neurological evidence is becoming available which shows that some pupils perceive and process numbers in ways which may make their acquisition of numeracy, in a minority of cases at least, rather difficult (Ansari et al., 2006; Jacob & Nieder, 2009; Ischebeck et al., 2009). This also has implications for teacher training, individual testing of pupils, and individualized instruction strategies.

NINETEEN: ACHIEVEMENT AND SCHOOL FAILURE IN BRITAIN: SOME INTERNATIONAL COMPARISONS

The first international research of note is that by Blanden and colleagues (Blanden & Gregg, 2004; Blanden & Machin, 2004a, 2004b; Blanden, Gregg & Machin, 2005) which compared the degree to which children from economically poor families were successful in upward social class mobility (from childhood to adulthood) in eight countries: Britain, United States, Canada, Germany, Norway, Denmark, Sweden and Finland. Countries with a high amount of upward mobility of children born into the poorer social classes, into higher education and into economically successful roles, were judged to be more open and egalitarian cultures. In contrast, the degree to which social class of birth determined adult economic success was seen to be the mark of an inegalitarian culture (ONS, 2009). In order to measure this, data from British longitudinal surveys were acquired, and available data-sets from the eight countries were accessed for purposes of comparison. Children in each data-set were followed up into mid-life.

Finland, Denmark, Sweden, Norway and The Netherlands were found to be the most 'open' societies, with high degrees of upward mobility in children who were born into economically poor families. Canada was also largely successful in fostering upward mobility. Germany held a middle position, but children from Britain and the United States fared badly. Being born poor in these latter two countries was a major determinant of growing up poor, and remaining poor in adult life, with impaired educational and economic achievement. In America it was African-Americans who were most likely to be caught in this poverty trap (Hertzig, 2004). But in Britain it was the wealth of parents (or lack of wealth) which was the major determinant of adult achievement and income, regardless of ethnicity. Interesting findings from the British data indicated that the situation had been getting *worse* over time in that the correlation between parental income and child's income when adult, increased significantly in each succeeding year in those born between 1958 and 1970.

The reasons for this can only be speculated upon. Wealthier parents may have became much more likely to pay for their children's education in a parallel private system, or to support them to stay in 'better' schools and sixth-form colleges until the age of 18. The final consequence had been the emergence of a number of 'sink schools' serving areas of urban blight, sometimes offering poor quality instructional environments. To be sure, some state schools offer excellent instruction at the secondary level, but frequently middle class parents strategically located their residence so as to be in the catchment areas of these well-performing state schools. A survey by the Sutton Trust using data generated by the National Foundation for Educational Research on GCSE success and social class profiles of pupils' parents, confirmed earlier research (Sieghart, 1999), that "the middle classes fill our best state schools" (Taylor, 2005).

Longitudinal Scottish research of 8,500 individuals confirmed the link between parent's and child's social class, which indicated lack of upward mobility in children from the poorest families (Paterson & Iannelli, 2006). This finding was further corroborated by English data on GCSE (General Certificate of Secondary Education) passes classified by pupils in receipt of free school meals, a traditional poverty indicator. These data (Garner, 2008a) showed that poverty of a parent (inability to pay for school meals) was strongly linked to poverty of achievement in their child, as measured by failure to achieve any GCSE passes at age 16. This index of poverty was associated too, with truanting from school.

In Britain, middle class parents were able to be geographically mobile in choosing the best state schools; could purchase private education; and could manipulate social networks (i.e. draw on social capital) which ensured that their child had the most advantageous employment opportunities after school-leaving and graduation. Research on publicly-funded 'faith schools' (Anglican and Catholic) which controlled their own admissions (a third of all publicly-funded schools in Britain) had shown that they were ten times more likely than non-faith schools to exercise bias in favour of the entry of middle class pupils (IPPR, 2007).

One reason for this is that despite being in theory fully state-funded, a number of these "voluntary aided" schools charge parents fees for such luxuries as textbooks, computers, and classroom furniture (Ross, 2008). These are fees that economically poor parents can ill afford. The reason that these faith schools within the state system can ask parents to pay fees is that they serve a largely middle class parent group, who can afford to pay for the best kind of education, at the expense of the poor. Parents are often desperate to find a school with high quality standards at the transfer to secondary schooling when their child is 11 (Asthana, 2008). Being allocated to a "poor quality" secondary school in a nearby neighbourhood may set in train not only legal appeals (costing up to £2,000) but also lobbying of heads of 'good' schools, which are often religious ones (Allen & West, 2008).

Religious schools for their part may enquire about parental social class and family composition as a semi-legal way of screening out pupils who might be low achievers. This would account for the fact that religious secondary schools (with Anglican and Roman Catholic foundation) admitted 10 percent fewer pupils eligible for free school meals (a commonly used criterion of poverty background) than did non-faith state schools. Another form of bias occurs when religious schools with a good sixth form tradition, charged up to £50 to transfer in of a pupil at age 16 (Hunter, 2008).

Children attending non-faith schools serving poor quality housing estates are, by implication, receiving a third class education. In 2005 according to government inspection reports at least one million primary school children were taught in "poorly performing schools" (Taylor, 2006). By 2007 the number of failing schools "in special measures" had increased by a fifth, so that according to the Office for Standards in Education one in eight secondary schools, and one in four primary schools was judged to be offering an inadequate level of education (Blair, 2007). Very few of these schools fell into the category of "voluntary aided" faith schools, the large majority of these "failing schools" being ones that served economically poor neighbourhoods, with a high proportion of pupils failing to achieve success in public examinations.

In a survey of educational achievements of school students conducted by The Organisation for Economic Co-operation and Development (OECD, 2004) Britain ranked fifteenth in achievements in reading, science and mathematics amongst the 41 countries who submitted data, despite Britain being, at that time, third or fourth in world rankings for wealth per head of population. This statistic was another indicator of the 'poverty of education' in Britain, a pattern of under-funding of an important resource in a wealthy country.

In fact, there were grounds for supposing that these figures overestimate the achievements of British pupils (Smithers, 2004). This was because some schools deliberately excluded, suspended or expelled students who were underachieving, apparently in many cases to improve their school's achievement profile. If the achievements of this small army of excluded (and also truanting) pupils were included, Britain's ranking would, apparently, be closer to twenty fifth than fifteenth out of the 44 countries surveyed.

OECD's periodic survey of the United Kingdom's economic performance (Hoeller et al., 2007) focussed specifically on educational expenditures and performance. Within a comparison of the 12 wealthiest OECD countries the UK ranked last in terms of upward social mobility that was fostered by educational achievements. The best performing countries were Denmark, Austria, Finland and Canada. This economic survey commented that, reflecting these marked and chronic income inequalities: "Students in Britain ... continue to perform particularly poorly relative to students in the best performing educational systems. Overall the socio-economic gaps in Britain remain large. One explanation may be that local authorities and schools are not distributing deprivation funds as intended, resulting in outcomes which can be seen as inequitable. Stronger measures may be required to correct this imbalance ..."

The measures advocated in the OECD Report of Hoeller et al. (2007) included recruiting the best teachers for poorly performing schools through salary incentives, giving more focussed funding for equipment, fabric and class size reductions, providing subsidized routes into training and employment for poorly performing students, and enhancing local community development through better local transport links, and tax subsidies to encourage more local employment.

TWENTY: SOME REASONS FOR BRITISH UNDERACHIEVEMENT

Some reasons for British underachievement have been adduced by a leading British education expert (Wragg, 2004). Schools in Britain in the period under review were subject to a heavy-handed bureaucratic control through a prescribed National Curriculum, with formal examinations for pupils at ages 7, 11 and 14. Schools were frequently inspected and their performance in the periodic tests were publicly ranked. Far from ensuring higher levels of achievement and learning, the opposite seemed to have resulted, with high levels of teacher malaise in under-funded schools with large classes of dispirited pupils. Subjects such as music, sport, history and physical education were increasingly left out of the curriculum to make way for yet more classes of formal instruction in government-required instruction in 'basic skills'.

In 2007 The General Teaching Council for England and Wales, an independent advocacy body, submitted to the House of Commons Select

Committee enquiry on pupil assessment, the opinion that *all* formal examinations prior to age 16 should be ended. The arguments in favour of this policy were that frequent, externally monitored examinations (at ages 7, 11 and 14) distorted patterns of teaching and the search for a broad, inclusive curriculum – such examinations often alienated pupils, especially the least able who often left school (or absented themselves) by age 16. The GTC pointed to the positive experience of education in Wales, where several local educational authorities had abandoned such frequent testing (Woodward, 2007).

Ironically, SATs (Standard Assessment Tests at ages 7, 11 and 14) had been used by the National Audit Office to identify 402 primary and secondary schools in England (some three percent of all schools, containing about 200,000 pupils) which were not just failing, but were chronically producing catastrophically poor outcomes in their pupils, with more than half failing in basic tests of numeracy, literacy and general subjects before age 16. All of these "exceptionally failing" schools were in inner city or decaying urban areas.

Harley and Tymms (2008) reviewed evidence which showed that the understanding of, and enthusiasm for, the study of science has declined significantly since 1995, a reflection, they argued, of the rote learning imposed by SATs which was undermining children's "natural curiosity" about the natural world. This in turn led to markedly fewer pupils taking science in the public examinations which are precursors to university entry.

Partly because of the publicity surrounding published league tables and the 'shaming' of underachieving schools in the standardized examinations at ages 7, 11 and 14, there was strong pressure to exclude learning-disabled, disruptive, and emotionally maladjusted pupils. It was perhaps no coincidence that in the summer term in which government SATS (Standard Assessment Tests) were held, the number of excluded pupils reached a peak – more than 9,000 pupils were permanently excluded from school in 2003, the majority of them in the summer term, prior to sitting these formal exams (Blair, 2004).

The main reasons given for these expulsions were pupil misbehaviour, but this was intimately linked to failure to take advantage of the instruction offered, and previous failure on formal tests of achievement. By 2005 the number of permanently excluded pupils in the previous year had risen to 9,880, with 334,000 pupils receiving 'fixed term' exclusions or suspensions (Literacy Trust, 2006). Permanent exclusions prior to public examinations were particularly likely to occur in the new 'city academies', set up to replace 'failing' inner-city schools, apparently in order to artificially enhance the public examination record of the new academies (Garner, 2007b).

The top country in the international league tables on comparable tests of reading, science and mathematics was Finland (sharing honours with several Scandinavian countries). This prompted Curtis (2004) to examine Finnish school policies which might explain this. She cites Prof. Erno Lehtinen, education policy advisor to the Finnish parliament. According to Lehtinen the idea that schools should be run from the centre, or even have their test results published was unthinkable in Finland. The only public examinations were those taken by students at age 18. Secondary schools were entirely comprehensive, taking all ability bands, and they attempted to teach to the student's highest potential. Private schools were unknown in this small country. Teachers themselves had high status and salaries (on a par with lawyers and doctors), and all were qualified at the master's level or beyond. Schools themselves had priority in government funding, and class sizes were much smaller than in Britain.

Finland also had an excellent record in its educational policies for the reception and absorption of children of immigrants and refugees in comparison with several other European countries, including Britain (Matinheikki-Kokko & Pitkanen, 2002). Britain's comparative failure in the integration of children of migrants is demonstrated by the exclusion statistics (DfES, 2004a). These showed that that highest rates of exclusion were of Gypsy and Roma children, followed by students with cultural origins in the Caribbean, this latter group being more than three times as likely as other ethnic groups to be excluded from school (Wanless, 2006).

The influence of parental income upon child test scores is demonstrated in the work of Blanden and Machin (2004b). Using data from large scale British longitudinal surveys, they examined the progress of the 'brightest' children in the economically poorest cohort of children at age 3, in comparison with test performance levels in children of the richest quintile of parents. By age five, the bright, working class children had dropped from a score equivalent to the 88th percentile at age three to 65th percentile (compared to norms for the whole group) at age five. By age seven the 'dullest' section of children of the wealthy had overtaken the cognitive performance levels of the very bright children of the poor at age three. The message from this and other data reviewed by Blanden and Machin (2004b) is that parental social class is a major determinant of scholastic success, a process that begins early in a child's life and becomes more pronounced as advantage piles upon advantage, and vice versa for the poorest social classes. These trends were *not* observed in similar types of data from Canada and the Nordic countries, including Finland.

In conclusion, the poor scholastic performance of British children in state schools had multiple causes – a variety of social background factors, large classes, teacher malaise, underfunded schools, and a rigid curriculum with frequent testing. Chronically failing schools were likely to serve economically poor areas, and successful teachers with marketable skills were unlikely to stay very long in such schools. Suspensions and temporary and permanent exclusions was one way of coping with chronic disorder in marginal schools. However, given the resources allocated to education the underperformance and poor motivation of British children in comparison with those in other countries is somewhat puzzling. A case study of Finland, which consistently came top of the international league tables in terms of achievement provided interesting explanations. British underachievement seemed deeply rooted within its class system, and longitudinal research showed that initially "bright" children from the poorest economic groups rapidly lost their scholastic advantages, while "dull", middle-class children very soon become scholastically advantaged.

TWENTY ONE: UNDERACHIEVING SCHOOL LEAVERS?

Of particular concern with regard to mainstream British students were reports from the Confederation of British Industry (CBI, 2004, 2008) of newly-recruited school leavers. Cumulatively since 1997, two million school leavers had by 2007 "insufficient skills in literacy and mathematics" which would enable them to advance occupationally – they were judged to be fit only for the lowest level of occupation, since they had failed to achieve adequate basic skills in their schooling. Overall, 47 per cent of British firms were dissatisfied with the educational quality of the school-leavers they recruited. These figures did not include the small army of permanently excluded (or self-excluding) pupils, who rarely entered the job market in any capacity. These figures are consonant with a 1999 report from the Basic Skills Agency (Moser, 1999) which found that one fifth of British adults had "severe problems" with basic literacy and numeracy, with skills in these areas lower than in any other European country except Poland and Ireland. Government data (Smithers, 2006) indicated that some 12 million British workers could not read beyond the level expected of 11-year-olds in the national literacy tests. In contrast, in other developed European countries (including Germany) the problem of functionally illiterate school-leavers was virtually absent (Machin, 2005).

Further data suggest that about four million aged 16 to 19 had only the reading skills expected of an 11-year-old (Bignell, 2006). About a million adolescents left school each year with these limited reading skills, and most were likely to have attended 'sub-standard' secondary schools in economically poor neighbourhoods (Taylor, 2006). The cost in terms of 'failed productivity' of an adolescent with few or mediocre public examination passes at age 16 was, within 20 years, £49,000 per individual in 2006 costs, or more than £2 billion in total (TOL, 2006). As the Confederation for British Industry argued, early interventions to prevent this 'drift into illiteracy' might be highly cost-effective.

This thesis is further underlined by work by Jean Gross (2006) for The National Literacy Trust. This showed that more than five percent of children failed to acquire any reading skills in the primary school, and this fed into a downward spiral of lack of confidence, school drop-out, delinquency and welfare dependency. These costs over three decades would on average, exceed £50,000 per individual. Gross proposed a programme of early identification of children unable to read, with focussed diagnostic work and individualized instruction. This would likely cost about £2,500 per child, but was likely to be very cost effective in the long run.

Further economic research suggests that at current prices each 'delinquent career' in youth barely able to read would over the lifetime of the individual, cost the state in excess of £64,000 in costs of crime, imprisonment, welfare benefits, payments to single mothers, and lack of taxable incomes (Brookes et al., 2007; Clark, 2008b). Assuming that a quarter of "failing students" will make maximal demands on state services for their care, imprisonment and control, the lifetime costs of frequent truants from secondary school (absent for at least five weeks) together with the costs over their lifetime, of excluded students gave a total figure of £800 million per annum (at *current* costs), in the costs of these 'failed' students in their adolescent and adult years (Brookes et al., 2007). The report calculated that for each £1 spent on enhanced social and instructional programmes, the lifetime savings will be about £11.50, at current costs.

A report by the government body OFSTED (Office for Standards in Education) in 2008 indicated that a fifth of all of pupils in state schools failed to achieve the basic levels set for achievement in English and Mathematics (Judd, 2008). These children, the report stated, were likely to go on to make up a high proportion of the so-called NEET adolescents (16 to 24 year-olds who were "Not in Education, Employment of Training"). Moreover, a high proportion of this NEET group (some 200,000 in total – Gilbert, 2007a) lived in areas of economic deprivation, where many adults of all ages were dependent on state benefits (Thomas & Dorling, 2007). The data imply that welfare dependency begins in adolescence and often continues throughout the life cycle in urban areas marked by chronic levels of disadvantage. A 2007 report (Prince's Trust, 2007) estimated that in certain urban areas, in every British city, at least a fifth of youth aged 16 to 24 fell into the NEET category, and the costs of their economic dependency and of their potential criminal careers could be at least £2 billion over their lifetime. This makes any kind of intervention which could improve the "life chances" of such youth would be highly cost effective.

A review by the Confederation of British Industries (Cridland, 2008) found that the proportion of 16 to 18-year-olds "not in education, employment or training" had remained unchanged over 25 years, and in this regard Britain ranked 24th amongst 28 developed countries, exceeded only by Greece, Italy, Mexico and Turkey. Halving the number of NEETS would save £250 million a year in later benefit payments, and would significantly add to Britain's productivity through adding to numbers of skilled people in the workforce.

The national Cambridge Review of Primary Education (Noden & West, 2009b) gathered together a mass of evidence which showed that the seeds of scholastic failure were sown in the primary school, in which the focus on creative literacy was all too often sacrificed in favour on a narrow and slavish pursuit of preparation for government examinations, at the expense of a broad-based curriculum in which the excitement of learning would not be lost.

In conclusion to this section, the evidence shows that at least a tenth of British school-leavers have few examination passes, and only minimal competence in basic literacy and numeracy. They are in danger of joining the large group of NEETS (aged 16 plus, who are not in employment of training, and face a lifetime of welfare dependency). European comparisons indicate that this is a British phenomenon, and reflects Britain's rigid class structure and lack of upward social mobility. When measured against lifetime social service costs, individualised educational programmes for this underachieving group, though expensive in the short-term, would be highly cost effective within a few years.

The economic recession beginning in 2008 was likely to have made the situation of unemployed teenagers worse. A survey of 500 firms by the Chartered Institute of Personnel Development (CIPD, 2009) found that only one in five would consider recruiting school-leavers for employment in 2009.

The numbers aged 16 to 25 who were unemployed and drawing the "job seeker's allowance" was 450,000 in May, 2009, an increase of 80 percent over the previous year. These figures were likely to swell with the ranks of newly unemployed school and college leavers in July, 2009. Youth without qualification are those least likely to be hired, and to become permanently unemployed.

TWENTY TWO: THE FATE OF EXCLUDED STUDENTS

Parsons (1999) identified the educational exclusion of British children as a major social problem, with far reaching implications for policy makers in education and in other fields. Figures on exclusions from British schools for 2003–2004 showed a six percent increase in the numbers excluded. Many of these 344,510 students were approaching the final year examination stage, examinations which they would never take (Halpin, 2005; Smithers, 2005). Figures for the school year 2005–2006 indicated yet another rise in the number of exclusions, to 434,280 (Garner, 2007f; Woolcock, 2008). New government policy required that a school which permanently excludes a student must accept another one in his or her stead. What this effectively meant was that as soon as a new Academy school opened, pupils who were seen as slow, unwilling or disruptive learners were immediately expelled and their places taken by "more promising" students (Major, 2008). What followed was a drift down of unpromising students between secondary schools until eventually the least promising individuals were partially absorbed by the lowest quality schools. But significant numbers of these most alienated teenagers dropped out of schooling permanently, many by the age of 14 – but there was little sociological evidence on the fate of these "disappeared" populations (Skidmore, 2008). Another strategy used by schools to respond to the "no exclusions" directive was to "suspend" unacceptable pupils for a specific time period (Garner, 2009a). It is likely that some of these students would get the message very soon, and might suspend themselves permanently.

What happens to excluded students in Britain? The answer to this important question was not very clear, since the government's Department for Education and Skills (2004) acknowledged that each year educational systems 'lose track' of some 10,000 students before they are aged 16. Some who are 'known about' are temporarily expelled, and find places in other schools, and this has been attributed to school policies which aim to enhance achievement profiles by expelling under-performing pupils (Brighouse, 2004). The fate of permanently excluded students is less clear – such pupils are usually referred either to special 'referral units'. These referral units offer remedial courses in basic skills (reading, writing and arithmetic) and vocational training. However, the atmosphere in these centres is often less than professional, and students are frequently absent ("… provision for pupils who were excluded or placed in temporary, specialized provision was of very variable quality …" Gilbert, 2006). In her annual report for 2007, the Director of OFSTED (Gilbert, 2007b) found that although 52 percent of the pupil referral units were "good", in 20 percent they were of very poor quality, with frequent absenteeism by the referred pupils. Gilbert (2009) further commented on OFSTED's inspection of Pupil Referral Units for excluded youth, that only a half were providing an adequate education. Oftentimes a youth had to wait for weeks for a vacancy in a PRU to become available.

Data on school exclusions for 2006–2007 (Clark, 2008b) for England and Wales showed a slightly changing picture. The number of pupils temporarily or permanently excluded from schooling in 2006 numbered 343,840 (DfES, 2007): 10,239 of these pupils had been permanently excluded (Brookes et al., 2007). The number of secondary school pupils permanently excluded from school has fallen by some seven percent, but this was largely due to changes to government policy which although allowing pupils to be permanently expelled, did require that other schools should attempt to educate these alienated pupils.

The result is that the final destination for these frequently excluded pupils are those secondary schools serving the most depressed, most alienated and least achieving pupils. These, as we stressed earlier, are often schools with a high teacher turnover and larger classes which serve the most depressed urban areas. 2008 government data showed an increase in limited term exclusions (up by about four percent) on the grounds of frequent aggression (including attacks on teachers), sexual assaults (male on female), racist language, and physical and verbal attacks on peers and teachers. Again, these disturbed pupils sink to the bottom of the school hierarchy, and many, although not permanently excluded are frequently absent.

Permanent drop-out (and voluntary absenteeism) is often not followed up. It is likely that many of the permanently excluded form a cadre of street youth, alienated and depressed, making money from petty crime from early adolescence onwards, and increasingly becoming prey to drug pushers and those who wish to sexually exploit the young (Bagley & Pritchard, 1998a; Bagley & King, 2003).

Some schools in Britain's major conurbations serve areas marked by economic depression, and social and ethnic division. Drop-out (or expulsion) rates from these schools are high, and youth aged less than 16 were not eligible for any kind of financial support from the state. At 16 they might be eligible for a weekly grant (about £30) which was less than a third of the minimum wage for young people in work. The alternative for some of these young people was participation in drug using and distribution subcultures, with associated thefts to pay for drug use, and the carrying of knives and guns which resulted in high rates of severe injuries and fatalities in these disaffected youth (Batmangheldjh, 2007).

Singh (2007), Chair of the Prime Minister's *Commission on Integration and Cohesion* advocated a form of "national service" for young people who could opt for a period of work in an area of social, civic or military service. This was an idealistic solution, but it seemed unlikely to be of relevance for youth of school age who rarely attended the schools in which they are nominally affiliated.

Parsons (2009) and Woodcock and Fishburn (2009) showed that the situation regarding school exclusions appeared to be worsening. The new government policy of allowing only short-term exclusions rather than permanent expulsions from schooling had resulted in a "revolving door" in which excluded students returned after a week or two, but were often expelled once again. There were 176,000 of these "multiple short term exclusions" in 2007–2008. Investigation of pupil referral units (PRUs), which expelled and excluded students should in theory attend, revealed an unsatisfactory picture. Communication between schools and the PRUs was poor, and many youth stayed at home or wandered the streets because the PRUs had not been informed of their existence. A single PRU could serve a large city, so problems of transport might also prevent youth attendance. "Lack of funding resources means that some pupil referral units are overwhelmed and can only offer a few hours a week to teenagers. At some units pupils turn up for only a couple of hours a week." (Woodcock & Fisburn, 2009). According to government figures, nearly 15,000 children were excluded more than five times in a single year.

Further data showed "an alarming link between exclusion and prison." According to the Prison Reform Trust, 86 percent of imprisoned young offenders (aged less than 18) had been previously excluded from school. Parsons comments that: "These kids are often on the edge of the criminal justice system before they are excluded. Exclusion will push them further." Parsons (2009) argued that only a minority of PRUs offered an adequate educational programme. "Exclusion from school, either permanently or for a fixed period, is a quiet mockery of the government's *Every Child Matters* policy." Parsons offered a number of "strategic alternatives" to exclusion, all of which although expensive in the short run, could produce human and financial savings if they could they prevent at least some of these youth from drifting into a life of delinquency and crime. Martin Narey (Director of the National Offender Management Service) commented (2009): "Once you take someone out of a class of 30 children, they can prosper very well in a smaller class and have a good chance in life. Once a child is excluded permanently, or repeatedly for a fixed term, it is very difficult to prevent later criminal careers."

In a later section of this document we will outline in detail an experimental British programme which had marked success in retaining youth in school who would otherwise have been excluded, preventing their drift into crime. Before this we would like to outline evidence from some remarkable American studies on reduction in class sizes, and individualized tuition for 'failing students', since this work has important implications on how educational practices in Britain should be framed and reformed.

TWENTY THREE: THE TENNESSEE AND TEXAS EDUCATIONAL EXPERIMENTS ON SCHOOL CLASS SIZE

The State of Tennessee, in America's deep south, is not noted for its progressive social policies, yet the "Tennessee class size experiment" is both notable and famous. This experiment began in 1985 (Picus, 2000), and was soon followed by somewhat similar experiments in California and Washington State. The Tennessee experiment began by selecting a school district with a relatively high proportion of disadvantaged and underachieving schools and students, and matching the district for purposes of comparison with a demographically similar district. In the focus district, class sizes in Kindergarten through to Grade 3 (containing children aged 5 to 8) were reduced from 25-plus to less than 18, usually to 15 in each class. Children in focus and control classes were then tested regularly until Grade 8 (average age 14).

Results were both spectacular and important (Achilles, 1997; Finn & Achilles, 1999; Picus, 2000). Compared with control children who remained in larger classes, the several thousand pupils in the reduced-size classes had significant gains on tests of basic ability and in learning of general subjects; they were more fluent and proficient in writing, listening and speaking; they displayed more creativity and types of divergent thinking; they were less likely to engage in fighting, shoving, pushing and crowding others in class; they had fewer fears about being ridiculed or bullied; they were better motivated and had significantly better self-concept; they participated more in voluntary activities; they were generally more eager and enthusiastic about school and schooling; and they were less likely to be absent from school.

Although the reduced class sizes did not extend beyond grade 3 (age 8), follow-up when the focus pupils were aged 14 showed that many had retained their significant gains. Pupils from disadvantaged social backgrounds made the most gains (compared with similar children in the control schools) and these previously disadvantaged children retained their achievements and motivation in the long run (Finn et al., 2005).

Observation of teachers in the reduced-size classes showed that they still taught using their traditional methods; but they were able to give their pupils much higher levels of individual attention, and were able to focus on pupils who were potentially disruptive or underachieving, without sacrificing levels of instruction for the remaining children in the class. It was important however that reductions in funding for equipment, support services and space were not made in order to fund the extra number of teachers required (Picus, 2000). Further follow-up of the original 95,000 children in more than 100 schools in the original class size reduction experiment found that the K-3 cohort, even though they entered regular class sizes following Grade 3, were more likely to remain in school until the age of 18, and were more likely to apply for college or university entrance (Achilles, 1999).

The most detailed follow up of the STARS programme by Finn et al. (2005) of 5,335 students to late adolescence showed that small class size (less than 20 per class) in the first four years of schooling had strong and highly significant effects on numbers graduating from high school. This effect was particularly strong with regards to pupils who came from economically poor backgrounds. Amongst those graduating from high school (76.3% in those who had attended large classes, 87.8% in those who attended small classes) measured reading and mathematical ability was significantly higher at age 18 in the "smaller classes" cohort.

Results from the California, Indiana and Washington reduced-class size experiments provided similar results, and teachers, educational administrators and public alike have become enthusiastic supporters of K-3 class size reductions, which are now widespread in the United States. Reducing class sizes in the early years of schooling is expensive, and by 2000 the Federal government was subsidizing costs within 20 States at the level of about $1.2 billions, since it was clear that class-size reductions are cost effective in the longer term (Krueger, 1999).

The individualized instruction model, and dividing larger classes into smaller groups, developed in Texas can be an adjunct to, or an alternative to the class size reduction model (Slavin, 1990). While several American states have deployed the individualized instruction strategy for elementary and junior high schools (Kindergarten to Grade 8) with an above average proportion of disadvantaged pupils, that in Texas has been described and evaluated the most systematically (Farkas, 1996, 2000).

In these experiments 'failing' students identified by teachers are given supplementary instruction of about 40 minutes a day on three to four days a week. The tutors were usually university and college students who are given short courses of preparation, and they then use specially prepared materials for reading instruction. Continuous evaluation on the child's progress by the tutor led to a highly individualized curriculum approach. Children in these specialized individual instruction programmes acquired reading levels which were nearly twice those of matched controls who merely received standardized educational instruction. By 2000 similar programmes were operating in six US States (ECS, 2002).

The lessons from the Tennessee class size experiments are salutary – in small classes teachers are able to give more individualized attention to the learning needs of pupils, as well as addressing very early on, problems of poor behaviour. In very small classes (15 or less) pupils feel more responsible and are less alienated. They achieve better, are more motivated to complete school and have better self-concept with regard to the learning environment. The alternate model from Texas of individualized instruction for some pupils also has demonstrated effectiveness.

In another American study, Allhusen et al. (2004) examined in detail how teachers and their 651 pupils behaved in US first grade classes. The smaller classes received significantly more "high quality instruction", and the pupils in these smaller classes achieved a higher level of literacy skills. Teachers gave pupils in small classes "more emotional support", while the pupils in turn demonstrated more closeness to their teacher, and less externalising or hyperactive behaviour.

The American Education Association (NEA, 2008) summarized the available American research as follows: "Teachers with small classes can spend time and energy helping each child succeed. Smaller classes also enhance safety, discipline and order in the classroom. When qualified teachers teach smaller classes in modern schools, kids learn more. It's common sense, and the research proves it works to increase student achievement." The optimum level for a school class is 15, says the NEA.

TWENTY FOUR: ACHIEVEMENT AND SCHOOL CLASS SIZES IN BRITAIN

For some time the myth prevailed in British educational policy that "class size doesn't matter", and it was the qualifications, experience and dedication of the teacher that was most important (OFSTED, 1995). Of course, well-qualified and highly motivated teachers are important, but unfortunately the morale of many British teachers had been undermined (up to 2008–2009) because of poor pay, difficult working conditions and the popular perception that teaching is an unrewarding profession, not just in financial terms.

While a legal regulation in 1998 specified that early school classes in Britain should be no larger than 30, in practice class sizes in the primary school are often much larger than this. A 1999 report indicated that in Inner London, class sizes were the largest in the country, twice the level in countries such as Norway and Finland (Foster, 1999). In Bangladesh, a prominent NGO The Bangladesh Rural Advancement Committee (BRAC), offered primary education in many areas based on a maximum of 23 children a class in rural primary schools (Nath, 2008).

The connection between class size and school exclusions is, we argue, linked to the fact that teachers in Britain are often unable to address the learning problems of some bored, alienated and potentially rebellious students. It is no coincidence that the highest proportion of exclusions from school occur in local authority areas which have the poorest teacher-pupil ratios. Again, there is a vicious circle here – in these areas which have the lowest achieving and most poorly behaved students, teacher turnover is highest and in consequence classes frequently become very large because of chronic teacher shortage.

In Britain Iacovou (2001) has argued that previous British research on class failed to control for the reasons why some children were in small small classes – often it had been pupils with educational difficulties, underachievement due to underlying cognitive problems, and/or behavioural maladjustment who had been assigned to very small classes. Including the achievements of these pupils with those who were retained in larger classes gave a skewed result, showing that smaller classes contained more poorly achieving pupils – but this finding was an artefact of referral procedures. It has been acknowledged by researchers that children in private schools in Britain, where class sizes are on average less than half of those in publicly-funded schools have much higher achievements than pupils in the state system: but this effect has usually been attributed to the social class bias in the student intake of private schools.

Iacovou's (2001) British research followed up some 12,100 children in the National Child Development Study, a cohort of children born in one week in 1958, and who were studied systematically at birth and at ages 7, 11 and beyond. First of all, she found as expected that pupils assigned to lower streams in primary schooling had poorer initial reading ability, and these lower streams had smaller numbers of children. Iacovou found that smaller class size – resulting from the normal variation in numbers in regular streams, not that resulting from any specific assignment policies – was associated, when streaming policy and a variety of other social factors were controlled for, with *higher* achievement. The smaller class-size effect accounted for an enhancement of about one-third of a standard deviation in reading test scores, a highly significant result. This important finding suggests that even quite small levels of class size reduction can have positive effects.

Furthermore, a reduction in class size of eight pupils below the average was associated with a highly significant 40 per cent increase (of one standard deviation) in reading score (other factors controlled for), slightly larger than the achievement advantage of coming from an advantaged social class, and ten times the advantage bestowed by having a mother with an additional year of completed education. The advantage in reading ability through being in a smaller class at age 7 was retained at age 11, particularly in children from larger families. While the variation in class sizes in this British study reflected a naturally occurring variation in the policies and resources of different schools, and was not the result of a carefully contrived experiment as in the Tennessee STARS project, the effect size in enhancement of achievements was quite similar to those observed by Achilles (1996) in Tennessee.

Dustman et al. (2002) analyzed a sub-sample from the National Child Development Study, of 4,000 participants living in England and Wales, followed up at ages 16, 23, 32 and 42. They found that even quite small reductions in class size significantly increased the possibility of a child staying on in school after 16, other factors (including attendance at grammar school) controlled for. Staying on at school increased the chances of attending college or university, reflected in significantly higher mean earnings over the individual's lifetime.

The British NCDS study reflected an era of very large classes (average primary school class sizes were 35.9), and since that time average primary school class sizes have fallen to a little over 30. There are strong grounds for supposing however that since the STARS experiment and the NCDS statistical study produced similar results in school achievement, the social advantages produced by the Tennessee experiment (better morale, higher self-concept, better behaviour, higher motivation, lower school drop-out) would also occur in pupils in smaller classes in Britain. This suggestion is important for the discussion in a later section on school exclusions and their sequels in our 'two-schools experiment'.

We note in this context the results of a study which focussed on the individual cognitive needs of boys in four inner-city primary schools in London. These underachieving boys made significant gains in achievement as a result of the inputs (CLPE, 2004). These findings tend to replicate those of the Texas individualized reading programmes, and show that individualized educational inputs could also significantly influence the enhancement of academic achievements of British pupils.

Preliminary results were available from a large experimental study which has focussed on 235 children aged four to seven in state schools, in small classes (average size 19 children) who were compared with children in large classes (average size 33 children) (Blatchford, 2003). This research by Blatchford et al. (2003) found that children in the larger classes were more often distracted, and spent more time 'off task'. In the later monograph emerging from this project (Blatchford et al., 2007), details are given of the largest experimental study of class size effects in Britain (effectively, a replication of the American STARS project). In this British study, 10,000 experimental and control pupils in 500 classes, in 300 schools were followed up from the time of their initial enrolment (at ages 4 to 5) until the end of Key Stage One (at ages 6 and 7). Key findings were:

1. There is a "disruption effect" when children move from reception classes into larger classes in Year 1 which is magnified when they move into a bigger class. Therefore, Blatchford urges, class sizes should remain stable (and ideally, small in size) from reception into future years of education.
2. Large groupings within classes can have an adverse effect on the amount and quality of teaching and the quality of pupils' work and concentration. Best outcomes are when teachers, with the aid of classroom assistants, divide children into smaller groups. Classroom assistants in and of themselves do not improve pupils' concentration and reading skills, unless classes are small at the outset.
3. In smaller classes there is more teacher support for learning and "less pupil inattentiveness and off-task behaviour". Children in larger classes spend more time interacting with each other, and less time attending to their teacher, and to work tasks.

Overall there were significant gains in literacy skills in the smaller classes. The optimum level for effective teaching was a class size of less than 20, the study concludes. This not only helped the teacher to instruct more effectively, but also helped them to individualize teaching for SEN pupils. Blatchford et al. (2007) used a multi-method, qualitative and quantitative study, in studying teacher-student interaction when children were aged 7 to 11. Sixteen 'small' classes (fewer than 25 students per teacher) were compared with 31 'large' classes (31 or more students per teacher). "Results showed that there was more individual attention in smaller classes, a more active role for pupils, and beneficial effects on quality of teaching."[4]

Blatchford et al. (2007) concluded:

> There may also be longer term effects of class size differences, beyond that evident from study of the first three years of school, and in the current research we are following the same children over the next stage of their schooling i.e. from 7–11 years (KS2) and documenting both class sizes and educational achievement. (p. 144)

Research by Croxford and Raffe (2007) which examined data for a cohort of adolescents in the period 1984 to 2002, found that Scottish adolescents were significantly more likely to attend university or college (at a rate of 37%), than were English adolescents (at a rate of 25%). Statistical analyses suggest that a major cause of this disparity were the larger secondary school class sizes in English schools (26 pupils per teacher on average) compared with Scottish adolescents (23 pupils per teacher). Smaller class size was linked in the first instance to proportions of pupils staying at school until 18. These findings like the earlier NCDS studies suggested that even small reductions in class size can yield favorable, long-term outcomes in achievement.

Further Scottish initiatives (Chapman, 2007) underline the paucity of educational provision in Britain (by 2006, 22,800 pupils in English schools were contained in classes larger than 30). The new Scottish policy should result in nursery and primary education classes (for those aged 4 to 8 years) which would have no more than 18 pupils per class. Nursery education for the four-year-olds would be free. These policy initiatives would begin in the most deprived areas, and would cost an additional £25 millions a year, compared to previous educational spending in Scotland. In 2007, Scotland had 31 percent fewer pupils per teacher than England and Wales (ONS, 2008).

The overall effects of the school class size studies are clear. In smaller classes teachers are more able to focus on the individual emotional, behavioural and learning needs of each pupil. Pupils are less distracted and overactive, and are more likely to concentrate on the learning process. Even when pupils move on to larger classes in secondary school, the early advantages from small classes at the primary level are retained, and they are significantly more likely to stay on in school to 18, and achieve at a higher level in formal examinations.

The British government by 2008–2009 was struggling to keep school classes below 30 per teacher. Even with a teaching assistant, it was difficult to see how a teacher could instruct effectively in such an environment. Inevitably, some children who desperately needed the teacher's focused attention would be neglected.

State-funded English schools in the period under review rarely offered their pupils the advantages of small class sizes, and it was left to the private sector of education, affordable only for well-off parents, to provide what should have been a basic educational right for *all* children. The under-funding of schooling in Britain (and particularly in England) is another aspect of the structures of social class, by which many of the poor and underachieving remain poor and underachieving throughout their lives.

The figures for the academic year 2006–2007 collected by OECD (OECD, 2008) indicated that in Britain more than 23,000 infants were still taught in classes which exceeded 31 pupils. Class sizes at all ages in Britain were, on average, 13.1 percent greater than the average for all of the other OECD nations. The situation in England (but not in Scotland) with regard to class sizes was getting worse rather than better. Data for the academic year 2007–2008 indicated the 24,820 children in primary schools in England and Wales were being taught in classes of 31 or larger, an increase of 1,610 classes compared with the previous year (Noden & West, 2009b). This, the Cambridge Review of Primary Education showed, had a depressing influence on children's achievement on basic numeracy and literacy tasks. Teachers of larger classes were less able to focus on class management and on difficult or distracting behavior of individual pupils. Both pupils and teachers were more often absent from these very large classes, which often seemed to be infected by a feeling of malaise. It is unclear whether this was because of high numbers of children from "problem" backgrounds combined with teachers who simply could not cope, or were at the end of their useful professional life, or some combinations of these factors. These teachers often soldiered on bravely, perhaps making envious glances towards schools in the private sector in which class sizes rarely exceeded fifteen.

327

In March 2008, the Minister for Schools was "jeered" at the annual meeting of a teachers' union when he maintained that primary class sizes of 38 were acceptable, provided a teacher's aide was present; and that secondary school mathematics classes of 70 were "perfectly acceptable" (Lipsett & Curtis, 2008). In May, 2009 the Department for Children, Schools and Families released figures showing that the number of children aged 5 to 7 in classes of more than thirty had doubled in the previous year. These numbers were expected to rise because of demographic changes, and government failure to allocate additional funds for class size reduction (Garner, 2009b).

TWENTY FIVE: THE PRIVATE SCHOOLS OPTION

According to the OECD (2007, 2008) overviews of educational statistics in the 29 OECD nations, Britain ranked 24th in terms of school class size in state-funded primary schools, with an average of 25.8 pupils per teacher. According to these data Britain had more pupils attending privately funded schools, which were entirely independent of any state funding, than any other OECD nation. These privately funded schools (which normally charge fees for a child's attendance), are chosen by a significant number of the upper and middle classes in Britain. In these private, fee-paying schools, average class sizes were often less than half of those in state-funded schools.

Freedman, research analyst for *The Independent Schools Council* (Freedman, 2006) showed that as expected the large majority of parents who sent their children to these well-endowed, small class-size schools come from the well-paid middle and upper classes. Nevertheless, around a quarter of pupils come from parents with below average incomes, implying that they were prepared to make sacrifices in order to give their child a quality education.

The number of parents opting to pay for their child's education had, by 2008 been increasing year by year. Some reasons why more than 500,000 parents each year were now prepared to pay for their child's education were the promise of smaller classes, and the availability of well-qualified teachers of languages, maths and physics (Garner, 2007e). The largest increase in pupils going to private education was in students aged 14 and above, since this appeared to be an age when the deficiencies of state secondary schools become, in pedagogic terms, more apparent.

Gilbert (2007a) produced for the New Labour government a "vision for schooling" in which the teacher produced an individualized plan for each pupil based on an individual profile, goal-setting and tutoring, rather than employing a group-instruction, "one size fits all" model. What Gilbert did not add was that such an ideal model required very much smaller class sizes, and more highly trained teachers. Certainly, for some children who have "normal" intelligence but who are failing to read or handle numerical concepts adequately, individualized instruction may be necessary, following appropriate diagnostic work on how they process information.

This an expensive model, and so far it is only available to parents who can afford to pay the fees required (Freedman, 2006). Ironically, it is parents who are served by the poorest quality schools in 'working class' areas who need such 'quality' education (in which fees often exceeded more than £3,300 a term for a day pupil) the most. Instead, parents living in the most depressed economic areas have been offered the poorest quality schools for their children. But if these children are to be upwardly mobile in social and economic terms, the opposite should be the case – they need the *highest* quality of schooling.

An alternative, advocated by Trevor Phillips (2007) was to employ the American model of "bussing" of students from disadvantaged areas into high quality state schools. Phillips, Chair of the British Commission for Social Equality and Human Rights cited an American study showing the success of this model. Ironically, this policy of bussing pupils between schools, at least on the grounds of "race" had been made illegal in the United States (Bagley, 2008b).

Another possibility which has been tried experimentally with the support of a private foundation, is to subsidize access to 'private' schools for promising students from economically poor families (Sutton Trust, 2001). This initiative is unlikely to reach the majority of alienated and disruptive students from smaller secondary schools, serving marginal areas of cities.

Another trend is for local consortia of parents to "home school" their children in groups of up to half a dozen in size, for a variety of reasons – parents may object to a lack of religious ethos in the available schools, or to the fact that their children would be bullied, or would acquire attitudes to violence, drugs and sexuality which would be undesirable. The estimated number of pupils in home education are about 50,000 at any one time, although much larger numbers may have experienced part of their schooling in this way (Curtis, 2008c). Websites exist through which parents can access curriculum guides, textbooks and details of examination entry, and there is no evidence (from visits by Office for Standards in Education Inspectors) that home education is harmful scholastically. Often these home educated students will enter sixth form colleges for more advanced work. There is some evidence that parents who choose to educate their children at home are largely middle class, and are choosing such education (sometimes with local authority subsidies of about £1,700 a year for each child) in order to save their child attending persistently failing secondary schools (Bartholomew, 2009).

In Britain Muslim parents increasingly see these small groupings of pupils in a parental home, or in a larger setting as providing the initial basis for larger schools offering a curriculum informed by the moral and spiritual teachings of Islam. According to research (Al-Refai & Bagley, 2008) these schools can, despite the prejudiced attitudes of some critics, lay the foundation for excellent citizenship.

In an age of austerity, some private schools in an effort to hold down fee levels or to increase recruitment of pupils were merging with nearby schools or increasing class sizes (Lipsett, 2009). Nevertheless, pupil-teacher ratios in private schools rarely exceed two thirds of those in the state system.

TWENTY SIX: INEQUALITY AND TERTIARY EDUCATION

There is a strong social class bias in England in state secondary school students who continue on to university studies, ranging in extreme cases from 8 per cent of the age group following this path in the poorest group of urban areas, to 62 per cent in the most prosperous areas (HEFCE, 2005). In Britain as a whole, young people living in the more advantaged areas were more than four times as likely to go on to university than are young people in areas where average family incomes are in the lowest quintile (Blanden & Machin, 2004b).

By the end of 2005 the proportion of children with parents in the highest wealth quintile had increased their chances of university entry by up to six times, compared with those whose parents were in the lowest income quintile (Cassidy, 2005). Research cited by Cassidy indicated that an important mediating factor was the poorer quality of the secondary schools attended by many of the students from economically poor homes. Even when they did enter university, children of the poorest parents tended to have poorer degree outcomes, largely because they had to work part-time because their parents (unlike well-off parents) were unable to provide for their child's living allowance (Van Dyke & Little, 2005).

A marked increase in fees for students attending university in England and Wales in 2006 was reflected in a decline of 13,500 students entering university whose parents were in the lowest income quintile, despite the fact that overall the number of applicants to university continued to increase (Blair, 2006). University education in Scotland remained free for Scottish residents, again underlining the paucity of educational provision in England. The New Labour government had announced a programme of limited bursaries for students from the poorest families entering university. However, research by the Institute for Fiscal Studies (Fitzimons & Chowdry, 2007) estimated that this £400 million programme would be of little use for those from poverty backgrounds, since their depressed circumstances mean that they rarely achieved the standards for university entry. This money would be better spent, the IFS researchers argued, on school programmes for youth aged 16 to 18 who would otherwise drop out of education, having no chance of college or university entry.

In her annual report, the Chief Inspector of Schools (Gilbert, 2007b) stated that schools in areas with a high proportion receiving free school meals (an indicator of overall poverty) were particularly likely to produce pupils with few 'good' passes in the General Certificate of Secondary Education, so that relatively few in turn took Advanced level GCSEs (the usual requirement for university entry). Disadvantage began at the infant-school level, according to Gilbert's (2007b) analysis, and fed through to a much poorer chance of going to university: children of the economically poor tended to be concentrated in disadvantaged areas, and were much less likely to achieve university entrance. The underachievement on the Standard Achievement Tests in pupils from poverty-background schools (compared with those pupils who attended 'better off' schools) was well-established at age seven, and *increased* at all phases of formal testing (at ages 11, 14 and 16). Children in these poverty-area schools from which very few went on to university, were more often absent (or had been excluded in 12 percent of cases), compared with two percent of students attending all other types of state school.

Paton (2008a) cites research showing that white males from working class backgrounds are significantly under-represented in university populations: even when they are qualified, they disproportionately failed to apply, despite the availability of special access funds (up to £1000 a year for each student) administered by the universities themselves. When they did attend university, students from poverty backgrounds were significantly more likely to attend former polytechnics, rather than OxBridge and the high status Russell Group universities (Goldthorpe & Jackson, 2007; Blanden et al., 2007).

TWENTY SEVEN: WORLD PERSPECTIVES ON BRITAIN'S FAILURE TO
SERVE THE NEEDS OF CHILDREN AND ADOLESCENTS

A major UNICEF report published in February 2007 placed Britain's failure in serving the needs of disadvantaged children and adolescents in a clear, comparative perspective. This report compared WHO and OECD data for the world's 21 richest countries. In terms of absolute wealth, and on GNP per head Britain ranked very highly – but in terms of the well-being of young people, Britain ranked last, and compared unfavourably with less wealthy nations such as Ireland, Greece, Poland and the Czech Republic. The country with the best record in the treatment of children and adolescents was The Netherlands, followed by Sweden, Denmark, Finland, Spain, Switzerland, Norway and Italy.

Data were assembled in six sections:

Firstly, *Material Well-Being* – defined as the percent of children living in poverty – homes with an income less than 50 percent of the median income for the nation; percent of children in which all of the adults were unemployed; percent of children living in homes with few educational resources; and percent of children in which there were fewer than 10 books of any kind. Of the 21 wealthy countries Britain ranked 18 on these aggregate indicators, with a high proportion (16%) in relative poverty, who were also living in homes with few educational resources.

Secondly, *Health and Safety* – defined by rates of infant mortality, children born with birth weight of less than 2,500 grams, percent of infants being immunized, and percent of deaths in children from 'accidents'. Britain's rate of infant deaths at 5.3 per 1,000 was nearly twice that of Finland's; and percent with birth weight of less than 2,500 grams was again nearly twice that in several Nordic countries.

Thirdly, *Educational Well-Being* – defined by level of school achievements at age 15+; percent staying on at school aged 16+; numbers aged 16–19 in training and vocational courses; percent expecting only unskilled employment. Overall, Britain ranked 17 out of the 21 nations, with a particularly high proportion (25%) of those aged 16+ dropping out of education, failing to receive vocational training, or having low occupational aspirations: 36 percent in Britain expected only unskilled employment, compared with 17 percent in the USA.

Fourthly, *Relationships* – defined by percent in one-parent families, percent in step-families; frequency of eating a meal with the whole family; percentage reporting positive interactions with parent(s); and percent at ages 11, 13 and 15 reporting their peers to be "kind and helpful". British children ranked last amongst the 21 nations studied on these various indicators, only 42 percent seeing their peers as kind or helpful, compared with 73 percent of Dutch and 81 percent of Swiss children and adolescents. British children were most likely to be in a family with only one parent, or with a non-biological parent, and had very low rates of direct or positive interactions with other family members. Britain and the US stood out among the 21 nations as having high proportions of one-parent and disrupted families.

Fifthly *Behaviours and Health Risks* – defined by percent eating breakfast; percent eating fresh fruit daily; percent physically active; percent overweight; percent who smoked in past week; percent drunk twice or more in past year; percent using cannabis in lifetime; percent having had intercourse by age 15; percent using condoms during sex; percent becoming pregnant between ages 15 and 19; percent aged 11, 13, and 15 in a fight in past year; and percent bullied in past two months. On these aggregated indicators British adolescents fared *worst* among the 21 nations by a considerable margin, Sweden, Poland and The Netherlands reporting the least problems of poor health and risk-related behaviours. Judging by these data, life for teenagers in Britain is often difficult and unpleasant, with frequent retreats into the self-indulgence of alcohol, drugs and sex.

Sixthly, *Subjective Well-Being* – defined by percent of young people rating health as no more than 'fair' or 'poor'; percent who 'like school a lot'; and percent with a low score on a measure of life satisfaction. More than a quarter of British girls ranked their health as only 'fair' or 'poor', and overall British youth scored poorly on the measures of life satisfaction. The Netherlands ranked best on these combined indicators, Britain the worst.

The UNICEF report concludes: "Children who grow up in poverty are more vulnerable: specifically, they are more likely to be in poor health, to have learning and behavioural difficulties, to underachieve in school, to become pregnant at too early an age, to have lower skills and aspirations, to be low paid, unemployed and welfare-dependent." In other words, the six areas of deprivation studied by UNICEF are systematically related. Children often begin their vulnerable careers *in utero*, and in economically poor and disorganised families often did not receive social and psychological supports which would prepare them for successful and healthy adult careers. They will likely form the parents of the next deprived generation.

The Children's Commissioner for England (Aynsley-Green, 2007) commenting on the findings of the UNICEF report, argued that there has been systematic under-funding in services and financial supports for children and families since 1979, a year coincident with the rise of neo-conservative policies of extreme individualism, which a New Labour government since 1997 had, he said, done little to modify. The British government in 2007 claimed that the UNICEF figures were out-of-date. This disingenuous defence was refuted by Aynsley-Green (2007) who pointed to the fact that the UNICEF Report Cards 1 (2000) and 6 (2006) showed similar differences between countries, indicating the chronic nature of the profound disadvantages for children and families in Britain, relative to other countries. Even though the situation in Britain had improved somewhat, the welfare of children had also improved in most other OECD nations. With regard to relative poverty, the situation in Britain appeared to be getting worse (Seager, 2007).

The UNICEF data have been subjected to additional analysis in ecological comparisons by Pickett and Wilkinson (2007), who added two further countries (Australia and Canada) to the original 21 OECD countries, and then after statistical modelling, replicated the analyses with data for 50 American States. Key variables were an aggregate measure of child well-being (rate of births to teen mothers; rate of children killed through murder; infant mortality; low birth weight rates; levels of educational performance; drop-out from high school; proportion overweight; and proportion with mental health problems). These indicators, making up the aggregate measure, were significantly and positively linked with one another.

The two independent predictor variables explored were average income per head, and the Gini measure of income inequality. Average income levels in a state or in a country did *not* predict levels of child well-being. However, the measure of *income inequality* (the proportion of people in relative poverty) correlated at a highly significant 0.67 with child well-being, indicating a fairly linear relationship between inequality and level of child problems.

The country with the *highest* level of inequality, and the *poorest* level of child well-being on the aggregate measures, was Britain. The countries which had least income equality and the highest levels of child well-being were Sweden, Netherlands Finland, Norway and Denmark. Replication across American States found largely similar results in terms of income inequality and low levels child well-being. The authors of the study conclude that the most likely effect is that high levels of relative poverty undermine the quality of family life, with numerous negative consequences for children's welfare.

The dismal findings from the UNICEF study with regard to children's welfare in Britain were corroborated in the 41-country study of survey data for 2005–2006 by Currie et al. (2008), which analysed findings on some 200,000 children aged 11, 13 and 15, in developed nations in North America and Europe. In this study, teenagers in Britain came well below the median (i.e. scored more poorly) in the national league tables with regard to proportion drinking alcohol regularly, and experimenting with cannabis. British children were also likely to be particularly anxious about school work, possibly a reflection of a regime of frequent school testing and examinations.

The British children were particularly likely, amongst the national groups studied, not to turn to parents for help and advice. Rather, they sought advice and support from peer groups, which provided support for (or initiation in) many of the health-risk behaviours. Children from The Netherlands, Finland and Denmark emerged as those with the lowest level of risky health behaviours, and with close relations with their parents.

Another example of Britain's worsening international position came from a study which compared the links between child mortality (in those aged 0 to 4), and income inequality (ratio of incomes of the poorest quintile to those of the richest quintile of population, as measured by the Gini coefficient). This study by Collison et al. (2007) of the 24 wealthiest OECD nations showed a strong correlation between income inequality and child mortality, using data for 2003 to 2006. Britain shared with the USA (another country with much income inequality) the highest rates of child mortality. In Britain increasing levels of income inequality over time were reflected in higher rates of child mortality.

Those countries with the lowest child mortality rates – Sweden, Iceland, Denmark, Japan, Finland – were those maintaining the least income differentials between the richest and poorest quintiles: in Britain by 2006, rates of child and infant mortality were *twice* those in Sweden.

In their submission to UNICEF for 2007, a consortium of 380 English advocacy groups campaigning for the full implementation of the UN Charter on Children's Rights, concluded that the British government had "wilfully neglected" the rights, safety and equality of many children, contrary to the UN Charter of which Britain is a signatory. Each year according to CRAE (2007) more than 12,000 younger children were processed in police custody, and at least 300 who were still minors were detained in adult jails. Diagnosable rates of poor mental health in adolescents were increasing (Skuse, 2006), and a substantial number (some 400,000) in Britain lived in crowded households, or in "unsafe" neighbourhoods; at least 3.4 million children continued to live in households with incomes below the official poverty line (CRAE, 2007).

Figures from OECD showed that Britain stood 24th in the ranking of Gini coefficients for the 30 wealthiest OECD nations. Only USA, Italy, Romania and Poland ranked more poorly than Britain. According to recent data, the richest 10 percent in Britain owned nine times more wealth than the poorest 10 percent. The wealth gap in Britain had grown steadily since the 1970s, and the gap between rich and poor in 2005 was 20 percent greater than this gap in 1985 (OECD, 2008).

A study conducted by the World Health Organization (Friedli, 2009) using data from the world's developed nations showed, once again how strongly was income inequality linked to poor health in children and adolescents. Scandinavian countries and The Netherlands were amongst the most equal and the healthiest of nations; Britain fell near the bottom in these league tables with a high degree of inequality, and above average measures of poor health, psychopathology, and poor social adjustments. Lakhani (2009) drawing on the work of Friedli and others points to the remarkable rise in deliberate self-harm among young Britons aged 16 to 24, which indicated an 80 percent increase since 2000, with a rise of one third in the previous 5 years. In addition 4,337 children aged 14 or less were admitted to hospital emergency departments for self-harm between 2003 and 2007. Possible reasons for Britain's high rate of youthful self-harm were high rates of unemployment and poverty in some urban areas in contrast with others, low educational attainments and a hopeless view of achievements later in life, a fear of crime and neighbourhood violence, premature sexual behaviours (and physical and sexual abuse), drug and alcohol abuse, and high rates of criminality and suicidal behaviour in an individual's extended family or neighbourhood. "Dropping out of school" and "dropping out of life" may have some conceptual similarities. Britain may have one of the highest rates of deliberate self-harm in youth due to specific socio-cultural factors, but the phenomenon does exist, according to an international survey, in a number of other developed nations (Madge et al., 2008).

An expanded replication of the UNICEF study undertaken by the University of York for the Child Poverty Action Group (Westhead, 2009) found after analysing 43 indicators of child and adolescent well-being grouped under seven headings (health; subjective well-being; relationship quality; access to material resources; behaviour and risk-taking; educational quality; housing and the environment) that Britain still ranked 24th out of the 29 developed nations that were studied. The passing of two years since the original UNICEF Report was issued in 2007, suggested that Britain had done nothing to diminish the relative poverty which diminished the lives of so many British children. The Netherlands, once again, came top of this child well-being league, followed by the Nordic countries. The researchers found that households in Britain which were in chronic poverty were particularly likely to have children with highly adverse aggregated scores on the seven measures off deprivation and disorganised behaviour. The British Child Poverty Action Group therefore advocated a number of clearly defined and easy to implement, government measures to diminish child and family poverty, income inequality, and adults without jobs whose children would otherwise enter the cycle of poverty. Whether this advocacy would have any better impact than the earlier, well-researched advocacy document edited by Fimister (2001) for the Child Poverty Action Group (a report that was ignored by New Labour) remained to be seen.

Layard and Dunn (2009) on behalf of the English charity, The Children's Society had taken forward the UNESCO (2007) study in a major review drawing on evidence from 30,000 children, adults and professionals. They identified family problems, family instability, and socialisation problems for most of the learning and behavioural problems identified, problems which now afflicted more than ten percent of British 5 to 16 year olds – including anxiety, depression, self-harm, anorexia, hyperactivity, and conduct disorder. Children with single or step-parents or who were separated from both their biological parents, were 50 percent more likely to suffer low academic achievement, poor self-esteem, unpopularity and being victims of bullying, and depression. Underlying these family problems were income inequality and relative poverty, which put a great strain on family life .

After the United States, Britain was the most unequal of the developed countries. In Britain 22 percent of children lived in economically poor families (incomes less than 60 percent of the median wage), compared with eight percent in Sweden, and ten percent in Denmark. Thirty years previously 'only' 13 percent of British children fell into this very poor sector. On interventions for children with conduct disorder and early patterns of delinquency, Layard and Dunn (2009) reflect on earlier research in showing how cost effective early interventions could be: "A child with conduct disorder costs the taxpayer £70,000 in crime, social care and remedial costs by the time they are 28, compared with £7000 for the effective treatment of the average child with problems of conduct disorder." Reviewing this report, Stephenson (2009) argued that it had important implications for action in a time of financial austerity – preventing expensive problems through early interventions was particularly important when money for servicing deviant and disorganized behaviour becomes increasingly scarce.

TWENTY EIGHT: THE SPATIAL DIMENSIONS OF DISADVANTAGE AND DISORGANIZED BEHAVIOUR

In his view of "geographies of young people", Stuart Aitken (2001) maps "the morally contested spaces of identity" in cities, using a Marxian analysis. Cities as stratified, zones 'contain' populations segregated by class and race, youth are socialized and controlled. It is functional for the ruling classes, in this analysis, when the segregated precariat classes 'turn in on themselves', encouraged to join gangs and harm one another, rather than joining political parties and bringing down the power structures that oppress them. Aitkin's view is an American one, but he reveres the work of Paul Willis in Britain for his acclaimed *Learning to Labour*, "which couches the lives of working-class youths in terms of covert resistance to schools ... and the larger structure of capitalism ... By translating an abstract framework of Marxism into the everyday cultural terms of his working class subjects, Willis is concerned with a tension between their knowledge and their rebellion against it." (p. 56) Aitken borrows metaphors from the English anarchist Colin Ward's description of *The Child in the City* (1978) in his account of how the child "learns through the body" to live in the city. This experience can be pleasing, or violent, according to class position.

An examination of the maps of Manchester included in Engels' account of "the condition of the working class in England" shows that several of the areas of extreme stress and poverty that Engels identified in 1845 remained as areas of poverty, stress and alienation of youth in 2008 – although there were now new "overspill" estates in Wythenshawe and Handforth in which problems of poverty and delinquency had been transported, and inherited through slum-clearance and rehousing from Greater Manchester.

The classic Chicago studies of spatially organised normative behaviour (Abbott, 1999) have inspired British scholars, such as the criminologist Terence Morris (1957) in his seminal work on *The Criminal Area*. Since then generations of students of the spatial correlates of crime, disadvantage, and oppression have studied British cities in some detail – research summarized by Bagley (1984).

For some years researchers have used ecological models in mapping rates of social deviance and disadvantage in urban settings in Britain (Bagley 1972 to 1992), India (Bagley, 1989) and Canada (Bagley, 1992). This research has shown that indices of social and behavioural disadvantage (poverty measured by various indicators) unemployment, population-adjusted rates of adult crime and juvenile delinquency, mental illness in adults and children, emergency admissions for psychiatric disorder, suicide and deliberate self-harm, numbers of children taken into care following neglect or abuse, family disruption, alcoholism and drug abuse, rates of unsolved crimes, high population density, household crowding, lack of environmental amenities, childhood injuries from 'accidents' including deaths and serious injuries as pedestrians and cyclists – all of these tended to co-occur within the same neighbourhoods to a degree which greatly exceeded chance expectation.

Moreover, while these are 'ecological correlations' (which puts limits on the kinds of statistical analyses that can be employed), further analysis of data for individuals showed that these indicators co-occur not merely in the same neighbourhood, but also in the same street, in the same multi-occupied dwelling, in the same family, and sometimes in the same individual. Adults who manifest one or more of these behaviours which the social order deems problematic, frequently have manifested or experienced 'negative' behaviours and conditions as children and adolescents (perhaps, in Willis' term "learning *not* to labour").

These 'zones of disadvantage' tended to be self-perpetuating and enduring from one generation to another unless there are major rehousing or community support policies. Even then, as in Exeter (Bagley, 1965) inhabitants from older slums were often rehoused into poor quality public housing projects. Local authority housing departments often exacerbate this process by further rehousing 'problem families' into particular streets on housing estates, which other families refuse to accept. The result, over time, is the evolution not merely of the 'sink estate', but also of the stigmatized street, and the 'mentally ill' tenement block. Schools serving these areas often struggle to deliver services to pupils who are ill-motivated to learn, including pupils whose behavioural maladaption reflects their disadvantaged and often disorganized home background.

An unanswered question is what causes the emergence of non-adaptive behaviours within neighbourhoods. Certainly, poor environment can elicit conduct and other behaviour disorders in neurologically vulnerable children who in better circumstances would not manifest negative disorders (Bagley, 1972; Bagley & Mallick, 2000).

Other factors which may cause rebellious behaviours (particularly crime) in zones of disadvantage, are structural: stress which results from living within crowded houses and neighbourhoods ill-served by local amenities – this was a major finding from the work in Brighton (Bagley et al., 1976). Another possible factor was the interaction of negative environmental factors, and the child's individual psychology. This possibility was demonstrated in a study of deaths and injuries which child pedestrians and cyclists experienced in Brighton, in replication of a Canadian study (Bagley, 1992, 1993a). Children in these "sub-zones" often have to cross busy roads to get to school and play spaces, and the overactive child becomes easy prey for the fast moving vehicle, whose speedy transit through the city takes precedence over child safety.

Identifying deprived neighbourhoods is an obvious basis for multiple-level interventions for community development, addressing both structural and individual problems. This was the basis for a programme initiated by the British government called National Strategy for Neighbourhood Renewal (Glass, 1999; ODPM, 2005; Eisenstadt, 2011), which aimed over 20 years to regenerate *all* of Britain's highly deprived local neighbourhoods (which constitute about ten per cent of all neighbourhoods identified at the enumeration district level). *Sure Start* programmes too were initiated on an area basis (Belsky & Melhuish, 2007; Eisenstadt, 2011) using census data to identify areas with populations potentially at risk. The neighbourhood regeneration programmes died with New Labour. *Sure Start* has taken a little longer to be discarded by central government (Sammons et al., 2015). An updated version of the section of this review chronicles the progress of Sure Start children's centres, and the resulting publication (Sawyerr & Bagley, 2017b) is contained in Appendix B of this book.

TWENTY NINE: THE TWO SCHOOLS EXPERIMENT IN EDUCATIONAL AND SOCIAL WORK INTERVENTION TO PREVENT SCHOOL EXCLUSIONS AND THE 'CYCLE OF POVERTY'

There is substantial evidence that schools which serve neighbourhoods with a high proportion of indicators of deprivation and social problems (poverty and unemployment; overcrowded and impermanent housing; child welfare interventions; high delinquency and crime rates; and rates of high rates of mental illness) have, on average significantly poorer achievement in their school students, and much higher rates of school exclusions than in schools in stable or prosperous neighbourhoods. Farrington's (1995) important British research concluded: "The whole process is self-perpetuating, in that poverty ... and early school failure lead to truancy and lack of educational qualifications, which in turn lead to low status jobs and periods of unemployment ... all of which make it harder to achieve goals legitimately."

The experiment described below was funded through the Home Office 'Safer Cities' programme, and aimed through focussing on schools, to reduce pupils' disruptive behaviour and expulsions, and to increase their motivation to achieve legitimate goals. In this the researchers attempted to replicate the experimental English work of Rose and Marshall (1975) which showed that social work interventions at the school level could have a strong role in reducing delinquency.

The experimental study (Bagley & Pritchard, 1998a, 1998b; Pritchard, 2001) selected two schools (linked primary and secondary serving some 1,300 children) in a city in southern England and matched them with two similar schools in another area of the city. In both experimental and control school settings there were similar levels of deprivation, with poverty rates of 60 per cent (judged by proportion of pupils receiving free school lunches). The neighbourhoods serving these two school areas had well above average proportions of social service interventions, and criminal convictions.

Inputs over three years in the experimental schools were an additional teacher in the primary school, a half-time additional teacher in the secondary school, and a project social worker who operated with families and children attending both primary and secondary schools. The additional teachers worked in both the areas of instruction and counselling, and also worked closely with the project social worker in co-ordinated strategies. The additional primary teacher worked intensively with children in the infant reception classes and with their families, trying to ensure that incipient problems of learning and behaviour could be addressed. In the secondary school the additional teacher focussed on both bullying and behavioural problems, seeking a variety of solutions to avoid the need for exclusion of disruptive students.

The social worker ensured that all families received maximum benefit from available income, support and social services, with the focus on preventing family disruption. Families of pupils whose under-performance in scholastic areas reflected their frequent absenteeism were engaged. Again, the focus was on helping the parents to emphasize the need for achieving educational goals by full attendance. Health education in the secondary school focussed on risky sexual behaviours, and drug use with a stress on long-term achievements rather than on short-term gratifications.

Evaluation consisted of self-report questionnaires and tests completed by pupils at the beginning and end of the three-year project. Similar measures were completed by pupils in the experimental and control primary and secondary schools (Bagley & Pritchard, 1998a). There was a highly significant fall in self-reported delinquency, fighting, experience of bullying, truanting and drug-use in the project schools, but the incidence of these events actually increased in the control schools. Positive attitudes to school increased significantly in the project schools, but there was no parallel increase in the control schools. In the project schools, for children's families there was a significant decline in problem behaviours, including movement of children into care, adult criminality, and unwanted pregnancies. Significantly fewer children from the project schools were excluded for any reasons.

A follow-up of children from the secondary schools to age 19 indicated that the positive effects of the school social work experiments were retained, with significantly fewer young people becoming pregnant, delinquent, leaving school early, or being unemployed. Careful estimates of the costs to the public purse of processing delinquents, supporting unmarried mothers, costs of keeping children in care, and maintaining older children in youth detention indicated that although initially expensive, the intensive social work and educational inputs had, over a five-year period *saved* the public purse £156,310 using the most conservative estimates of cost saving.

Generalising these figures to the country as a whole the researchers estimated that "at least a billion dollars" of public expenditure could be saved in the long-term nationally in Britain, by programming of this type through early interventions and the reordering of chaotic and wasted lives which were the lot of many of the pupils who graduated from the control secondary school (Bagley & Pritchard, 1998b). The elements of the programme are straightforward: additional teachers, social workers operating within schools, and focussing on referrals from teachers in order to help struggling families.

Somewhat similar figures were presented by the Scottish Executive (1997) with older adolescents and young adults, who pointed to the relatively low costs of "preventing reoffending" (including cognitive behavioural projects; social skills training; aggression reduction programmes; treatment of mental health and drug use conditions; and pre- and post-natal support and counselling).

Our own results have been substantially verified in a three-year study of seven British secondary schools by Webb and Vuillamy (2004). In this experiment a full-time, trained support worker was allocated to each school with the role of preventing exclusions of "difficult" children. As well as preventing many temporary exclusions, the experimental interventions were able to prevent 26 pupils from permanent exclusion, a 25 percent reduction across the seven schools.

Several studies of the costs and benefits of preventing school exclusions and associated disruptive behaviour provide substantive support for the cost-benefit analyses of Bagley and Pritchard (1998b). Scott and Knapp (2001) followed up 124 10-year children into adulthood, comparing children excluded from school for "antisocial disorder", and "normal controls". By young adulthood, *each* young person with conduct disorder had (in the absence of any special interventions) in 1998 prices cost the public purse £70,019 on average, in educational, psychiatric, social service costs.

In America Pelham, Foster and Robb (2007) provide an overview of 13 studies of children with attention deficit hyperactivity with varying levels of seriousness. From childhood to young adulthood the cost to the public purse for the average child in the study was $14,576 – implying a $42.5 billion cost for the country as a whole. These figures had an obvious implication – intervention services, even if successful with only some of the disruptive youth, could be hugely cost effective. Further American research also suggested that various programmes of youth mentoring could be highly cost-effective (DuBois & Karcher, 2005).

Brookes, Goodall and Heady (2007) in Britain provided estimates of the costs of both school exclusions and of truancy, since these two statuses often overlap – truancy often precedes forced exclusion from school, and also often stems from or continues after expulsions – being excluded from school simply adds to the alienation of the young person. The short-term cost (to age 18) of the persistently truanting and often excluded youth amounted, on average, to £63,851 per individual when costs of crime, social service interventions, and additional health needs as well as lost productivity due to examination and skill development failures were taken into account. 'Scaling up' these figures to the national level, these costs amounted to about £800 millions per annum. Brookes et al. (2007) estimate that there was a 124 percent return in the medium term, on initially expensive interventions, such as providing specialised workers in schools along the lines established by Bagley and Pritchard (1998a) and Webb et al. (2004).

RESET (2007), a consortium of employers funded by the EU Social Fund provided detailed figures on the annual costs of a young offender aged 15 to 17: £46,460 for the cost of the crimes, and their detection, they committed in one year; and £31,580 for the further costs of housing and processing each young offender – a total of £78,040. The annual costs of short custody with maximised resettlement programmes RESET put at £65,707. Even if these interventions by RESET in mid to late adolescence were successful with only half of the youth involved, the cost savings over the lifetime of *each* youth would amount to at least £100,000, depending on the type of services needed.

Waller (2009) a Canadian criminologist writing about Britain confirmed these figures, arguing that even only partially successful crime prevention strategies would save several billion pounds within a decade. Based on these figures, he advocated that five percent of the prison budget should be diverted into prevention and rehabilitation work.

THIRTY: COMPARISON OF THE EXPERIMENTAL SCHOOLS PROGRAMME AND SURE START INTERVENTIONS

It is pertinent to ask why the experimental work in schools had, apparently been so successful (Bagley & Pritchard, 1998a; Pritchard, 2001) and so cost-effective, and why *Sure Start*, aimed at preschoolers from deprived families, has in its initial stages at least, been relatively ineffective (Belsky & Melhuish, 2007). First of all, *Sure Start* may be underfunded, and could offer only limited support and counselling for families experiencing problems. Secondly, the Sure Start programme was not linked systematically to social work action, or the treatment of the family as a systemic reality, treating older as well as younger siblings who might have problems linked to their school, peer group and the wider community.

Thirdly there was only partial take-up of the parent support and education programmes offered by *Sure Start*. In contrast, the school-based project was able to access all pupils attending the focus primary and secondary schools, and operated within the legal framework of Acts governing the care of children, their regular attendance at school, and the consequences of their delinquent acts. In other words our programme was both comprehensive, and to a certain degree authoritarian as well as supportive.

That *Sure Start* might be spreading scarce economic resources too thinly comes from the various evaluation programmes, summarized in Appendix B. Significant numbers of parents of children with a high risk of developing conduct disorder might be missed, or required long-term, intensive follow-up. Thus Jones et al. (2008) in describing counselling and behavioural interventions for children with ADHD and developing conduct disorder, found that these interventions could only be partially successful – with 40 percent of the treated group continuing to be highly challenging for their families, environments and schooling. Coe et al. (2008) emphasized this too in their study of parents living in *Sure Start* areas who avoided enrolling their children, despite the service being free and non-threatening. Extremely disorganized families presumably need a more intensive type of contact and intervention. These issues are discussed in some detail in Appendix B, below, which examines the evaluations of the Sure Start programme (and its demise) up to 2016.

THIRTY ONE: NEW LABOUR GOVERNMENT INITIATIVES

Responding to the various demonstration projects described in the sections above, in December 2005 the New Labour government announced the *Early Help* programme (Brown, 2005). This aimed to create social work support for children and families in difficulty, using a school-based worker who would co-ordinate a range of services for referred families. Acknowledging that the current government had failed to meet its targets for the reduction in the amount of child and family poverty (Branigan, 2006), the British Prime Minister (Blair, 2006) stated that: "... We intervene too late. We spend without asking how effective is the spending. These are the children who are the clients of many agencies, but the charges of no-one, prey to drugs, into crime and anti-social behaviour, lacking in self-belief, lacking a basic stake in the society into which they are born ... It isn't right, and we can't afford it."

In March, 2006 the Prime Minister elect (Brown, 2006) presented a budget programme in which increased spending on education was a major part. Gordon Brown acknowledged the favourable effects of small classes and announced a five-year programme in which spending on education would be increased by £2.4 billions in order to reduce class sizes to those which pertained in private, fee-paying schools. By September, 2008 only £200,000 of this promised funding had been made, to ten areas with particularly poor outcomes in terms of achievements and staying in school to 16 and beyond (TeacherNet, 2008).

In 2006 the British government announced a £40 millions programme in London for individualised support for parents of primary and secondary school children who were persistently truanting from school, but announced in parallel that parents who failed to co-operate in programmes for helping children stay in school would be fined (Frean, 2006). For the school year 2006–2007, rates of truanting had risen by four percent to a record level (Garner, 2008b).

The success of the London schools programme was, apparently, indicated by enhanced GCSE results in the targeted schools, and in 2007 a similar £50 million programme was announced for Manchester (Ottewell, 2007). The need for such programmes in Manchester was underscored by figures which showed that the city's pupils, on average, lost 3.3 percent of class time because of truancy and exclusions, compared with a national average of 1.4 percent. In Manchester 3,300 children were "persistent truants" while another 21,500 were frequent or occasional truants (Qureshi, 2007). Manchester did employ some educational welfare officers, but it seemed that the way in which their activities were organized had done little to diminish truancy rates, particularly in areas marked by poor housing or urban decay.

These new expenditures were a fraction of other educational programmes abandoned by the New Labour government (Browne, 2007). A £55 billion programme of school building refurbishment which promised the production of 3,500 'good as new' schools by 2020 had almost certainly been abandoned, because of broad cutbacks in educational expenditures.

In the face of a marked growth in violent crime and social malaise involving young people, and the failure of its punitive justice system, the British government in July, 2008 announced a two-year programme of initiatives which would focus on at-risk youth (Sparrow, 2008). In doing so the national government appeared to have accepted the estimates of various researchers, that a young person who drops out of (or is excluded from) school in early adolescence will over his or her lifetime cost the state at least £100,000 in current costs because of illiteracy and innumeracy, lost employment, welfare dependency, lawless behaviour, court processing, poorer health, time spent in imprisonment, and the costs of servicing children of this group in the long-term.

The new programme which was designed following various experimental initiatives and cost-benefit analyses, aimed to "Develop a comprehensive and coordinated national package of short and long term policy options to tackle youth crime and disorder and its causes, in order to provide maximum protection to the public whilst providing appropriate support and assistance." The initiative would provide £250,000 for each local authority in England and Wales. Four social workers within each local authority would, across England identify about 30,000 very high risk young people. Diverting a 1,000 of this group into normal career pathways would, according to government, make the programmes highly cost-effective. The criteria for identification of these children in the early years of primary school were a diagnosis of Attention Deficit Hyperactivity Disorder (ADHD), inconsistent or abusive parenting within a dysfunctional family, and scholastic failure in both primary and secondary school, with frequent absenteeism from school, and disruption when in school.

Our reservations in 2008 were that this programme did not specify funds for keeping families together, and preventing the often disastrous option of children coming into care; nor did it specify any funding for individualized tuition to overcome problems of literacy and numeracy which may be associated with the subtle neurological pictures which underlie ADHD.

Presumably this new programme was to run in parallel to *Sure Start*. The need for this multi-level intervention comes from work by the *Sure Start* team on a parallel cohort of 2,857 children followed up to age 11 (Melhuish et al., 2008). This showed that the combination of child's placement in high quality preschool together with parental support for learning was associated with significantly higher achievement in tests at ages 10 to 11. But children born with low birth weight, developmental delay in the first three years of life, and with mothers with minimal educational achievement were unlikely to make such gains.

The British Prime Minister had further promised a programme of "individual tuition" to the 300,000 or more pupils who were struggling with literacy and numeracy – but by the end of the school year in 2008, only 3,438 pupils had received such help with mathematics, and 3,514 with English (Paton, 2008b). There was no prospect for any increase in these numbers, and the government programme for enrolling some 300,000 struggling pupils seemed, like so many other governmental proposals, destined to fail because of lack of funding, in the face of the world economic crisis.

A recurring theme in the literature reviewed has been the negative impact of income inequality in Britain which is much greater than that in most other developed nations. This inequality is both enduring, and difficult to change through existing policy interventions and fiscal interventions. Recognising this, the Cabinet Office (2008) had launched a programme called *Getting Ahead*, which aimed to capitalize on trends which showed that inequalities in Britain might finally be narrowing. Important case studies of schools which were relatively successful in boosting academic performance in white, working class youth were analysed by Mongon & Chapman (2008). There was, concluded these authors "no silver bullet" for success, although an inspirational and determined head teacher who linked with agencies for neighbourhood improvement could be of key importance.

In January, 2009 the New Labour government announced a range of measures aimed at enabling teenagers (including teenaged mothers) to enter the world of work, with the aim of breaking intergenerational cycles of disadvantage (Bennett & Bahra, 2009). These included the promise of £57 millions to extend the amount of free childcare for disadvantaged 2-year olds; a dedicated nurse for each pregnant women deemed to be at risk; 35,000 new apprenticeships for youth who might otherwise drop out of education and training; special university access courses for disadvantaged youth; £10,000 "golden handcuffs" to keep (or recruit) successful teachers into "difficult" schools in marginal areas; and a new *Narrowing the Gaps* programme, in which £400 millions was promised for allocation to increasing the achievements of white, working class boys, those most likely to fail at the GCSE stage, with prior or subsequent school drop-out (Curtis, 2008e; Morgan, 2009).

Whether these measures would actually be initiated in a climate of fiscal confusion, and would go any way to reducing the profound lack of social mobility and the persistence of social class disadvantage remained to be seen. In considering the evaluation these programmes we should take note of the government warning that "schools must plan for an austere future" (Paton, 2009a). At a time of tight budgets, government funding for new social and educational supports might be operating in a "zero sum" climate, in which money for new programmes had to be obtained at the expense of reducing government spending elsewhere. In the April 2009 budget statement, the Chancellor of the Exchequer announced many programme cuts, but promised to retain education and training programmes for those less than age 25 who had been unemployed for at least a year. However, the New Labour government did not survive the subsequent general election, and few if any of these plans were effected. Subsequent governments (Coalition, and Conservative) have not initiated new programmes of social regeneration, or of help for disadvantaged families and universities. "They asked for bread, and they were given Brexit."

THIRTY TWO: CONCLUSIONS: EDUCATIONAL FAILURE, POVERTY, CHILD WELFARE AND SCHOOL EXCLUSIONS IN BRITAIN

This review of trends up to the fiscal year 2008–2009, has documented the chronic crisis in British education from the highest to the lowest levels. Universities faced a crisis of under-funding, secondary schools failed to prepare disadvantaged pupils for occupational achievement, and infant and primary school classes were too large for fully effective teaching, as were classes in many state secondary schools. Teacher morale was low, and classes were getting larger. In such contexts alienated pupils and those with special needs (including children from the care system) were ignored, bullied, suspended or expelled. This lack of positive educational policies was a feature of an extremely wealthy country, but in one in which incomes and resources were unequally distributed, with degrees of inequality which were much greater than in many countries with similar or lesser sources of national wealth. Income inequalities, rather than national income as such strongly predict child morbidity and mortality in international comparisons (Wilkinson & Pickett, 2009).

The ecological dimension of unequal schooling meant that poor quality schools, both primary and secondary often served deprived areas marked by very high levels of poverty, infant mortality and morbidity, poor housing, unemployment, delinquency and adult criminality, and mental health problems. Schools in these areas struggled not only with a high proportion of disaffected and underachieving pupils, but also experienced a poverty of resources and a high turnover of teachers who found working in such schools particularly difficult. This in turn led to chronically larger classes than the 30 pupils per class, required by government policy.

British research indicated that even relatively small reductions in school classes could be reflected in a significant enhancement in reading abilities. American research clearly showed that halving class sizes in primary schools in the early years (to between 15 to 18 pupils per class) resulted in significant and enduring scholastic gains, better behaviour and motivation, better self-concept, less school drop-out, and greater college attendance. The reasons for these improvements seem to be that teachers of small classes in the early years are able to focus more readily on the individual learning, behavioural and social needs of their pupils. Although halving class sizes in the age group 5 to 8 years is expensive, these expenditures are highly cost-effective in the medium-term.

It is not surprising that pupils in Britain's overcrowded classrooms perform on average, rather poorly on internationally standardized tests of ability, and clearly below the level expected of a nation with Britain's national wealth. Inequalities of income make these problems worse, and children from the poorest families attending the poorest schools are also likely to experience significantly higher rates of illness and premature death (from infections, accidents, and incidents of abuse), child neglect, delinquency, underachievement, and school exclusions. Economic and social disadvantage in Britain was often transmitted between generations, and upward mobility rates were low compared with several other countries. In other words, being born into a disadvantaged social class tended to be a deterministic status.

A review of experimental programmes to prevent school exclusions and to improve the welfare of families and children from poverty neighbourhoods showed that despite their initial expense, these programmes could be highly cost effective in preventing children moving into a cycle of family poverty in which their own children were neglected, demotivated, marked down for careers of petty crime, unemployment, and drug-taking. Thus, vigorous interventions which are school-based and family-oriented could be successful in breaking the deterministic patterns of being born into a disadvantaged family in an underprivileged neighbourhood.

This was the dilemma of social policy of Britain. A rich nation could afford to vastly improve the quality of education and the welfare of families and children. Far from being expensive this would actually be cost-productive in the medium to long-term, saving the public purse many millions of pounds. But governments seemed reluctant to make major social investments whose return might not yield measurable returns within the normal life of a parliamentary five year term.

Projects such as *Sure Start*, and the urban regeneration programme might well succeed as long-term programmes, but they were nevertheless inadequately funded. There were some grounds for optimism with regard to new initiatives which would target disadvantaged children at the school level, and new developments which promise to reduce class sizes in all schools. Nevertheless, the fiscal year 2008–2009, the endpoint of this policy review was the beginning of a period of fiscal crisis in the world economy, and as we now know, the ending of New Labour's attempts to intervene on behalf of the most disadvantaged groups. Writing in 2017, we can only conclude that the situation of children and youth from economically deprived families has become worse, rather than better. Capital rules, and the poor (and their children) stay poor.

Nevertheless, Britain could still learn lessons on social policy initiatives on behalf of children from countries such as Sweden, The Netherlands, Finland, Norway and Denmark which are marked by much lower levels of income inequality, higher rates of upward social mobility, far fewer pockets of extreme poverty, and school systems which are well-funded and not constrained by the burden of continuous examinations. Unfortunately, as Wilkinson and Pickett (2009) argue, unequal societies such as Britain reflect a set of values which are not socially cohesive, and which do not support ideas of movement towards better health, family stability and educational achievement for the poorest groups of society. Their data suggests that class divisions are deeply rooted in British social structure, and will be difficult to change in the direction of a more equal society, with diminished degrees of child and family poverty.

Finally, we have argued that in an age of financial austerity, preventive programs whose efficacy has proven, cost-benefit efficiency in both the long and the short-term, and which increase the life chances of the poorest children and adolescents should not be sacrificed in an era of increasing unemployment and cutbacks.

This review considered policies up to the end of the fiscal year 2008–2009. Since that time the effects of the cutbacks in funding of education, health and welfare imposed by Coalition and Conservative governments are having their expected consequences. Almost all of the educational and social disadvantages suffered by the most disadvantaged sectors of Britain's population have become worse. An illustration of this is the underfunding and closing of many of the Sure Start children's centres, documented in Appendix B.

In education, major reductions in government funding will amount to cuts of £3 billion by 2019. Previous cuts since 2012 had meant that by 2017–2018 a half of all class sizes secondary schools would increase in size, many to 35 or more. There are cuts too in Special Needs educational support, and in the hiring of teachers for "esoteric" subjects such as drama, music and foreign languages (Pellis, 2017). Parallel reductions in income and housing benefits for individuals of working age of £46 billion in the next four years (2017 to 2020) would mean a significant increase in numbers who fall into officially defined poverty (Cowburn, 2017).

In health care between 2012 and 2017, £50 million had been cut from children's mental health service budgets in Britain despite an increasing demand for such services; and £200 million had been cut from public health funding. A further 0.6% cut in government funding for the National Health Service would occur in the financial year 2018–2019 (Stone, 2017). A report published by the Royal College of Paediatrics and Child Health (RCPCH, 2017) gives a series of international comparisons for childhood illnesses and death rates, and shows that health inequalities outlined in the OECD and other reports summarized earlier in this review, have either prevailed, or become worse (Boseley, 2017). In 2015 there was a significant increase in premature mortalities, attributable after a range of factors was controlled for in international comparisons, to UK cutbacks in health funding (Hiam et al., 2017). The "spike" in premature deaths (most notable in the elderly) was the greatest year-on-year experienced since 1965.

Compared with 2010, in 2017 the number of children in families living below the officially defined poverty level in Britain had increased by at least 100,000. Given fiscal and welfare benefit changes, this number was expected to increase by 10 percent, by 2020 (Emberg-Dennis, 2017). Another estimate suggested that numbers of children in very poor families would increase by 200,000, by 2020 (Burns, 2017). Summing up the effects of these various funding cuts in the face of increasing needs of vulnerable children and young people for better schools and social and health services, Ryan (2017) observed that "the child social care system is quietly being dismantled". The situation for abused children, children in care, children with psychiatric problems, children challenged by learning tasks within the context of poor schools, children in poverty-level families, has since 2009, become much worse.

Inequality in health, education and welfare in Britain continues to have a profoundly negative impact on the lives of the poorest families and children, and year by year their situation becomes worse, rather than better.

THIRTY THREE: A MARXIAN POSTSCRIPT

An examination of the maps of Manchester included in Engel's account of "the condition of the working class in England" shows that a number of the areas of extreme stress and poverty identified in 1845 remain areas of poverty, stress and the alienation of youth – although there are now new "overspill" estates in Wythenshawe and Handforth to the south of Manchester, in which problems of poverty and delinquency have been transported, and inherited.

We have argued in this review that Britain remains a society deeply divided by social class privilege on the one hand, and continued poverty on the other. The deprivations of the poorest fifth of the nation are associated with high rates of morbidity, mortality, inferior education, reduced life chances, delinquency, and alienation from school, learning and employment. Engels (1845, 1978) argued that the continued deprivation of working people resulted in primitive rebellions of crime, and self-destructive actions such is alcoholism and violence within the ghettoized areas to which the working classes were assigned. What has changed? Today poverty is relative rather than absolute; yet outcomes are often similar to those described by Engels.

Our task, we submit, is to raise the consciousness of working class youth, and to stimulate their energies in ways which both foster their educational commitment and their upward mobility in order to finally "unmask" the alienation which besets their lives. The goal is not the Marxist one of overthrowing the class system; rather we should seek to raise *all* citizens to the status of the highest classes, maximizing the citizen's freedom as well as their fulfillment. In this we follow T.H. Green's model of an ideal society (Greengarten, 1981) in which every citizen, free of want, is raised to through the process which Archer (2007) calls "social mobility" to the status of equality with the bourgeoisie: this is the critical realist, Marxian solution to inequality, rather than the Marxist one of "dictatorship of the proletariat".

Finally, it is clear from this review that the majority of "the permanent underclass" of Britain are "white", traditional proletariat of English, Scots, Welsh and Irish origin. This is much easier group for the ruling classes to control on a permanent basis, as the useful 'reserve army of labour'.

Ethnic minorities are, for the ruling classes, potentially dangerous for they can organize themselves on *cultural* lines, as radical intellectuals who pose a danger to the forces of establishment. A case in point are African Caribbean settlers in Britain, who with their white partners (fellow scholars, fellow professionals, fellow Artisans) have exposed the outrages of racist educational and social policies, such as the false-labelling of Black children as "Educationally Subnormal", and the invention of deviance which results in Black adolescents being disproportionately excluded from school (Pearson, 2009). Once this kind of crude institutional racism is identified, exposed, and debated it slips away. Tomorrow all Black and Asian-Heritage people in Britain will be artisans, craftspeople, entrepreneurs, artists, professionals, politicians. They are upwardly mobile because that is the path that most immigrants and their children have created for themselves.

Many of "the poor whites" and their children, and their children, and their children, are likely to remain poor whites because that is how British society is structured. Fenetke (2009) writes angrily about the new racism of Islamophobia: but the irrationalities of such prejudice and the biased actions which result are easy to expose. In the span of one generation ten percent of the British population will be Muslim: they too may be upwardly mobile, and their employees will be the poor whites lucky enough to be employed. The best option for Britain's ruling economic class seems to be to co-opt ethnic minorities into their ranks, so that the functional practice of maintaining the poor in poverty can proceed, unhindered.

This detailed overview of inequality in British social structure, and in particular inequality in its educational achievements and social care provision, offers we hope, valuable information on an important period in modern British history. As Atkinson (2015). has asserted, any diagnosis of inequality with constructive proposals for its ending, must "learn from history".

NOTES

[1]   This is a revised and updated version of a paper which appeared on the web site of The Manchester Educational Research Network in 2008.

[2]   In a 'back to the future' footnote: Stahl (2015) reports that 333,000 pupils were 'temporally' excluded in the year 2010–2011.

³ In an era where most gains in employment were at the minimum wage level, by 2017 the goals proposed by Wanless seem more remote than ever. For updates see the Rowntree Trust website at: www.jrct.org.uk

⁴ For an interesting overview of Blatchford's findings, in the context of cross-cultural comparisons see Blatchford and Chan (2016).

REFERENCES

Abbott, A. (1999). *Department and discipline: Chicago sociology at one hundred.* Chicago, IL: University of Chicago Press.

Abisgold, C. (2008). *Supporting pupils with dyslexia.* Retrieved from www.schoolzone.co.uk

Achilles, C. (1996). *Summary of recent class-size research with an emphasis on Tennessee STAR and derivative research studies.* Nashville, TN: Tennessee State University, Centre of Excellence for Research Policy on Basic Skills.

Achilles, C. (1997). Small classes, big possibilities. *The School Administrator, 54*, 6–15.

Achilles, C. (1999). *Let's put kids first, finally: Getting class size right.* Thousand Oaks, CA: Corwin Press.

Adam, S. (2007). *The UK tax system.* London: Institute of Fiscal Studies.

Adam, S., Brewer, M., & Shepherd, A. (2006). *The poverty trade-off: Work incentives and income redistribution in Britain.* Bristol: The Policy Press.

Aitken, S. (2001). *The geography of young people: Morally contested spaces of identity.* New York, NY: Wiley.

Al-Refai, N., & Bagley, C. (2008). *Citizenship education: The British Muslim perspective.* Rotterdam, The Netherlands: Sense Educational Books.

Alderson, P. (2013, 2016). *The politics of childhoods real and imagined: Practical application of critical realism and childhood studies, volumes I and II.* Abingdon: Routledge.

Allen, R., & West, A. (2008). *Religious schools in London: School admissions, religious composition and selectivity.* London: Institute of Education, University of London.

Allhusen, V., & 28 Others. (2004). Does class size in the first grade relate to child's academic and social performance and observed classroom procedures? *Developmental Psychology, 40*, 651–664.

Ansari, D., Fugelsang, J., Dhital, B., & Ventatramen, V. (2006). Dissociating response conflict from numerical magnitude processing in the brain: An event-related fMRI study. *Neuroimage, 15*, 799–805.

Archer, M. A. (2007). *Making our way through the world: Human reflexivity and social mobility.* Abingdon: Routledge.

Atkinson, T. (2015). *Inequality: What can be done?* Boston, MA: Harvard University Press.

Avineri, S. (1970). *The social and political thought of Karl Marx.* Cambridge: University of Cambridge Press.

Avis, M., Buchanan, D., & Leighton, P. (2007). Factors affecting participation in Sure Start programmes: A qualitative investigation of parents' views. *Health, Social Care and Community, 15*, 203–211.

Aynsley-Green, A. (2006). *Report on educational services for autistic children.* London: Office of the Children's Commissioner for England.

Aynsley-Green, A. (2007, February 14). Comment on the UNICEF report on child poverty. *BBC Newsnight.*

Bagley, C. (1965/1972). Juvenile delinquency in Exeter: An ecological and comparative study. *Urban Studies, 2*, 39–50. (London: Longman. Reprinted from J. Mays (Ed.) *Juvenile delinquency, the family and the social group.*)

Bagley, C. (1984). Urban delinquency: Ecological and educational perspectives. In T. Freeman (Ed.), *Mental health and the environment* (pp. 204–259). London: Churchill-Livingston.

Bagley, C. (1989). Urban crowding and the murder rate in Bombay, India. *Perceptual and Motor Skills, 69*, 241–1242.

Bagley, C. (1992). The urban environment and child pedestrian and bicycle injuries: Interaction of ecological and personality characteristics. *Journal of Community and Applied Social Psychology, 2*, 1–9.

Bagley, C. (1993a). The urban setting of juvenile pedestrian injuries: A study of behavioral ecology and social disadvantage. *Accident Analysis and Prevention, 24*, 673–678.

Bagley, C. (1993b). Transracial adoption of aboriginal children in Canada: A disturbing case study. In C. Bagley (Ed.) *International and transracial adoptions: A mental health perspective.* Aldershot: Ashgate.

Bagley, C. (2002). *Child abusers: Research and therapy.* Miami, FL: Universal Publishers.

Bagley, C. (2008a). An end to apartheid? The oppression and educational inclusion of India's Dalits. In C. Bagley & G. Verma (Eds.) *Challenges for inclusion: Educational and social studies from Britain and the Indian sub-continent.* Rotterdam, The Netherlands: Sense Educational Publishers.

Bagley, C. (2008b). The logic and morality of educational inclusion. In C. Bagley & G. Verma (Eds.), *Challenges for inclusion: Educational and Social Studies in Britain and the Indian sub-continent.* Rotterdam, The Netherlands: Sense Educational Publishers.

Bagley, C. (2008c). The educational and social inclusion of disadvantaged children in Britain. In C. Bagley & G. Verma (Eds.) *Challenges for inclusion: Educational and social studies in Britain and the Indian sub-continent.* Rotterdam: Sense Educational Publishers.

Bagley, C., & D'Augelli, A. (2000). Gay, lesbian and bisexual youth have elevated rates of suicidal behaviour: An international problem associated with homophobic legislation. *British Medical Journal, 321*, 767–768.

Bagley, C., Jacobson, S., & Palmer, C. (1973). Social structure and the ecological distribution of mental illness, suicide and delinquency. *Psychological Medicine, 3*, 177–187.

Bagley, C., & Jacobson, S. (1976). The ecological variation of three types of suicide. *Psychological Medicine, 6,* 429–438.

Bagley, C., & King, K. (2003). *Child sexual abuse: The search for healing.* London & New York, NY: Taylor and Francis.

Bagley, C., & Mallick, K. (2000). Spiralling up and spiralling down: Implications of a long-term study of temperament and conduct disorder for social work with children. *Child and Family Social Work, 5,* 291–301.

Bagley, C., & Pritchard, C. (1998a). The reduction of problem behaviours and school exclusion in at-risk youth: An experimental study of school social work with cost-benefit analyses. *Child and Family Social Work, 3,* 219–226.

Bagley, C., & Pritchard, C. (1998b). The billion dollar cost of troubled youth: Prospects for cost-effective prevention and treatment. *International Journal of Adolescent and Youth, 7,* 211–225.

Bagley, C., & Verma, G. (1979). *Racial prejudice, the individual and society.* Aldershot: Ashgate.

Bagley, C., Verma, G., Mallick, K., & Young, L. (1979). *Personality, self-esteem and prejudice.* Aldershot: Ashgate.

Bagley, C., Young, L., & Scully, A. (1993). A follow-up of adopted children in the national child development study. In C. Bagley (Ed.) *International and transracial adoptions: A mental health perspective.* Aldershot: Ashgate.

Baker, D., Taylor, H., & Henderson, J. (1998). Inequality in infant morbidity: Causes and consequences in England in the 1990s. *Journal of Epidemiology and Community Health, 52,* 451–458.

Ballard, A. (2008, September 3). Inaugural address to association of teachers and lecturers. *Party and Policy Communications.* Retrieved fromwww.epolitix.com

Barnes, J., Belsky, J., Broomfield, K., Dave, S., Frost, M., & Melhuish, E. (2005). Disadvantaged but different: Variation among deprived communities in relation to child and family well-being. *Journal of Child Psychology and Psychiatry, 40,* 952–962.

Barnett, W. S., & Hustedt, J. J. (2005). Head start's lasting benefits. *Infants and Young Children, 18,* 16–24.

Barker, I. (2008, September 26). Asbestos rules land Head in court. *Times Educational Supplement Online.*

Batmangheldjh, C. (2007, February 6). This mindless shooting is a direct result of our failure (Editorial). *The Guardian Online.*

Bartholomew, J. (2009, April 11). Home schooling: A vision of the future. *The Telegraph Online.*

BBC. (2005, April 25). US prison rate soars even higher. *BBC Online.*

Bell, M. (2002). *Understanding English spelling.* Cambridge: Pegasus Elliot MacKenzie.

Bell, M. (2004). *Learning to read.* Cambridge: Pegasus Elliott MacKenzie.

Bell, M. (2008, June 7). *The most costly English spellings.* Paper given to Literacy Conference, Coventry University, England.

Belsky, J., & Melhuish, E. (2007). Impact of sure start local programmes on children and families. In J. Belsky, J. Barnes, & E. Malhuish (Eds.), *The national evaluation of sure start: Does area-based early intervention work?* Bristol: The Policy Press.

Bennett, R. (2005, February 25). Labour 'failed poorest children'. *The Times Online*.

Bennett, R. (2006, October 10). Foster children to gain right to stay in care until 21. *The Times Online*.

Bennett, R. (2008, May 29). Fostering a little more care. *The Times Online*.

Bekhradnia, B. (2006). *Demand for higher education to 2020*. Oxford: Higher Education Policy Unit.

Belsky, J., Melhuish, E., Barnes, J., Leyland, A., & Romaniuk, H. (2006). Effects of Sure Start local programmes on children and families: Early findings from a quasi-experimental, cross-sectional study. *British Medical Journal, 332*, 1476.

Bennett, R. (2006, October 10). Foster children to gain the right to stay in care until 21. *The Times Online*.

Beveridge, W. (1968). *Social insurance and allied services, 1942*. London: Her Majesty's Stationery Office.

Bhaskar, R. A. (1992/2008). *Dialectic: The pulse of freedom*. Abingdon: Routledge.

Bignell, P. (2006, December 12). Millions can't read well enough for karaoke. *The Independent Online*.

Blair, A. (2004, July 21). Violence leads to exclusion of 17,000 pupils in one term. *The Times Online*.

Blair, A. (2006a, June 12). 1,500 schools are left headless and adrift. *The Times Online*.

Blair, A. (2006b, October 19). Poor put off college by fee rise. *The Times Online*.

Blair, A. (2007, February 1). More schools fail to make the grade. *The Times Online*.

Blair, P., Sidebotham, P., Berry, P., Evans, M., & Fleming, P. (2006). Major epidemiological changes in sudden infant death syndrome: A 20-year population-based study in the United Kingdom. *The Lancet, 218*, 314–319.

Blair, T. (2006, February 25). Speech reported. *Daily Telegraph Online*.

Blanden, J., & Gregg, P. (2004). Family income and educational attainment: A review of approaches and evidence for Britain. *Oxford Review of Economic Policy, 2*, 245–263.

Blanden, J., Gregg, P., & Macmillan, L. (2007). Accounting for intergenerational income persistence: Non-cognitive skills, ability and education. *Economic Journal, 117*, 43–60.

Blanden, J., & Machin, S. (2004a). Educational inequality and the expansion of UK higher education. *Scottish Journal of Political Economy, 51*, 230–249.

Blanden, J., & Machin, S. (2004b). *Recent changes in Intergenerational mobility in the United Kingdom*. London: The Sutton Trust.

Blanden, J., Gregg, P., & Machin, S. (2005). *Intergenerational mobility in Europe and North America*. London: Centre for Economic Performance, University College, University of London.

Blatchford, P. (2003). *The class size debate: Is smaller better?* Maidenhead: Open University Press.

Blatchford, P., Edmonds, S., & Martin, C. (2003). Class size, pupil attentiveness and peer relations. *British Journal of Educational Psychology, 73*, 15–36.

Blatchford, P., & Chan, K. (Eds.). (2016). *Class size: Eastern and western perspectives.* London: Routledge.

BMA. (1999). *Growing up in Britain: Ensuring a health future for our children.* London: British Medical Association.

BMA. (2006). *Child and adolescent mental health – A guideline for health professionals.* London: British Medical Association.

Boateng, P. (2000). Foreword. *Policy action team national strategy for neighbourhood renewal.* London: HMSO.

Booth, J. (2008a, October 22). UK still one of the world's most unequal societies. *The Guardian Online.*

Booth, J. (2008b, June 10). Child poverty rises for second year in a row. *Times Online.*

Booth, T., & Ainscow, M. (2002). *Index for inclusion: Developing learning and participation in schools.* Bristol: Centre for Studies on Inclusive Education.

Bosely, S. (2017, January 25). Child health in jeopardy, landmark report warns. *The Guardian Online.*

Bowcott, O. (2008a, September 22). Jail rates of under-fourteens among Europe's highest. *The Guardian Online.*

Bowcott, O. (2008b, December 14). UN report criticises Britain's 'demonizing' and jailing of children. *The Guardian Online.*

Branigan, T. (2006, March 19). Labour checks Britain's widening poverty gap. *Guardian.*

Bradshaw, J., & Chen, J.-R. (2002). *Poverty in the UK: A comparison with nineteen other countries.* York: Social Policy Research Unit, University of York.

Bradshaw, J., & Lynes, T. (2009, May 15). Benefit negligence. *The Guardian Online.*

Brewer, M., & Gregg, P. (2003). *The welfare we want? The British challenge for American Reform.* Bristol: The Policy Press.

Brewer, M., Goodman, A., Shaw, J., & Shepherd, A. (2005). *Poverty and inequality in Britain 2005.* London: The Institute of Fiscal Studies.

Brewer, M., Browne, J., Joyce, R., & Sutherland, H. (2009). *Ending child poverty in a Changing Economy.* London: Institute of Fiscal Studies.

Brighouse, T. (2004). *Policy Statement.* London: Office of The Commissioner for London Schools.

Brogi, L., & Bagley, C. (1998). Abusing victims: Detention of child sexual abuse victims in secure accommodation. *Child Abuse Review, 7,* 315–329.

Brookes, M., Goodall, E., & Heady, L. (2007). *Misspent youth: The costs of Truancy and Exclusion.* London: New Philanthropy Capital.

Brown, G. (2005, December 6). The Chancellor's prebudget speech in full. *The Times Online.*

Brown, G. (2006, March 22). The Chancellor's prebudget speech. *The Times Online.*

Browne, A. (2006, December 12). New Deal not working for youth. *The Times Online.*

Browne, A. (2008, January 15). Pupils kept in crumbling classrooms by red tape. *Times Online.*

Buie, E. (2009, January 23). Schools close, but no more new ones. *The Times Educational Supplement Online.*

Burches, D. (2008). *A comparative study in mathematics teachers' training.* Plymouth: Centre for Innovation in Mathematics Teaching.

Burns, J. (2017, April 3). Benefit changes 'could push 200,000 children into poverty. *BBC News Online.*

Cabinet Office. (2006). *Policy review: Crime, justice and social cohesion.* London: Cabinet Office, Prime Minister's Strategy Unit.

Cabinet Office. (2008). *Getting on, setting ahead.* London: Cabinet Office, Prime Minister's Strategy Unit.

CAFCASS. (2009). *Care statistics continue to rise* (Press Release). London: Child and Family Court Advisory Support Service.

Cambell, D., & Travis, A. (2007, March 31). UK headed for prison meltdown. *The Guardian Online.*

Cameron, C., & Moss, P. (2011). *Social pedagogy: Working with children and young people.* London: Jessica Kingsley.

Carter, H. (2005, March 12), Third of children in north-west live in poverty. *The Guardian Online.*

Cassen, R., & Kingdon, G. (2007). *Disadvantage and GCSE achievements.* York: The Rowntree Foundation.

Cassidy, S. (2005, November 30). University entrance getting more difficult for poor pupils. *Independent Online.*

Cassidy, S. (2008, Septemer 19). Half of maths lessons 'not good enough'. *The Independent Online.*

CBI. (2004). *Educational standards of British school-leavers.* London: Confederation of British Industry.

CBI. (2008). *The Costs of Unemployed Teenagers.* London: Confederation of British Industry.

Craig, G. (2007). *Sure Start and Black and minority populations.* London: Department for Children, Schools and Families.

Craig, G. (2009). *Institutional ris still alive and hriving in Britain.* Hull: Centre for Social Justice and Social Inclusion, University of Hull.

CSJ. (2006). *Breakdown in Britain.* London: Centre for Social Justice.

Chapman, J. (2007, June 20). Scots to cut class sizes. *Daily Mail Online.*

Chevalier, A., & Dolton, P. (2004). *Teacher shortage: Another impending crisis?* London: London School of Economics, Centre for Economic Performance.

Clark, L. (2008a, March 7). Ed Balls: Parents denied 'fair choice' because 1 in 5 secondary schools is failing. *The Daily Mail Online.*

Clark, L. (2008b, June 20). Not in education or training, the 189,000 teenagers who are idle on benefits. *The Daily Mail Online.*

Clarke, N. (2007, January 8). Special educational needs. *The Guardian Online.*

CLPE. (2004). *Boys on the margin.* London: Centre for Literacy in Primary Education.

Coe, C., Gibson, A., Spencer, N., & Stuttaford, M. (2008). Sure Start: Voices of the 'hard-to-reach'. *Child Care Health and Development, 34,* 447–453.

Collier, A. (2002). Dialectic in Marxism and critical realism. In A. Brown (Ed.), *Critical realism and Marxism*. Abingdon: Routledge.

Collison, D., Dey, C., Hannah, G., & Stevenson, L. (2007). Income inequality and child mortality in wealthy nations. *Journal of Public Health, 13*, 1093 (March, preprint).

Commons Education and Skills Select Committee. (2006). *Report on special education*. London: The House of Commons.

Cowburn, A. (2017, April 2). Spending freeze to cut extra £46 bn from benefits as raft of new benefit cuts kick in. *The Independent Online*.

CRAE. (2007). *State of children's rights in England*. London: Children's Rights Alliance for England.

Cridland, J. (2008, October 2). Statement of research carried out by the confederation of British industries. *The Telegraph Online*.

Croxford, L., & Raffe, D. (2007). Young people's experience of compulsory schooling in England and Scotland during two decades of educational reforms. In G. Bhatti (Ed.), *Social justice and intercultural education: An open-ended Dialogue*. Stoke: Trentham Books.

Currie, C., Gablainn, S., Godeau, G., Roberts, C., Smith, R., Currie, D, Pickett, W., Richter, M., Morgan, A., & Barnekow, B. (2008). *Inequalities in young people's health: Health behaviour in school-aged children – International Report from the 2005–2006 Survey*. Copenhagen: WHO Regional Office; and Edinburgh: Adolescent Health Research Unit, University of Edinburgh. Retrieved from www.euro.who.int/Document/E91416.pdf

Currie, J., & Thomas, D. (1993). *Does head start make a difference?* Cambridge, MA: National Bureau of Economic Research.

Curtis, A., Power, S., Whitley, G., Exley, S., & Sasia, A. (2008). *Primed for success: The characteristics and practices of state schools with good track records of entry into prestigious United Kingdom universities*. London: The Institute of Education, University of London, and The Sutton Trust.

Curtis, P. (2004, December 7). Best schools are in Finland and the far east. *The Guardian Online*.

Curtis, P. (2008a, June 30). Physics teachers dying out in some state schools. *The Guardian Online*.

Curtis, P. (2008b, August 8). Rich-poor education gap wider under Labour, claim Tories. *The Guardian Online*.

Curtis, P. (2008c, February 8). State schools shunned from home education. *The Guardian Online*.

Curtis, P. (2008d, December 12). Million poor pupils denied free meals. *The Guardian Online*.

Curtis, P. (2008e, Decmber 11). White working class boys among worst achievers. *The Guardian Online*.

Dale, R., Esland, G., & MacDonald, M. (Eds.). (1976). *Schooling and capitalism: A sociological reader*. London: Routledge.

Dawson, R. (2008, July 3). Poor state of schools is getting desperate. *Stockport Times West.*

DfES. (2004a). *Statistical profile of school exclusions.* London: Department for Education and Skills.

DfES. (2004b). *Building schools for the future.* London: Department for Education and Skills.

DfES. (2006). *Looked-after children the struggle for stability.* London: Department for Education and Skills.

De Vogli, R., Mistry, R., Gnesetto, R., & Cornia, G. (2005). Has the relation between income inequality and life expectancy disappeared? Evidence for Italy and top industrialised counties. *Journal of Epidemiology and Community Health, 59,* 158–162.

DoH. (1998). *A wealthier nation.* London: HMSO for The Department of Health.

Dorling, D. (2007). *Poverty, wealth and place in Britain, 1968–2005.* York: The Rowntree Foundation.

DuBois, D., & Kercher, M. (2005). *Handbook of youth mentoring.* London: Sage Publications.

Dustman, C., Rajah, N., & Van Soest, A. (2002). *Class size, education and wages.* London: Institute of Fiscal Studies.

Dutton, E., Warhurst, C., & Fairley, J. (2005). *New Britain – Old politics: Devolved post-16 education and training.* Glasgow: University of Strathclyde, Department of Human Resource Management.

Dyer, O. (2005). Gap in life expectancy between classes narrows, but disparity in disease-free years remains. *British Medical Journal, 330,* 498.

Dyson, A. (2001). Special needs in the twenty-first century: Where we've been and where we're going. *British Journal of Special Education, 28,* 24–29.

ECS. (2002). *Reading one-to-one.* Denver, CO: Education Commission of The States. Retrieved from www.ecs.org/clearinghouse/18/90/1890.htm

Education Guardian. (2004). Rise in school class sizes. *The Guardian Online.*

Edwards, P., Roberts, J., Green, J., & Lutchman, S. (2006). Deaths from injury in children, and employment status in family: Analysis of trends in class specific death rates. *British Medial Journal, 333,* 119.

Edwards, P., Green, J., Lachowycz, K., Grundy, C., & Roberts, I. (2008). Serious injuries in children: Variation by area deprivation and settlement type. *Archives of Diseases in Childhood, 93,* 485–489.

Edwards, R., Ceillachair, A., Bywater, T., Hughes, D., & Hutchings, J. (2007). Cost benefit analysis of interventions with parents for family and parenting support in Sure Start local programmes. *British Medical Journal, 334,* 682.

Eisenstadt, N. (2011). *Providing a Sure Start: How government discovered early childhood.* Bristol: Policy Press.

Emerson, E., & Hatton, C. (2007). Poverty, socio-economic position, social capital and the health of children and adolescents with intellectual differences in Britain: A replication. *Journal of Intellectual Disability Research, 51,* 866–874.

Embury-Dennis, T. (2017, March 16). UK child poverty hits highest levels since 2008 financial crisis. *Independent Online.*

Engels, F. (1945/1978). *The condition of the working class in England.* London: Penguin Books.

Farah, M., & Seven Others (2006). Childhood poverty: Specific associations with neurocognitive development. *Brain Research, 1110,* 166–174.

Farrington, D. (1995). The development of offending and anti-social behaviour from childhood: Key findings from the Cambridge study on delinquency behaviour. *Journal of Child Psychology and Psychiatry, 36,* 929–964.

Fekete, L. (2009). *A suitable enemy: Racism, migration and Islamophobia in Europe.* London: Pluto Press.

Fimister, G. (Ed.). (2001). *An end in sight? Tackling child poverty in the UK.* London: Child Poverty Action Group.

Fitzsimons, E., & Chowdry, H. (2007). *Higher education funding.* London: Institute of Fiscal Studies.

Frankel, H. (2009, May 1). School toilets play a crucial part in pupils' health and well-being. *Times Education Supplement Online.*

Freedman, S. (2006). (Ed.). *Independent Schools Bulletin,* No. 1.

Elliott, F. (2005, Decemer 12). Infant mortality gap between rich and poor worsens. *The Independent Online.*

Finn, J., & Achilles, C. (1999). Tennessee's class size study: Findings, implications, misconceptions. *Education Evaluation and Policy Analysis, 21,* 97–109.

Finn, J., Gerber, J., & Boyd-Zaharias, J. (2005). Small classes in the early grades, academic achievement, and graduating from high school. *Journal of Educational Psychology, 97,* 214–223.

Foster, D. (1999). *Classes are getting bigger.* London: The Liberal Democrats' Policy Statement.

Frean, A. (2006, September 22). Parents of under-twelves face fines as truancy hits record levels. *The Times Online.*

Frean, A. (2008, October 14). Government drops SATS for 14-year-olds. *The Times Online.*

Frean, A. (2009, April 4). 35,000 pupils may lose A-level places. *The Times Online.*

Friedli, L. (2009). *Inequality is bad for Your health.* Geneva: The World Health Organization.

Garner, R. (2007a, January 10). Teachers say they cannot cope with needs of the dyslexic child. *The Independent Online.*

Garner, R. (2007b, January 29). High expulsion rates 'massage' academies' results. *The Independent Online.*

Garner, R. (2007c, February 20). Alarming slump in number of pupils studying history. *The Independent Online.*

Garner, R. (2007d, July 18). Disabled children targeted by bullies. *The Independent Online.*

Garner, R. (2007e, May 4). Record numbers sent to private schools. *The Independent Online.*

Garner, R. (2007f, January 27). High expulsion rates 'massage' academies' results. *The Independent Online.*

Garner, R. (2007g, December 24). Alarm over exclusion of pupils with special needs. *The Independent Online.*

Garner, R. (2008a, April 4). GCSEs expose increasing gap between rich and poor. *The Independent Online*.

Garner, R. (2008b, June 28). Ministers attacked as truancy rises by 4%. The *Independent Online*.

Garner, R. (2008c, April 14). 40,000 not entered for GCSE mathematics in England. *The Independent Online*.

Garner, R. (2008d, December 12). School buildings scheme massively over budget. *The Independent Online*.

Garner, R. (2009a, April 1). Schools suspend three times as many persistent troublemakers. *The Independent Online*.

Garner, R. (2009b, May 19). More than 300 infant classes break Labour's 30-pupil limit. *The Independent Online*.

Garner, R. (2009c, May 19). Specialist schools accused of failing their specialist subjects. *The Independent Online*.

Gentleman, A. (2009, February 18). Majority of children in poverty have at least one parent in work, says study. *The Guardian Online*.

Gilbert, C. (2006). *Better education and care*. London: Annual Report of the Chief Inspector of Schools.

Gilbert, C. (2007a). *A vision for schooling*. London: Department for Education and Skills.

Gilbert, C. (2007b). *Annual report*. London: Office of the Chief Inspector for Schools.

Glass, N. (1999). Sure Start: The development of an early development of an early intervention programmes for young children in the United Kingdom. *Children and Society, 13*, 257–264.

Glennerster, H., Hills, J., Piachaud, D., & Webb, J. (2005). *One hundred years of poverty and policy*. York: The Joseph Rowntree Foundation.

Godlee, F. (2007). Our unequal society. *British Medical Journal, 334*, 432.

Golding, K., Dent, H., Nissim, R., & Stott, E. (2006). *Thinking psychologically about children who are looked after and adopted*. Chichester: Wiley.

Goodman, R., Ford, T., & Meltzer, H. (2002). Mental health problems of children in the community: 18-month follow-up. *British Medical Journal, 324*, 1496–1497.

Gray, R., & Francis, E. (2007). The implications of US experiences with early childhood interventions for the UK Sure Start programme. *Child Care Health and Development, 33*, 655–663.

Greengarten, J. (1981). *Thomas Hill Green and the development of liberal-democratic thought*. Toronto: University of Toronto Press.

Gross, J. (2006). *Every child a reader: Reading recovery*. London: The National Literacy Trust.

Hackett, G. (2005, June 26). Blair's £1billion literacy drive fails GCSE test. *Sunday Times Online*.

Hackett, G. (2007, February 4). Maths classes add up to 60 in staff crisis. *Sunday Times Online*.

Haile, D. (2005, May 19). Supersize classes blow for school-kids. *Manchester Evening News Online*.

Hales, G., Lewis, C., & Silverstone, D. (2006). *Gun crime in Brent*. London: Home Office Research Study.

Halpin, T. (2005, June 24). Almost 10000 pupils expelled as violence against teachers escalates. *The Times Online*.

Hansard (2008). *Written answer to parliamentary questions, from the secretary of state for education*. London: Hansard, Proceedings of the House of Commons.

Harker, J. (2007, February 16). This isn't about guns. *The Guardian Online*.

Harlen, W., & Tymms, P. (2008). *Perspectives on education: Primary science*. London: The Wellcome Trust.

HEFCE. (2005). *Young participation in higher education*. London: Higher Education Funding Council for England.

Hertzig, T. (2004). Rags, riches and race: The intergenerational economic mobility of Black and White families in the United States. In S. Bowles, H. Gintis, & M. Osborne (Eds.), *Unequal chances: Family background and economic success*. New York, NY: Russell Sage and Princeton University Press.

Heyderman, R., Ben-Shlomo, Y., Brennan, C., & Somerset, M. (2004). The incidence and mortality of meningococal disease associated with area deprivation. *Archives of Diseases in Childhood, 89,* 1064–1068.

Hiam, L., Dorling, D., Harrison, D., & McKee, M. (2017, February 16). What caused the spike in mortality in England and Wales in January, 2015? *Journal of the Royal Society of Medicine, 110,* 131–137.

Hirsch, D., & Sutherland, H. (2009). *Ending child poverty in a changing economy: Projections of child poverty in 2010 and 2020*. York: The Joseph Rowntree Foundation with the Institute of Economic and Social Research, University of Essex, and Institute of Fiscal Studies, London.

HM Revenue and Customs. (2006). *Social trends*. London: HMSO.

HM Treasury. (2007). *Budget 2007*. London: HMSO.

Hobson, D. (2001). *The national wealth: Who gets what in Britain*. London: Harper Collins Business.

Hoellar, P., Brook, A., Johanssn, A., Vujanovic, P., & Sollie, M. (2007). *Economic survey of the United Kingdom 2007: Raising educational achievement within a tighter budget constraint*. London & Paris: Organization for Economic Co-Operation and Development.

Horwood, J., & Eleven Others (2008). IQ and non-clinical symptoms in 12-year-olds: Results from the ALSPAC birth cohort. *British Journal of Psychiatry, 193,* 185–191.

Howden-Chapman, P., & 14 others. (2007). Effect of insulating houses on health inequality: Cluster randomised study in the community. *British Medical Journal, 334,* 460.

Howden-Chapman, P., & 16 others (2008). Effects of improved heating on asthma in community dwelling children: Randomised trial. *British Medical Journal, 337,* 1141.

Hughes, B. (2005, October 15). *Sure Start*. Statement by the Minister for Families and Children.

Hunt, G. (2007, January 8). Minister who sent child to private school 'has let the party down'. *The Times Online*.

Hunter, P. (2008, October 10). *Statement from the Office of the Chief Schools Admission Adjudicator*, London.

Hutchings, J., & seven others (2007). Parenting intervention in Sure Start services for children at risk of developing conduct disorder: Pragmatic randomized controlled trial. *British Medical Journal, 334,* 678.

Iacovou, M. (2001). *Class size in the early years: Is smaller really better?* Wivenhoe: University of Essex, Institute for Social and Economic Research.

IPPR. (2007). *School admissions should offer parents fairer choice.* London: Institute for Public Policy Research.

Ischebeck, A., Shocke, M., & Delazer, M. (2009, March 25). The processing and representation of fractions within the brain: An fMRI investigation. *Neuroimage, 47,* s89.

Jacob, S., & Nieder, A. (2009). Notation-independent representation of the fractions in the human parietal cortex. *Journal of Neuroscience, 8,* 4652–4657.

Jones, K., Daley, D., Hutchings, J., Bywater, T., & Eames, C. (2008). Efficacy of the incredible years programme as an early intervention for children with conduct problems and ADHD. *Child Care Health and Development, 84,* 389–390.

Joshi, H. (2007). *School readiness and social disadvantage in the millennium cohort of children.* London: Center for Longitudinal Studies, Institute of Education, University of London.

Joshi, M. (2008). *The millenium cohort study children at age six.* London: Centre for Longitudinal Studies, Institute of Education, University of London.

Keegan, M. (2009, January 14). Shock as deadly asbestos found in nine out of 10 school buildings. *Manchester Evening News Online.*

Khan, U. (2008, October 20). Half of all trainee teachers are failing basic numeracy test, according to government figures. *The Telegraph Online.*

Kmietowicz, Z. (2005). Children face same social problems as they did 100 years ago. *British Medical Journal, 330,* 163.

Kyffin, R., Goldacre, M., & Gill, M. (2004). Mortality rates and self-reported health: Database analysis by English local authority area. *British Medical Journal, 329,* 887–888.

Krueger. A. (1999). Experimental estimates of educational production functions. *Quarterly Journal of Economics, 114,* 497–532.

Lakhani, N. (2009, March 22). Self-harm: A British disease. *The Independent Online.*

Lawlor, S. (Ed.). (2007). *Teaching matters: The recruitment, employment and retention of teachers.* London: The Politeia Trust.

Layard, R., & Dunn, J. (2009). *The good childhood inquiry: Searching for values in a competitive age.* London: The Children's Society.

Lee, J. (2009, April 24). £300m more for building and £251m for 16 to 19s. *Times Educational Supplement Online.*

Leeming, C. (2007, June 22). White boys trail minority pupils. *Manchester Evening News Online.*

Lewis, F. (2009). *The age of foster care.* Cardiff: Fostering Network Wales.

Lipsett, A. (2008, February 2). Teacher shortage in key subjects feared. *The Guardian Online*.

Lipsett, A. (2009, April 9). Private schools axe teaching staff as recession bites. *The Guardian Online*.

Lipsett, A., & Curtis, P. (2008, March 20). Schools ministered jeered by teachers for backing large class sizes. *The Guardian Online*.

Literacy Trust. (2006). *School exclusions*. London: The Literacy Trust. Retrieved from www.literacytrust.org.uk

Lyall, S. (2007, March 10). How the young poor measure poverty in Britain: Drink, drugs and their time in jail. *The New York Times Online*.

Machin, S. (2005, April 25). Demise of grammar schools leaves poor facing uphill struggle. *The Times Online*.

Mackinnon, S. (2009, May 5). German and French exams show drop. *BBC Online*.

Maddern, K. (2009, March 23). Shrinking primary beset by problems, asks local authority to close it down. *The Times Educational Supplement Online*.

Madge, N., & Eight Others (2008). Deliberate self-harm within an international community sample of young people: Comparative finding from the Child and Adolescent Self-Harm in Europe (CASE) study. *Journal of Child Psychology and Psychiatry, 49*, 667–677.

Marley, D. (2009, April 17). Asbestos victim facing death: Heed my warning – she urges removal from schools and says heads lack training to evaluate risk. *Times Educational Supplement Online*.

Marmot, M. (2008). *Report of the commission on social determinants of health*. Geneva: World Health Organisation.

Marks, J. (2008). *The value of mathematics*. Buckingham: The University of Buckingham.

Martin, R., & Kitson, M. (2008, August). *Income deprivation and the North-South divide in Britain*. Paper presented to Annual Conference of the Royal Geographical Society, London.

Mayor, S. (2007). WHO report recommends tighter legislation and better road design to reduce injuries and deaths. *British Medical Journal, 334*, 867.

McFarlane, A., Stafford, M., & Moser, K, (2004), The health of children and young people. In *Social inequalities in health*. London: Office of National Statistics.

McLeod, A. (2007, February 1). Unskilled workers will have no jobs in a decade, says Brown. *The Times Online*.

Meen, G., Gibb, K., Goody, J., McGrath, T., & McKinnon, J. (2006). *Economic segregation in England: Causes, consequences and policy*. Bristol: The Policy Press.

Meikle, J. (2007, March 27). Bullying: Calls for a national enquiry. *The Guardian Online*.

Melhuish, E., & the SSLP Study Team. (2007). Variation in community intervention programmes and consequences for children and families: The example of Sure Start local programmes. *Journal of Child Psychology and Psychiatry, 48*, 543–551.

Melhuish, E., & Seven Others. (2008). Preschool influences on mathematics achievement. *Science, 29*, 1161–1162.

Melhuish, E., & the SSLP Study Team. (2008). Effects of fully-established Sure Start local programmes on 3-year-old children and their families living in England: A quasi-experimental, observational study. *Lancet, 373*, 1641–1647.

Meltzer, H., Gatward, R., Goodman, R., & Ford, T. (2000). *Mental health in children and adolescents in Great Britain*. London: HMSO for the Office of National Statistics.

Meltzer, H., Gatward, R., Corbin, T., Goodman, R., & Ford, T. (2003). *The mental health of young people looked after by local authorities in England*. London: Department of Health.

Micklewright, J., & Schnepf, S. (2006). *Response bias in England in PISA 2000 and 2003* (Research Report No. 771). London: Department for Education and Science.

Mitchell, R., Shaw, M., & Dorling, D. (2000). *Inequalities of life and death: What if Britain were more equal?* Bristol: The Policy Press.

Mongon, D., & Chapman, D. (2008). *Promoting achievement of white working class pupils*. Manchester: National College for School Leadership, School of Education, University of Manchester.

Morgan, D. (2009, January 4). Statement from the parliamentary under secretary for children, young people and families.

Moser, C. (1999). *Illiteracy and innumeracy in Britain's adults*. London: Institute of Education, The Basic Skills Agency Resource Centre.

Mourant, A. (2007, May 25). End crisis on repairs. *The Times Online.*

NAO. (2007a). *Helping people from workless households into work*. London: HMSO for the National Audit Office.

NAO. (2007b). *Sure Start children's centres*. London: HMSO for the National Audit Office.

NAO. (2009). *Improving road safety for pedestrians and cyclists in Great Britain*. London: HMSO for The National Audit Office and The Department of Transport.

Narey, M. (2008). *Locking up of giving up: Is custody for children the right answer?* London: Barnardo's Childrens Society.

Narey, M. (2008). *School exclusions: Preventing the drift into crime*. London: Barnardo's Childrens Society.

NASUWT. (2008). *Health and safety at work*. London: National Association of Schoolmasters and Union of Women Teachers.

Nath, S. (2008). Quality of Bangladesh rural advancement committee education programmes: A review of research studies. In C. Bagley & G. Verma (Eds.), *Challenges for inclusion: Educational and social studies from Britain and the Indian Sub-Continent*. Rotterdam: Sense Educational Publishers.

NLT. (1999). *The first national survey of school exclusions*. London: The National Literacy Trust.

NEA. (2008). *Issues in education*. Washington: National Education Association. Retrieved from www.nea.org/classsize/

Neustatter, J. (2004). *Locked in, locked out: The experience of young offenders out of society and in prison*. London: Calouste Gulbenkian Foundation.

New Scientist. (2007, July 7). Editorial - Reasons to be cheerful: Under Gordon Brown's government, UK science finds itself in a novel place. *New Scientist.*

Noden, P., & West, A. (2009a). *Attainment gaps between the most deprived and advantaged schools*. London: Educational Research Group, London School of Economics for The Sutton Trust.

Noden, P., & West, A. (2009b). *Learning and teaching in primary schools: The curriculum, an alternative vision – The Cambridge primary review*. Cambridge: The Faculty of Education, University of Cambridge.

Oden, S., Schweinhart, L., & Weikart, D. (2000). *Into adulthood: A study of the effects of head start*. St Pauls, MN: Red Leaf Press for High/Scope Publications.

ODPM. (2004). *Homelessness in Britain*. London: Office of The Deputy Prime Minister, for the Social Inclusion Unit.

ODPM. (2005). *National strategy for neighbourhood renewal*. London: Office of The Deputy Prime Minister, for the Social Inclusion Unit.

O'Dowd, A., & Coombes, R. (2008). Government will not meet its health inequalities targets in England. *British Medical Journal, 336*, 633.

OECD. (2004). *International survey of achievement in 15-year-olds*. London & Paris: Organisation for Economic Co-Operation and Development.

OECD. (2006). *Education at a glance*. London & Paris: Organisation for Economic Co-Operation and Development.

OECD. (2007 & 2008). *Education at a glance*. London & Paris: Organisation for Economic Co-Operation and Development.

OECD. (2008). Income inequality in OECD countries. London & Paris: Organisation for Economic Co-Operation and Development.

OFSTED. (1995). *Class size and the quality of education*. London: Office for Standards in Education.

ONS. (2004). *Permanent exclusions from schools and exclusion appeals, England 2002–2003*. London: Office for National Statistics.

ONS. (2008). *Education statistics for 2007*. London: Office for National Statistics.

ONS. (2009). *Social trends*. London: Office for National Statistics, and Palgrave-MacMillan.

Osuh, C. (2005, April 1). City suffers some of worst child poverty. *Manchester Evening News Online*.

Ottewell, D. (2007, June 11). £50M boost for weak schools. *Manchester Evening News Online*.

Parsons, C. (1999). *Education, exclusions and citizenship*. London: Routledge.

Parsons, C. (2009). *Strategic alternatives to exclusion from School*. London: Routledge.

Parker, J., & Hughes, H. (1970). *Democratic Sweden*. London: New Fabian Research Bureau.

Paterson, L., & Iannelli, C. (2006). *Education and social mobility in Scotland in the Twentieth Century*. Edinburgh: Centre for Educational Sociology, Edinburgh University.

Paton, G. (2008a, February 25). Poor students 'failing to get to university'. *The Daily Telegraph Online*.

Paton, G. (2008b, June 18). Gordon Brown's pledge on one-to-one tuition condemned as spin. *The Telegraph Online*.

Paton, G. (2008c, September 30). OECD education report: British classes amongst the biggest in the developed world. *The Telegraph Online*.

Paton, G. (2009a, January 6). Schools told to plan for an 'austere future'. *The Telegraph Online*.

Paton, G. (2009b, Jnauary 7). OFSTED: Half of schoolchildren bullied. *The Telegraph Online*.

Pearson, C. (2005). *Re-orienting parent education with a local sure start programme.* Chester: Centre for Public Health Research, University College of Chester.

Pelham, W., Foster, E., & Robb, J. (2007). The economic impact of attention-deficit/hyperactivity disorder in children and adolescents. *Journal of Pediatric Psychology, 32*, 711–727.

Pellis, R. (2017, April 4). More than half of schools forced to increase class sizes as a result of underfunding. *The Independent Online*.

Petrou, S., Kupek, E., Hockley, C., & Goldacre, M. (2006). Social class inequalities in childhood mortality and morbidity in an English population. *Paediatric and Perinatal Epidemiology, 20*, 14–23.

Phillips, T. (2007, November 26). *Poor schools should have bussing quotas.* Paper presented to Runnymede Trust Symposium on Policies for Equality, London.

Pickett, K., & Wilkinson, R. (2007). Child well-being and income inequality in rich societies; ecological cross-sectional study. *British Medical Journal, 335*, 1080.

Picus, L. (2000). *Class-size reduction: Effects and relative costs* (Policy Report No. 1). Eugene, OR: ERIC Clearing House.

Pitkanen, P., Kalekin-Fishman, D., & Verma, G. (2002). *Education and immigration: Settlement policies and current challenges.* London: Routledge-Falmer.

Pritchard, C. (2001). *A family-teacher-social work alliance to reduce truancy and Delinquency - the Dorset Healthy Alliance Project* (RDS Occasional Paper No. 78). London: The Home Office, .

Prince's Trust. (2007). *The cost of exclusion: Counting the Cost of Youth Disadvantage in the UK.* London: Centre for Economic Performance, London Shool of Economics, for The Prince's Trust.

Pring, R. (2006). *Review of 14–19 education and training.* Oxford: The Nuffield Review of Education. www.nuffield14-19review.org.uk

Pugh, R. (2008, April 4). Lonely road: Why school is hell for transgender pupils. *The Independent Online*.

Quershi, Y. (2007, April 19). City's absent pupil shame. *Manchester Evening News Online*.

Rahman, M., Palmer, G., Kenway, P., & Howarth, G. (2000). *Monitoring poverty and social exclusion.* York: Joseph Rowntree Foundation.

Raymond, J. (2009). 'Creating a safety net': Women's experiences of antenatal depression and their identification of helpful community support services during pregnancy. *Midwifery, 25*, 39–49.

RCPCH (2017). *The state of child health.* London: Royal College of Paediatrics and Child Health.

Redfern, G. (2005). Ministers urged not to jump the gun on Sure Start findings. *new start - Community regeneration*. Retrieved from www.newstartmag.co.uk/news858.html/

Reed, J. (2004). *Toward zero-exclusion: Beginning to think bravely*. London: Institute for Public Policy Research.

RESET. (2007). *The business case for youth esettlement: Better outcomes for young people and communities*. London: RESET - National Youth Homeless Resettlement Scheme.

Riddell, M. (2006, July 2). We shamefully fail our children by locking them up. *The Observer Online*.

Rose, G., & Marshall, T. (1975). *Counselling and school social work*. Chichester: John Wiley.

Ross, T. (2008, March 11). Shock of schools breaking admissions law. *The Independent Online*.

Rustemier, S. (2008a). Social and educational justice: The human rights framework. In C. Bagley & G. Verma (Eds.), *Challenges for inclusion*. Rotterdam: Sense Educational Publishers.

Rustemier, S. (2008b). The case against segregation in special schools – A Look at the Evidence. In C. Bagley & G. Verma (Eds.), *Challenges for inclusion*. Rotterdam: Sense Educational Publishers.

Runciman, W., & Bagley, C. (1971). Status consistency, relative deprivation and attitudes to immigrants. In W. Runciman (Ed.), *Sociology in its place*. Cambridge: Cambridge University Press.

Rutter, M. (2007). Sure Start Local Programmes: An outsider's perspective. In J. Belsky, J. Barnes, & E. Melhuish (Eds.), *The national evaluation of Sure Start*. Bristol: The Policy Press.

Ryan, F. (2017, April 6). The child social care system is quietly being dismantled. *The Guardian Online*.

Sammons, P., Hall. J., Smees, R., & Goff, G. (2015). *The impact of children's centres: Studying the effects of children's centres in promoting better outcomes for young children and their families (Summary Report)*. London: Department for Education. Retrieved from www.gov.uk/government/publications

Schneider, J., Ramsay, A., & Lowerson, S. (2006). Sure Start graduates: Predictors of attainment on starting school. *Child Care Health and Development, 32*, 431–440.

Scott, S. (2007). Conduct disorders in children. *British Medical Journal, 334*, 646.

Scott, S., & Maughan, B. (2008). *The good childhood inquiry*. London: The Children's Society.

Scott, S., & Knapp, M. (2001). Financial cost of social inclusion: Follow-up studies of antisocial children into adulthood. *British Medical Journal, 323*.

Scottish Office. (2005). *For Scotland's children*. Edinburgh: The Scottish Office.

Scottish Office. (2006). *Low birth weight babies in Scotland*. Edinburgh: The Scottish Office.

Seager, A. (2007, March 27). Blow for brown as poverty figures increase after years of decline. *Guardian Online*.

Sergeant, H. (2006). *Handle with care: An investigation into the care system*. London: The Centre for Policy Studies.

Sethi, D., Racioppi, F., & Bertollini, R. (2007). Preventing the leading cause of death in young people in Europe. *Journal of Epidemiology and Community Health, 61*, 842–843.

SEU. (1998a). *Reducing teenage pregnancy*. London: Office of The Deputy Prime Minister, Social Exclusion Unit.

SEU. (1998b). *Truancy and school exclusion*. London: Office of The Deputy Prime Minister, Social Exclusion Unit.

SEU. (1998c). *Homelessness and social exclusion*. London: Office of The Deputy Prime Minister, Social Exclusion Unit.

SEU. (2006). *Reaching out: The government action plan on social exclusion*. London: Office of The Deputy Prime Minister.

Shaw, M., Davey-Smith, G., & Dorling, D. (2005). Health inequalities and new labour. *British Medical Journal, 330*, 1016–1021.

Sheerman, B. (2009). *Report of The Select Committee on children, schools and families.* London: The House of Commons.

Shepherd, J., & Farrington, D. (2003). The impact of antisocial lifestyle on health. *British Medical Journal, 326*, 834–835.

Sidebotham, P., Herson, J., & ALSPAC Study Team. (2006). Child maltreatment in the "Child of the Nineties": A cohort study of risk. *Child Abuse and Neglect, 30*, 497–522.

Sieghart, A. (1999, September 19). Making our schools work again: The class divide is starker than 30 years ago. *The Times*, p. 10.

Simkhada, P., & Bagley, C. (2008). Excluded and exploited: The sexual trafficking of girls and women from Nepal to India. In C. Bagley & G. Verma (Eds.), *Challenges for inclusion: Educational and social studies from Britain and the Indian Sub-Continent*. Rotterdam: Sense Educational Publishers.

Singh, D. (2007). *Our shared future*. London: The Commission on Integration and Cohesion, Communities and Local Government Publications.

Singleton, C. (2008). *Screening for Dyslexia and specific reading difficulties: Saying no to failure*. Bracknell: British Dyslexia Association.

Singleton, C. H., & Trotter, S. (2005). Visual stress in adults with and without dyslexia. *Journal of Research in Reading, 28*, 365–368.

Skidmore, C. (2008). *The failed generation*. London: The Bow Group.

Slavin, R. (1990). Class size and student achievement: Is smaller better? *Contemporary Education, 62*, 6–12.

Smith, G. D. (2003). *Health inequalities: A life-course approach*. Bristol: The Policy Press.

Smithers, A. (2004). *Policy statement*. Buckingham: University of Buckingham, Centre for Education and Employment Research.

Smithers, A., & Robinson, P. (2005). *The crisis in school hysics*. Buckingham: Centre for Education and Employment Research, University of Buckingham.

Smithers, A., & Robinson, A. (2006). *Physics in Schools and Universities*. Buckingham: Centre for Education and Employment Research, University of Buckingham.

Smithers, A., & Robinson, P. (2008). *The good teacher training guide 2008.* Buckingham: Centre for Education and Employment Research.

Smithers, R. (2005, June 24). Permanent school exclusions rise. *Guardian Online*.

Smithers, R., & Bawden, A. (2005, February 25). Big fall in language students. *Guardian Online*.

Smithers, R. (2006, January 24). Twelve million workers have reading age of children. *Guardian Online*.

Smithers, R. (2007, February 20). Poor maths and literacy skills cost £800m. *Guardian Online*.

Smithers, R. (2007). *Blair's education: An international perspective*. London: The Sutton Trust.

Sparrow, A. (2008, July 15). Youth crime: How 982 children will save us all £300m. *The Guardian Online*.

Starkey, P. (2002). Innovation and experiment with deprived families in Britain, 1940s to 1980s: The work of the Family Service Units. *British Journal of Social Work, 32*, 573–587.

Stephenson, T. (2009). Children's health and the financial crisis. *British Medical Journal, 338*, 1783.

Stone, J. (2017, January 25). NHS spending per person will be cut next year. *The Independent Online*.

Strand, S. (2008). *SEN and ethnicity: What we know*. Warwick: Institute of Education, University of Warwick.

Sure Start Research Team. (2008). *The impact of sure start local programmes on three year olds and their families*. Nottingham: DfES Publications.

Sutton Trust. (2001). *Educational apartheid: A practical way forward*. London: The Sutton Trust.

Taylor, C. (2006). *Quality of secondary schools*. London: Report to House of Commons Public Accounts Committee.

Taylor, M. (2005, October 10). Top state schools colonized by middle classes. *Guardian Online*.

Taylor, M. (2006, January 11). One million pupils taught in struggling schools, MPs told. *Guardian Online*.

Teacher Net. (2008). *The extra mile: How schools succeed in raising aspirations in deprived communities*. London: Department for Children, Schools and Families, for Teacher Net, Online Publications for Schools.

TES. (2009a, April 3). Colleges have difficult equation to balance. *The Times Educational Supplement Online*.

TES. (2009b, April 3). Double trouble for colleges as main funds cut and capped: Train to Gain budget under pressure and no allowance made for growth in student numbers. *Times Educational Supplement Online*.

TES. (2009c, April 3). Financial crisis: We haven't seen the worst yet. *Times Educational Supplement Online*.

TES. (2009d, June 12). Who's up for a 10K bonus? *Times Educational Supplement Online*.

Thomas, B., & Dorling, D. (2007). *Identity in Britain: A cradle-to-grave analysis*. Bristol: The Policy Press.

Thomas, G., & Vaughan, M. (2004). *Inclusive education: Readings and reflections*. Buckingham: Open University Press with McGraw-Hill.

Tomlinson, M. (2009, February 24). Address to Conference of Chartered Teachers, London, by former Chief Inspector of Schools.

TOL. (2006, December 11). Cost of illiteracy £2 billion a year. *The Times Online*.

TOL. (2007, February 19). Teachers want out. *The Times Online*.

Townsend, P. (Ed.). (1970). *The concept of poverty*. London: Heinemann.

Townsend, P. (1979). *Poverty in The United Kingdom: A survey of household resources and standards of living*. London: Penguin Books.

Townsend, P., & Davidson, N. (1992). *Inequalities in health: The black report*. London: Penguin Books.

UN. (2005). *United Nations development program report for 2005*. New York, NY: The United Nations.

UN. (2006). *Report of the convention on rights of disabled persons*. New York, NY: The United Nations.

UNESCO. (2007). *Child poverty in perspective: An overview of child well-being in rich countries* (Report Card 7). Florence: UNESCO Innocenti Research Centre.

Van Dyke, R., & Little, B. (2005). *Debt, part-time work and university achievement*. London: University of The South Bank, for Higher Education Funding Council.

Vaughan, R. (2009, May 1). Cuts jeopardise plan to rebuild nation's schools. *Times Educational Supplement Online*.

Verma, G., Woodrow, D., Darby D,.Shum, S., Chan, D., Bagley, C., & Skinner, G. (1999). *Chinese Adolescents in Hong Kong and Britain: Identity and Aspirations*. Aldershot: Ashgate.

Waller, T. (2009). *Less law, more order: The truth about reducing crime*. Ottawa: Institute for the Prevention of Crime, University of Ottawa.

Wanless, D. (2004). *Securing good health for the whole population*. London: Her Majesty's Stationery Office.

Wanless, P. (2006). *Getting it right*. London: Office of the Director of School Performance and Reform, Department for Education and Skills.

Warden,S. (2005, November 18). Pupils stop learning foreign languages. *Manchester Metronews*.

Warnock. M. (2008). Special educational needs: A new look. In C. Bagley & G. Verma (Eds.), *Challenges for inclusion: Educational and social studies from Britain and the Indian Sub-Continent*. Rotterdam: Sense Educational Publishers.

Webb, R., & Vuillamy, G. (2004). *A multi-agency approach to reducing disaffection and exclusions from school* (Research Report No. 568). London: Department for Education and Science.

Westhead, J. (2009, April 20). UK ranked low on youth well-being. *BBC Online*.

Wilkinson, R. (2005). *The impact of inequality: How to make sick societies healthier*. London: Routledge.

Wilkinson, R., & Pickett, K. (2009). *The spirit level: Why more equal societies almost always do better*. London: Allen Lane Penguin Books.

Williams, P. (2004, December 12). Science crisis: Statement by chairman, the engineering and technology board. *The Sunday Times Online.*

Woodhouse, L. (2005, August 17). Postcode lottery knocks 10 years off life. *Manchester Evening News Online.*

Woodward, W. (2007, June 11). End examinations for children under 16, says watchdog. *The Guardian Online.*

Woodcock, N. (2008, March 27). Schools to be forced to keep a quota of problem pupils. *The Times Online.*

Woodcock, N., & Fishburn, A. (2009, May 28). School exclusions 'merry go round' shows that reforms are failing. *The Times Online.*

World Bank. (2008, July 1). *World development indicators database.*

Wragg, T. (2004). *Education, education, education.* London: Routledge.

ENGLAND'S *SURE START* PRE-SCHOOL CHILD CARE CENTRES

Public Policy, Progress and Political Change

INTRODUCTION

Identifying deprived neighbourhoods is an obvious basis for multiple-level interventions for community development, addressing both structural and individual problems, in order to enhance children's physical and mental health, and cognitive development: this was the basis for a programme initiated by the British government, called National Strategy for Neighbourhood Renewal Glass, 1999; ODPM, 2005; Eisenstadt, 2011 which aimed over 20 years to regenerate *all* of Britain's highly deprived local neighbourhoods (which constitute about ten per cent of all urban neighbourhoods identified at the 'voter enumeration district' level). *Sure Start* programmes, as part of this initiative, were established on an area basis (Eisenstadt, 2011; Belsky & Melhuish, 2007) using census data to identify urban areas with populations potentially at risk.

The neighbourhood regeneration programmes were greatly diminished after 2010, when the New Labour government was replaced by a Coalition, and then by a Conservative government. *Sure Start* itself has taken a little longer to be discarded by central government, since phasing out the many neighbourhood child care centres was politically difficult, so the reduction and changes in funding affecting these centres has been more gradual (Sammons et al., 2016a, 2016b).

The aim of this policy review is to examine the numerous challenges to the Sure Start initiative – methodological, political, and organisational – which surrounded a major public policy initiative on behalf of children up to age five. As Melhuish et al. (2010) acknowledge in their overview of the first phase of Sure Start a change of national government in Britain meant that ideological pressures meant that the focus, design and reporting of Sure Start had to change within a changing political climate, and identification of "success" in programme delivery may not have been welcome news for subsequent UK governments for whom reducing public expenditure, rather than enhancing the life chances of children born into the poorest social classes, even though this initially expensive venture would have been highly cost effective in the medium and long-term (Allen, 2011).

Initial Evaluation Studies of Sure Start

The New Labour government of Britain had paid some attention to the abundant medical and social evidence on the corrupting, demoralizing and demeaning effects of chronic poverty on family life, and on children's health and welfare (Bagley & Sawyerr, 2008). The New Labour government thus initiated the *Sure Start* programme in 1998, as part of its goal of halving the incidence of child poverty by 2010.

The declared goals of *Sure Start* were: "To work with parents-to-be, parents and children, to promote the physical, intellectual and social development of babies and young children – particularly those who are disadvantaged – so that they can flourish at home when they get to school, and thereby break the cycle of disadvantage for the current generation of young children" (Sure Start Research Team, 2008). This initial three-billion pound programme, modelled to some extent on the American *Head Start* initiatives, aimed to provide improved parenting skills in areas of high deprivation, focussing on the first five years of a child's life (Barnes et al., 2005). Unfortunately, the systematic integration of *Sure Start* with various medical interventions was dropped following the initial pilot work, largely on grounds of cost, although such integration did remain (and was shown to be highly effective) in some centres (Sammons et al., 2015a).

The initial workings of *Sure Start* (in the integrated model, using medical, social work and educational resources) were described, for example, in an evaluative study in the North West region of England (Pearson, 2005). Within the selected areas, participant families were identified and referred by community midwives, and the programme offered support to parents (particularly mothers) to improve their health and emotional and social development, and their parenting abilities. In addition to group sessions for effective parenting before and after the child's birth, parents were usually offered a maximum of four individual counselling sessions, although further sessions might be offered for families considered at high risk of neglect or abuse of children. Involvement in the programme was voluntary, and in the settings studied by Pearson (2005) some 70 per cent of parents approached initially agreed to participate. However, of those parents considered most at risk for 'problem parenting', 50 per cent chose not to attend any of the individual counselling sessions, and less than a quarter completed all four sessions. Among the reasons given for not attending were "illness of self or family member".

Fathers were particularly difficult to engage, and because evening sessions were not usually offered, parents working full-time often had difficulty in attending. The initial evaluation of this programme was qualitative rather than quantitative, and there were few indicators of outcome, apart from the fact that most parents who had participated said that the experience had been enjoyable and positive. But this kind of 'halo effect' is common in evaluation work, and merely tells us that those who participated fully in a voluntary programme were probably those least likely to have required such a service.

Attached to the national *Sure Start* programme was a major evaluation programme based at Birkbeck College, University of London. This team first of all, examined service delivery to 15,000 families and their focus child in 150 Sure Start nursery centres in order to provide a description of services actually delivered. Secondly the team attempted to assess whether children, families and communities had actually benefited according to various indicators. Twenty six centres were randomly selected from the 150 centres for intensive study, children and families in these centres being compared over six years with initially similar families in fifty "Sure-Start-to-be" comparison areas (Eisenstadt, 2011).

Belsky et al. (2006) published details of the first statistical evaluation of *Sure Start*, based on interviews and tests involving 3,927 mothers and their children who were enrolled in the programme, at the age nine months and three years. The target group were compared with 1,509 mothers and children from similarly deprived neighbourhoods, who were not yet enrolled in *Sure Start*. The main dependent variables were mother's perception and use of community services; her family functioning; her reports on her child's health and development; and a measure of the child's verbal skills at age three.

The results of this initial evaluation were disappointing: differences between target and comparison groups were small, and when statistically significant pointed to *adverse* outcomes for the most deprived mothers and children enrolled in *Sure Start*. Children of teenaged, single mothers, and unemployed single parents who participated in *Sure Start* had children with poorer verbal ability in the third year of life. *Sure Start* had the most beneficial effects for the least deprived, intact families living in areas with lower levels of deprivation. Apparently these mothers were able to elicit additional helping and support networks unavailable to the most deprived mothers. Overall, outcomes were slightly better in *Sure Start* programmes which were delivered within a health services framework. A follow-up of a pre-2003 *Sure Start* cohort into the early years of schooling showed that the focus children had better social skills, but were no better at scholastic attainments than were control children (Schneider, Ramsay & Lowerson, 2006).

The Minister for Children and Families defended the *Sure Start* programme, arguing that positive outcomes should be seen in the longer-term, rather than in the first few years of the programme (Hughes, 2005; Redfern, 2005). The authors and evaluators of *Sure Start* might have been looking to the evaluations of the US *Head Start* programme, which also showed few short-term benefits, but nevertheless showed highly significant gains for the child participants when they were in their teens – in terms of school achievements, adaptive behaviours, and educational and occupational aspirations and achievements – compared with controls (Oden, Schweingart & Weikart, 2000).

The need for a fully effective programme which could fulfil the idealist goals of *Sure Start* was underlined by the longitudinal research by Joshi and colleagues (Joshi, 2007). This study used data from the Millennium Cohort of 15,500 British children born in the years 2000 to 2002, and indicated that children from the most socially advantaged social groups were on average, a year ahead of children from the least advantaged group on the School Readiness Test, which assessed a child's recognition of words, numbers, shapes and colours, regardless of whether or not they had been enrolled in preschool nurseries. This series of studies was unable to show that *Sure Start* programmes had been effective in enhancing 'school readiness' in children from the most disadvantaged families. A further report from the Millennium Cohort in 2008 showed that before they entered schools, children of young, poorly educated mothers were nearly a year behind in the their vocabulary scores, a difference that increased for each year that they remained in school (Joshi, 2008). In this study, boys with conduct behaviour disorders, with depressed and often punitive mothers, were the most disadvantaged in terms of reading readiness, and it was clear that these were mothers and children whom *Sure Start* should focus on in particular.

It may be countered that *Sure Start* focused not on cognitive goals, but on parenting capacity and the development of behavioural and emotional competence in children. Ideally of course, cognitive and emotional goals should be simultaneously addressed in a comprehensive programme for the most disadvantaged families (Eisenstadt, 2011).

One problem which emerged in evaluative studies of *Sure Start* was that of integrating the work of health care, social work, child care and clinical psychology specialists involved (Anning & Ball, 2008; Edgley & Avis, 2006, 2007). Apparently programming in some areas was working better than in others, and this could have been due to varying degrees of integration of the professionals involved, or of the differing nature of the communities in which intervention was attempted (Barnes, 2007; Melhuish et al., 2007; Melhuish, Belsky & Barnes, 2010; Raymond, 2009). In addition, some severely disadvantaged clients may have felt stigmatized by the proposed interventions, accounting for their low take up of services (Coe et al., 2008). Failure of *Sure Start* programmes to recognize, or intervene with severe maternal depression (especially likely for single, abused or deserted mothers) was another problem which could be associated with reduced impact (Raymond, 2009; Coe et al., 2008). Another identified problem was that some *Sure Start* centres were failing to link effectively with black and other ethnic minorities (Craig, 2007).

The planned expansion of *Sure Start* centres after 2004, from some 1,400 to 3,500 over ten years (Eisenstadt, 2011), faced the problem that not enough qualified workers were readily available to staff such expansions; and the budgetary allocation for *Sure Start* appeared to be inadequate for training such new staff (NAO, 2007 Anning & Ball, 2008).

A useful policy analysis by Gray and Francis (2007) goes some way to explain both positive and negative aspects of *Sure Start's* initial roll-out phase. They draw specific lessons from a comparison of *Sure Start* with the American *Head Start* programmes. Their analysis offers the following conclusions:

1. Early interventions, as the American experience shows, can significantly improve the life chances of many children throughout their lifespan; but failure to provide adequately expanded funding can impair both the quality and impact of early intervention programmes of this type. These positive outcomes occurred despite some differences in the American and British models.
2. There is a temptation for evaluators to focus on narrow, measurable objectives; but this runs the risk of ignoring broader aspects of success, and a combination of quantitative and qualitative evaluation techniques may be needed.

3. Programmes must be flexible in meeting local conditions, and the needs of individual families, while remaining faithful to the original programme goals.
4. Be aware that multiple programme objectives may conflict with one another, and political demands to divert early intervention programmes to meet new or multiple goals should be avoided.
5. Evaluation may show that the programme works better with some client groups, and in some areas. The failure to be effective with all client groups should not be seen as a general failure of the programme in it its initial years.
6. The English and Welsh *Sure Start* programme was probably rolled out too fast, in order to fulfil political goals. Funding, although initially generous, failed to recognize problems of recruiting and training staff for a programme which was, at that stage, unproven.
7. Now that *Sure Start* was entering its second phase and building on experience, it was crucial that funding matched the needs of what was still a developing programme. Failure to fully fund the programmes because of for example, a recession and cutbacks in public funding, could be disastrous for the long-term success of *Sure Start*.

The methodological challenges facing the Sure Start evaluation team should be acknowledged, and Melhuish et al. (2010) in their final report on the first phase of Sure Start clearly acknowledge these challenges. The methodological design, influenced by the best standards of educational psychology, using validated measures analysed by the latest statistical techniques is laudable in theory, but may have problems with large-scale data sets, since the researchers have to rely on non-research trained field workers to collect data. Thus the *reliability* of data may at times be questionable; and certainly, minimally trained field researchers were not 'blind' to the research setting (Sure Start versus controls) when they administered instruments and collected data. Melhuish and his colleagues (2010) coped with this problem to some extent by sub-sampling groups of Sure Start centres for more intensive and controlled investigation.

It is of importance that the distinguished scholar, Michael Rutter (2007) who had conducted many large scale epidemiological studies in child psychiatry, praised the Sure Start team led by Melhuish and Belsky for their careful methodology, and accepted the overall validity of their findings.

Sure Start's Developing Success

Notwithstanding the earlier problems of programme organization and service delivery [3], *Sure Start* seemed to have 'bedded down', gaining a 'second wind', as evidenced by later evaluation studies (Edwards et al., 2007; Melhuish et al., 2008, 2010). Overall evaluation of the *Sure Start* programme when the children were aged five-plus, according to Melhuish & the Sure Start Research Team (2010) provided rather more optimistic findings than the 2005 evaluations. There were now more than 9,000 families involved in SSLPs (Sure Start Local Programmes) in 150 areas. Comparison between SSLP participants, and matched non-SSLP families and children enabled a wide range of family and area background factors to be controlled. The main findings were:

1. Parents of 3-year-old children in the programmes showed less negative parenting, while providing their children with a better home learning environment.
2. Children in SSLP areas had better social development, with higher levels of positive social behaviour and independence/self-regulation.
3. The SSLP effects for positive social behaviour appeared to be a consequence of enhanced parenting behaviours.
4. SSLP children had higher immunization rates and fewer accidental injuries.
5. SSLP families used more child and family-related services.
6. Positive effects associated with SSLPs applied to all of the participants, rather than to different subgroups identified in 2005.
7. The more consistent benefits associated with SSLPs in 2008 compared with 2005 might well reflect the greater exposure of children and families to the programme, and to the evolution of a more focussed and sophisticated type of programme delivery.

Sure Start, like the American *Head Start* programme (Currie & Thomas, 1995; Bennett & Hustedd, 2005; Cameiro & Ginja, 2014) *might* have global advantages which spread out from earlier gains, reflected in better achievement in later years. The American programme found that by their mid- to late-teens the children enrolled as infants made better school progress, dropped out of school less, were more likely to go on to college, were less delinquent, and less often became pregnant. These gains made the early investment in Head Start highly cost effective (Cameiro & Ginja, 2014).

Further evidence that *Sure Start* Local Programmes (SSLP) were learning valuable experience over time, came from the longer term evaluation programme by Melhuish and his team (Melhuish et al., 2008, 2010; Melhuish, Belsky & Barnes, 2010). A quasi-experimental study which compared 5,883 3-year-olds and their mothers who were enrolled in *Sure Start* nurseries, with a comparison group of 1,879 3-year-olds of similar backgrounds, not enrolled in *Sure Start*. The *Sure Start* children had statistically significant advantages in the following areas, after all relevant background factors (e.g. family size, presence of father, dependence on financial benefits) were controlled for: better social behaviours; more self-confident independence in the child; less negative parenting; better home learning environment; more use of relevant family support services. These advantages held across different regions, ethnic groups, and social class backgrounds.

However, the SSLP children had no significant advantages in several other desired outcomes: mothers smoked as much as before; children's language skills were similar; mean BMI indicators (predictors of obesity) for child and mother were similar across the two groups; father's involvement was no greater; personal life satisfaction was no greater; and mothers in both SSLP and control populations, often rated their housing and urban environment negatively. A similar proportion of children from both groups still had incipient behaviour problems. It remained to be seen whether prolonged exposure to SSLPs, and added programme experience and feedback based on evaluations such as these could yield better results in the longer term.

The medical focus of *Sure Start* had been emphasized in a successful intervention with parents in deprived areas whose children were at risk of developing conduct disorder (Hutchings et al., 2007). In this controlled study 153 parents were offered behavioural support and focussed counselling to help them cope with their child's incipient problem behaviour. Results showed clear and significantly different positive outcomes for children in the focus families, compared with those in the wait-list controls, in terms of reduction of problem behaviours.

This important new direction for *Sure Start* was emphasized by further work of the team led by Hutchings, Bywater and Daly (2009, and Bywater et al., 2009, and came from a follow-up of this experimental programme, based in Wales and North West England which identified children at particular risk of developing conduct disorder (and later delinquency) because of their identified symptoms of Attention Deficiency and Conduct Disorder (ADHD) at age three. This team identified 50 children with serious levels of ADHD and instructed and monitored their parent(s) in giving appropriate feedback to the child in ways which reduced the chronicity of symptoms. The approach is similar to that described by Bagley and Mallick (2000) of providing "goodness of fit" between child behaviour and parental feedback in ways which lead to the "spiralling down" of difficult behaviour to normal levels. Jones et al. (2008) achieved an improvement of 57 percent in the focus group (criterion, falling below the clinical level as indicated by scores on the Connors Rating Scale) compared with 21 percent in the untreated, waiting list controls. These gains were maintained, in comparison with controls, at follow-ups 12 and 18 months later.

These interventions were shown to be clearly cost-effective (Bywater et al., 2009; Jones et al., 2008). Scott (2007) commented, on the basis of this and earlier research, including Scott et al. (2001), that although these interventions were relatively expensive (about £1,800 per family), in the long run these interventions could be very cost effective, given the known costs of children who enter cycles of juvenile delinquency and rebellion in school and community. *Sure Start* could be most effective not principally as a service agency, but also as a screening agency which refers for intensive help families with children most at risk.

Melhuish, Belsky and Barnes (2010) summarised their evaluations of the first phases of Sure Start in the following terms:

> Sure Start has been evolving, and ongoing research has partly influenced this process. Later developments have considerably clarified guidelines and service delivery. It is plausible that the improved results in the evaluation of Sure Start reflect actual changes in the impact of Sure Start programmes resulting from the increasing quality of services, greater attention to the hard to reach, the move to children's centres, as well as the greater exposure to programmes, of children and families in the latest phase of the impact evaluation. The results are modest but suggest that the value of Sure Start programmes is improving. The identification of factors associated with the more effective programmes has propelled recent improvements in Sure Start Children's Centres and may be in part the reason for the improved outcomes for children and families now found in Sure Start. (p. 160)

The Second Stage of Evaluation: The Oxford's Team Results

Eisenstadt (2011), the civil servant responsible for overseeing the setting up of Sure Start in the early years of the New Labour government, gives an insight into the fierce competition in bids to evaluate the early years of Sure Start – the awarding of the research contract was certainly valuable for the university or research group which took on the task, and many influential publications were likely to follow. Indeed, there was 'controversy' at the contract being awarded to Birkbeck College, University of London, perhaps because these scholars promised a quantitative form of evaluation, rather than a more global, qualitative perspective (although the two perspectives are of course complement rather than compete with one another). The social psychiatrist Michael Rutter (2007) was asked by government to conduct an independent audit of the earlier research emerging from the Birkbeck group, and he observed:

> Given the constraints imposed by government, this was a rigorous and careful an evaluation as could be undertaken … The research team are to be congratulated on their high quality research. As a consequence, there is every reason to trust the research findings. (pp. 197–209).

The second major contract for the evaluation of Sure Start, now relabelled for political reasons as Children's Centres (Lewis, 2011) was awarded to a group at the University of Oxford. In the event, this group carried out a methodologically careful quantitative approach, reflecting the rigours of research in educational and clinical psychology. The team was joined by Melhuish, who had been a key member of the Birkbeck group. And Eisenstadt, having retired from her civil service post, joined the Oxford group, writing an extremely interesting account of the political sociology of Sure Start in her (2011) book: *Providing a Sure Start: How Government Discovered Early Childhood.*

The major series of reports on the second wave of evaluation were issued in 2015[1] under the authorship of the four key researchers, with acknowledgments to a number of specialist or consultant researchers (Sammons et al., 2015a, 2015b). These new evaluations did not use the term "Sure Start Centres", but instead termed their work on centres by the new, politically correct terminology as "ECCE", meaning "Evaluation of Children's Centres in England". The research was divided into five "Strands" for the period of evaluation, 2009 to 2017, and a number of evaluations were to be published over this timespan.

The Strands were:

Strand 1: Delivery and use of ECCE in 509 'most disadvantaged' areas, 2011 to 2013.

Strand 2: Interviews with a sample of 2,608 staff in 128 ECCE centres in 2013.

Strand 3: Reports of visits to a sample of 121 of the 128 'focus' ECCE centres (Goff et al., 2013).

Strand 4: The impact of ECCE programmes on child and family functioning in 1,305 boys and 1,305 girls attending 117 of the 128 focus centres, studied at three points in time, when children were aged between 9 months and 38 months.[2]

Strand 5: Cost-benefit analyses (Briggs, Kurtz & Pauli, 2012); and a yet unpublished, later report.

The Strands 1 and 2 evaluations focussed on a broad range of non-child outcomes examining the underlying goals of Children's Centres "... to support all children and families living in particularly disadvantaged areas, by providing a wide range of services tailored to local conditions and needs" (Sammons et al., 2015a).

Results from the Strand 1 evaluation reported: "... high levels of parent satisfaction, and clear evidence of improved 'personal, social and emotional development', with 92 percent of mothers interviewed being 'very happy' with the programmes offered" (Evangelou et al., 2014). The delivery of services on a neighbourhood basis was offered to a broad range of families, including those not currently experiencing material or social stress. The aim was to avoid stigmatising low-functioning families, through services which were inclusive of the whole community (Sammons et al., 2004a, 2004b). Nevertheless, within this broad range of services, those "most in need" were identified, so that for such families a more focussed approach could be offered, in terms of mothers' material and mental health problems, problematic parent-child relationships, and material difficulties (Lord et al., 2011; Sylva et al., 2015).

The major evaluation, Strand 4, was based on longitudinal data collected at three points in time in the pre-schoolers' lives (from 18 months through to four years of age), using a number of validated measures of children's behaviour and cognition, parent-child interactions, and maternal and family functioning. Among the measures was one intriguingly termed the CHAOS scale which measured family "parental distress and dysfunctional parent-child interaction", based on a validated measure using in American Head Start projects (Matheny, 1995), estimating (through mother's self-report) "confusion, hubbub and (dis)order in family life." Overall, 13 child, mother and family outcomes were measured. The longitudinal design allowed the researchers to identify what services were available and were used, and their possible outcome (and influence) over a 30-month period.

The broad research question was: "What aspects of children's centres (management, working practices, services offered, services used) promoted better family, parent and child outcomes?" (Sammons et al., 2015a).

The researchers used advanced statistical modelling (based on multiple regression analyses) which allowed them to partial out the influence of any predictor variable on any outcome variable, all other factors controlled for. The demographic and health factors controlled for included the family's socioeconomic status, ethnicity, family size and birth order, maternal age and education, child's perinatal health status, degree of neighbourhood deprivation, and mother's initial mental and physical health status.

Significant predictors of negative CHAOS scores (Matheny, 1995) and related parental distress indicators when the child was aged three were (all other factors controlled for): Mother's poor mental and physical health when first interviewed; family's lack of material resources or chronic unemployment at the outset; larger families; and mother's low educational achievement. This model applied to mothers of both genders, but was more marked in the mothers of preschool boys.

The ECCEs did have a significant influence on problematic family functioning in the focus child's fourth year of life. The more that the families used the child care centres, the less likely were they to have negative outcomes in terms of CHAOS scores, and problematic parent-child interactions. When a health visitor was based in the ECCE centre, outcomes were also better. The better the worker-child staff ratio in a centre, the better the outcome, but only when the centre was operated on an "Educational Leadership" model, with kindergarten classes run by qualified teachers (Sammons et al., 2016b).

The period over which the research was undertaken was one in which Sure Start funding was being offered on a changing legal and fiscal basis, and this resulted in both some contraction of services offered in CC centres, and the closure of a number of centres: Sammons and her colleagues (Sammons, 2015a) observed:

> Since 2010 [Sure Start] child care centres have experienced considerable turbulence and volatility as a result of changing organisational models, funding constraints linked to budget cuts, and addressing new children's centres 'core purpose'. Local authorities were given responsibility for making decisions on which services were most required per locality. The ring-fence for Sure Start funding was removed and the Early

Intervention Grant (EIG) was introduced in 2011, so it is not possible to put a figure on central government funding for Sure Start from 2011–2012 onwards ... and many children's centres reduced their services. (p. 2)

Government Policies Undermining the Funding Base, and the Effectiveness, of Centres

A survey in 2010 by The Day Care Trust, an independent charity (Bennett, 2011) of 3,578 Sure Start children's centres in England, found that more than 2,000 had reduced the programmes offered because of diminished funding in the previous year: some 250 centres had already closed, or were planning to close in the forthcoming financial year. These reductions in service reflected two factors: transfer of financial responsibility for the Centres to local authorities from national government; and a cumulative reduction in local authority budgets of 7 percent per annum.

By 2015, in England Sammons and her colleagues (2015b) reported, that another 142 children's centres had closed, leaving 2,816 centres remaining in the country. Between 2010 and 2013 government funding for the Sure Start initiative had fallen by 28 percent; it was not possible to calculate the extent of funding cuts in England after 2013, because the changes in the 'block grants' to local authorities did not allow this fiscal breakdown, although spending in the national health service budget on child and adolescent mental health also reduced by around five percent over a 4-year period (Sammons et al, 2015b).

The evaluation research by the Oxford University team found that when child care and other services were reduced in quantity and quality during the period of their 3-year evaluation, outcomes in terms of parental distress, and poor parental functioning had *significantly increased*, compared with centres which maintained the full range of staffing and services. The best outcomes for parents and children were delivered by centres which offered not only a stable and fully staffed service, but which also linked to health care supports, and were led by an educationally-trained professional.

Not surprisingly, parental distress and high-CHAOS families tended, overall, to have children with poorer cognitive and emotional outcomes – effects which were stronger for boys than for girls. However, overall cognitive gains or deficits resulting from family and children's centre variables were marginal. The strongest effects were those concerning externalising (e.g. conduct) behavioural disorders, and internalising (e.g. anxiety) problems.

The "neediest families" in contact with Centres clearly got the most help. For most (but not all) families this paid dividends in terms of positive outcomes, particularly for boys at the threshold of serious conduct disorders (Sammons et al., 2015a).

Health visitors (combining the role of public health nurse and social worker) were particularly effective in helping mothers who had problems with alcohol or drug abuse. Being in financial distress was systemic in causing various family dysfunctions, and when intervention was able to stabilise a family's finances, maternal mental health and mother-child relationships also improved, as did child behavioural outcomes. The greater the level of family disadvantage, the more likely was the family to use the services offered by the child care centres. It is implied that if the Centres were more generously funded, and could offer a wider range of specialist services, then outcomes for children would have been more favourable. Centres which employed a multiagency model, linking with health, social and educational services had the best outcomes.

There was one negative finding however. Mothers whose social and mental health and material conditions, and lack of partner support were profoundly negative at their first contact with a Centre, actually deteriorated over time (to the disadvantage of their children) despite their high level of dependency on anything the Centres had to offer. This did not mean that the Centres were making things worse for some families. Rather, it implied that a small fraction (perhaps five percent) of mothers needed *more* intensive and more highly skilled help than could be offered by even the best-staffed Centre: "... Children's Centres typically did not have highly qualified specialist staff to support complex mental health or social problems" (p. 23) (Sammons et al., 2015b). Furthermore, according to the evaluation team "Cuts to mental health services further hit child care centres' ability to treat and refer those with complex social or mental health problems." The five percent of mothers whom *Sure Start* did not help had very poor physical and mental health at the outset, had rarely succeeded in school, were not usually supported by a stable partner, and endured chronic material poverty. Their mental health and their parent-child relationships steadily deteriorated over a two-year period, this decline being particularly marked when the children's centre services were reduced or withdrawn.

The research found that 14 of the 117 centres studied had experienced cuts in their budget, or loss of staff. However, because of local authority support 32 of the centres were actually expanding services, and child and parent outcomes were most favourable in these expanding centres, and least favourable in the contracting or underfunded centres. Moreover, the negative effects of reduction or withdrawal of services for highly-stressed families was significantly greater than the overall positive effects of continued services. It appeared that programme reduction or withdrawal acted as an additional stressor in the lives of already highly-stressed families (Hall et al., 2016). This has been emphasized in a qualitative study of *Sure Start* child care centres in Liverpool (Campbell et al., 2016) which showed that as child poverty was *increasing* in areas of deprivation, available services including *Sure Start* centres, were experiencing (as were other social and health services for children and families) a *reduction* in funding, making child and parent outcomes appreciably worse.

The main evaluation study by the Oxford team (Sammons et al., 2015b) acknowledged that although moderately disadvantaged families who made maximal use of the facilities offered, did seem to be "on track" for improved life chances, in general the Sure Start programme had not altered the overall impacts of inequality on child and family health in the most disadvantaged sectors of population in England. Very disrupted and disturbed families were often not helped by the children's centres, and in an era of reductions in social work and mental health programming, a likely outcome was that many of these children would eventually be removed into care, since resources which could support these families were not available. Families who had additional resources of "social capital" seemed to have gained most from Sure Start (Bagley, 2011).

Sure Start child care centres were established in areas serving 'mixed' communities, both in terms of economic and ethnic status. The Oxford team's evaluation sample reported that 71.1 percent of families served were traditional "white British", and these included most of the "very deprived" families. Some 12 percent of the children served came from black or "mixed-race" backgrounds. Mothers and children from these backgrounds were *not* identified as having particularly poor or good outcomes in terms of social adjustment, cognition and behaviour. This underlines the fact that the neighbourhood-delivery model of *Sure Start* would inevitably offer services to some families who were climbing out of poverty, or indeed did not require child care other than for enabling mothers to pursue career options. Although Sammons and colleagues (2015b) did not specify ethnic profiles of the economically poor and disrupted low-functioning families, we infer that these are largely inter-generationally disadvantaged families of "poor whites", in whom problems of children are likely to predict the development of those children when they are adolescents and young adults, and have children of their own.

Sammons et al. (2015b) compare their evaluations with those of the earlier *Sure Start* (NESS) evaluations, and concluded: *"The ECCE results support and extend those of the earlier NESS study. They demonstrate that children's centres do have the potential to promote better outcomes for families and to a lesser extent, for children who are engaged in specific programmes (such as high quality childcare). At present the focus is on family and parenting services, and perhaps unsurprisingly, such outcomes show more evidence of impact in this evaluation."*

But funding and service changes since 2010 were clearly making evaluation using straightforward statistical models extremely difficult. It could be however that in the very long-term, follow up of *Sure Start* and Children's Centre "graduates" will show that as young adults, they will manifest some positive gains in educational achievement, employment, and stable family formation – as demonstrated in the American Head Start research (Currie & Thomas, 1993).

CONCLUSIONS

Offering a comprehensive programme of child and family support (including income and housing support) in neighbourhood family centres, with links to local schools, and offering individualised support for each child is an ideal – and the Oxford team point, enviously, to the 'universal care' models in Finland (and also in Norway) (Kekkonen, 2015). Such programmes are generously funded, and comprehensive in nature and are linked to Finland's overall programmes of income equality, and the high scholastic achievement levels of children and adolescents later on (Bagley & Sawyerr, 2008).

The English *Sure Start*, in comparison with this Finnish model, is poorly funded and subject to the political forces which prevail in a country in which neo-liberal economic and policy models dominate social care options. The emerging conservative-liberal alliance in 2010, and the subsequent conservative government rebranded *Sure Start* as Child Care Centre programmes, and withdrew the evaluation contract from the University of London.

Sure Start child care centres began, idealistically, as neighbourhood programmes but also offered services to families and children who did not actually need those services. The evaluation programme focussed on families using the services, rather than on families who were in greatest need, but who might have not accessed the services offered. The kind of school-based research identifying particular families in whom problems are intergenerational in nature, which we applied in a government-funded demonstration project (Bagley & Pritchard, 2008a, 2008b) would, in contrast, result in comprehensive services being focussed on those *most* in need. There is irony in that the UK government appears to have ignored the obvious benefit of investing in disadvantaged families by focussing on schools in disadvantaged areas, identifying children and families who were clearly in need of supportive intervention using a much cheaper option than that employed in Sure Start, which offered services to families who were clearly not in need of social and psychological supports. This alternative model (focussing on particular schools, and on sub-groups of 'problematic' children and their families, including the provision of services for pre-schoolers) (Bagley & Pritchard 1998a, 1998b; Williams & Pritchard, 2006) has been shown to be highly cost-effective. The follow-up studies of 'graduates' of these school-based programmes have shown that by late adolescence, these young people have significantly fewer indications of problematic behaviour (e.g. criminality, substance use, unwed pregnancy). In the medium term these programmes are highly cost-effective (Williams & Pritchard, 2006).

The Sure Start/Children's Centres programme was, paradoxically too ambitious and idealistic, and spread its limited funding over too large a client group. An alternative model would have been to use the primary school and the neighbourhood it serves as the centre of social work intervention, identifying pupils with problems of learning and behaviour, and then offering intensive engagement (including free preschool day care) for the families' other children, with special support from teachers and therapists. Ultimately, as Standing (2014) advocates, the problems of the very poor can only be successfully addressed in the longer term within the context of a stable and generous "basic living allowance" available to all citizens. Evidence continues to emerge that providing low income families with a stable income can have significant public health benefits (Gray, 2013; Muenning et al., 2016). And as the Allen Report urged the UK government in 2011, influences on a child in the first five years of life are very hard to undo, and can have negative impacts throughout adult life, at great cost for a variety of service providers. The same model also shows that enhancement of the material, social and psychological circumstances of a child's development in these crucial preschool years, can be highly cost-effective.

NOTES

[1] The Reports were released by the Department for Education on "the night before Christmas" in December 2015, allegedly so that they would attract little press attention (*Guardian*, January 14, 2016). In the event, the press did, by and large, ignore the Reports.

[2] Fathers were not interviewed, since they are difficult to interview when they are working full time; or when they are absent from the family.

REFERENCES

Allen, G. (2011). *Early intervention: Next steps – An independent report to her majesty's government*. London: Her Majesty's Government.

Anning, A., & Ball, M. (2008). *Improving services for young children: From Sure Start to children's centres*. London: Sage.

Avis, M., Buchanan, D., & Leighton, P. (2007). Factors affecting participation in Sure Start programmes: A qualitative investigation of parents' views. *Health, Social Care and Community, 15*, 203–211.

Bagley, C. (2011). From Sure Start to children's centres: Capturing the erosion of social capital. *British Journal of Educational Psychology, 37*, 95–113.

Bagley, C., & Mallick, K. (2000). Spiralling up and spiralling down: Implications of a long-term study of temperament and conduct disorder for social work with children. *Child and Family Social Work, 5*, 291–301.

Bagley, C., & Pritchard, C. (1998a). The reduction of problem behaviours and school exclusion in at-risk youth: An experimental study of school social work with cost-benefit analyses. *Child and Family Social Work, 3*, 219–226.

Bagley, C., & Pritchard, C. (1998b). The billion dollar cost of troubled youth: Prospects for cost-effective prevention and treatment. *International Journal of Adolescence and Youth, 7*, 211–225.

Barnes, J., Belsky, J., Broomfield, K., Dave, S., Frost, M., & Melhuish, E. (2005). Disadvantaged but different: Variation among deprived communities in relation to child and family well-being. *Journal of Child Psychology and Psychiatry, 40*, 952–962.

Barnes, J. (2007). Targeting deprived areas. The nature of Sure Start local programme neighbourhoods. In J. Belsky, J. Barnes, & E. Melhuish (Eds.), *The national evaluation of Sure Start: Does area based intervention work?* Bristol: The Policy Press.

Belsky, J., & Melhuish, E. (2007). Impact of Sure Start local programmes on children and families. In J. Belsky, J. Barnes, & E. Melhuish (Eds.), *The national evaluation of Sure Start: Does area-based early intervention work?* Bristol: The Policy Press.

Belsky, J., Melhuish, E., Barnes, J., Leyland, A., & Romaniuk, H. (2006). Effects of Sure Start local programmes on children and families: Early findings from a quasi-experimental, cross-sectional study. *British Medical Journal, 332,* 1476–1478.

Bennett, R. (2011, January 26). Sure Start centres to close in 'slaughter' of child services. *The Times,* p. 25.

Bennett, W., & Hustedd, J. (2005). Head Start's lasting effects. *Infants and Young Children, 18,* 16–24.

Briggs, N., Kurtz, A., & Paull, G. (2012). *Evaluation of Children's Centres in England (ECCE) Strand 5: Case studies on the costs of centres in the most deprived areas.* London: Department for Education.

Bywater, T., Hutchings, J., Daley, D., Whitaker, C., Yeo, S., Jones, K., Eames, C., & Edwards, R. (2009). Long-term effectiveness of a parenting intervention in Sure Start services in Wales for children at risk of developing conduct disorder. *British Journal of Psychiatry, 195,* 318–324.

Cameiro, P., & Ginja, R. (2014). Long-term impacts of compensatory preschool programs on health and behaviour: Evidence from head start. *American Economic Journal: Economic Policies, 6,* 135–173.

Campbell, M., & Six Others (2016). Austerity cuts are eroding benefits of Sure Start children's centres. *British Medical Journal,* 352: i335.

Coe, C., Gibson, A., Spencer, N., & Stuttaford, M. (2008). Sure Start: Voices of the 'hard-to-reach'. *Child Care Health and Development, 34,* 447–453.

Craig, G. (2007). *Sure Start and Black and minority Populations.* London: Department for Children, Schools and Families.

Currie, J., & Thomas, D. (1993). Does head start make a difference? Cambridge, MA: National Bureau of Economic Research.

Edgley, A., & Avis, M. (2006). Inter-professional collaboration: Sure Start, uncertain future. *Journal of Interprofessional Care, 20,* 433–435.

Edgley, A., & Avis, M. (2007). The perceptions of statutory service providers of a local Sure Start programme: A shared agenda. *Health, Social Care and Community, 15,* 379–386.

Edwards, R., Ó Céilleachair, A., Bywater, T., Hughes, D., & Hutchings, J. (2007). Parenting programme for parents of children at risk of developing conduct disorder: Cost-effective analysis. *British Medical Journal, 334*(7595), 682–687.

Eisenstadt, N. (2011). *Providing a Sure Start: How government discovered early childhood.* Bristol: Policy Press.

Evangelou, M., & Ten Others. (2014). *Evaluation of Children's Centres in England (ECCE) – Strand 3: Parenting services.* London: Department for Education.

Glass, N. (1999). Sure Start: The development of an early development of an early intervention programmes for young children in the United Kingdom. *Children and Society, 13,* 257–264.

Goff, J., & Nine Others (2013). *Evaluation of Children's Centres in England – Strand 3: Delivery of family services.* London: Department for Education.

Gray, R., & Francis, E. (2007). The implications of US experiences with early childhood interventions for the UK Sure Start programme. *Child Care Health and Development, 33,* 655–663.

Gray, M. (2013). The swing to early intervention and prevention and its implications for social work. *British Journal of Social Work, 44,* 1750–1769.

Hall, J., & Six Others (2016). Disadvantaged families are at greatest risk from austerity cuts to Children's Centres. *British Medical Journal, 352,* i897.

Hughes, B. (2005, October 15). *Sure Start.* Statement by the minister for families and children.

Hutchings, J., & Seven Others (2007). Parenting intervention in Sure Start services for children at risk of developing conduct disorder: Pragmatic randomized controlled trial. *British Medical Journal, 334,* 678.

Hutchings, J., Bywater, T., & Daley, D. (2007). Early prevention of conduct disorder: How and why did the North and Mid Wales Sure Start study work? *Journal of Children's Services, 2,* 4–14.

Jones, K., Daley, D., Hutchings, J., Bywater, T., & Eames, C. (2008). Efficacy of the incredible years programme as an early intervention for children with conduct problems and ADHD. *Child Care Health and Development, 84,* 389–390.

Joshi, H. (2007). *School readiness and social disadvantage in the Millennium Cohort of Children.* London: Center for Longitudinal Studies, Institute of Education, University of London.

Joshi, M. (2008). *The Millennium Cohort Study Children at age six.* London: Centre for Longitudinal Studies, Institute of Education, University of London.

Kekkonen, M. (2015). *Family centres in Finland: A strategic way to provide universal promotion and early support.* Helsinki: National Institute for Health and Welfare.

Lewis, J. (2011). From Sure Start to children's centres: An analysis of policy change in English early years programmes. *Journal of Social Policy, 40,* 71–88.

Lord, R., Southcott, C., & Sharp, C. (2011). *Targeting children's centre services on the most needy.* Slough: National Foundation for Educational Research.

Matheny, P. (1995). Bringing order out of chaos: Psychometric characteristics of the confusion, hubbub and order scale. *Journal of Applied Development Psychology, 16,* 429–444.

Melhuish, E. (2016). Longitudinal research and early years policy development in the United Kingdom. *International Journal of Child Care and Education Policy, 10,*

Melhuish, E., & the SSLP Study Team. (2007). Variation in community intervention programmes and consequences for children and families: The example of Sure Start local programmes. *Journal of Child Psychology and Psychiatry, 48,* 543–551.

Melhuish, E., & the SSLP Study Team. (2008). Effects of fully-established Sure Start local programmes on 3-year-old children and their families living in England: A quasi-experimental, observational study. *Lancet, 373,* 1641–1647.

Melhuish, E., Belsky, J., & Barnes, J. (2010). Evaluation and value of Sure Start. *Archives of Diseases in Children, 95,* 159–161.

Melhuish, E., Belsky, J., Leyland, A., & Nine Others. (2010). *The impact of Sure Start local programmes in five year olds and their families: Report of a longitudinal study* (Research Report DFE-RR067). London: Department for Education. 3 (online open access).

Muenning, P., Mohit, B., Wu, J., Jia, H., & Rosen, Z. (2016). Cost-effectiveness of the earned income tax credit as a health policy investment. *American Journal of Preventative Medicine*. doi:10.106/ampere.2016.07.001

NAO. (2007). *Sure Start children's centres*. London: HMSO for the National Audit Office.

Oden, S., Schweinhart, L., & Weikart, D. (2000). *Into adulthood: A study of the effects of head start*. St Pauls, MN: Red Leaf Press for High/Scope Publications.

ODPM. (2005). *National strategy for neighbourhood renewal*. London: Office of The Deputy Prime Minister, for the Social Inclusion Unit.

Pearson, C. (2005). *Re-orienting parent education with a local Sure Start programme*. Chester: Centre for Public Health Research, University College of Chester.

Raymond, J. (2009). 'Creating a safety net': Women's experiences of antenatal depression and their identification of helpful community support services during pregnancy. *Midwifery, 25*, 39–49.

Redfern, G. (2005). Ministers urged not to jump the gun on Sure Start findings. *New Start – Community Regeneration*. Retrieved from www.newstartmag.co.uk/news858.html/

Rutter, M. (2007). Sure Start local programmes: An outsider's perspective. In J. Belsky, J. Barnes, & E. Melhuish (Eds.), *The national evaluation of Sure Start*. Bristol: The Policy Press.

Sammons, P., Hall, J., Smees, R., & Ten Collaborators. (2015a). *Children's centres: Their Importance for children and families: Evaluation of children's centres in England (ECCE, Strand 4)*. London: Department for Education. Retrieved from www.gov.uk/government/publications

Sammons, P., Hall, J., Smees, R., Goff, J., & Four Co-Authors and Consultants. (2015b). *Children's centres: Their importance for children and families: Evaluation of children's centres in England summary report*. London: Department for Education. Retrieved from www.gov.uk/government/publications

Schneider, J., Ramsay, A., & Lowerson, S. (2006). Sure Start graduates: Predictors of attainment on starting school. *Child Care Health and Development, 32*, 431–440.

Scott, S. (2007). Conduct disorders in children. *British Medical Journal, 334*, 646.

Scott, S., Knapp, M., Henderson, J., & Maughan, B. (2001). Financial cost of social inclusion: Follow-up studies of antisocial children into adulthood. *British Medical Journal, 323*, 191.

Standing, G. (2014). *The precariat: The new dangerous class* (2nd ed.). London: Bloomsbury Academic.

Sure Start Research Team. (2008). *The impact of Sure Start local programmes on three year olds and their families*. Nottingham: Department for Education and Science Publications.

Sylva, M., & Seven Others (2015). *Organisation, services and reach of children's centres: Evaluation of children's centres in England*. London: Department for Education.

Williams, R., & Pritchard, C. (2006). *Breaking the cycle of educational alienation: A multi-professional approach*. Maidenhead: McGraw-Hill Educational.

ABOUT THE AUTHORS

Alice Akoshia Ayikaaley Sawyerr has African-Canadian ancestry, from freed slaves in Nova Scotia and Nigeria. Alice was born in Sierra Leone, and grew up in Ghana. She studied nursing in England, followed by psychology and social work degrees in Canada. Her postgraduate work in England has included qualifications in systemic family therapy, teaching and learning in higher education, and a PhD from the University of London. She has been a child, adolescent and family mental health clinician with the National Health Service, and a lecturer in developmental psychology and systemic family therapy, at Royal Holloway, University of London. She now lectures in psychology in the Department of Continuing Education, University of Oxford.

Christopher Adam Bagley is a Muslim-Quaker, and has qualifications in social policy and education from Exeter and Essex Universities in the UK. His doctorates in social psychology, and sociology are from Sussex University, and Essex University. He has held Chairs of Social Work, Child Welfare and Social Policy, and Applied Social Studies at universities in Canada, England and Hong Kong. He is now Professor of Social Science in the Public Health Institute of Liverpool John Moores University.

INDEX